A PRACTITIONER'S GUIDE TO RISC MICROPROCESSOR ARCHITECTURE

This text is printed on acid-free paper.

Library of Congress Cataloging in Publication Data:
Stakem, Patrick H.
    A practitioner's guide to RISC microprocessor architecture
Patrick H. Stakem.
        p.   cm.
    "A Wiley-Interscience publication."
    Includes index.
    ISBN 0-471-13018-4 (cloth : alk. paper)
    1. RISC microprocessors.   I. Title.
QA76.5.S6957   1996
004.165—dc20   95-4732
                                               CIP

0-471-13018-4

Printed in the United States of America

10 9 8 7 6 5 4 3 2 1

A PRACTITIONER'S GUIDE TO RISC MICROPROCESSOR ARCHITECTURE

Patrick H. Stakem

Loyola College

A WILEY-INTERSCIENCE PUBLICATION

JOHN WILEY & SONS, INC.

New York / Chichester / Brisbane / Toronto / Singapore

More Haste, Less Speed,
Seutonius, Augustus, Sec. 25, Augustus Caesar, 63 BC–AD 14

To Conquer without RISK is to triumph without glory
LeCid (1636), Act II, sc. ii, Pierre Corneille, 1606–1684

Good Speed to your youthful valor, boy! So shall you scale the stars!
Aeneid, Bk. IX, I. 641, Virgil (Publius Vergilius Maro), 70–19 BC

Our life is frittered away by detail. Simplify, Simplify.
Walden [1854], Henry David Thoreau, 1817–1862

Art should Simplify, finding what convention of form and what detail
one can do without and yet preserve the spirit of the whole..
Willa Cather, 1873–1947

We be fast, they be slow.
Ghostbusters II, 1989

CONTENTS

Preface

BACKGROUND

This book is an outgrowth of a course I developed and taught at Loyola College in the engineering science graduate program. In 1989 it was obvious that the reduced instruction set computer (RISC) was becoming a significant new force in the marketplace as well as a design approach of great importance. With the Engineering Science Department's blessing, I developed the courseware, relying on a general introduction to the subject, followed by a comparative look at competitive architectures from the marketplace. Students were required to do a project in the field. The course was given during the summers of 1990–1992, and the Spring and Summer semesters in 1993 and continues to generate enough interest among students to justify offering the course every semester.

Originally I thought that RISC as a design paradigm was a passing fancy, and would disappear as a separate field as it was absorbed into the mainstream. Well, I still think that, but the timeframe has stretched out. RISC chips will provide the implementation basis for the High Performance Computing and Communication infrastructure initiative, which was kicked off by then-Senator, now Vice-President Al Gore. RISC chips are found in high-end desktop workstations, massively parallel machines, laser printers, LAN routers, and other communication switches. RISC chips are paving the information superhighway. RISC techniques are being applied to the aging 80x86 instruction set architecture which currently dominates the desktop. This is an exciting time in RISC systems.

I took on the thankless task of putting together this book because there is no comprehensive discussion of RISC architecture. There are collections of key papers in the field, and Hennessy and Patterson's work is certainly the architecture bible. However, no one text gives the overall view of RISC as a design philosophy, as a market force, and as a technology driver. It is important to realize that in a rapidly moving, trendy area such as RISC, information changes quickly. We intend to counter this with a fairly agressive update schedule. Issues such as Intel's Pentium

Pro Processor and Pentium's floating-point division problem (section A1.20.3) are discussed.

This book is intended for the hardware or software practitioner to use as an introduction to the subject. It assumes a working knowledge of the internals of computer systems, architecture, and instruction execution. It would be relevant for an advanced undergraduate or graduate level course in computer design or architecture. It discusses a chip level view of RISC processors, and looks at the design tradeoffs and penalties that RISC processors place on their memory subsystems and their support software.

I actively solicit feedback from users and readers of this book because systems without feedback are not stable. The author may be contacted via the Internet address STAKEM@LOYOLA.EDU.

SCOPE AND COVERAGE

This book covers the field of *reduced instruction set microprocessors*, a subset of the field of reduced instruction set computers. We will emphasize the comparative architecture of processors, memory and software.

The goal of this book is to give the reader an introductory look at the fundamentals of RISC microprocessor design and to allow the reader to understand the tradeoffs, limitations, speed, cost, complexity, and architectures.

The reader will learn:

1. Who are the key players in RISC?
2. What are the key architectural features of RISC?
3. What are the strengths and weaknesses of the technology, and what are its limitations?
4. Where did RISC come from, and where is it going?

To achieve these goals, we'll review the basics and background of the technology and examine where the tradeoffs are. We'll then look at real-world design examples to see how the tradeoffs were made. It is essential to realize that in RISC technology, as in many cutting-edge endeavors there are few wrong answers, but a multitude of right ones. The wrong answers either never make it to the market, or don't last long there.

This is not a book for chip designers, because the level of detail presented is not sufficient. However, it will be useful for engineers and engineering managers that must make use of this technology in systems. They need to know the capabilities and limitations of this important field to be able to apply the technology in their particular domains of expertise. This book should provide at least a first-level replacement for several bookcases' worth of manufacturer's data books.

Since RISC is a rapidly evolving field, software has not begun to catch up with the processors, and the life cycle for a processor chip from introduction to obsolescence may be as short as eighteen months. This is not enough time for mature software and support systems to be developed and to evolve.

In many cases, we'll see decisions that were not really influenced by the technological issues, but rather by marketing considerations. To the design engineer, this is heresy; but in the cold, cruel world of commerce, this is the basis of economic survival. Some companies are pioneers at the "bleeding edge" of technology development; others prefer to hold back and address mature markets. As Nolan Bushnell, founder of Atari, says, "The pioneers are the ones with the arrows in them."

HOW THIS BOOK IS ORGANIZED

Chapter 1 presents the background, scope, and organization of the book, and discusses some of the history of RISC technology. It attempts to define what is RISC and what is not, presents some metrics we can apply to systems, and discusses some of the limitations of the technology.

The basics of RISC are presented in Chapter 2. We need to review the elements of a computer, the basic fetch/execute cycle, and memory architectures. We'll begin to see what makes RISC tick.

Chapter 3 presents the RISC approach to high-performance computing, first by identifying the bottlenecks and then by showing how each of those is addressed and overcome. The *performance equation* is introduced and analyzed. The concepts of *superscalar* and *superpipelined* are introduced. Various RISC schools of thought are examined. We look at several of the market drivers for RISC, including embedded systems. Also, we examine the software tools to develop, debug, and maintain RISC systems. In essence, software makes or breaks the RISC approach (as some companies have painfully learned), because software enables us to harness the raw throughput of the hardware to do useful work.

Chapters 5 through 19 are devoted to specific design examples, drawn from industry, in which case studies are used to illustrate specific points. A roadmap for Chapters 5 through 19 is discussed in Chapter 4. All of these chapters were written to the same outline. A bibliographic listing of books, manufacturers' data books, and relevant articles follows each chapter. By Chapter 5 we are ready to see how real-world companies have approached RISC processor products. Intel's embedded RISC family, the i960, is discussed in Chapter 5. Chapter 6 addresses the MIPS machines. The Inmos Transputer, and the concepts of parallel processing and scalability are introduced in Chapter 7. The architecture of Advanced Micro Devices (AMD) 29k family is presented in Chapter 8. Chapter 9 discusses Intel's RISC computation engine, the i860. In Chapter 10, we see the various varieties of the SPARC architecture. The Advanced RISC Machine (ARM, formerly Acorn) from VLSI Logic Inc. is covered in Chapter 11 while Chapter 12 considers the Digital Equipment Corporation (DEC) Alpha machines. Chapter 13 covers the Hewlett-Packard (HP) precision architecture (PA) approach to RISC. The International Meta Systems (IMS) model 6250 is addressed in Chapter 14. In Chapter 15, we look at the Motorola/IBM PowerPC architecture. The Nippon Electric Corporation (NEC) V800 approach is covered in Chapter 16. Chapter 17 details Hitachi's SH-7000 family. The Microchip PIC details are given in Chapter 18. Chapter 19 is a catchall for those chips not deserving of a full chapter. We discuss the discontinued Clipper, 88k, AT&T Microprocessor, and the iWarp. We look at the influences of RISC on DSP and mainline CISC. Several proprietary architectures, including IBM's RIOS, and the chips from nCube, Kendall Square Research (KSR), and MasPar are discussed. Chapter 20 contains a listing of contact information for manufacturers and RISC organizations. There follows a glossary list of terms, jargon, and abbreviations. We also take an in-depth look at the issue of floating-point calculation and its implementation in Appendix 1. In Appendix 2, we see examples of student projects from the EG-769 RISC course at Loyola College. Appendix 3 talks about the use of RISC in various aerospace projects, which is the author's background.

USE OF THIS BOOK

For the Working Professional

This book is written at the advanced undergraduate or graduate engineering level. Practicing information technology professionals, engineers, system architects, and software designers will be able to pick it up and read it, or use it as reference guide. Technical management and technical sales will also find it of use. Commodity RISC chips are the basis for engineering workstations and large, massively parallel machines. They are found on the laptop, and in large, enterprise-level class rooms. RISC processors are the technology engines that form the basis for the current and emerging generation of systems. Unix is the software system of choice, and C/C++ are the preferred languages. Other contenders seek to attain the necessary critical mass in the marketplace. The only serious threat to RISC chips comes from the instruction-set compatible 80×86 processors from Intel. This may become a moot point as 80×86 emulation hardware is built into RISC cores. RISC chips themselves are influencing the embedded control and digital signal processor (DSP) market, and RISC techniques are being found in mainstream *complex instruction set processor* (CISC) machines. Systems based on RISC chips are challenging traditional large mainframe systems for the lead in supplying computing power to enterprises. This is a technology that has to be monitored, as the advances occur rapidly.

The various technical representatives and technical salespeople I have spoken with have universally praised the basic idea of this book. Their view is that they have a very narrow focus on their own product, and no good mechanism to see what the competition is doing or to garner compare-and-contrast information. Sales representatives, even though they may not have a technical background, understand the jargon and have expressed interest in this format.

In a Course

This book can serve as the text for a course in RISC computer architecture, or as a supplemental text for a general computer architecture course. The student should be intimately familiar with the material presented in Chapters 1 through 3 before proceeding. We assume that the student is familiar with industry jargon and understands how an instruction is executed. I recommend reading the book starting from Chapter 1, and slowing down as necessary. If the material is not familiar, consider answering the questions at the end of the first three chapters. For use as a reference, the reader may proceed directly to the detailed examples in Chapters 5 through 19. For specific issues or terms, use the index to find where the theory for those issues or the definition was discussed in Chapters 1 through 3.

After a thorough examination of the basics the student will be ready to examine comparative architectures drawn from industry. Chapters 5 through 19 summarize the respective architectures, but don't present all of the details. It is suggested that this material be supplemented with data books from the corresponding manufacturer. When scheduling permitted, a technical representative of the company should present the architectural material to the class. My students and I have found this to be an excellent approach, and the companies are very cooperative. We get hardcore technical presentations, not marketing slicks.

For the class at Loyola, a major portion of each student's grade was determined by an independent project that he or she did. This was conducted as a real-world project. Each student determined a topic and a problem, possibly related to his or her personal interests or work assignments. They were then responsible for assembling the resources to do the job, with help from the instructor, as needed in a "superconsultant" role. There were negotiations, software licenses, nondisclosures, equipment loans, late nights, late deliveries, disappointments, and excellent results. A few of the projects are summarized in Appendix 2.

A few students, who were doing a project closely related to their work assignments, received awards from their companies in addition to the grades. Some projects were continued into independent research. The hardware students built and programmed hardware while the software types built simulators and tools. Those not directly working in the industry did surveys of particular topics in depth, or considered a particular application area, such as databases or manufacturing, and examined how RISC would apply. I was constantly surprised and amazed by the amount of work that these students put into projects of their own interest and choosing. We reached the point where students were picking up and extending previous students' work.

HOW THIS BOOK WAS PRODUCED

I used WordPerfect for Windows versions 5.2 and 6.0 software, on a variety of personal computer (PC), (non-RISC) systems. The figures were collected from various sources, or produced on the PC with the CorelDraw package by my daughter, Meredith.

ACKNOWLEDGMENTS

This book would not have happened without the support and contributions of the following people and organizations and others that I have forgotten: Dale Simmonds at AMD; Greg McDonald at Cypress Semiconductor; Deb Richmond at Digital Equipment Corporation; IBM Corporation; Inmos Corporation; Ray Lloyd; Jeff Wilson; Marco Figueiredo; Texas Instruments; Doug May at Integrated Device Technology; Dr. Pramode Agarde at AT&T; John Taverna at Microchip; Tom Man and Phil Grove from Motorola; Andy Suchosky of HP; Carl Shaw at LSI Logic; Bill Whelan at Intel; Bob Baltz and Chuck Roberts at VLSI Technology; Steve Sprehn of Lystad Ltd.; and Dr. Bernard Weigman, Director of the Masters Program in Engineering Science, and Dr. Paul Coyne, Associate Director of the Masters Program in Engineering Science, at Loyola. Many thanks to everyone that helped in this effort.

Pat Stakem

Laurel, MD

TRADEMARKS

The following trademarks, listed in alphabetical order, are the property of the respective owners.

Am 29000	Advanced Micro Devices Inc
Am29027	Advanced Micro Devices Inc.
AMD	Advanced Micro Devices Inc.
ASM29K	Microtek Research, Inc.
Coreldraw	Corel Corp.
CLIPPER	Intergraph Corp.
CRAY 1	Cray Research Inc.
DEC	Digital Equipment Corp.
Embedded System Processor	National Semiconductor
Hyper SPARC	SPARC International, Inc.
i286	Intel Corp.
i386	Intel Corp.
i387	Intel Corp.
i486	Intel Corp.
i750	Intel Corp.
i860	Intel Corp.
i960	Intel Corp.
iAPX	Intel Corp.
IBM	International Business Machines Corp.
IBM PC	International Business Machines Corp.
ICE	Intel Corp.
IMS	Inmos Group
inmos	Inmos Group
INTEL	Intel Corp.
Intergraph	Intergraph Corp.
iWARP	Intel Corp.
LOTUS	Lotus Development Corp.
MC68000	Motorola
Microsoft	Microsoft Corporation

Micro SPARC	SPARC International, Inc.
Motorola	Motorola
Motorola 88100	Motorola
Occam	Inmos Group
PARC	Xerox Corp.
PDP-11	Digital Equipment Corp.
Pentium	Intel Corp.
PIC	Microchip Technology
PowerPC	International Business Machines Corp.
PowerPC Architecture	International Business Machines Corp.
PowerPC 601	International Business Machines Corp.
RISCompiler	MIPS Computer Systems Inc.
RISCwindows	MIPS Computer Systems Inc.
RS/6000	International Business Machines Corp.
Solaris	SunSoft
SPARC	SPARC International, Inc.
PARClite	SPARC International, Inc.
Sun	Sun Microsystems, Inc.
SuperSPARC	SPARC International, Inc.
TI	Texas Instruments, Inc.
UltraSPARC	SPARC International, Inc.
UNIX	UNIX Systems Laboratories Inc.
VAX	Digital Equipment Corp.
VMS	Digital Equipment Corp.
Windows	Microsoft
WordPerfect	WordPerfect Corp.

The mention of other product or brand names is solely for identification purposes and may involve trademarks or registered trademarks of the respective companies. Trademarked names are used for editorial purposes, to the benefit of the trademark holder.

1

INTRODUCTION

1.1 HISTORY OF THE TECHNOLOGY

The Reduced Instruction Set Computer (RISC) as a design philosophy has been around since the beginning of computers, but has only become mainstream in the last few years, as the quest for raw speed has dominated the highly competitive computer industry. Most of the early machines, such as the PDP-8 from Digital Equipment Corporation, had a very reduced instruction set. There was a desire to simplify the hardware for reasons of cost. At the same time, the number of registers was also limited by cost. As we will see, modern RISC machines have large numbers of registers. Central processing unit (CPU) evolution progressed in families of instruction-set-compatible elements with increasing speed and capability. The 80X86 family from Intel, the VAX family from Digital Equipment Corporation (DEC), and the Motorola MC680X0 family are examples. Instruction-set compatibility was an overall design goal, to tap into a perceived large installed base of existing system and applications code. Machine users were notoriously averse to reprogramming any application, once it more-or-less worked. This was known from mainframe days as the "dusty deck" syndrome, referring to shelves of old punch card programs. The manufacturers of new hardware were reluctant to introduce new instruction sets, and new ways of doing things to managers and programmers reluctant to alter working programs.

The cost of maintaining instruction-set compatibility began to emerge in the early 1990s as an artificial barrier to performance. If one could support a C language compiler, for example, one tapped into a large base of applications and experience. With support for the C language, the Unix operating system was easily implemented. When a new architecture offered an order-of-magnitude performance increase, it was worth the pain of reprogramming.

The technology of digital computers is interesting in that it feeds upon itself; it is *bootstrapping*. In other words, the companies with the best computer architectures use these to build machines with which to design and simulate the next generation of chips and machines. This means the cost of entry into the field is high for non-participants, and grows with time. The chances for success of a garage-shop operation in RISC design are almost nil, and getting worse.

The requirements driving RISC designs and the quest for speed and density come from several sources. The military requirements for radar and sonar signal processing during the Cold War drove the development of fast digital signal processors. The commercial marketplace, from cellular phones to video games, is primarily cost sensitive. Automotive manufacturers began to influence the design, as the need for increasingly complex controllers for automobiles became apparent. The blend of these markets has produced the RISC machines that we know. "RISC" doesn't specify a set of rules as much as it describes a paradigm or methodology for implementation for high-performance, high-throughput computers.

We are currently into the fourth generation of RISC machines, characterized by clock speeds in the 100 MHz range, true 64 bit architectures, densities exceeding multiple millions of transistors, and superscalar/superpipelined architectures. The next few years should be very interesting. Texas Instruments estimates that by the year 2000 it will produce an architecture of 100 million transistors, with performance in excess of two giga-ops per second. They have already attained the performance figure (Section 19.4.1).

1.2 RISC VERSUS CISC

Sometimes it is easier to tell what is not RISC than what is. The alternate to RISC is CISC, the *complex instruction set computer*. These machines have a large, rich instruction set with multiple addressing modes, and numerous ways of doing the same thing. CISC machines have evolved in families such as Intel's 80X86, or Motorola's 680X0. These families are upwardly compatible, and instruction-set compatible. For example, the Pentium® Pro Processor will execute 8086 code written in 1978. CISC machines have evolved with faster clock rates, and have reduced the number of clock cycles for the same operation compared to previous members of the processor family. Features such as on-chip caches are built into modern CISC architectures. CISC processors, while staying instruction-set compatible with previous family members, attempt to gain performance by making instructions more powerful. Generally, microcoded instructions are used, such that one operand code (opcode) can initiate a long sequence of micro-operations without further memory access. However, the time penalty of a microcode access for instruction decode is applied to all instructions, simple and complex. Studies of code have shown that complex instructions and complex addressing modes are rarely used. We can apply what is known as the 80/20 (or sometimes 90/10) rule: 20 percent of all instructions do 80 percent of all operations. RISC chooses to focus on the simple 20 percent of the instruction set, to gain performance 80 percent of the time. Of course, we do lose performance 20 percent of the time, but this is more than balanced out, as we shall see when we consider the performance equation in Chapter 3.

1.3 TAXONOMY

This section strives to put RISC machines in categories and classifications. There are essentially two major schools of thought in RISC design: the Stanford and the Berkeley. Almost all RISC designs trace back to the work of John Hennessy and David Patterson [1]. Hennessy's work at Stanford University resulted in the MIPS family discussed in Chapter 6, and Patterson's work at Berkeley spawned the SPARC processor line, covered in Chapter 10. The RISC taxonomy fits into a larger taxonomy of computer systems, defined by M. J. Flynn [2]. Flynn's classic taxonomy describes processor types used in characterizing machines and is illustrated in Table 1.1.

1.4 DEFINITIONS

The Harvard architecture machines are derived from early work done at Harvard University during and immediately after World War II. These machines typically had the instructions and the data stored in separate memory. This is because the word lengths and formats were different, and because some level of security was provided by not having the ability to execute the data, or to write inadvertently over program coefficients. This type of machine formed the basis for the early missile guidance computers that sat in silos, and waited to guide the ICBMs. However, the commercial data processing industry followed another path.

The Von Neumann machines, named after the famous computer scientist and mathematician at Princeton, accompanied his observation that there is no inherent difference between the program and the data; the program is simply data. This has

Table 1.1 Flynn's Taxonomy

• SISD	Single-instruction, single data; example: uniprocessor
• SIMD	Single-instruction, multiple-data uniprocessor with time-multiplexed data streams, or multiprocessors running the same program; examples: NASA MPP, Connection Machine (early models), array processors
• MISD	Multiple-instruction, single-data multiprocessor with one data stream
• MIMD	Multiple-instruction, multiple-data multiprocessor; multiple programs; multiple data streams

given us the ability to write self-modifying code, and to execute our data ever since. It greatly simplified the memory interface. Almost all modern computers are of the von Neumann style. However, higher-performance systems eventually ran into the von Neumann limit. Essentially, the capacity between memory and the CPU is limited. One can increase the capacity of this channel by making it wider or faster, but eventually the CPU is limited in its ability to access the memory. There are many solutions to this problem, and we'll discuss the architectural ones later. However, an obvious solution is to return to the Harvard architecture, and divide the code and the data into separate memories. This doubles the channel capacity, because there are now two channels. There are complexities introduced, of course, because some programs must be able to write their "data" into program memory. Compilers are the obvious example. In modern design practice, the program and data memories are usually the same word width and format. They may be of the same size. However, there are advantages to caching them differently, taking advantage of the different natures of program flow and data flow. This will be discussed in more detail in the section on caching in Chapter 2.

We will not discuss the field of dataflow (as opposed to traditional control flow) machines, although the RISC paradigm is applicable here as well. Dataflow machines are radical architectures, usually special-purpose in nature, and still remain a research topic.

1.5 METRICS

We need some way to compare systems, and what is usually considered is operations per second. This has lead to misuses, benchmarkmanship among companies, and confusion among users and potential buyers. What we want is to compare apples to apples, but all we have is a fruit salad. Rumors abound of machine architectures optimized for particular industry benchmarks. A clever programmer can devise a benchmark program to present the best side of any processor, while emphasizing the weakness of the competition.

On the memory side, what we want is access in one clock cycle to all data of interest. This is not economically feasible. Thus, we use hierarchical memory, with a small, affordable amount of fast memory next to the processor, with access speed increasing but cost per bit decreasing as we get further from the processor. We also give up random access for sequential access (such as is found with magnetic tape systems) at some point.

Memory speed must be commensurate with the processor, and input/output (I/O) speed need only be commensurate with the corresponding device. We won't dwell on RISC I/O, because there is really nothing special about it. We will find that memory-mapped I/O is the norm, and special consideration must be taken to make I/O accesses "noncacheable." In RISC-embedded architectures, I/O features become important, as integrated solutions are used to reduce chip count, and thus cost. Some RISC controllers include sophisticated I/O capability on-chip, including ana-

log-to-digital converters. Embedded processors, as opposed to desktop workstations, will be discussed in Chapter 3.

1.6 LIMITS

One area to explore is the limits to the performance of the technology. Since the
thrust of the RISC ideology is the quest for speed of computation, it is informative
to explore what limits are imposed on this parameter, and from where these limits
derive.

Technology has begun to hit the fundamental physical limitations in hardware development. These include the speed of light as an upper limit to communication
speed and the uncertainty principle as a lower limit to feature size in storage and
processing media. In the near term, hardware capability will continue to develop at
an increasingly rapid rate, but will begin to decrease in complexity rate without fundamental breakthroughs. In particular, processor capability will outstrip the ability
to provide fast memory access and sufficiently fast I/O, and to develop code. One
solution is to develop methodologies for applying multiple processors in parallel to
large and complex problem sets of interest. This approach is applicable at any point
in the technology curve. Moore's Law presents the empirical observation that chip
complexity has doubled and is doubling roughly every 18 months. Obviously, this
can't continue forever. But it is continuing, at considerable cost. A recent addendum
by Gordon Moore, co-founder of Intel Corporation, may present a limit to the
growth. He observes that the cost of production facilities doubles for each microprocessor generation [3].

What are the limits to the basis technology? The answer to this question sets limits
on sequential processors. The speed of light is roughly 12 inches per nanosecond in
vacuum, and slower than that in other media. The mobility of charge carriers in silicon, gallium arsenide (GaAs), or other semiconductors is significantly less than the
speed of light. Similarly, we need to consider the fabrication technology. What is the
limit of resolution of visible light, X-rays, e-beams, and so on? Features are currently below one-half micron in size, and with busing less than 0.1 micron. One factor
working in our favor is that, as devices get smaller, and features get closer together,
communication times drop, and operating speed rises. At the same time, power density goes up, and devices are in danger of melting from their own operation. This is
a driver for the recent push from the traditional 5 volt devices to 3.3 and even lower
voltages, as the power goes as the square of the voltage. For this reason, the Intel P6
chip was introduced at 2.9 volts. Another factor is the ability to distinguish between
logic levels and to sense transitions. The binary system uses two levels, and we must
be able to distinguish between them for system operations.

There are several key questions to consider in assessing this technology. These are
presented, without answers, to provide a basis for further thought.

1. Is there a practical upper limit to processing speed? And, are we nearing that
   limit?

2. Is there an upper limit to memory size? Thirty-two bits of addressing used to be thought sufficient, but recently the trend is toward 64-bits. How many bits are really needed?

3. Is there an upper limit to connectivity or I/O speed? What do we have to communicate with, and at what speed? What latency is acceptable?

4. What are the requirements for "intelligent" systems? What level of processing is required for systems for vision, human-level processing, dolphin-level sonar, and so on?

5. Where are the computational barriers that prevent or limit progress in the physical and biological sciences?

One limitation to constantly increasing performance of RISC machines is the communication problem between the CPU and memory known as the *von Neumann bottleneck* [4]. It is not unique to RISC machines, but is part of the overall performance problem in computer design. It was recognized by computer pioneer John von Neumann in his work at Princeton's Institute for Advanced Studies, after World War II. He recognized that there is a communication channel between memory and the CPU, which has a limited capacity. To make things go faster, we increase that channel capacity, or we implement multiple channels. We can essentially double the channel capacity by using a Harvard architecture, with two paths between the CPU and memory. By using a 64 bit data path between the CPU and memory, we have twice the channel capacity of a 32 bit path, at the cost of increased complexity of the memory system. Contention for communication resources such as shared buses adds to the complexity and overhead of arbitration.

The heart of RISC is derived from what is termed "Flynn's anomaly," or "Flynn's bottleneck" [2] which states that, at best, a processor element (PE) can do only one thing per clock cycle. One solution is to speed up the clock rate, so we get more clock cycles per unit time. This simply goes with the flow in modern digital design, where basic system clock rate has been increasing according to a variation of Moore's law since chips were first made. Another approach is to have multiple processor elements, each doing one thing per clock cycle. This results in a parallel or vector machine, the multiple-instruction single-data (MISD) or multiple-instruction-multiple-data (MIMD) of Flynn's taxonomy. Although the discussion of parallel processors per se is beyond the scope of this book, several RISC architectures lend themselves particularly well to this approach. One of these will be discussed in Chapter 7. In addition, "fourth-generation" or superscalar RISC machines include multiple execution units that, at the chip level, provide more than one instruction per cycle throughput by providing more than one processing element in the same package.

However, the main concept of RISC is to get more done per processor element per clock cycle, regardless of the actual clock value. To maximize this, we have to examine what happens during a clock cycle. We do this in Chapter 2, which dissects the fetch/execute cycle. It is recommended that the reader be thoroughly familiar with this material, or the rest of the book won't make much sense.

1.7 QUESTIONS

1. What is the benefit of fixed-length instructions? What is the cost of variable-length instructions?

2. What are the advantages and disadvantages of a microcoded instruction decoder, versus a hard-wired one? What are the impacts on the code generation portion of the compiler for both cases?

3. What is the bandwidth advantage of the Harvard over the von Neumann (or Princeton) architecture, and how is it achieved?

4. What is the effect of eliminating microcoded instructions? What penalties are incurred?

5. What are the advantages and disadvantages of large on-chip register sets?

1.8 REFERENCES

[1] Hennessy, John L., and Patterson, David A. *Computer Architecture A Quantitative Approach.* San Mateo, CA: Morgan Kaufmann 1990. ISBN 1-55860-069-8.
[2] Flynn, M. J. "High-Speed Computing Systems," *Proc, IEEE* 54:12, 1901–1909 1966.
[3] Gilder, George, "The Bandwidth Tidal Way," *Forbes,* Dec. 5, 1994 154(13) S158.
[4] Aspray, W. and Burks, A. (eds.). "Papers of John von Neumann," Cambridge, MA: MIT Press, and Los Angeles, CA: Tomash, 1987.

1.9 BIBLIOGRAPHY

Bailey, David H., "RISC Microprocessors and Scientific Computing," RNR Technical Report RNR-93-004, March 26, 1993, NASA-Ames Research Center, Mountain View, CA.
Brooks, Eugene D., Heston, Barbara J., Warren, Karen H., Woods, Linda J. (eds.), "The 1992 MPCI Yearly Report: Harnessing the Killer Micros," August 1992, Massively Parallel Computing Initiative, Lawrence Livermore National Laboratory.
Brooks, Eugene D. and Warren, Karen H. (ed.), "The 1991 MPCI Yearly Report: The Attack of the Killer Micros," March 1991, Massively Parallel Computing Initiative, Lawrence Livermore National Laboratory.
Clarkson, Mark A. "The Quest for the Molecular Computer," May 1989, *Byte,* 14(5) 268–73.
Cole, Bernard C. "Scaling the Limits," Feb. 15, 1993, *Electronic Engineering Times.*
Geppert, Linda, "Not your Father's CPU," Dec. 1993, *IEEE Spectrum,* p. 20.
Gunn, Lisa, "The Problems of RISC-Based Designs," Nov. 1989, *Electronic Design,* 37: 69–72.
Heudin, J. C. and Panetta, C., *RISC Architecture.* New York: Chapman & Hall, 1992. ISBN 0-442-31605-4.
"High-Performance Computing and Communications: Technology for the National Informa-

tion Infrastructure," supplement to the President's Fiscal Year 1995 Budget, Committee on Information and Communication, National Science and Technology Council, 1995, 2nd printing.

"High Performance Computing and Communications: Toward a National Information Infrastructure," Committee on Physical, Mathematical, and Engineering Sciences, Federal Coordinating Council for Science, Engineering, and Technology, Office of Science and Technology Policy, 1994.

"HPCC FY 1995 Implementation Plan," April 1994, National Coordination Office for HPCC, Executive Office of the President, Office of Science and Technology Policy, NCO HPCC 94-02.

Howard, Bill, "All's Quiet on the CPU Front," Dec. 6, 1994, *PC Magazine,* 13n(21) 105.

Machrone, Bill, "Machrone's Law Repealed After 10 Years," July 11, 1994, *PC Week,* 11n(27) p. 69.

Mitchell, H.J., *32-bit Microprocessors.* New York: McGraw-Hill, 1986. ISBN 0-07-042585-X.

Patterson, David A. and Hennessy, John L., "Computer Organization & Design The Hardware/Software Interface." San Mateo, CA: Morgan Kaufmann, 1994. ISBN 1-55860-281-X.

Reed, Mark, "The Quantum Transistor," May 1989, *BYTE,* vol. 14n(5) 275–81.

Slater, Michael (ed.), "Understanding RISC Microprocessors," *Microprocessor Report,* Emeryville, CA: Ziff-Davis, 1993. ISBN 1-56276-159-5.

Weiss, Ray, "RISCy History," Jan. 1995, *Computer Design,* 34: 105.

Weiss, Ray, "Superscalar RISCs Battle for High-End Perch," Nov. 1994, *Computer Design,* 33: 34–36.

2

RISC BASICS

2.1 INTRODUCTION

This chapter examines the basics of the RISC design philosophy. First, we need to reexamine the classical fetch/execute cycle to see where the time-consuming elements and phases reside. Then, we can isolate those elements that are best for optimization. Recall that RISC as a design philosophy tags along with the general trend in digital architectural design toward denser structures and faster clock speeds. The bulk of this chapter discusses memory techniques. Most of these are not unique to RISC, or even to microprocessor-based systems. Recently, RISC has been the major driver of memory performance. CISC systems have benefited from this as well.

Currently, most computers are not RISC, but this is rapidly changing. The distinction between RISC and non-RISC is blurring. Perhaps we should define RISC-influenced designs. In any case, RISC is a hot, current design trend in processors. It will likely disappear as a separate entity in a few years, as the RISC features are incorporated more and more into the mainstream. The marketplace dictates upward compatibility with family instruction sets, such as Intel's 80X86, Motorola's 680X0, the SPARC, the MIPS, or DEC's VAX. The large value, or perceived value, of existing code (referred to as the "dusty deck" syndrome) drives instruction-set compatibility. Programmers, engineers, and their managers do not want new instruction sets (reduced or not), with new toolsets to master, new bugs to discover, new procedures to learn. However, every end user benefits when the existing instructions execute faster. RISC as a design paradigm provides this.

Current computer architectures evolved from machines designed when memory was an expensive resource. Instruction sets were encoded to reduce memory usage.

Unfortunately, these instructions are time consuming to decode. Coupled with multiple addressing modes that may involve multiple accesses of memory to resolve the final operand address, the decoding of these complex instructions presented a major bottleneck. The same technological limits to memory complexity limited the amount of silicon dedicated to instruction decoding, forcing microprogramming, or decoding using lookup tables and microsteps. Figure 2.1 illustrates the trend in system performance increases for several classes of machines, showing the more rapid increase for RISC systems compared to other types of computer systems.

2.2 RISC MACHINES

RISC machines, with their simple addressing modes and simple, fixed-size instructions, address the complexity issues in the software, at the compiler level. The issue is that programs usually will be compiled once and run many times. Thus, a longer compile time is a reasonable price to pay for fast run times. Of course, during develop and debug, the compile-time cost is felt more. Optimization can be turned off during development to avoid this issue.

To understand RISC computers, we must understand how computers operate, and just what it is we are reducing. In this section, we will review the elements of a computer, the fetch/execute cycle, and how instructions are executed. In RISC processors, we must be very aware of the relationship between the executing instructions and the hardware. The register and pipeline details must be visible to the compiler. The distinction between hardware and software issues begins to blur.

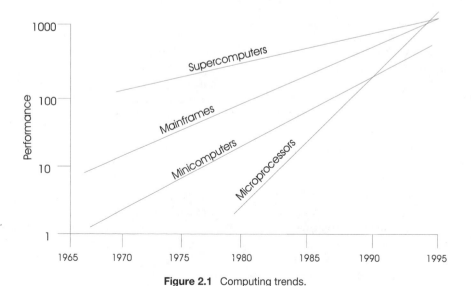

Figure 2.1 Computing trends.

2.3 ELEMENTS OF A COMPUTER

Any computer can be thought of as having three main elements or building blocks. These are the processing element (PE), the memory, and the input/output (I/O) section. The processing element handles the mathematical and logical operations on data, and the flow of control. The memory, which is probably organized hierarchically, holds the data and instructions. The I/O section allows for the user interface, and provides a communication path to other systems or devices. These elements are shown in Figure 2.2, and the functions of the elements are defined in Table 2.1.

It is important to remember that, at any given time, processor and memory speeds are not always well matched. At the current time, processors are much faster than affordable memory. The goal of RISC is to have all instructions execute in one processor clock cycle but, at the same time, to have a rich, complex instruction set. This is the first of many conflicting requirements that force tradeoffs in the design. The one-instruction-per-clock-cycle requirement at the heart of RISC puts a tremendous burden on memory systems design.

Memories are dense, regular silicon structures. Processors are dense, not very regular structures. Processors tend to be regular along the word size, but memories are millions of the same cell design, replicated to the limits of manufacturing technology. Memory production lends itself to economies of scale much more than do processors. Processors are harder to design, test, and build than memory.

The actual fetch/execute cycle can be broken down into several microcycles. The basic microphases are defined in Table 2.2.

We will define each of the steps shown in Table 2.2 to take one clock cycle. Now, an obvious way to speed up the whole fetch/execute process is to overlap each of the steps. In essence, we assign a sub-PE to each step, and let these six units do six things collectively in one clock cycle. But the above steps are not independent. For

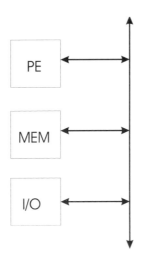

Figure 2.2 Elements of a computer.

TABLE 2.1   Elements of a computer

- Processing Element (PE)
  - Math and logic operations
  - Flow of control

- Memory (MEM)
  - Primary
    - RAM - Fast, Random Access, Expensive
  - Secondary
    - Nonvolatile, Archival, Cheap, Slow

- I/O
  - User Interface
  - Connection with other systems

example, we can't do step two until step one is complete. We can't really do step five until step four is complete, in case we have a branch or jump instruction. Steps three and six may not even be present. What is the solution? We pipeline or assembly-line process the microcycles. This introduces a latency, because of the pipeline depth. However, once everything is working smoothly in sequential code, we get a result every clock. This implies we must do an instruction read, maybe two operand reads, and perhaps an operand write every clock. The burden of speedup has been placed on the memory subsystem. Pipelining and other techniques will be discussed in detail in Chapter 3.

2.4 RISC ARCHITECTURES

The first goal of RISC is to have all instructions execute in one clock cycle. This necessarily gives a small instruction set, because some instructions just can't be done in one clock, while others are computationally expensive to do. The approach to the complex instructions (such as divide) is to synthesize them from primitive, fast instructions.

TABLE 2.2   Fetch/Execute Cycle

- Opcode fetch (memory read)
- Instruction decode (CPU)
- Operand fetch (memory read) if applicable
- Instruction execution (CPU)
- Update program counter (CPU)
- Operand store (memory write) if applicable

RISC also uses a fixed, simple-instruction encoding that can easily be decoded. Thus, microcoded instructions are avoided.

In RISC, the fetch/execute cycle looks like this:

1. instruction fetch
2. instruction decode
3. execute, operand(s) fetch, operate, operand store

There is a natural parallelism in well-selected instruction sets with a simplified (i.e., load/store) addressing. However, the burden on the memory from this stream-lined execution model is immense. The rest of this chapter is devoted to discussing the memory system in general, and specifically for RISC. In the next chapter, we will examine other, system-level approaches to gain speed and throughput performance.

2.5 MEMORY ARCHITECTURE HIERARCHY

The storage hierarchy of a computer system may be viewed as a triangle, as shown in Figure 2.3, with access speed and cost increasing in the upward direction, access time increasing, and cost per bit decreasing in the downward direction. The width of the pyramid corresponds to the amount of storage.

Two major horizontal divisions of the pyramid may be seen. The upper corresponds to the on-chip versus off-chip boundary, and the lower corresponds to the random-access versus sequential-access methodology. *On-chip versus off-chip* refers to features collocated on the same silicon chip or module as the processor. In most cases, we are talking about features on the same die as the processor, but the recent advances in multichip modules allow multiple dies to be combined on one substrate, essentially a silicon circuit board, into one monolithic structure. Having storage on the same chip as the processor provides the fastest access, because there is no need to drive large, external capacitances, and go large distances. On-chip, we will find data registers, instruction queues, data and instruction caches, and read/write buffers. Usually, we refer to the cache on the chip as primary cache, with secondary cache being off the chip. Because silicon real estate is expensive, relatively few bits are provided for on-chip storage. This contrasts with the essentially unlimited amount of storage on removable media such as tape. Disk, tape, and CD-ROM units will not be discussed further in this book. For a discussion of the topic of removable media, an excellent choice is Kempster [1]. On the topic of CD-ROM, see reference [2].

First, we examine some issues in the actual implementation of memory on silicon. We can use static or dynamic memory. From the software point of view, this is transparent to us. However, DRAM, *dynamic random access memory,* takes fewer transistors to implement a given amount of memory. Thus, for a fixed number of available transistors, we get more bits of storage from DRAM. Most on-chip memo-

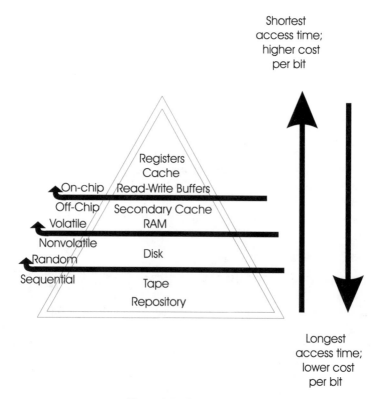

Shortest
access time;
higher cost
per bit

Registers
Cache
On-chip Read-Write Buffers
Off-Chip Secondary Cache
Volatile RAM
Nonvolatile
Random Disk
Sequential
Tape
Repository

Longest
access time;
lower cost
per bit

Figure 2.3   Storage triangle.

ry in processors, such as registers, is implemented as SRAM, *static random access memory.*

First we will examine static memory, and then dynamic. In essence, the memory we need has to be random access; that is, we need to access any piece of data in one clock time. During a read operation, the processor provides the memory with a data item called an address, and the memory responds with the corresponding datum. During a write operation, the processor provides the memory with a corresponding pair of {address, datum}. The memory remembers this correspondence, so it can reproduce it later when asked. Now, this describes the overall process, whether the data are inscribed on clay tablets, granite blocks, as waves in a pool of mercury, or quantum charges in silicon. The key is that the memory device is random access, not sequential access like magnetic tape. With a sequential-access medium such as tape, one has to read from the beginning to get to items of interest.

Parity techniques are sometimes applied to detect memory errors. Even on-chip caches and translation lookaside buffers (TLBs) can be parity protected. The added complexity of a parity bit to detect single or an odd number of errors cannot always be justified. It must be considered whether an appropriate action can be taken after the error is detected. As an example of parity application, the main memory in IBM PC machines and compatibles is usually organized as 9 bits to the byte to provide parity. A parity error on read or write will cause a system interrupt. The parity feature can be disabled.

Another approach is to use more overhead bits for true error detection and correction (EDC). This has implications for systems cost and access times, and is usually not applied except in the most critical applications.

2.5.1 Static Random Access Memory (SRAM)

Original computer memory was ferromagnetic. Once you wrote into it, it retained the value until you wrote into it again. It didn't care if the power went off and came back again, as long as transients were minimized. Unfortunately, ferromagnetic memory was expensive to manufacture in large quantities. Many of the early arrays were hand assembled, in a process akin to knitting. Semiconductor technology provided a cheap, mass-produced alternative. The problem with the semiconductor variant is that it forgets when the power is turned off. In actuality, the contents usually get scrambled when the power is turned back on. It is volatile memory.

Recently, in a blend of technologies, techniques have been developed to use ferromagnetic elements, assembled with integrated circuit techniques to produce nonvolatile, random-access chips. The densities do not compare with all-silicon alternatives, however. An interim solution is to include small lithium batteries within the memory device packaging for a 5- to 10-year nonvolatility period that is well beyond the useful life of the parent system. The recent popularity of flash memory devices as read-mostly devices may lead to their reduced cost and substitution for ROM in many systems.

In SRAM, the basic unit of storage is the flip-flop, a silicon bistable element, as shown in Figure 2.4a. It takes about four metal oxide semiconductor (MOS) transistors to make one bit of storage, and some designs use more. Static random access memory (SRAM) has a faster access time than dynamic random access memory (DRAM) (discussed below), but uses more of the available transistors per bit. Static RAM cells are organized into a two-dimensional array, as shown in Figure 2.4b.

2.5.2 Dynamic Random Access Memory (DRAM)

Dynamic random access memory (DRAM) has some cost and density advantages over static memory, but does have one major drawback—it forgets in a period of milliseconds unless refreshed. This might seem a fatal flaw until you consider that a typical RISC processor can execute a million or so instructions before having to refresh the memory. The DRAM storage cell is as simple as a transistor and a capacitor, as shown in Figure 2.5. The cells are organized in a two-dimensional structure, like the SRAM. The capacitor stores a charge that represents the desired value to be maintained, a "one" or a "zero." The capacitor's charge leaks off, and before long, we can't tell the difference between the original values anymore.

The solution to this is to refresh the memory. This operation, done every few mil-

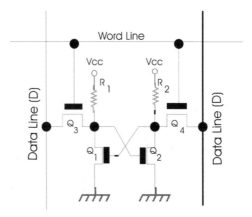

Figure 2.4a Static RAM memory cell.

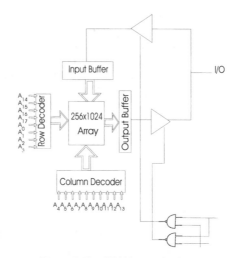

Figure 2.4b SRAM organization.

liseconds, reads the data while it is still possible, and writes it back. Then the refresh clock is ticking again. In practical systems, memory refresh imposes a burden of one to five percent of the available time. This is usually tolerable, but dynamic memory greatly complicates system design of features such as direct memory access, and deterministic interrupt response.

The memory is organized as a two-dimensional structure, that is, addresses along rows and columns as shown in Figure 2.6. The incoming address is split in half. One half is applied to the row address, latched with a *row address strobe* (RAS), and the other half of the address is applied to the columns and latched with a *column address strobe* (CAS).

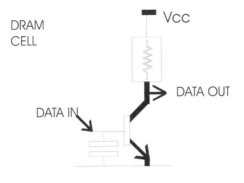

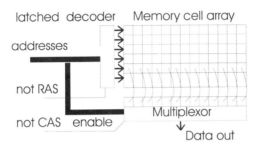

Figure 2.5 DRAM cell.

The important parameter of memory is the cycle time, as opposed to the read or write time. This represents the minimum time between two operations. In essence, we can't do single-cycle accesses repeatedly. We need the memory cycle to be less than the processor cycle, but in actual practice, it is the reverse. Some solutions to this dilemma are discussed in section 2.6. Recent advances in DRAM technology have lead to approaches such as self-refreshed DRAM, and burst mode accesses, which return a series of consecutive bytes for each address.

2.5.3 Registers

Registers are data storage elements on-chip, built up from SRAM cells, to hold data. Different register lengths are used to accommodate different word lengths. Usually, a register holds all of the bits (32, 64, ...) of one word. Registers are also used to hold internal state information. A separate set of registers may be provided for floating point and for integer data. A large number of registers is a RISC trait. Most architectures have settled on about thirty-two integer registers, but AMD's 29k family (Chapter 8) implements 192 registers. The Intel i960 (Chapter 5) has 112 registers. Register access speed is usually commensurate with the arithmetic/logic elements that require or generate the data. In most RISC designs, the sources and destinations for data operations are the registers.

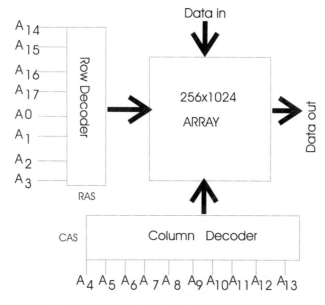

Figure 2.6 Two-dimensional memory organization.

2.5.4 Queues

A *queue* is a first-in, first-out data structure, usually built up from SRAM cells. It is not random access. Queues can be used on-chip to hold fetched instructions, decoded instructions, operands that have been read, or data waiting to be written. The read/write buffers discussed below are a type of queue. The queue provides some smoothing of access times, essentially an impedance matching for asynchronous processes.

2.5.5 Read/Write Buffering

Read/write buffering may be provided on the CPU chip itself. Since reading or writing are lengthy operations compared with the pipeline cycle, it is reasonable to buffer the pending reads and writes on-chip to a depth that allows continuous pipeline operation. Recent implementations allow several pending reads and writes to be stored.

If we examine the issue of memory access, regardless of reads or writes, we see that it is a lengthy process in which we must provide an address, set control signals, and provide or accept data. In some systems, memory reads are given preference over writes on the theory that reads will stall pending operations, whereas writes are results of completed operations. So, the actual order of reads and writes to memory is dynamically reordered to optimize program flow. Of course, if a pending read depends on data to be set by a pending write, we have a coherency problem. This is addressed by result forwarding (at the pipeline and register level), and a sophisticated address snooping in the write buffer. In implementations that offer this feature, there is always an instruction provided to flush the write buffers before any further memory accesses for data are made.

2.5.6 Cache

In the hierarchical memory approach, cache fits between the processor and the main memory, as can be seen in Figure 2.7. It is faster but smaller than main memory, and is usually implemented in SRAM. It may be implemented on the same chip as the CPU. The purpose of cache is to improve the average memory response time to the processor, because much memory with a cycle time commensurate with the processor is not affordable. Cache memory is a technique long used on minicomputers and mainframes to solve this problem.

The CPU runs at cache memory speed as long as the data are available. When the requisite data are not present in cache, the cache is filled from the main memory in burst mode. A cache decouples memory and processor speeds. When the system is operating, the cache will contain the most frequently and recently referenced memory locations.

A cache consists of the actual memory, additional "tag" bits for directory, and logic for content management. This latter is essentially address-compare logic. The tags contain status bits checked by the logic. Keep in mind that the cache is not a separate section of the address space. The cache has the same address as sections of the main memory. How is this possible, you ask? All read and write access is to cache, and it is the responsibility of the memory mapper/controller to keep the contents of the cache and the main memory the same. This is the cache coherency problem, to be discussed later. It becomes particularly important where multiple caches are involved.

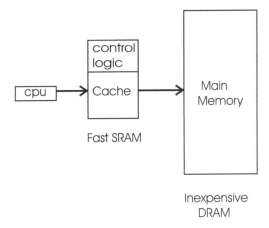

Figure 2.7 Cache memory.

All memory requests from the processor pass through the cache. The cache logic determines if the requested address is present in the cache. If so, we have a cache hit, and the requested data are passed back to the processor. If the data corresponding to the address are not present in the cache, we have a cache miss, and the data must be fetched from main memory. There is a small but finite overhead added to all memory references by the cache process, but the overall benefits outweigh the costs. The overhead of cache misses can be hidden by address pipelining.

When a cache miss occurs, and the data are fetched from main memory, it is stored in the cache as well, for future references. Where does it get put? If the cache is full, something must be stored back into main memory to make room for the new data. Most controllers use the least-recently-used (LRU) algorithm to make this decision. If the data item to be stored back has not been changed since it was read from main memory, it does not have to be written back, saving a step. Thus, one of the tag fields is a "dirty bit" that tracks whether the data items in the cache have been modified since they were read.

The "hit rate" of the cache, which measures how often the reference item is actually present, is a performance measurement. The higher the number the better, and designers hope for 95 percent or better. The hit rate depends on the size of the cache, and the "locality of reference" of the code. This refers to the distance from one referenced item to the next sequentially accessed item, in terms of memory addresses. Sequential accesses of sequential addresses are good for a caching scheme; numerous branches are not, forcing frequent invalidations and refilling of the cache from main memory. Code has a greater locality of reference than data, and there are different approaches to caching data versus caching instructions. The larger the cache the better, but cache memory is an expensive resource. At some point between 64 and 256 kilobytes, diminishing returns set in. A cache may hold virtual addresses, as seen in Figure 2.8a, or physical addresses, as seen in Figure 2.8b. Some systems use both schemes.

There are problems unique to each caching approach. Since in a virtual cache the same virtual address may point to different physical addresses, this causes thrashing, or unnecessary memory references. If different virtual addresses point to the same physical address, the virtual cache is said to be incoherent, due to aliasing. A solution is to increase the virtual tag field to include a context field to identify uniquely virtual addresses. Hardware and software can detect and eliminate aliasing problems. Virtual address caching is more complicated than physical caching, but is more effective in preserving processor-memory access throughput.

The cache block or line size greatly affects performance. Upon a cache miss, the cache is refreshed not just with one byte or one word, but with a group of sequential addresses called a *line*. This is the minimum block transferred from main memory to cache, ideally in burst mode. Increasing the size takes advantage of locality of reference, particularly of code. Increasing line size generally increases hit rate. However, too large a minimum involves excessive time to update the cache line. The line size should be commensurate with the memory system bus width.

Another parameter that affects cache performance is associativity, which ranges from one to one, or direct mapped, through set-associative to complete, or fully as-

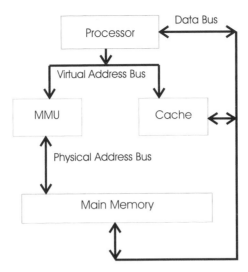

Figure 2.8a Virtual cache system.

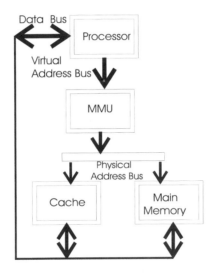

Figure 2.8b Physical cache system.

sociative. A direct mapped cache, as seen in Figure 2.9a is one-way set associative. Each location in cache is mapped to one line in main memory. This reduces the number of searches required in cache to one.

Direct-mapped systems are susceptible to thrashing, wherein every memory access generates a cache miss. Higher levels of associativity tend to control this problem, at the cost of more complex logic in the cache control. The simplest case is

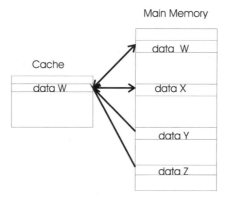

Main Memory maps to only one cache location

Figure 2.9a   Direct-mapped cache.

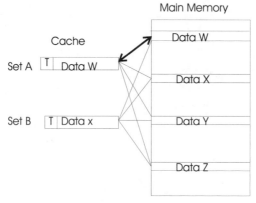

2-way Set-Associate
each Memory maps to two cache locations
T=tag

Figure 2.9b   Set associativity in cache.

two-way set associative, as seen in Figure 2.9b. This acts like two direct-mapped caches in parallel. Two possible cache memory locations are mapped to one line in main memory. In four-way set-associative cache we have, in effect, four caches in parallel. In the fully associative case, each main memory location has a unique cache entry. In most cases, the fully associative cache has higher performance than a lesser, set-associative architecture.

The replacement policy of cache refers to the action taken upon a cache miss. Direct-mapped caches usually use an update-always scheme and the LRU approach (explained above).

With cache, one must also decide a memory update policy. This depends on the whether the cache is unified, instruction only, or data only, among other things. The write-through approach specifies that all processor writes update both the cache and the main memory. A posted-write scheme avoids wait states by allowing the write to main memory to be buffered, so the processor can continue. In the copy-back mode physical memory is updated only when cache lines are flushed.

For multiprocessor systems, each with its own cache, the caches must be kept consistent with each other and with main memory. A multiprocessor system with cache can be seen in Figure 2.10. This is the issue of cache coherency. There must be identical data values for a given address. Each cache unit has to track the activity of the other units to ensure coherency. This is called "bus snooping," as the cache units look on the system bus for references to addresses contained in themselves. Memory references are made by all bus masters, not just CPUs. Thus Direct Memory Access (DMA) devices may cause a difference in the contents of main memory, not reflected in a cache. A higher-performance system would allow the processor to operate out of the local cache while the DMA is proceeding into the main memory. The tags must be expanded to indicate whether a cache has exclusive use of a data item, and whether the item in main shared memory has changed. The snooping logic adds complexity to the cache controller, but should not add any latency to accesses.

In the exclusive, unmodified case, no other caches contain a copy of a particular cache line, which is the same as memory.

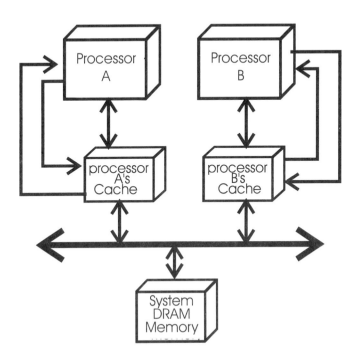

Figure 2.10 Cache coherency in multiprocessors.

A popular protocol for multiprocessor cache coherency is referred to as MESI. This stands for the four elements *modified, exclusive, shared,* and *invalid.* Modified refers to cache entries that are available only in one cache, and are different from the corresponding element in memory. Exclusive refers to cache entries that are available in one cache and main memory. Shared refers to items that are available in multiple caches as well as main memory, and invalid refers to data items not available in a specific cache. These four items define the entire set of possible cache entries. Table 2.3 illustrates the MESI cache status, and the allowable state transitions.

Ideally, cache is software transparent, and software need not be aware of its existence or operation. However, for maximum results, if a program and its associated data can be configured to operate completely out of cache with no references to main memory, maximum performance will be achieved.

2.5.7 Main Memory

In the old days, this was called *core* memory, not because of its central position, but because of the fact that it was built up from small magnetic cores. Now, main memory is almost always built up from DRAM. Memory of this nature is now a mass-produced commodity product. The economies of the older systems were such that memory was an expensive resource. Now this is less true, and older restrictions can be relaxed. The impact of memory as an expensive resource is seen in encoded instruction fields and multiple, complex addressing modes, which are now viewed as impediments to fast execution of instructions.

Table 2.3 MESI Cache States

RH=Read Hit
RMS=Read Miss,Shared
RME=Read Miss,Exclusive
WH=Write Hit
WM=Write Miss
SHR=Snoop Hit on a Read
SHW=Snoop hit on a Write or
 Read-hit-with-Intent-to-Modify

2.5.8   Addressing

When we speak of addressing, we almost always mean byte addressing. We may choose to pick up more than one byte at a time, but we specify the word address (a word is of arbitrary length) as the address of the byte containing bit zero—least significant bit (LSB).

2.5.9 Byte Ordering

There is a general philosophy that if there are two ways of doing things, the field of endeavor will polarize into two schools of thought, if not two religions, supporting both approaches. The order in which we store the bytes in a word in memory may go from low-to-high (little-endian) or high-to-low (big-endian) [3]. Now, it really doesn't matter which we use (heresy!), as long as we are consistent. It is easy to translate between the two schemes. Recently, architectures have contained features to handle either representation. Figure 2.11 illustrates byte ordering, and endianess.

To put it in perspective, recall that *big-endian* and *little-endian* were terms coined by Jonathan Swift in *Gulliver's Travels* [4] to describe two warring camps who disagreed over which end of an egg should be opened first.

To explain the confusion over this issue, let us first observe that almost everyone

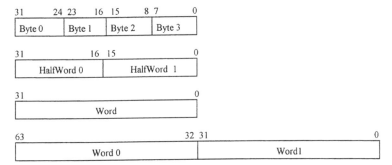

Big Endian Byte Ordering

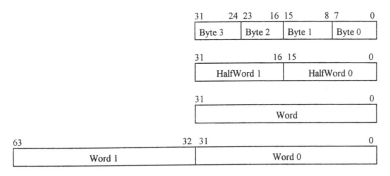

Figure 2.11   Little endian byte ordering.

agrees that bit zero is the least significant or rightmost bit. Thus, bits are numbered little-endian. It is the ordering of bytes in larger word structures that is the source of confusion. Motorola chips and IBM mainframes use the big-endian system, in which byte zero is on the left. Intel chips and Digital Equipment Corporation use the little-endian scheme, in which byte zero is on the right. Most current generation products can use either format, selectable in hardware or software.

2.6 ARCHITECTURAL APPROACHES

In this section we address architectural approaches to reducing system-level memory access time. Most of these approaches will work with any underlying technology, and are useful after the maximum speed of a given technology has been wrung out. Approaches discussed in this section include interleaving, virtual addressing, and memory management units. None of these approaches are unique to RISC, and most have been used on large mainframes ever since the processors began to outrun the access times of the magnetic core memories in use in the 1960s.

2.6.1 Interleaving

One approach to faster memory access, and to reducing apparent cycle time, is interleaving. This is not a new concept, and was used successfully in the early mainframes with core memory. Noninterleaved memory is shown in Figure 2.12a. In essence, we assume that memory will be accessed sequentially. We then use the lowest address bit to address different banks or devices, as shown in Figure 2.12b. Usually, the least significant address bit specifies adjacent locations within the same device. However, we can use the LSB to specify different devices, thus reducing the apparent cycle time. In sequential code, each device would be accessed only half as much, or at one-half the rate. Of course, if we access every other location, the scheme falls apart. We are not limited to using only the least significant bit. Four-way, eight-way, and higher-order interleavings are also possible. Shuffling the memory addresses involves no hardware impact, except on memory board layout.

2.6.2 Virtual Addressing

This section will discuss the technique of virtual addressing, which allows a program to address more memory than it actually has. This mapping of memory addresses from a large virtual space to a smaller physical space (see Figure 2.13) is the job of the memory management unit (MMU). However, MMUs can also do a lot more. Besides providing isolation among the user programs and operating system program, MMUs can provide remapping capabilities for redundancy and security, as well as fault recovery. They can provide restricted access to data and/or code, and restrictions on control transfers. In addition, we can relieve the software from worrying about the amount of memory available. However, virtual addressing will not solve the memory access timing problem; in fact, it makes it worse.

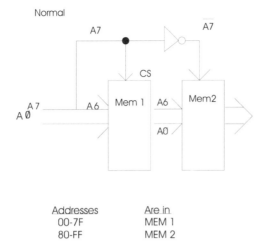

Figure 2.12a   Noninterleaved memory.

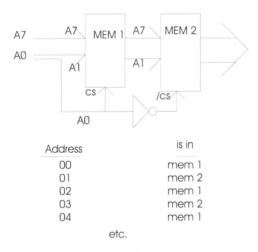

Figure 2.12b   One-way interleaved memory.

2.6.3 Memory Management Units

Memory management units not only provide the translation of virtual addresses to physical addresses, as shown in Figure 2.14, but provide access protection as well. For each access, we can define access rights. We can arbitrarily divide the memory space in user and supervisor spaces, and define access or read/write privileges on each space. We can mark some sections as execute-only, providing no mechanism for reading the code. The penalty in memory management is a translation time overhead associated with each memory access. Obviously, we try to minimize that over-

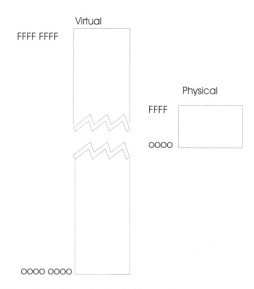

Figure 2.13 Virtual and physical address spaces.

head. Operating systems such as UNIX support demand-paged virtual memory, but not segmentation.

Some applications, such as embedded control, don't really need the large address spaces, and may turn memory mapping off. However, the protection mechanisms are applicable to embedded applications, and the ability to use memory remapping for redundancy can't be ignored.

There are two types of memory management schemes: segmentation and paging. They are similar but distinct approaches to providing the capabilities we need. Both techniques can be used together, and generally are.

Paging is transparent to the running program. It is used to simulate a large, flat address space from smaller, possibly fragmented spaces. It allows programs to define and use data structures larger than available memory, without explicit mapping or overlays at the application software level. Virtual memory will be mapped partially into available real memory, and partially to disk. With the hierarchical memory model, disk memory is simply slower RAM. Paging involves a fixed page, usually four kilobytes in extent.

Segmentation divides available memory into manageable independent address spaces. Segmentation can be applied to the physical address space, or the larger virtual space provided by paging. There are various models of segmentation, the simplest being the flat model, which provides a one-to-one mapping but with all the protection mechanisms that are built into the process. A segment is of variable size, up to a maximum imposed by the hardware.

Translation lookaside buffers (TLBs) are the mechanisms used by the MMU to convert virtual to physical addresses; thus they support paging. In essence, TLBs are special caches that store the most recently accessed page table entries. Although

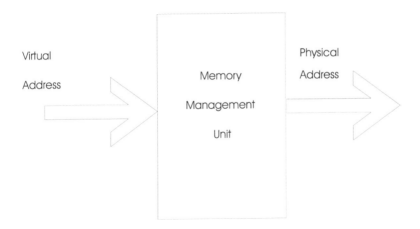

Figure 2.14   Memory management.

the TLB could reside in main memory, usually a special section of the MMU is dedicated to the TLB. The position of the TLB in the system is shown in Figure 2.15.

Besides the translation information, the TLB contains flags that define the page characteristics. There is an "accessed" flag, which defines whether the page has been read or written to. There is a dirty bit (at last, we get to the dirty bits), which defines whether the page has been written to. If the page has been accessed but is not dirty, it needn't be written back to disk when a page swap is necessary.

The "present" bit indicates whether a referenced page is present in physical memory. If the page is present, address translation can proceed. If it is not present, and an exception is generated, the exception handler (the "pager") must choose one page to swap back to disk. This makes space for the requested page. Usually, the page least recently used (LRU) is chosen to be swapped.

2.7 RISC CHARACTERISTICS IN REVIEW

In this chapter, we have focused on the memory systems that are required to satisfy the voracious appetite of RISC chips. The various design features incorporated into the RISC chips are discussed in the next chapter.

In summary, we can list the characteristics of RISC machines that we will examine in detail starting in the next chapter. Not all examples will share all of the characteristics, and most will violate some.

RISC Characteristics

1. Single-cycle instruction execution, as a goal. Superscalar architectures will achieve single-cycle execution per processor element.
2. Consequently primitive but uniform instruction set; uniform word width, uni-

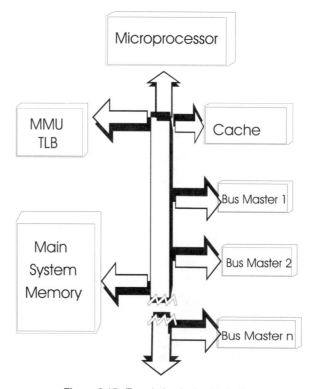

Figure 2.15 Translation lookaside buffer.

form field placement. Uniform instruction formats are easier and faster to decode, and easier to pipeline.

3. Minimal addressing modes; usually load/store architecture. This simplifies the virtual memory translation as well.
4. Interrupt response improved by single-cycle execution:
   a. Deterministic
   b. Short
5. Register-intensive calculations: Numerous registers with math and logic operations on these registers only. This helps keep the pipelines full.
6. CPU is tightly coupled to memory.
7. Pipelined instruction execution.
8. Parallel hardware; multiple-execution units.

2.8 QUESTIONS

1. What features of RISC architecture are finding their way into the mainstream of CISC design? Which features are not really applicable?

2. RISC machines make extraordinary demands on their memory subsystems, which are usually addressed by certain architectural features in the memory subsystem design. Discuss some of the different memory systems architectural approaches, and how these alleviate the memory bandwidth problem.

3. Besides faster execution time, what advantages does a RISC system have in real-time applications?

4. What is the depth of the prefetch queues on the various 80X86 family members? What are the consequences for nontaken branches on these machines?

5. Take a representative CISC instruction set and eliminate all instructions that take more than one cycle to execute. What is the resulting instruction set, and would it be sufficient for useful work? What is gained by allowing instructions of time two or three cycles?

2.9 REFERENCES

[1] Kempster, Linda, Media Mania! The Fundamentals and Futures of Removable Mass Storage Media. Avedon Associates: Potomac, MD. 1994.

[2] Starrett, Robert and Parker, Dana J., CD-ROM Fundamentals. Danvers, MA: Boyd & Fraser, 1994, ISBN 0-87709-168-4.

[3] Gillig, James R., "Endian Neutral Software, Part 1: System Concepts and Implications," Oct. 1994, *Doctor Dobb's Journal,* 19(11) 62, and "Endian-Neutral Software, Part 2: Program Design and Coding Practices, Nov. 1994, (19) (13) 14.

[4] Swift, Jonathan, The Travels of Lemuel Gulliver. London: Motte, 1726.

2.10 BIBLIOGRAPHY

Adamson, Malcom, *Small Real-Time Design: From Microcontrollers to RISC Processors.* UK Sigma Press, 1990.

Bailey, David H., "RISC Microprocessors and Scientific Computing," March 26, 1993, RNR Technical Report RNR-93-004, NASA/Ames Research Center, Mountain View, CA.

Bell, Gordon and Newell, Allan, *Computer Structures, Readings & Examples.* New York: McGraw-Hill, 1971. ISBN 0-7-004357-4.

Cache Tutorial, 1990, Intel 296543-001.

Crichlow, Joel M. *An Introduction to Distributed and Parallel Computing.* Hertfordshire, UK: Prentice-Hall, International (UK) Ltd. 1988. ISBN 0-13-481086-4.

Furber, Steven B. *VLSI RISC Architecture & Organization.* New York: Dekker, Electrical Engineering and Electronics Series #56, 1989. ISBN 0-8247-8151-1.

Harrison, M. A. et al., "Advanced Computing in Japan," Oct. 1990, Japanese Technology Evaluation Center of Loyola College in Maryland, NTIS Report PB90-215765.

Heath, Steve, *Microprocessor Architecture and Systems: RISC, CISC, and DSP.* Oxford: Jordan Hill, 1991. ISBN 0-7506-0032-2.

Hennessy, John, and Patterson, David A., *Computer Architecture A Quantitative Approach.* San Mateo, CA: Morgan Kaufmann, 1990. ISBN 1-55860-069-8.

Heudin, J. C., *Les architectures RISC.* London: Chapman & Hall, 1992.

Johnson, Mike, *Superscalar Microprocessor Design.* Englewood Cliffs, NJ: Prentice Hall, 1991. ISBN 0-13-875634-1.

Levy, Markus, "A Thumbnail Sketch of Cache Memory," Jan. 19, 1995, *EDN,* pp. 30–38.

Milier, Richard K, Walker, Terri C., "RISC Architecture," 1989, Future Technology Survey No. 87, LC88-81639.

Patterson, David A. and Hennessy, John L., *Computer Organization and Design: The Hardware/Software Interface.* San Mateo, CA: Morgan Kaufmann, 1994. ISBN 1-55860-281-X.

Ricchetti, Dominic, "The Emergence of the RISC PC," Oct. 1994, *OEM Magazine,* 11, pp. 36–49.

Slater, Michael, *A Guide to RISC Microprocessors.* New York: Academic Press, 1992. ISBN 0-1649140-2.

Slater, Michael (ed.) "Understanding RISC Processors," *Microprocessor Report,* Emeryville, CA: Ziff-Davis, 1993. ISBN 1-56276-159-5.

Stallings, William, Reduced Instruction Set Computers. 2nd ed., *IEEE Computer Society Press Tutorial,* 1990, ISBN 0-886-0713-0.

Tabak, Daniel, *Advanced Microprocessors.* New York: McGraw-Hill, 1993. ISBN 0-07-062807-6.

Tabak, Daniel, *RISC Systems.* New York: Wiley, Research Studies Press, 1990. ISBN 0-471-92694-9.

"Trends in Computing," 1988, *Scientific American,* vol. 1.

Veronis, Andrew M., *Survey of Advanced Microprocessors.* New York: Van Nostrand Reinhold, 1991. ISBN 0-442-0120-7.

3

RISC APPROACHES
AND TECHNIQUES

3.1 INTRODUCTION

This section discusses various approaches and techniques used in RISC processor design. First, we'll examine where the bottlenecks are in processing, to derive a set of targets to optimize. We'll look at rate balancing, then some concepts of RISC. We next need to examine how these RISC characteristics are achieved. The performance equation will give us insight into the tradeoffs made with RISC. At the same time, we can examine the performance limitations inherent to CISC architectures. We'll examine architectural approaches for performance, then look at specific examples, such as pipelining. We need to examine the main schools of thought on RISC architecture, represented by the Stanford and the Berkeley approaches. Then, we look at how RISC has evolved beyond engineering workstations to embedded applications. An important topic is the support software, which we will examine in the section on optimizing compilers. We wrap up with a discussion of the built-in test features.

3.2 WHERE IS THE BOTTLENECK?

In any scheme designed to improve performance, we need to ensure that we are concentrating on those system elements that need optimization. First, we must derive requirements by examining where the bottlenecks are in our problem set. Do we need faster integer or floating-point calculations? Do we need faster double precision arithmetic, or faster graphics manipulation? Are we bound in the amount of information we can access, and not in the amount we can process?

3.3 PROCESSOR-TO-COMMUNICATIONS BALANCE

Most problem domains have an inherent requirement for processor throughput and communication bandwidth. In embedded applications, we shall see that the metric of interest is usually interrupt response determinism and latency. In large scientific or engineering problems, it is usually millions of instructions per second (MIPS) or megaflops. We also have to consider memory capacity and speed. No matter how many registers we have on-chip, we are unlikely to have enough to be able to invert a fifty-thousand by fifty-thousand-element matrix without an access to memory. What we want is enough registers to minimize cache accesses, enough cache to minimize main memory accesses, and enough main memory to minimize disk accesses. For high external I/O bandwidth processing, such as video data, we need an architecture that lets the data flow through the processor, because we won't have enough memory to buffer more than a few seconds' worth of data. However, we can examine the inherent "graininess" of the problem to decide whether it can be partitioned and operated upon in parallel.

Although faster uniprocessors are one answer, and certainly the trend of technology, they do not provide an answer to the essential problem of getting around the von Neumann bottleneck (Chapter 1). This is, in essence, a communications channel restriction problem between the processor and memory. Coupled with Flynn's anomaly (Chapter 1), which states that one processor element can do only one thing at a time, an upper bound is placed on the throughput of uniprocessor systems. Let's look at some definitions. If we have more than one processor working on a problem, we have multiprocessing.

Multiprocessor systems tend to convert compute-bound problems into communication-bound problems by stressing the interprocessor interconnect topology. A usual solution is the use of high-bandwidth channels such as shared memory. A key interprocessor communication question to answer is whether the communication resource is shared in time, by means of time division multiplexing (TDM), or in space, by means of cross-bar switching. Regardless of the scheme used, the interprocessor communication channel has an upper limit (a la Shannon [1]), and most processors are not well balanced in terms of processing capability with respect to I/O capability. A metric in this area is the number of operations that can be performed on each byte of incoming data, in mega-operations per second per megabyte per second, simplified to operations per byte. Certain architectures concentrate on this metric, most notably the Transputer (Chapter 7) and the iWarp (section 19.3).

3.4 RISC CONCEPTS

The basic concepts of the RISC paradigm are presented below. Although they may seem obvious and simplistic, they provide the basis for what we term RISC machines. Recall that this is not a book for RISC chip designers. However, the user community needs to understand where the design tradeoffs were made. To speed up processing, we need to:

1. *Eliminate all those instruction that can't execute in one cycle.* First, simplify all Arithmetic Logic Unit (ALU) operations to execute only from registers. This probably means we need a lot of registers. Then, eliminate all instructions that don't execute in one cycle. From the set of simple instructions that are left, can we do real work? Can we synthesize complex instructions, such as divide, from sequences of more primitive instructions?

2. *Move complexity from hardware to software.* Use the compiler to schedule use of the registers, and use of the other internal hardware, to optimize the execution of instructions. Look for the obvious, and rearrange the code to go fast. Allow for dynamic reordering of code and memory accesses.

3. *With more hardware, include more instructions.* As more transistors or silicon real estate becomes available, add more instructions. For example, implement a barrel shifter, which is a combinatorial circuit for doing from one to n (usually, thirty-two) shifts in one clock. Throw hardware at the problems. Include multiple execution units.

4. *Go with the flow on higher clock speeds.* As clock speeds increase, take advantage of this. For RISC, MIPS = MHz. That is, since we can execute one instruction per clock, we should be able to do as many instructions per second as there are clock ticks per second.

Given these guidelines, what characterizes a fast RISC machine?

1. A fast clock rate, as a result of very large scale integrated (VLSI) design, lean instruction set architecture, and tight integration of memory system

2. Low instruction counts; balanced instruction set design coupled with an optimizing compiler

3. Low cycle count per instruction, with a goal of one or less

4. A regular instruction set architecture with no microcoding; a large number of registers; simplified addressing modes

Actually, each of these traits is violated by one or more of the real RISC architectures we will examine in subsequent chapters. However, we use these as guidelines to help us decide in general what is RISC and what is not.

3.4.1 How RISC Characteristics Are Achieved

Instructions are simple and hardwired. Microcode is not needed for decoding, because the bit fields are regular, and the instruction width is fixed. This contrasts with a CISC architecture such as the Intel 80386, where an instruction varies between one and seven bytes in length. In RISC, instructions are chosen to execute in one machine cycle. Emphasis is placed on pipeline efficiency. There are few addressing modes; most RISC architectures are load/store, where internal registers hold the operands. Parallelism is exploited at a low level by overlapping loads and stores and by delayed jumps. There is a minimum processor state, such that context switching can be accomplished quickly. The actual number of instructions doesn't matter, as long as they all execute in one cycle.

3.4.2 Why RISC Is Better

1. Streamlining of the instruction set improves the clocks per instruction by a factor of two to six.
2. Clock speeds are commensurate with or better than non-RISC architecture.
3. The price of this simplification is the increase in the number of instructions executed per task. This increase can be kept smaller than the corresponding decrease in clocks per instruction, for a net gain, as we'll see in the next section. We can express this net increase in a quantitative fashion, using the performance equation (described below). It will show us how optimizing one factor can have adverse effects on another.

3.4.3 Performance Equation

$$\text{time} = \text{instructions/task} * \text{cycles/instruction} * \text{time/cycle}$$

The time to perform a given task on the machine is set by the product of these terms. The terms are not independent. The instructions/task term is set by the compilers and the algorithms. The cycles/instruction term is set by architecture. The time/cycle term is set by the clock speed capability of the base technology.

Decode time delays each instruction. Instructions must be hardwired decoded, not microcoded or decoded by lookup. Memory access time also affects this parameter. Instruction decode time is a function of the complexity of the instruction set, the encoding method, and the number and variety of bit fields within the instruction. Fewer options and possibilities allow for faster operations. Memory access time can be minimized by use of hierarchical memory with fast cache. A Harvard architecture doubles the effective memory channel bandwidth. Multiple caches on each line allow for fast operation. The locality principle is higher for instructions than for data or a code/data mix. All instructions must be a uniform length, aligned on word boundaries, and accessed by a single fetch.

Routes to Higher Performance

1. Faster clock
2. Larger on-chip caches
3. Branch prediction; branch-miss penalty minimization
4. Superscalar techniques; parallelism at a low level; multiple execution units
5. Superpipelined techniques
6. Wider data paths and/or instructions

Analysis of large amounts of raw source code reveals that about 90 percent of all instructions executed are simple load/stores, ALU operations, and branches. The other 10 percent are complex instructions such as divide, or complex addressing modes such as base indexed. For CISC designs, the instructions/task term is low, but the cycles/instruction term is high, sometimes seven to eight, or more. For RISC, cycles per instruction is one, but instructions per task may be larger than for CISC. RISC leverages the product of instructions per task and cycles per instruction better than CISC. CISC machines are driven by different forces, and must remain instruction-set compatible with previous family members and compilers.

3.4.4 Performance Limitations for CISC

CISC architecture machines tend to have rich, complex instruction sets that minimize the instructions/task term. In the simplest case, consider a divide instruction. If we concentrate on reducing the instructions/task term, we get a repertoire of complex instructions, which tends to increase the cycles/instruction term for all instructions. For example, complex instructions require a complex encoding that increases the decoding complexity for the entire instruction set. Even the simple instructions share this penalty.

3.4.5 RISC Model for Performance

RISC designs allow for better compiler optimization, which reduces the instructions/task term in the performance equation. Cycles/instruction, with a goal of one, is enhanced by high-performance memory architecture, bigger pipelines with better issue and scheduling logic, and wider architectures allowing the initiation of multiple instructions per clock. The underlying process technology provides better time/cycle through advances in production techniques, use of faster technologies, and denser devices.

Pipelining allows the processor to initiate a new instruction every clock. However, not all instructions can be completed in one clock; some have data dependencies, and some have a built-in latency. Examples of these are load/stores, branches, and floating-point operations. The pipeline allows the apparent removal of this latency.

3.5 ARCHITECTURAL APPROACHES FOR PERFORMANCE

There are many architectural approaches we can apply to enhance performance. We can even apply more than one at a time. We are still faced with the allocation of available transistors (silicon real estate) among these features. This involves trades among the available tricks and within the available implementation area. Some techniques work well with others; some are mutually exclusive. In the architectures we will examine later, we will see one or more of these techniques applied. Among the techniques we can consider are pipelining, on-chip caching, and very long instruction word.

Pipelining is discussed next, followed by a discussion of duplication of execution units, a technique referred to as *superscalar.* Caches were discussed in the previous chapter, along with on-chip instruction queues and read/write buffers. We have seen how we can double the memory bandwidth by applying the Harvard architecture, using separate paths to memory for instructions and data. We can also widen the memory path to 64, 128, or more bits. We can widen the fetched data, or widen the instructions (a technique referred to as very long instruction word—VLIW), or both. The cost of widening the access path is the complexity of the packaging; more pins per chip are required.

Minimizing the impact of changes in the flow of control involves the use of delayed branches, branch prediction, and possibly the use of a branch target cache. None of these issues involves hardware alone, as we will see in the section on optimizing compilers.

3.5.1 Pipelines

Pipelines allow for overlapped instruction execution, by dividing the instruction into steps, and doing these steps in parallel in an assembly line fashion. The number of cycles per instruction will be reduced by the depth of the pipeline once the pipeline is full. The time to fill is the latency period. After this, a new instruction is executed each cycle. The pipeline process is disrupted by branches/jumps, interrupts, and other exceptions to the linear progression of the flow of control. Several instructions are simultaneously present in the pipeline, in various stages of execution as shown in Figure 3.1. Here we observe a very simplified four stage pipeline, with a four-step fetch/execute cycle. The aggregate execution delay is reduced, because execution of multiple instructions has been overlapped.

Pipeline management is complicated if instructions take a varying number of cycles. Thus, pipeline management is more difficult for traditional CISC machines than for RISC. A compiler cannot schedule instruction execution to optimize pipeline flow in the CISC case. To minimize the delays and interruptions in the

FETCH, DECODE, EXECUTE, WRITE

Instruction 1	F	D	E	W						
Instruction 2		F	D	E	W					
Instruction 3			F	D	E	W				
Instruction 4				F	D	E	W			
Instruction 5					F	D	E	W		
Instruction 6						F	D	E	W	
Instruction 7							F	D	E	W
CYCLE	1	2	3	4	5	6	7	8	9	10

Figure 3.1 Operation of a four-stage pipeline.

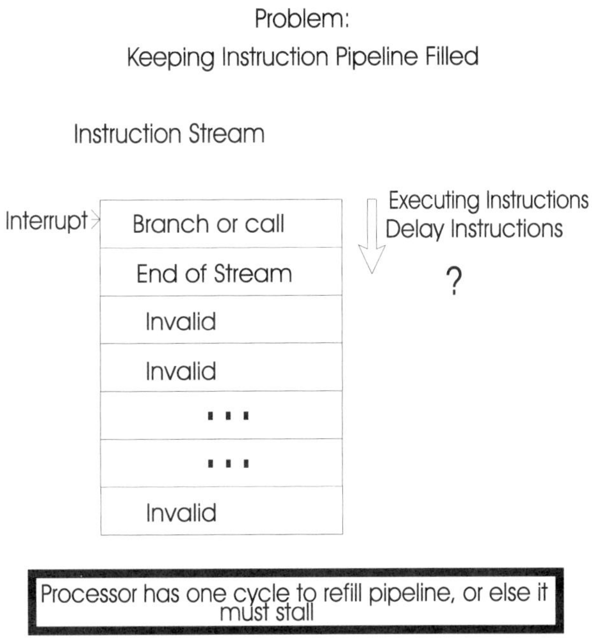

Problem:

Keeping Instruction Pipeline Filled

Instruction Stream

Interrupt →

Branch or call
End of Stream
Invalid
Invalid
▪ ▪ ▪
▪ ▪ ▪
Invalid

Executing Instructions
Delay Instructions

?

Processor has one cycle to refill pipeline, or else it must stall

Figure 3.2 Pipeline interrupt by branches or interrupts. Reprinted by permission from Advanced Micro Devices, Inc., 29K001-78, 29K Family Briefing.

pipeline, the instruction execution times must be uniform. Emphasis must be placed on special handling for those events that upset the smooth operation of the pipeline: branches and interrupts. After a branch, call, or other interruption to sequential operation, the rest of the pipeline contents are no longer valid. This is illustrated in Figure 3.2.

The pipeline must be kept filled, or the advantage of the pipeline is not realized. When a branch is encountered, the contents of the pipeline are invalid and the processor has one clock cycle to refill it. Of course, this is not possible, so the pipeline stalls. Pipeline can be kept filled by fast, zero-wait-state external cache, but this is a costly approach. Remember that the pipeline is sensitive to differences in operation times of instructions, not to their actual lengths. For instructions that take any arbitrary number of clocks to complete, a pipeline can be devised to make it appear that a stream of these instructions executes in one cycle after the latency of the pipeline is overcome. This means that a 37-step pipeline would expedite a flow of 37-clock floating-point arc-hyperbolic sine operations, but with a latency (or a delay to load the pipeline) of 37 clocks. It would be a slow system to interrupt as well.

Branches also cause pipeline problems, because the effective target address of a branch must be calculated. The solution to branch delays in the pipeline is to recognize that there is a branch delay slot immediately following all branches (taken or not), and to rearrange the code to put some useful instruction in this branch delay time. This approach is taken by AMD's 29000 family (Chapter 8), among others. Even though a particular instruction appears in the instruction stream after a branch, it gets executed before the branch is taken, because of the time to complete the effective address calculation.

Conditional branches compound the problem, because the effective target address of a branch must be calculated after (or in parallel with) the evaluation of the condition to decide whether the branch will be taken. If we could predict this at compile time, life would be simpler. Several approaches to this seemingly impossible task are possible and will be discussed in section 3.9 on optimizing compilers.

3.5.2 Superpipelined and Superscalar

The two techniques that are used for performance enhancement, superpipelining and superscalar, are not mutually exclusive. Either technique can tax the designer's ingenuity and the capabilities of the available silicon and toolset. We will discuss both in turn, and then the combination. We will also comment on the applicability of these techniques to "mainstream" CISC processor design. Actually, both came from the CISC world. Superscalar techniques were used in the circa-1960s IBM System S/360 model 91.

The superscalar architecture has multiple execution units, and multiple pipelines in parallel. Multiple independent instructions per cycle can be issued, one into each pipeline. This can be a simple process, like having a separate integer and floating-point pipeline, or a separate add/subtract and multiply pipeline, or it can be complex, by having multiple identical pipelines. The unit in Figure 3.3 has three execution units, each of which could be pipelined. The compiler and the instruction-issuer hardware must work together to examine data dependencies. Delayed branches cause a problem, because there is not enough parallelism in this case to leverage multiple pipelines. In essence, an order superscalar design can start N instructions per clock, and provide N times the performance of a nonsuperscalar machine. There are almost always issue restrictions on the instructions that can be simultaneously issued, even allowing for data dependencies. *Opportunistic superscalar* refers to architectures that issue only to different functional units, such as to one integer and one floating point.

Superscalar, because it duplicates the functional units, requires more complex logic than a superpipelined approach. Delayed loads and branches are a nuisance for superscalar. They don't provide enough parallelism to keep the functional units busy while a target address is fetched from memory. Various architectural approaches, such as branch target caches and speculative execution, are employed to overcome these cases. If we want to issue N instructions, we need to fetch N instructions, and the correct number of corresponding operands. This could be three times N (two inputs and one output). This process is made easier and faster if all of the fetched items are of a fixed size, and aligned in memory.

With superscalar, we have a combinatorial dependence problem. Instructions can be issued only if they are independent. If we wish to issue four instructions, none of them can depend on any of the other three. The average execution rate will be less

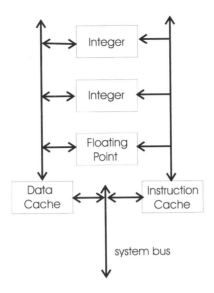

Figure 3.3 Superscalar architecture.

than or equal to the issue rate. One approach to this bottleneck is speculative issue, discussed in section 3.5.9.

Dual-issue superscalar approaches include the Motorola 88k, Ross HyperSPARC, the DEC Alpha 21064, and the HP PA-7100. Triple instruction units include some Intel i960 models and Texas Instruments' SuperSPARC. The IBM RIOS-II is four issue.

The superpipelined scheme uses a longer pipeline with more stages to further reduce cycle time. This exploits fine grain pipelining; the cost is increased latency and a bigger hit for exceptions. According to Jouppi and Wall [2], superpipelined and superscalar processors of the same degree have roughly the same performance. It is possible, although complex, to apply both techniques at the same time. This is referred to as the super-super architecture. This architecture is complex, hard to manage, and hard to keep fed. Superpipelining requires higher clock speeds, whereas superscalar requires more complex logic. Superpipelining requires only slightly more logic than a regular baseline processor. Delayed branches and delayed loads still work in the superpipelined approach. RISC performance is determined by the actual completion rate of instructions, not by the issue rate. Superpipelining is harder to apply to CISC-type architectures, due to their variable-length instructions. In a CISC architecture, the currently executing instruction may define the length of the subsequent instruction. The MIPS R4000 and R8000 use a superpipelined approach, whereas the R10000 is superscalar.

Recall from the performance equation in section 3.4.3 that RISC tries to minimize the product of terms. Different architectural approaches emphasize different terms of the equation. At least two major philosophies have evolved. One emphasizes the last term, the clock speed. This group has been dubbed the "Speed Demons." Digital Equipment Corporation is currently predominant in this group, along with MIPS, and Hewlett-Packard. The other group emphasizes the cycles/instruction term. This group, including SPARC, Motorola, and IBM, is termed "Braniacs." Their metric is SPEC-int per MHz.

Right now, the Speed Demons have a performance edge. That will change in time. Speed Demons tend to be superpipelined, and use a high clock rate, which implies a high power consumption. They require expensive memory. The Braniacs tend to throw hardware at the problem, and have inverted the cycles/instruction term to a superscalar instructions/cycle. It remains to be seen which approach will pay off more in the long run.

3.5.3 Load/Store Architecture

The load/store architecture is a simplification of the addressing modes, and only allows the loading of an internal register from memory, or the storage of a register to memory. The alternatives include a register-memory exchange architecture, a stack architecture, and an accumulator architecture, among others. The load/store architecture reflects the latest trends in compiler optimization techniques, and allows the single-cycle execution of RISC instructions to be achieved. In the load/store architecture, no ALU operations are allowed on memory contents, but only on or between fast internal registers. This can simplify the on-chip logic, freeing transistors (silicon real estate) for pipelines or caches.

Instructions that access external memory can play havoc with a well-tuned pipeline, because it is almost impossible to get these to execute in one cycle, even with fast caches and write-back buffers. RISC architecture usually specifies that all arithmetic or logic operations operate only on or between on-chip registers. "Load" specifies a read from memory to register, and "store" specifies a write from on-chip memory to memory. This is referred to as a "load/store" architecture. However, if a particular load operation is followed by an operation on the data expected to be in the register, the pipeline will stall while the read is completed. Instructions following a load are said to be in a load delay slot for the number of clocks it takes to do the load from memory. There can be no instructions in the load delay slot that depend on the data being loaded, or the pipeline flow must be stalled for the period of the latency. Of course, if the instructions in the load delay slot are not dependent on the data being loaded, the pipeline proceeds smoothly. This suggests that at compile time, the compiler could rearrange the code to achieve this goal. Loads could be moved earlier and grouped. In fact, this is one approach used by optimizing compilers.

3.5.4 Scoreboarding

Scoreboarding is a technique used to keep track of currently used resources by busy processors. Each step in a pipeline uses different resources; a control mechanism must keep track of these. The instruction dispatcher uses this information to determine when and how to issue instructions, which registers to use, and so on. Scoreboarding applies to registers and condition codes as well. Scoreboarding may involve a mechanism as simple as a single bit, as shown in Figure 3.4, or several bits to track whether a resource is in use. A closely associated topic is register renaming, to be discussed next.

3.5.5 Register Renaming

What if we had multiple sets of generic registers in the architecture, and we could change the names of the registers as we desired? What is more important, at any given time, we could have multiple copies of "register R14," for example. This is the basis for register renaming. In essence, we have logical and physical names for the registers, and the resolution is done at the final pipeline, or write-back step. Register renaming reduces register dependencies at runtime, and allows for simultaneous execution of instructions, at a cost of increased complexity. This technique can be applied in a programmer-invisible fashion to mainstream CISC processors, such as the 80x86-compatible M1 from Cyrix (section 19.7.1).

3.5.6 Very Long Instruction Word (VLIW)

Very long instruction word techniques [3] date back at least to Josh Fisher's work at Yale in the 1970s. Fisher went on to found Multiflow to exploit VLIW. After Multiflow shut down, Fisher and some of his design team wound up at Hewlett-Packard. VLIW is essentially visible horizontal microprogramming. If we can fetch more instructions onto the chip in a given time, we will have more instructions ready to decode and execute. In addition, current instruction formats usually involve encoded fields, driven by the earlier need to reduce memory requirements. If we relax the memory usage requirements, we can use a longer, nonencoded instruction format

in-use	resource
1	Register 0
1	Register 1
1	Register 2
0	Register 3
0	Register 4
1	Register 5
0	Register 6

1	Register 58
0	Register 59
0	Register 60
0	Register 61
1	Register 62
0	Register 63

Figure 3.4 Scoreboarding.

that is easier and faster to decode. VLIW is experiencing a comeback in popularity as a technique, and is being actively pursued by the Hewlett-Packard project for a follow-on to the 80x86 instruction set architecture.

VLIW depends heavily on the compiler to group instructions, since the instruction words may scope four to eight RISC-type instructions or more. If the compiler can arrange the instructions properly at compile time, the instruction issuer does not have to do it at runtime. VLIW systems are more dependent on their optimizing compilers (see section 3.9) than most RISC systems. However, VLIW is being actively investigated by several major players as a path to even more performance.

3.5.7 Issues in Instruction Set Design

Most often, hardware is designed to execute a particular set of instructions. The choice of instructions to be executed affects the timing of the machine. As we have stated, our goal is to have a regular set of instructions that all execute in the same time—ideally, one cycle. If all the instructions execute in the same time, the design becomes easier to pipeline. However, we don't always have a completely free choice in instruction sets. Sometimes, instruction sets are inherited from previous efforts. One approach is detailed in the next section.

3.5.8 Hardware Emulation of Foreign Instruction Sets

The value in having multiple instruction sets executable by the hardware is to provide for the efficient execution of other instruction set architectures. This approach drove the design of the IMS 3250 chip (Chapter 14), which is basically a RISC machine with a native RISC instruction set. However, it was designed to be able to execute 80x86 and 680x0 instructions as well. A favored approach is to translate CISC dynamically into RISC instructions. This technique is employed in Intel's Pentium® Pro Processor chip, AMD's K5, and NexGen's Nx586 (section 19.7.1), and is said to be the basis of the PowerPC 615 (Chapter 15).

Emulation of one instruction set by another machine is an old technique, dating back at least to the 1960s. Writable control store (WCS) and microcoded instruction sets made such experimentation possible. It was easy to envision but impossible to implement a generic hardware set with a big rotary switch for different instruction set architectures. Now it is not only possible, but perhaps necessary to implement the 80x86 ISA in this fashion.

3.5.9 Speculative Execution and Issue

Speculative execution occurs after a data-dependent branch, and involves predicting the branch direction and executing accordingly. The Motorola 88110 (section 19.2) supported speculative execution, and it is a favored approach for most high-performance applications.

A much easier technique is speculative issue. This is used in the Texas Instruments' SuperSPARC (Chapter 10) and some i80960 (Chapter 5) family members.

With multiple sets of virtual registers and scoreboarding, a processor can actually follow both paths of a branch, and choose the correct stream of execution (and discard the other) when the sense of a data-dependent branch is resolved. Some architectures can execute through multiple branches, following eight or more threads of execution before resolution is required.

3.6 RISC CAMPS

RISC designs can be traced back to any of three sources in most cases: the work of David Patterson at Berkeley [4], the work of John Hennessy at Stanford [4], or the early IBM work on the 801 machine [5].

3.6.1 Berkeley Architecture

The Berkeley architecture traces its origins back to the work of David Patterson [4] at the University of California at Berkeley, which resulted in the SPARC (*scalable processor arc*hitecture; Chapter 10), currently in its fourth generation and ninth architectural specification. SPARC chips are made by numerous companies such as Ross Technology, Fujitsu, Bipolar Integrated Technology, LSI Logic, Texas Instruments, Matra, Phillips, Weitek, Solbourne, and others. The SPARC architecture forms the basis of Sun Microsystems' workstations. The key distinguishing feature of the SPARC architecture is its register windows.

3.6.2 Stanford Architecture

The Stanford architecture originates in the work of John Hennessy [4] at Stanford University, and has resulted in the MIPS family of chips (Chapter 6) and computers. MIPS (in this context) stands for microprocessor without interlocking pipeline stages. Today, the chips are made by Integrated Device Technology (IDT), Performance Semiconductor, LSI Logic, NEC, Sony, and others. Figure 3-5 shows the major manufacturers of the Stanford and Berkeley derived architectures.

3.6.3 Other Architectures

Numerous other RISC architectures developed and evolved during the 1980s. Some of these include the Inmos Transputer (Chapter 7), developed from Oxford University; Intel's iWarp (section 19.3), which was influenced by Intel's earlier work on the i432 project, and Kung's WARP architecture; and the IBM 801/ROMP/PC-RT/R-6000 projects. IBM holds a series of basic patents on aspects of RISC architecture, dating back to its 801 project.

Many other companies experimented with RISC techniques during the 1980s as well. Not all of this work found its way into products in the marketplace.

RISC is not a new technique. It had been applied to the IBM 801 series machines

Stanford Architecture   Berkeley Architecture

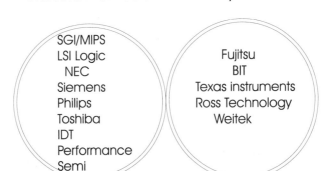

SGI/MIPS
LSI Logic
NEC
Siemens
Philips
Toshiba
IDT
Performance
Semi

Fujitsu
BIT
Texas instruments
Ross Technology
Weitek

Figure 3.5   Schools of RISC. Copyright © 1995 by LSI Logic Corp. Reproduced with permission.

in the 1970s. However, it wasn't until the late 1980s that RISC began to emerge as a dominant force in the industry.

In the first generation, RISC as an emerging technology was represented by the early IBM efforts, the Stanford school, and the Berkeley school. It was applied to technical computing for high performance workstations, and the software tools were poor and limited in scope. The performance was equal to or slightly better than mainstream CISC machines. RISC drove compiler technology and memory architectures.

In the next generation, RISC began to dominate technical computing in high-end engineering workstations, and for graphics-based design. The support software tools were much improved, and decided advantages were demonstrated over CISC machines. The RISC core was being integrated with peripheral controllers for custom applications. The war cries were "smaller, denser, faster, cheaper."

In the third phase, RISC emerged as a mainstream technology, and RISC techniques were applied to the CISC (read: *instruction-set-compatible*) machines. Applications broadened from technical computing to commercial and embedded markets. Performance gains for CISC came harder than for RISC. RISC designers tried superscalar or superpipelined designs, and had 64-bit or wider paths to memory. Architectures were optimized for multiprocessing. Interestingly, each of these generations lasted about two years.

Currently, RISC designers are using superscalar/superpipelined designs with clock speeds beyond 100 MHz. Companies like Digital Equipment Corp. and IBM are betting the farm on RISC, a departure from the mainframe mentality of years past. RISC is being incorporated into mainstream designs like Intel's Pentium Pro Processor. Computer companies like Digital Equipment Corporation (DEC) and IBM are fundamentally different from predominantly chip-making companies like Motorola and Intel. Whereas Intel and Motorola have expanded their role from silicon to systems, DEC and IBM have expanded their sights downward from systems to chips. The major difference is that DEC and IBM have considerable software expertise, and correspondingly, a stake in a large installed base of customers with existing applications code. Figure 3.6 shows some of the relationships between the various architectures.

3.7 DRIVERS IN THE MARKETPLACE

This section attempts to describe the market forces shaping RISC technology. These forces change and evolve in time. The market may not be ready to accept a particular technology, and market maturity takes a long time to develop. The best chip in the world is no good if it doesn't sell. An example of this is the failure of Inmos to recognize the importance of a good C compiler to the marketability of the Transputer. The T-800 languished for two years while Inmos salesmen preached the advantages of the OCCAM language. Too late, Inmos realized that most users don't want another language, no matter how good it is. Other manufacturers have made similar strategic errors.

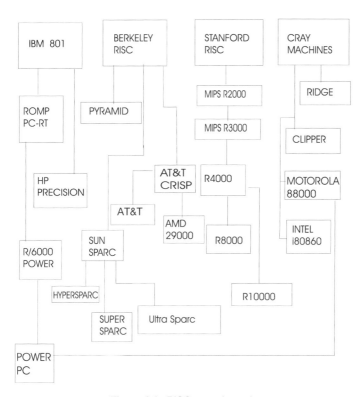

Figure 3.6 RiSC genealogy chart.

3.7.1 Embedded RISC—A Volume Market

What are embedded processors? Well, they are defined more by their applications than by their features. They are more likely to be found inside a larger assembly than on or beside a desktop. They have extensive I/O capability, but usually no direct user interface. They are a subsystem of a larger system.

Although the thrust of early RISC development was enhanced computation that usually found itself in engineering workstations, the market for such endeavors is limited in scope. A much larger market, and, what is more important, a volume market, is found in embedded control. Volume markets are cost driven. There is the primary cost of the part itself, and secondary costs related to sockets, power supply, and other required parts. Memory type and organization are strong cost drivers. The application engineer has to look at what the chip designers have done to achieve performance, and where the design tradeoffs were made. These will imply costs at the systems level. For example, more expensive, faster memory will be required. Some features that enhance workstation performance pose problems for the embedded systems designer. Embedded applications mostly involve elements of real-time control.

Another important concept emerges here: Although we usually associate RISC with 32- or even 64-bit machines, this is not necessarily always true. For a counterexample, consider the Microchip PIC (Chapter 18), which represents a minimalist 8-bit approach to RISC for embedded control. More importantly, conventional RISC manufacturers, who might produce from 50 to 100,000 units for the workstation market, are finding the multi-million-piece embedded systems market appealing. This is a production environment, with customer hand-holding done once, at development time. After that, the process involves turning out product and shipping it. Volume-embedded control markets include laser printers, fax machines, cellular communication devices, and so on. Emerging markets are automotive engine and transmission controls, smart appliances, anti-lock brake/traction control systems, high-end video games, X-terminals, fax machines, color printers and scanners, and more. RAID (redundant array of inexpensive disks) disk controllers and advanced networking techniques such as ATM (asynchronous transfer mode) also demand more capable embedded controllers.

Features of importance to embedded computers include interrupt latency, interrupt determinism, integrated solutions for low chip count, and good development for quick time to market. The devices that address this market are the Intel i960 (Chapter 5), the AMD 29k line (Chapter 8), the Transputer (Chapter 7), some of the SPARC chips such as the Fujitsu SPARClite (Chapter 10), and certain MIPS processors (Chapter 6). Embedded versions of the PowerPC have also appeared (Chapter 15).

3.7.2 RISC Moves into the Mainstream

Recently, RISC has begun to enter the mainstream computer marketplace in several ways. First, although RISC workstations had the highest performance, they lacked user acceptance because they ran proprietary operating systems, or had limited applications software available. This is changing, as the move to "universal" operating systems such as Windows-NT or a codified version of Unix is completed.

Then, there is the effect on the CISC market. It is easy to see the effect of Intel's i860 and i960 on their i486™, Pentium, and Pentium Pro Processor. This is discussed in section 19.7. Similarly, we see Motorola's influence of the 88k on 680x0, and PowerPC. Some RISC techniques, such as superscalar, apply to CISC, and some, such as superpipelining, do not. CISC's retrograde influence on RISC can be seen in the Motorola "Coldfire" (section 19.7.2), and AMD's K5 (section 19.7.1).

A whole other area of endeavor is digital signal processing (DSP) RISC. This is exemplified by Motorola's 96k family, and Texas Instruments' 320C0x0 family, and will be discussed in section 3.7.5.

A major looming mass market is that of (TV) set-top boxes for interactive multimedia, and Internet access. These units must be cheap, capable of mass-production, and plug-and-play in simplicity of operation. They will connect the cable TV–entertainment–home computing industries into a new, massive entity with overwhelming market potential. High-definition television (HDTV) will bring vastly increased demands on bandwidth. The set-top box will provide network interface functions, real-time video decompression, format conversion and control, and decryption. Major players in the entertainment, cable media, and telephone-service worlds are anxious to dominate this new market. Early RISC processor choices in this area include the MIPS, ARM, and PowerPC.

3.7.3 Personal Digital Assistants (PDAs)—An Emerging Market

The next volume market may well be the handheld personal digital assistants (PDAs) like Apple's Newton. These devices have the potential to create a volume market larger than any currently in place.

The class of handheld or palmtop computers known as PDAs or personal communicators imposes special requirements on RISC chips. Primary among these is intelligent power management. All of the contending units are of a fully static design. Another requirement is a small form factor, with a corresponding high level of integration. Thus, single-chip solutions are preferred. Primary contenders in this market include the AT&T Microprocessor (Chapter 19.6), the ARM (Chapter 11), the NEC V-800 (Chapter 16), and the Hitachi SH-7000 models (Chapter 17).

Thirty-two bits are not necessarily required in this application; actually, neither is RISC. Since the environment is entirely different, users will accept something other than a scaled-down version of their desktop system—as long as it interfaces and shares data with the desktop system. A key user demand in PDAs is connectivity—ideally, global wireless connectivity anywhere, at low cost. This is a natural extension of the pager/cellular phone/fax market. The units have to be lightweight, pocket-sized, and use their batteries sparingly.

In 1994, this market was beginning to shake out, with early adopters Apple (Newton, using the ARM processor) and Tandy/Casio (Zoomer, using a low power 80x86 variant from NEC) staying the course, while EO Corporation (Hobbit Processor) folded. A second generation of PDA units should have a better user interface, and thus better market acceptance. This depends on building a user base, an applications software base, and a communications infrastructure.

These units are too small to support a usable keyboard, so emphasis has been placed on handwriting recognition. Small, yet high-resolution screens are required for visibility in all sorts of lighting conditions.

3.7.4 RISC Influence on CISC

This section discusses the influence of RISC design on CISC processors. The Motorola 88k RISC chip (Chapter 19.2) influenced the design of the 68060, the latest in the 68k family (section 19.7.2).

Perhaps the most easily perceived influence of RISC-on-CISC is the development of the 80x86 family from Intel (section 19.7.1), particularly on the Pentium and its clones. Besides streamlining the operation of later family members in the instruction set architecture (ISA), another factor has appeared. Because of the popularity of this ISA for writing applications, a large existing base of code has been developed. A current trend is to emulate the execution of the 80x86 ISA, with assistance from RISC hardware. A software-only approach will work, but won't provide the power of a hardware approach. The software approach has been used by Apple in its first generation of PowerPC-based computers to provide a complementary DOS/Windows environment. IBM is supposedly providing hardware emulation of 80x86 ISA in an upcoming PowerPC model (Chapter 15), and it is a feature of the IMS 3250 chip (Chapter 14).

Binary compatibility is the overall goal. A large, loyal customer base is both a blessing and a curse. The issue is legacy drag, the massive inertia of existing software applications.

Some RISC approaches are more applicable to CISC than others. Those immediately applicable include superscalar, large on-chip caches, and single-cycle instructions. Surprisingly at first glance, many CISC instructions can be made to execute in one cycle. Other techniques used in RISC can be applied to CISC, with some difficulty. For example, we can use the superpipelining technique, but this has problems with variable-length instructions. We can also choose to supply a large register set, in terms of multiple scoreboarded sets of CISC registers. One pathological feature of some CISC architectures, and the 80x86 in particular, is that the currently executing instruction can modify subsequent instructions in the instruction stream. It is all von Neumann's fault.

Is there a performance gap between RISC and CISC, and if so, is it widening or narrowing? There still is a performance gap, with systems built from the high-end RISC chips having the performance advantage. In fact, massively parallel processors (MPPs) built from large numbers of "merchant" RISC chips are challenging traditional supercomputers for large research tasks. Symmetric multiprocessor (SMP) machines, with two to sixteen RISC-based processors, are challenging traditional mainframes and departmental servers. But the gap between RISC and CISC performance is narrowing, due to the software available for CISC that is not available in the RISC world, and the application of RISC design techniques to the latest in the families of mainstream CISC processors. In the future, RISC may disappear as a separate product line, but its influence will be seen in all processors.

3.7.5 RISC-Digital Signal Processing (DSP)

Digital signal processing (DSP) chips trace their origins back to the development of specialized architectures for sonar and radar data processing. The key developments came from Texas Instruments, AT&T, and Motorola. Initially fixed point, recent products have evolved to support floating-point data structures as well. Word sizes have increased from 16 to 24 to 32 bits. The important parameters in a DSP are set by the rate of data movement. Operations on the data tend to be simple and repetitive. A DSP chip doesn't do anything a general purpose CPU couldn't do; it just does it faster. The fact that specialized DSP chips still exist, and haven't been replaced by merchant RISC CPUs, indicates that they still have an edge in processing throughput.

Each company involved in DSP chips has its own view of the marketplace. Motorola has a full line of DSP parts, the 5600x family and 9600x families. The later models have been influenced by RISC design, although Motorola has kept these product lines differentiated. AT&T, with its DSP32C design, has focused on voice and signal processing applications. Texas Instruments, with its TMS320C0x0, has the most RISC-like of the DSPs, culminating in the MIMD system on a chip, the two-billion-operations-per-second TMS 320C080 (section 19.4.1). Analog Devices' SHARC processor (section 19.4.2) has gained a lot of attention for its capabilities as well. The Massachusetts Institute of Technology (MIT) is building a 64-node parallel processor based on the SHARC architecture.

In some applications, a DSP processor can be used as an applications accelerator. The DSP core, optimized for the multiply-accumulate operation key to digital filtering, is sufficiently general to handle a broad range of computation tasks as well. DSPs are finding application in the new multimedia field, processing sound and full-motion video. DSPs have been used for modulator/demodulator (modem) and coder/decoder (codec) applications in PCs for some time.

To muddy the waters, some mainline RISC chips like the HP7100LC (Chapter 13) add specialized instructions to support MPEG/JPEG compression operations on video data. In the short run, RISC and DSP technology will be synergistic—each side has a lot to gain from the other.

3.8 DEVELOPMENT AND DEBUG—SOFTWARE SUPPORT

When the complexity is removed from the instruction set of RISC machines' hardware, that complexity does not vanish. At the systems level, we see that the complexity reemerges in the software. There are many popular interpretations of RISC beyond *reduced instruction set computer.* One of these is *relegate important stuff to the compiler.*

Analysis of "typical" instruction streams has shown that complex instructions and complicated addressing modes are rarely used. Both compilers and assembly language programmers prefer the simplified addressing modes. Thus, the impact of a load/store architecture with one address mode for memory is not too bad. First-generation RISC design used early cache study data from mainframe programs. Now, analysis of instruction streams on the same architecture is leading to performance gains in third- or fourth-generation systems.

Numerous sources exist for tools to develop and debug RISC software. Not all are from the manufacturer; some are from third parties, and some are even free. For example, the GNU C compiler is a popular basis for software development. Since not many chip manufacturers have in-house compiler development teams, much RISC support code comes from specialized compiler-writer houses.

3.9 OPTIMIZING COMPILERS

One lesson painfully learned from the development of fast RISC hardware is that hardware and software development must be done in parallel. This is because of the previously hard-learned lesson that fast, impressive hardware without the supporting software tools is useless. End-users do not want fast, impressive, inexpensive hardware; they want fast, impressive, inexpensive *solutions.* They are unwilling to develop, or wait for the development of good toolsets. Some vendors of RISC hardware are simply chip designers that must contract with external compiler writers to support their products. Other companies, more vertically integrated, such as IBM and DEC, can do the job in-house. It has been a good decade for compiler-writing houses. These optimizing compilers are more difficult to write, and drive the state-of-the-art. A spinoff of the focus on good optimizing compilers for the RISC architectures has been a positive influence back into the world of mainstream CISC compilers. Tracking generations of chip architecture, optimizing compilers are now in their third generation. And optimizing compilers are probably more magic than technology.

It has been the case that good tools lag the hardware by three years or more. Since this is longer than a hardware generation, this implies that the tools don't become available until after the hardware is obsolete. What can be done to speed up this process? Well, first-generation RISC is at a disadvantage because a compiler for a new architecture is harder to write than improvements to an existing tool. Using simulation tools, compiler development can begin before hardware completion. In the best case, software considerations can influence and direct the hardware design. RISC's simple orthogonal instruction set is easy to implement in compilers. The compilers must have tremendous visibility into the hardware, and must have a synergistic relationship with the hardware. For example, the compiler must know the size and organization of caches to take advantage of locality of reference for code and data. The concept is to maximize the cache hits (or minimize the cache misses). This might require a restructuring and rearrangement of the entire program, to make loops commensurate with cache sizes.

Optimizing compilers can take more time to run than standard compilers. This can be an order of magnitude longer. This cost is paid once, at compile time; the benefits are seen every runtime. Compilers can also be used to migrate older code to new hardware platforms. Generally, optimizing compilers share a common back end, such that FORTRAN and C would use a common code generator module.

3.9.1 Optimization Techniques

Numerous optimization techniques for code are known. Almost all require in-depth knowledge of the hardware features in the target processor. Optimization techniques are either general purpose, or architecture specific. This section will touch upon the most popular techniques. Analysis of the source code by instruction profiling reveals which instructions are used, how often, and in what sequences. From these profiles, or code fingerprints, the compiler can begin to compute the optimum way to map the instruction stream onto the available hardware resources. Optimizations run from fine-grained (at the instruction level) through medium-grained (loop level) to coarse grained (program and module). Here is a listing of some of the important optimization methods, as compiled by the MIPSpro Compilation Team, for Silicon Graphics:

Architecture-Specific Optimization Techniques

- Software pipelining
- Instruction scheduling
- Automatic blocking
- Register blocking
- Array padding
- Global instruction distribution

State-Level Optimization

- Array expansion
- Common subexpression elimination
- Global constant propagation
- Dead code elimination
- Global code motion

Loop-Level Optimization

- Loop unrolling
- Loop interchange

- Unroll-and-jam
- Loop distribution
- Loop fusion
- Loop invariant code motion
- Sum reduction

Procedure-Level Optimization

- Procedure inlining
- Interprocedural analysis

Register allocation is used to reduce load/stores. This is also called register coloring or register coalescing. Register coloring takes its name from the minimal map coloring problem. The technique involves the allocation of variables to registers in an optimum manner. One must determine the lifetime of variables to predict when a register may be reused. The underlying approach is to keep all active variables in on-chip registers, and to minimize loads and stores. On-chip registers are a scarce and expensive resource. This technique interacts with hardware scoreboarding of on-chip register usage. Similarly, it is preferable to pass parameters in registers.

In redundancy elimination we reuse results. This allows for common expression elimination. Values are held in registers for subsequent reuse rather than being recalculated each time needed.

Instruction-level or fine-grained optimizations can include software pipelining, instruction scheduling, and register allocation. For loop optimization, we move outside the loop code that doesn't change. This may also be called *static address elimination.* In essence, we vectorize the computation to take advantage of pipelining. In loop-invariant analysis, items that are computed within a loop but do not change within the loop are moved outside the loop structure, and computed once. Another technique is constant folding or constant propagation. Here, expressions using constants can be computed at compile time. Assignment of a constant to a variable is propagated forward to the next use of the variable.

Different languages store and access arrays in different formats. Most languages, except for FORTRAN, store multidimensional arrays in row-major order. FORTRAN stores in column-major order. The accessing of elements in a matrix in a loop should be commensurate with the cache size and the access method, such that each loop iteration does not cause a cache miss.

Software pipelining involves the initiation of loops at constant intervals, without waiting for preceeding iterations to complete. Multiple-loop iterations in varying stages of completion are simultaneously in the pipeline. This makes maximal use of the pipeline.

Loop unrolling involves the decomposing of loop code to multiple copies of straight-line code, similar to macro expansion. Straight-line code runs faster because conditional branches do not need to be evaluated. Hardware is most efficient in accessing linear code. Twenty instructions seems to be the magic number for loop unrolling. This technique increases subsequent scheduling opportunities. Of course, the code gets larger. In certain cases, nested loops can be interchanged, with the inner loop becoming the outer loop. This is done to improve data locality to ensure cache hits and decrease memory bus traffic. A technique called strip mining breaks a single loop into a nest of two loops, with the increase in loop overhead more than offset by increases in data cache locality. In the technique of distribution, a single loop is split into a sequence of multiple loops that operate over different partitions of the original. Conversely, several loops may be combined into one to decrease overhead. In the skewing technique, loop starting and/or ending points are changed. The order of the iterations of a loop can be changed, to allow further processing for nesting reordering.

Unrolled Loop

do i = 1 to m

    x(i) = x(i) + Q * y(i)

next i

unrolled to:

do i = 1 to m by 4

    x(i) = x(i) + Q * y(i)

    x(i) = x(i+1) + Q * y(i+1)

    x(i) = x(i+2) + Q * y(i+2)

    x(i) = x(i+3) + Q * y(i+3)

next i

Similarly, subroutine calls can be eliminated by putting the subroutine code inline (subroutine unrolling). This is faster than the interruption of control flow involved in getting to and returning from a subroutine. The cost is that the code gets larger.

A common technique is to replace slow operations with fast ones. Avoid special cases and, where possible, replace a multiply by shifts and adds. Replace division by multiplication by the reciprocal. Multiply operations are pipelined. Divisions are special cases, hard to optimize in hardware. The reciprocal is division into a known entity. It is implemented in some architectures instead of divide, because the reciprocal followed by a multiply is still faster than a divide.

A very important technique that has a great effect on performance is instruction alignment. Alignment of taken branches on quad-word or 64-bit boundaries optimizes the pipeline refill operation for taken branches. Alignment of code and data for optimum fetches is a valid technique for CISC and RISC runtime improvement.

For optimum pipeline scheduling we do reorganization of code. The reason for scheduling or rearranging the code is to eliminate data dependencies in the flow of instructions that would cause the pipeline to stall. If the result of one operation is needed as an input to subsequent operations, a delay cycle or pipeline "no-op" may be needed. First-order dependency occurs in the case of adjacent instructions with the same destination. Another type of dependency involves an instruction with the same destination as a prior, stalled instruction.

In strength reduction, multiple operations within loops that involve the loop variable and thus change linearly with iteration count are replaced with additions. We replace expensive instructions with simpler ones. In dead (invariant) code removal, code that can never be executed is eliminated. Sometimes prior optimizations have made code fragments redundant and they can be removed in later stages. It is possible in certain cases to trade accuracy for speed. An example is to replace a division in a loop by a reciprocal operation outside the loop, and multiply operations inside the loop. The division is usually the most expensive operation to execute, with the reciprocal being easier.

Generally, we don't want to branch to a branch because of the cost involved in processing branches in the pipeline. The compiler can take care of this for us.

Delayed Load We perform a load from memory to register to provide an operand for subsequent operations. Memory operations are slow compared to internal processor operations, so the memory operand will not be immediately available to subsequent operations in the pipeline. There is a data dependency, or load latency. This delays the pipeline, or requires the use of pipeline no-ops, both a bad idea. The solution is to have the compiler rearrange the instruction stream (if possible) to fill in the gaps with useful work. These include subsequent instructions not dependent upon the pending load or its results. The process is diagramed in Figure 3.7.

Delayed Branch In branch instruction execution, there is a delay due to the effective address calculation. Conditional branches introduce additional delay. These can stall the pipeline or require the introduction of pipeline no-ops. The solution is to rearrange the code, if possible, to execute one or two instructions after the branch is encountered. Even though these instructions appear after the branch opcode, they are executed before the branch is taken. The process can be seen in Figure 3.8. Another technique is branch target prediction, which attempts to determine the data-dependent target of a conditional branch at compile time. Although at first glance this may seem impossible, there are some techniques to accomplishing this. Consider the case of a loop executed 100 times, with a branch at the bottom. One hundred times out of one hundred and one, the branch is taken, and one time the flow of control falls through.

3.9.2 Optimization Levels

Various levels of optimization are possible, depending upon how wide a view the compiler has of the code. Usually, the optimization proceeds bottom-up, with subsequent steps further refining the results of previous steps. The narrowest view is tak-

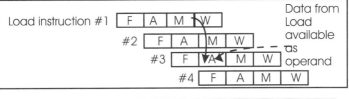

```
Load    R1,A
Load    R2,B
NOP        ◄··   This instruction fills delay slot

Add     R3,R1,R2
```

```
# Consider the code for C :=A+B;F :=D
    Load  R1,A
    Load  R2,B
    Add   R3,R1,R2  ◄ This instruction stalls because R2
    Load  R4,D         data is not yet available
    ...     ...
# An alternative code sequence (where delay length=1)
    Load  R1,A
    Load  R2,B
    Load  R4,D
    Add   R3,R1,R2   no stall since R2 data is available
    ...     ...
```

Figure 3.7 Delayed load. From Kane, MIPS RISC Architecture, © 1988. Reprinted by permission of Prentice Hall, Englewood Cliffs, New Jersey.

en by peephole optimization, which considers only a narrow context—perhaps, one instruction. Next, local optimization considers multiple-instruction sequences in the areas of register-usage management, simplify branch to branch, and such. At the global level, we consider the optimize program flow in the big picture. Table 3.1 shows C source code for a simple FFT routine, and the subsequent assembly language for the inner loop as produced by the optimizing compiler. Notice the grouping of the loads, the adds/subtracts, and the multiply routines. This may appear counter-intuitive, but has the effect of keeping the pipelines filled.

3.10 BRANCH PREDICTION

Since a taken branch represents a disruption, there is value in having the compiler predict the target of a branch. Although at first glance it would seem impossible to predict a data-dependent branch at compile time, there are some techniques that

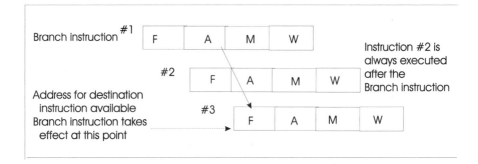

With this approach, the inherent delay associated with the branch instructions is made visible to the software, and compilers attempt to fill the branch delay slot with useful instructions. This task is usually not too difficult if there is only one instruction delay as in the case in the following code example:

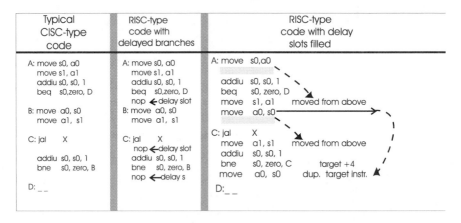

Figure 3.8   Delayed branch. From Kane, MIPS RISC Architecture, © 1988. Reprinted by permission of Prentice Hall, Englewood Cliffs, New Jersey.

work often enough to make them useful. For example, a rule of thumb is to predict all forward conditional branches as not taken, and all backward conditional branches as taken. The compiler needs to rearrange the code to match the hardware's expectations. Certain processors have a specialized loop instruction that does a decrement and test in one step.

The compiler can make intelligent guesses on the direction of data-dependent branches at compile time, and provide hints to the runtime logic. With hints from the compiler, the instruction decoder and dispatch logic can begin to make intelligent guesses about data-dependent branches at runtime. The cost of a bad guess is

TABLE 3.1 Translation of FFT source code

FFT C Source Code	FFT Inner Loop	

```
FFT( xr, xi, n, m, wr, wi)
single xr[], xi[], wr[], wi[];
unsigned n,m;
{
    unsigned n1, n2, ia, ie, i, j, k, l;
    single   c, s, xrt, xit;
    n2 = n;
    ie = 1;
    for( k=0; k < m; k++)
    {
        n1 = n2;
        n2 = n2 >> 1;
        ia = 0;
        for ( j = 0; j < n2; j++)
        {
            c = wr[ia];
            s = wi[ia];
            ia = ia + ie;
            for( l = 0; l < n; l += n1)
            {
                i = l + n2;
                xrt = xr[i] - xr[l];
                xr[i] = xr[i] + xr[l];
                xit = xi[i] - xi[l];
                xi[i] = xi[i] + xi[l];
                xr[l] = c * xrt - s * xit;
                xi[l] = c * xit + s * xrt;
            }
        }
        ie = ie << 1;
    }
}
```

```
L3:
    add      r16,r15,r8        *   i = l + n2
    ld       r19,r1,r15        *   xr[i]
    ld       r20,r1,r16        *   xr[l]
    ld       r21,r2,r15        *   xi[i]
    ld       r22,r2,r16        *   xi[l]
    fsub.sss r17,r19,r20       *   xrt = xr[i] - xr[l]
    fadd.sss r19,r19,r20       *   xr[i] = xr[i] + xr[l]
    fsub.sss r18,r21,r22       *   xit = xi[i] - xi[l]
    fadd.sss r21,r21,r22       *   xi[i] = xi[i] + xi[l]
    fmul.sss r23,r11,r17       *   c * xrt
    fmul.sss r26,r12,r17       *   s * xrt
    fmul.sss r24,r12,r18       *   s * xit
    fmul.sss r25,r11,r18       *   c * xit
    fsub.sss r20,r23,r24       *   c * xrt - s * xit
    fadd.sss r22,r25,r26       *   s * xit + c * xrt
    add      r15,r15,r7        *   l = l + n1
    cmp      r27,r15,r3        *   l < n
    st       r19,r1,r15        *   xr[i] = xr[i] + xr[l]
    st       r21,r2,r15        *   xi[i] = xi[i] + xi[l]
    st       r20,r1,r16        *   xr[l] = c * xrt - s * xit
    bb1.n    lt,r27,L3
    st       r22,r2,r16        *   xi[l] = s * xit + c * xrt
```

really nothing in time, just some wasted effort and increased circuit complexity. However, the benefit of a correct guess can be a tremendous advantage.

There are two basic approaches to guessing data-dependent branches at runtime. One involves making the best guess and following down that path unless and until proven wrong. Then the stream of execution must be backed up and restarted. Another approach is to start down both branches simultaneously, and choose the right one later. No results are saved until the sense of the branch is resolved. The complexity of this approach comes when a series of branches is encountered. Each branch adds two forks to the path of execution, and only very sophisticated processors can simultaneously maintain multiple speculative execution paths.

3.11 BENCHMARKING

Benchmarks are so misused in comparing computer systems, particularly RISC systems, that a few cautions are in order. Benchmarks represent an artificial environment that does not model any particular application. They are rough estimates, not absolute measures of performance. The best benchmarks are actual programs from out of your environment. Industry-standard benchmarks can indicate what processors deserve a second look. The indicated candidates should then be benchmarked with your own code.

Remember that benchmarks cover both a hardware and a software component. To

be valid, you have to know the hardware details (clock, memory type and organization, wait states, etc.), and the software details (compiler version, optimization level, etc.).

3.11.1 Lies, Damn Lies, and Benchmarks

Once computer manufacturers see that users are basing buying decisions on benchmark results, there is a scramble to achieve high benchmark results at all cost. Unfortunately, good benchmark results may correlate poorly with your real-world applications. There is no question that hardware/software combinations can be tuned
to optimize specific benchmark fragments. The problem is when this becomes the
dominant driving force in the chip design. There are documented cases of compiler
products that are tuned to recognize certain industry-standard benchmarks and produce the very best, hand-tuned results. The result is a benchmark-optimized system,
not necessarily optimized for any real application.

3.11.2 Industry-Standard Performance Measures

Integer benchmarks include the Dhrystone, developed in ADA by Weicker [6], and
Stanford integer suite, which includes samples of code from various applications,
developed by Stanford's computer science department.

Floating-point benchmarks include the Whetstone, developed in the late 1960s by
Curnow and Wichman at National Physical Lab, Whetstone, England [7]. It includes transcendentals and arrays computations, and is not vectorizable. The Linpack was developed by Jack Dongarra at Argonne National Labs in 1978, and is
floating-point intensive. It is intended to give users of Linpack software (basic linear algebra package) an idea of comparative runtimes.

The SPEC (Systems Performance Evaluation Cooperative) benchmarks come in
both integer and floating point flavors, and are widely cited. The SPEC-fp floating-
point benchmark is single precision.

For noncomputational applications, the Transaction Processing Council (TPC)
benchmarks are usually cited. These involve I/O-heavy applications that would be
found in commercial database environments. The TPC's address is given in Section
20.3.

Trace-driven simulations are used to evaluate the efficiency of an instruction set,
and can be used to tune a hardware implementation to an instruction set, or vice ver-
sa.

3.12 BUILT-IN TEST AND JTAG

Testability is a major issue for complex systems, and the complexity of processors
has shown that testability has to be designed in. Fortunately, an IEEE standard exists
in this area (IEEE Std. P1149.1/D6, Standard Test Access Port and Boundary Scan
Architecture). Usually not all of the internal logic of a chip can be completely test-

ed. The Joint Test Action Group (JTAG) has been active in defining the mechanics of testability, and most designs now incorporate this feature. JTAG represents a capability, and the specific tests and reporting must be defined for each individual device. Interface chips and display software are now available to support the JTAG standard on most computing platforms.

Some processors perform a self-test upon power-up, and report back the results in a register. This is referred to as BIST—built-in self-test. The JTAG approach involves the serial loading of predefined test vectors, and comparing expected versus actual results. The vectors may be available from the chip manufacturer. JTAG may be able to isolate specific problems within a chip, going beyond simple go/no-go testing.

Some processors implement a master/slave mode, in which one processor changes all its outputs into inputs, and monitors the outputs from a second, "buddy" processor. A difference signals that a mistake has been made by one or the other. This scheme works only when the processors operate in synchronization from the same instruction stream. The following is a listing of those processors that support a master/checker mode, and those that implement a full JTAG.

Processors with Master/Checker Feature

AMD 29k

Motorola 88k

MIPS 4400

Processors with JTAG Support

AMD 29030, 035, 200

AT&T 9201x

Fujitsu SPARClite

Motorola PowerPC

Intel i80860XP

Intel Pentium Pro

Motorola 88110

Texas Instruments MicroSparc

VLSI 86C060,061, ARM 600

3.13 QUESTIONS

1. Compare and contrast Berkeley and Stanford RISC. Which has the edge in interrupt processing? How do their branch approaches differ?

2. In the instruction set of the 80386 CISC processor, list the many ways to clear a

register to zero. List the cycle times for each of these options. Which is the fastest? Choose a list of ten representative instructions, and compare the clock times across the 80x86 family, from the 8086 to the Pentium Pro Processor.

3. Choose a member of the 80x86 family. Cross out all instructions that take more than one cycle to complete. What is required to synthesize the instructions you crossed out, from those that are left?

3.14 REFERENCES

[1] Shannon, Claude E., The Mathematical Theory of Communication. Urbana: University of Illinois Press, 1963. ISBN 0-252-72548-4.

[2] Jouppi, N.P. and Wall, D.W., "Available Instruction-Level Parallelism for Superscalar and Superpipelined Machines," *ASPLOS-III Proc.,* Boston, MA, April 1989.

[3] Fisher, Joseph A., "Parallelism Breeds a New Class of Supercomputer," March 15, 1987, *Computer Design,* 26.

[4] Hennessy, John L. and Patterson, David A., Computer Architecture A Quantitative Approach. San Mateo, CA: Morgan Kaufmann, 1990, ISBN 1-55860-069-8.

[5] Hopkins, Martin E., "A Perspective on the 801/RISC," Jan. 1987, *IBM Systems J.,* 26(1) 107–12.

[6] Weicker, R.P., "Dhrystone: A Synthetic Systems Programming Benchmark," Oct. 1984, *Comm. ACM,* 27(10)1013–30.

[7] Curnow, H.J., and Wichman, B.A. "A Synthetic Benchmark," 1976. *The Computer J.,* 19(1):80.

3.15 BIBLIOGRAPHY

Armstrong, Kenji, B., "Sun's SPARC Embedded Development Tools," Technical Marketing Note, TMN-0100-1290, Sun Microsystems.

Barrenechea, Mark, "Loop Unrolling: A RISC-y Business," 1991, TM 91-1, Microway Corp.

Baxter and Arnold, "Code Restructuring for Enhanced Performance on a Pipelined Processor," 1991, *IEEE COMPCON Spring '91 Proceedings.*

"A Big Fast Macintosh with RISC Graphics," May 1990, *Personal Workstation.*

Bourekas, Philip, "RISC Depends on its Memory," April 19, 1991, *EETimes.*

Bursky, Dave, et al., "Take the Risk Out of Using RISC," June 1990, *Electronic Design,* 38, pp. 53–58.

Case, Brian, "32-bit Microprocessor Opens System Bottlenecks," April 1, 1987, *Computer Design,* 26, 79–86.

Case, Brian, "Pipelined Processor Pushes Performance," March 1987, *ESD,* 30–34.

Cates, Ron, "Processor Architecture Considerations for Embedded Controller Applications," June 1988, *IEEE Micro,* pp. 28–38.

Chan, Scott, "Parallelism in the Instruction Pipeline," Dec. 1989, *High Performance Systems,* X(12).

Child, Jefferey, "Faster Processors Ignite SRAM Revolution," July 1994, *Computer Design,* 33, p. 97.

Child, Jeff and Wilson, Dave, "RISC Champions Challenge Moto in Embedded Control," Oct. 1991, *Computer Design,* 30.

Chow, Fred C., "Minimizing Register Usage Penalty at Procedure Calls," 1988, *SIGPLAN '88 Conf. on Programming Design and Implementation.*

Chow, Fred and Weber, Larry, "Optimizing the RISC Odds," Sept. 1988, *ESD,* 18(9), pp. 73–75.

Clarke, Michele, "RISC Drives Embedded Multimedia," Oct. 24, 1994, *EETimes,* 820 p. 1.

Cole, Bernard C., "New BRISC Beat, Bipolar/BICMOS RISC Processors," June 1989, *Electronics,* p. 110.

"Coping with RISC Processor Complexity," June 25, 1990, *Electronic Engineering Times,* p. 43.

"Design Applications, for Cost/Performance, Partition RISC System on Bus Parameters," Nov. 1987, *Electronic Design,* 35.

"Design Applications, Software Approach Broaden Options for Virtual Memory," April 1987, *Electronic Design,* 35.

Dewar, Robert B.K., *Microprocessors: A Programmer's View.* New York: McGraw-Hill, 1990. ISBN 0-07-076639-0.

Drafz, Ron "Turn a PC into a Supercomputer with Plug-in Boards," Nov. 23, 1988, *Electronic Design,* 36, pp. 89–93.

Falcone, Joseph R., "It's Becoming a RISC-based World," Sept. 19, 1994, *EETimes,* 815, p. 75.

Feigel, Curtis P., "High-End Embedded Processors Evolve in '93," Dec. 27, 1993, *Microprocessor Report,* 7(17):12.

"The Future of RISC," 1989, Cypress Semiconductor.

Gardner, W. David, "A New Twist in RISC vs CISC," Jan. 1990, *High Performance Systems,* XI(1), 51–52.

Gimarc, Charles E. and Milutinovic, Veljko M., "A Survey of RISC Processors and Computers of the Mid-1980s," Sept. 1987, *IEEE Computer,* pp. 59–69.

Gross, Thomas R. and Hennessy, John L., "Optimizing Delayed Branches," Oct. 1982, *IEEE Proceedings, Micro-15,* 114–120.

Gunn, Lisa, "The Problem of RISC-Based Designs," Nov. 23, 1989, *Electronic Design,* 37, p. 69.

Gwennap, Linley, "CPU Vendors Deploy Half-Micron Processes: MIPS Processor Vendors Lead in Race to Shrink IC Feature Sizes," April 18, 1994, *Microprocessor Report,* 8(5):16.

Gwennap, Linley, "Microprocessors Head Toward MP On a Chip; Future Processors May Use Multiple CPUs to Boost Performance," May 9, 1994, *Microprocessor Report,* 8(6):18.

Gwennap, Linley, "Speed Kills? Not for RISC Processors: Cost of Complexity Becomes Clear from SuperSPARC, 88110," March 8, 1993, *Microprocessor Report,* 7(3):3.

Gwennap, Linley, "Stupid Compiler Tricks: SPEC Results Inflated by Too Many Compiler Flags," Dec. 6, 1993, *Microprocessor Report,* 7(16):3.

Gwennap, Linley, "Visionaries See Beyond Superscalar; But They Disagree Over What Will Follow—MP On a Chip?" Dec. 6, 1993, *Microprocessor Report,* 7(16):28.

Gwennap, Linley, Ryan, Bob, Thompson, Tom, "RISC Grows Up," Jan. 1994, *BYTE,* 19, p. 91.

Hafeman, Dan and Zeidman, Bob, "Memory Architectures Compound RISC's Gains," July 11, 1991, *Electronic Design,* 39, pp. 71–82.

Hardenbergh, Hal W., "CPU Performance: Where Are We Headed?" Jan. 1994, *Dr. Dobb's Journal,* 19(1):30.

"Harris Adds Multiprocessing RISC System to Night Hawk Computer Family," June 1, 1990, *Aircraft Engineering and Aerospace Technology,* 62(6):20.

Hart, Frank, "Multiple Chips Speed CPU Performance," Sept. 1989, *High Performance Systems,* X(9).

High Performance Systems, March 1990, issue on embedded RISC, x1(3).

Hobbs, Marvin, *RISC/CISC Development and Test Support.* Englewood Cliffs, NJ: Prentice-Hall, 1992. ISBN 0-13-388414-7.

"HP PA-RISC Compiler Optimization Technology," August 1992, Technical White Paper, version 1.0, Hewlett-Packard Corporation.

Khan, Ashis, "Microprocessor Stall Handling," Oct. 1988, *MIPS* (White Paper).

Lampson, Brian, "Hints for Computer System Design," Oct. 1983, *ACM Operating Systems Review,* 17(5), pp. 33–48.

Lane, Alex, "Optimizing for today's CPUs," Feb. 1994, *BYTE,* 19(2):81.

Lieberman, David, "Microprocessor Incompatibility Poses Challenge: Designers Bridge the RISC, CISC Gap," Feb. 7, 1994, *EETimes,* 783, p. 49.

Levy, Markus, "A Thumbnail Sketch of Cache Memory," Jan. 19, 1995, *EDN.*

Mann, Daniel, "RISC Performance Depends on Compiler," Dec. 1991, *Computer Technology Review.*

Mann, Daniel, "The Universal Debugger Interface," Sept. 1992, *Dr. Dobb's Journal,* 17(9).

Margulis, Neal, "Single Chip RISC Eases System Design," Sept. 1989, *High Performance Systems,* X(9).

Marshall, Trevor, "Real-World RISCs," May 1988, *BYTE,* 13(5), pp. 263–268.

McGeady, Steven, "Embedding Superscalar RISC," April 15, 1991, *EETimes.*

McLachlan, Gordon, "Why Not RISC It?," August 1994, *HP Professional,* 8(8), pp. 72.

Moon, Soo-Mook, Ebcioglu, Kemal, "On Performance and Efficiency of VLIW and Super-scalar," 1993, *1993 International Conference on Parallel Processing,* pp. II–283.

Morrison, Scott, Waller, Nancy, "Register Windows vs. General Registers: A Comparison of Memory Access Patterns," May 13, 1988, U.C. Berkeley (white paper).

"The New Contenders," Dec. 1993, *IEEE Spectrum,* p. 20.

Ohr, Stephan, "Fast Cache Designs Keep the RISC Monster Fed," Jan. 1995, *Computer Design,* 34, pp. 67–93.

Paterson, D.S., Ditzel, D.R., "The Case for the Reduced Instruction Set Computer," Oct. 15, 1980, *Computer Architecture News.*

"PDAs Begin Shipping in 1993; Many Processor Vendors Target Small But Growing Market," Jan. 24, 1994, *Microprocessor Report,* 8(1):18.

"Portable Processors Balance RISC and CISC," July 1994, *OEM Integration (Computer Design)* p. OEMI 5.

Pountain, Dick, "PDA CPUs: New Form Demands New Functions," Oct. 1993, *BYTE,* 18(11):80.

Poursepani, Ali, "The PowerPC Performance Modeling Methodology," June 1994, *Communications of the ACM,* 37(6): 47.

Ricchetti, Domenic, "The Emergence of the RISC PC," Oct. 1994, *OEM Magazine,* pp. 38–49.

"RISC," April 2, 1990, *PC Week* special report, 7(13), pp. S1–S30.

"RISC Factors," Cypress Semiconductor, undated (white paper).

Rodriguez, Karen, "RISC Brings New Horizons into View for Business Users," June 15, 1992, *Infoworld,* pp. 59–60.

Seery, Doug, et al., "System-Level Strategy Attacks Key Multiuser Bottlenecks," Jan. 1, 1988, *Computer Design,* 27.

Silverthorne, Sean, "Accepting RISC," Oct. 18, 1993, *PC Week,* 10(41):A6.

"Six Case Studies of Real Machines," Jan. 1989, *IEEE Computer,* 22, pp. 12–90.

Slater, Michael, "Pick a PDA, any PDA," May 1994, *OEM Magazine,* p. 28.

Stockton, John F., "Making RISC Chips Work in Embedded Controllers," April 15, 1991, *EETimes,* p. 55.

"Technology Trends—The Hour of RISC Is Near," March 19, 1990, *Electronic Engineering Times.* Special Section.

Thompson, John, "Development Tools Tackle Embedded RISC," July 29, 1991, *EETimes.*

Toprani, Subodh, "RISC hits the Desktop," April 19, 1991, *EETimes.*

Twaddel, William B., "Optimizers Ignite New Battle in the Compiler Wars," Feb. 1993, *Personal Engineering & Instrumentation News.*

Wall, D.W., "Global Register Allocation at Link Time," Digital Equipment Corp.

Weiss, Ray, "Core Wars," April 1995, *Computer Design,* 34, pp. 113–114.

Weiss, Ray "RISC Chips Muscle into Embedded Applications," Aug. 5, 1993, *EDN,* 38(16):45.

Weiss, Ray, "RISC Processors: The New Wave in Computer Systems," May 15, 1987, *Computer Design,* 26.

Weiss, Ray, "Superscalar RISC's Battle for High End Perch," Nov. 1994, *Computer Design,* 33, pp. 34–36.

"Will Monolithic or Multichip Processors Win the Performance Race?" May 1, 1991, *Computer Design,* 30(8):100.

Willenz, Avigdor, and Bourekas, Philip, "RISC Architecture Affects Real-Time System Design," 1/10/89, IDT Corp. (White Paper).

Wilson, Dave, "Higher Speeds Push Embedded Systems to Multiprocessing," July 1, 1989, *Computer Design,* 28, 72–83.

Wilson, Ron, "Applications Determine the Choice of RISC or CISC," March 1, 1989, *Computer Design,* 28, 58–73.

Wilson, Ron, "Embedding 32-bits Power," April 15, 1991, *EETimes.*

Wilson, Ron, "MPUs Push Superscalar Limits," May 9, 1994, *Electronic Engineering Times,* p. 56.

Wilson, Ron, "RISC Architectures Take on Heavyweight Applications," May 15, 1988, *Computer Design,* 27, pp. 59–79.

Wolfe, Alexander, "The Supercomputer is Back," Feb. 13, 1995, *EETimes,* 835, p. 43.

"Wonder Chips," July 4, 1994, *Business Week,* p. 86.

Wynia, "RISC and CISC Processors Target Embedded Systems," June 27, 1991, *Electronic Design,* 39.

4

ROAD MAP FOR CASE
STUDY CHAPTERS

4.1 INTRODUCTION

This transitional chapter marks the end of the theory and definition sections, and the beginning of the practical design examples. This section explains the format of the following chapters, which present the specifics of selected RISC architectures. Each chapter follows the same overall plan, so architectures may be compared and contrasted. Some of the comparison and contrast information is presented in this chapter. This section also provides a road map to the "case study" chapters on specific RISC architectures. In addition, it provides backward references to show where specific features and characteristics were discussed in previous chapters. The definitions of terms will not be repeated in each individual chapter, for brevity's sake. We have been careful to define and explain all terms before their use, so look back to Chapter 2 or 3 if there is a question. Specific terms may be located in the glossary.

Major architectures rate their own chapter, and these are presented as Chapters 5 through 18. Chapter 19 serves as a catchall for those chips that for one reason or another didn't deserve the full treatment. We can argue which chips deserve to go where, but this is my first cut. In subsequent revisions of the book, new material will be introduced up front, and some of the current topics will be moved back to Chapter 19. Some of the chips discussed in Chapter 19 are no longer in production, but did set certain standards or influence follow-on designs. For example, Motorola's 88k family left its internal busing legacy in PowerPC. IBM's RIOS chips also blended into the PowerPC. Chapter 19 serves both to introduce new architectures, and eulogize older ones.

Chapter 19 also discusses some specific subsets of RISC chips. Specifically, there are some examples of DSP-RISC, and certain proprietary RISC designs used in high-performance computers. These chips, even though they are not available in the open market, are significant. They represent the outcome of a build/buy trade by a computer manufacturer that was settled on the side of custom design. Another hot topic is that of RISC emulation of CISC instruction sets in real time. This approach allows RISC vendors to address the massive installed base of 80x86 software, now addressed only by the 80x86 chips and their clones. This is discussed along with a presentation of the influence of RISC on mainline CISC, including the Intel Pentium Pro Processor, and the Pentium competitors.

4.2 BACKGROUND

In the background section of subsequent chapters, information on each architecture will be given. RISC chips tend to be produced by chip companies such as AMD or Integrated Device Technology (IDT), or computer companies such as Digital Equipment Corporation and IBM. Each has its own unique approach to the technology, and its own focus. Manufacturers' contact addresses, phone and fax numbers, and email addresses are given in Chapter 20. World Wide Web contact URLs (Universal Resource Locators) are also given.

Also in the background section, we will discuss the particular niche or market that each processor is addressing. Some architectures target the desktop engineering workstations, and some the embedded control universe, and some try to address a full spectrum, from the handheld personal digital assistant (PDA) to TV set-top boxes to supercomputers and massively parallel machines. The target market drives the architecture in certain directions, with certain features. For example, embedded controllers tend to be low power single-chip, highly integrated systems with little use for memory management. The emerging PDA market is both price and power sensitive. Thus, to understand the various architectures and the directions in which the technology is going, we have to have some understanding of the market being addressed.

Different members of the architecture family will be introduced, along with the compatibility standard or architecture specification that ties them together. Architecture derivatives will be discussed. Some families, like the MIPS, are built strictly to an architecture specification. Some, like the SPARC, are built to be instruction-set compatible with an open architecture. Most, like the 29k and 88k, evolve in time due to market forces and technological advances. We must distinguish between the architecture and specific examples or instantiations of the architects. As we establish in Chapter 1, the technologies feed upon themselves. A successful product can become a burden for the manufacturer, who must now maintain the architecture for the installed customer base. This "legacy drag" continues until a radical shift is called for, because at some time in the life-cycle, the benefits of change will outweigh the costs of maintaining compatibility. The 80x86 architecture may be approaching this point.

We will also discuss the architecture pedigree—where the chip family came from. RISC is not a new technique. It was applied to the IBM 801 series machines in the 1970s. However, it wasn't until the late 1980s that RISC began to emerge as a dominant force in the industry. There are essentially two major schools of thought in RISC design: the Stanford and the Berkeley. Almost all designs trace back to the early work of Hennessy and Patterson at Stanford and Berkeley.

4.3 ARCHITECTURE

In the architecture section of the subsequent chapters, we present the processor first from a hardware and then from a software point of view. All of the RISC processors are load/store in nature except for the ATT9201x, which is memory-memory. All manage single-cycle execution of almost all instructions. All except the Transputer feature hardwired instruction decode, although some choose to extend the basic instruction set via microcode. All have fixed-length basic instructions except the ATT9201x, which has three variations. The point is, for every rule we can postulate about RISC processors, we can also find at least one counterexample.

Table 4.1 summarizes the RISC processors in terms of registers, number of instructions, and certain "non-RISC" features. Registers are listed as a number times a bit size, with integer given first, and floating point second. Not all of the registers may be usable at the same time. The number of instructions is also tabulated. Some CISC processors are included for comparison.

4.3.1 Hardware

In the hardware sections of the subsequent chapters, we discuss the various pipelines that are used to reduce apparent latency in the flow of operations. Pipelines and superpipelines are discussed in Chapter 3. Table 4.2 shows the integer pipeline depth for the various architectures. Other pipelines may be seen in the floating point or loader units. A superpipeline, generally those with more than six stages, is characteristic of one approach to performance enhancement.

Next, the various execution units of the processor are presented. These can consist of the integer arithmetic-logic unit (ALU), the floating-point unit, possibly a graphics unit, a branch processor, and others. Multiple-execution units usually imply a superscalar architecture, as discussed in Chapter 3. In the early generations, the integer, floating point, and MMU units may have been on different chips, but are usually integrated onto one chip by now. Superscalar architectures are rated by the degree of multiple issue of instructions they support. However, it is not necessarily the number of instructions issued, but rather the number completed, that relates directly to performance. Table 4.3 presents the issue for the superscalar RISC processors discussed in subsequent chapters. Issues restrictions will be discussed in the individual chapters.

Integrated functions of the processor may include DRAM control, DMA support, interrupts, a counter/timer, a memory management unit (MMU) and others. Issues

TABLE 4.1 Register Architecture and Number of Instructions

Chip	Registers Int & FP	Number of Instructions	Non-RISC Features
88100/200	32x32+32x80	51	sfu's**
8 8110	32x32+32x80	66	sfu's**
R2000/2010	32x32+16x64	78+19	
R3000/3010	32x32+16x64		
R4000	32x32+16x64	170+39	
T800	3x32 (stack)	145	microcode
29k	192x32	112	mult. + divide by emulation
Mospar PE-2	64x32		
i860	32x32+32x32	88	
i960xx	112 x32	201	11 data addressing modes
iWarp	128x32		
SPARC	32x32***	84	multiple operand addressing modes
IMS 6250	72x32+8		emulation microcode
M1	32x32		only 8 visible at a time
TMS320C080	44x32		DSP engines
SHARC	32x32		
KSR-2	32x64+64x64		
RIOS	32x64+32x64		
ARM	27x32		
Alpha	32x64+32x64		PALcode synthesized instructions
68060	8x32+8x80	161	multiple data addressing modes
ATT9201x	none	44	mem-mem architecture, var. len instr
HP-PA	32x32+32x64	70	3 operand addressing modes
Clipper	32x32+16x64	101	9 addressing modes + decode ROM
PowerPC	32x64+32x64	184	3 operand addressing modes
PIC	80x8	33–55	3 operand addressing modes
i80486, Pentium	8x32	231*	7 operand addressing modes, variable length instructions

*not including variations of JCC (jump on condition code).
**sfu = special function unit.
***Multiple sets, in a register window configuration.

of the processor impact on the memory system are presented in Chapter 2. DMA involves the issues of hand-off of bus-mastership, and similar arrangements are needed for multiprocessor architectures. Interrupts, or exceptions, play havoc with carefully orchestrated pipelines. Memory management, the translation lookaside buffer, and virtual memory systems were discussed in Chapter 2. Next, we look at the memory/bus interface, whether it is a Harvard or a von Neumann format (Chapter

TABLE 4.2 Pipelined/Superpipelined Integer Instruction Depth

Pipeline Depth	Processor
12	P6
9	UltraSPARC
8	R4000, 4400, 68060, SuperSPARC
7	Alpha, PA-8000, M1
6	HyperSPARC, PA7100
5	RIOS-1, R2000, R3000, R4200, R4600, R8000, R10000, T9000, Pentium, PA7000, SPARC V8
4	80486, 29k, IMS6250, C400, PowerPC, 68060
3	i80960, TMS320C080, 88100, SHARC, i80860, 29050, ATT9201x, ARM, C-300
2	PIC

1), and the path width. Wider paths to memory increase the bandwidth at the expense of packaging and system-level complexity. We also examine read/write buffering, and read-before-write issues (Chapter 2). All of these features enhance performance and cost complexity. They must be carefully balanced in the design.

Not all RISC architectures are 32 bits. Most are, but the trend is to 64 bits, and wider. The PIC, discussed in Chapter 17, is a full-fledged 8-bit RISC processor. The SH7000 and the V800 are 16-bit RISC designs. And what is a 64-bit chip, anyway? At a minimum, it must have 64-bit-wide registers to handle 64-bit data structures with one instruction. The internal and external data paths must be 64 bits (or wider). Ideally, it should have 64-bit addressing, although this has not yet been fully implemented. Table 4.4 shows the word size for various RISC processors.

Most "64 bit" processors are trending toward a 64-bit virtual address with a smaller physical address. Most chips have gone to a Harvard bus internally, and use wide (up to 128-bit) data paths. Externally, wide data paths and a Harvard architecture can have a detrimental effect on packaging and pin count, as shown in Table 4.5.

For the system interface, we need to consider the reset initialization process, the processor clock, and any supplied test signals or debug support, including the Joint Test Action Group (JTAG) interface. This is discussed in Chapter 3. As clocks head

TABLE 4.3 Superscalar/Multiple Issue

Degree of issue	Processor
6	RIOS-2
4	RIOS-1, T9000, UltraSPARC, Alpha 21164
3	i80860, SuperSPARC, PowerPC 601, 88110
2	PowerPC 603, R4400, PA-7000, i80960CA, HyperSPARC 68060, Alpha 21064, IMS6250, Pentium, M1

TABLE 4.4 Word Size of Various Processors

8-bit

MicrochipPIC (data, instruction word size varies 12-16 bits)

16-bit

SH7000, V800

32-bit

680x0
88100, 88110
MIPS R2000, R3000
Transputer T800, T9000
29k
i80860 XR, i80860 XP
i80960xx
iWarp
SPARC version 8
ATT9201x
HP-PA 7000
PowerPC 601
TMS 320C080
SHARC (ADSP21000)
Clipper
RS6000
ARM
HyperSPARC, SuperSPARC
IMS 6250
Pentium, K5, M1

64-bit

SPARC V9-Ultra SPARC, SPARC-64
Alpha
PowerPC 620, 630
HP PA8000
MIPS R4xxx, R8000, R10000
nCube 3

TABLE 4.5 Pin Count of Processors with External Harvard Buses

Parts	Pin Count	
1. 88100	180x3 chips	CPU plus 2 CMMUs
2. 29k	168	
3. HP-PA	504	
4. PowerPC	304	

past 100 MHz, it gets harder to distribute the clock signals on a board without significant skew. The usual design approach is to distribute a lower-frequency clock that is phase-lock multiplied on the processor chip. Distributing higher-frequency clocks around a circuit board also leads to significant radiated electromagnetic interference (EMI). Some processors have a monitor/supervisor (or master/slave) hardware mode, in which the supervisor (slave) processor does not output signals, but compares its calculated outputs with the other processors. A discrepancy signals an error, but it is not necessarily known on whose part. It is incorrect to assume that the checker is always right. I recall an early space flight mission that became an underwater mission when the backup computer concluded that the primary upper stage guidance computer had made a mistake, and took over control of the launch vehicle. Actually, it was the backup unit that had made the mistake, and it proved to be a costly one. One big splash, and tens of millions of dollars of sophisticated hardware became a target site for future archeologists.

In the area of support functions and chips, we will look at issues of bus arbitration, secondary cache support, and peripheral control. Secondary cache is discussed in Chapter 2. RISC controllers, targeted at the embedded systems market, tend to include a wide range of support functions on-chip.

For electrical and packaging issues, we will examine power, thermal issues, operating voltage and packaging. Although 5-volt operation used to be the norm, units are going to 3.3 volts and lower to reduce power consumption and voltage-induced breakdown in narrow-featured geometry. Since power is a function of the voltage squared, going to 3.3 volts from 5 volts reduces the power by a factor of more than two.

4.3.2 Software

Next we will shift to a software and programmer's view of the architecture. We will look at the instruction set, and the classes and formats of instructions. Most (but not all) RISC machines are characterized by a single instruction format, or at least by having the opcode in the first byte. Instruction classes include integer math, floating-point math, load/store, shift/bit manipulation, flow control, processor state control, and miscellaneous or special types.

We need to consider the registers, including general purpose, floating point, status, and supervisor/control. Issues of addressing modes, byte ordering (endianness), and data types are examined. Byte ordering was explained in Chapter 2. Table 4.6 shows the endian-ness of various RISC processors. The trend is to support both modes with selection in software.

Of considerable importance are the software development and test tools. Software toolsets can enable or impede the use of the hardware. These typically include the cross-assembler, linker, loader, code profiler, cross-compilers, read only memory (ROM)–based monitors, emulation and simulation tools, and in-circuit emulation (ICE). These tools are available from the manufacturer and various third-party vendors. User groups may be available for the architecture; these are listed in Chapter 18. Software issues in development and debug are discussed in Chapter 3.

TABLE 4.6 Endian-ness of Various Processors

Little

T-800
Alpha (big endian support at compiler level)
i80960 (most models)
Clipper C100
ARM610
80x86
VAX

Big

SPARC-V8
HP-PA
680x0
IBM S/360, S370

Selectable in Hardware, at Boot Time

MIPS R-2000
MIPS R-3000, 4000 for Kernel or Supervisor Mode
Clipper C300
MIPS R4200

Selectable in Software, During Execution

88100, 88110—defaults to big-endian upon reset; uses bit in processor status register (PSR)
R3000, R4000—for user mode, "RE" bit (25) in status register
i80860—defaults to little-endian, set by bit in extended processor status word (EPSP)
ATT9201x—bit in processor status word (PSW)
PowerPC—bit-endian default; separate bits for user and supervisor mode (!) "LM" bit (28)
   of HID0 register, set by MTSPR instruction, after reset
80960 Jx
29k
SPARC V9
ARM 620,7xx
HP PA 7100 LC
R4400

4.3.3 Floating Point

Next, we will specifically examine the floating-point unit in the areas of registers, format, modes, operations supported, instructions, exceptions, the pipeline, and scheduling and latency. The theory and practice of floating point is set out in Appendix 1. Nowadays, all floating-point hardware implements the IEEE standard, and some include proprietary modes (Digital Equipment Corp., IBM) as well. Table 4.7 summarizes the floating-point characteristics of various RISC processors.

TABLE 4.7 Floating Point Characteristics of Various RISC Processors

Integral Floating Point

Not Included	*Associated FP Chip*
MicrochipPIC	n/a
ATT9201x	n/a
ARM600, 700	FPA10
MIPS R2000	R2010
MIPS R3000	R3010
29000	29027 (obsolete)
i80960 (most models)	n/a
SPARC version 8	various, from Weitek, Texas Instruments, and others
IMS 6250	n/a
HP-PA	Texas Instruments

Included (32 + 64 bit)

88100, 88110
68060
MIPS R4000, R4400, 3500, 8000, 4600, 4700
Transputer T800, T-9000
i80860 XR, i80860 XP
SHARC—single precision only
iWarp
R4650 —single precision only
HyperSPARC, SuperSPARC
RIOS-1,2
Alpha
HP PA 7100, 8000
TMS 320C080
PowerPC
Maspar MP-2
29050
nCube
i80960 KB, SB, MM
KSR-2
Clipper
80486, Pentium, Pentium Pro Processor, M1
POWER
SPARC V9

Support for Other than IEEE FP

Alpha (supports Digital Equipment Corp.)
PowerPC (supports IBM)

4.3.4 Cache

In the cache section of subsequent chapters we examine the cache in terms of organization (data/code, primary/secondary), arbitration, priorities, coherency, snooping, protocols, and control. Caching as a technique to increase the apparent memory bandwidth and reduce latency is discussed in Chapter 2. Table 4.8 summarizes the caching strategies of the various RISC processors.

TABLE 4.8 Cache Strategies of Various RISC Machines

Internal Level 1 Cache sizes

Architecture	I-cache	D-cache	Assoc.	Other
88100*	16k	16k	2	32 entry btc
88110	8k	8k	2	32 entry btc
MIPS R4000	8k	8k	1	
MIPS 4200, 4300	16k	8k	1	
MIPS R4400, 4600, 8000	16k	16k	2	
MIPS R10000	32k	32k	2	
29000	n/a	n/a	n/a	½k btc
29050	n/a	n/a	n/a	1k btc
29040	8k	4k	2	copy-back
i80860 XR	4k	8k	2	1k btc
i80860 XP	16k	16k	4	
NexGen Nx586	16k	16k		
i80960 Sx, Kx	1/2k	0	1	
i80960 Hx	16k	8k	4	
i80960 CA	1k	0	1	4 sets/16 regs
RIOS-1	32k	128k	4,2	
iWarp	0	1k	1	
RIOS-2	32k	256k	2,4	
SPARC Version-8	2-4k	2-4k		
68060	8k	8k	4	256 entry btc
HyperSPARC	16k	0	2	
MicroSPARC-II	16k	8k		
SuperSPARC	20k	16k	5,4	
UltraSPARC	16k	16k	1	
Alpha	8k	8k	1	***
nCube 3	8k	8k		
ATT9201x	3k	0	3	256 user stack
HP-PA 7000	n/a	n/a	n/a	all external
IMS 6250	1k	1k		
PowerPC 603	8k	8k	2	
PowerPC 604, 603e	16k	16k	4	
PowerPC 620	32k	32k	8	
TMS 320C080 RISC	2k	8k		
TMS 320C080 Master	4k	4k		
Alpha	8k	8k	1	

TABLE 4.8 *(continued)*

| Architecture | Internal Level 1 Cache sizes | | | |
	I-cache	D-cache	Assoc.	Other
ATT9201x	3k	0	3	256 user stack
Clipper C100, 300	4k	4k	2	
Clipper C400	n/a	n/a	n/a	
RS6000	32k	128k		
Pentium	8k	8k	2	btc
68060	8k	8k	4	
Unified				
M1	16k	4k		
80486	8k			
PowerPC 601	32k	8k		
HP PA 7100LC	1k			
ARM 620	4k	64k		
ARM 710	8k			
T9000	16k	256	4 banks	

*3 chip set 88100 + 2x88200
**7 chip set
***21164 has an additional 96k bytes of Level 2 cache on-chip.
btc = branch target cache
Note: ATT9201x keeps top 256 bytes of user data stack cached on-chip.

This table covers the primary on-chip caches. Some architectures (Intel Pentium Pro Processor, DEC Alpha 21164) are including secondary cache on-chip as well. A major design decision is how much of the silicon real estate to dedicate to cache.

4.3.5 Memory Management

An important topic is that of memory management, including modes of operation, multiprocessor support, virtual memory, the translocation lookaside buffer (TLB), address translation, the coherency model, prefetch, read/write ordering, segmentation models, out-of-order execution, cache access modes, protection mechanisms, and input/output (I/O). Memory management techniques are discussed in Chapter 2.

4.3.6 Exceptions

The exceptions section discusses exceptions (interrupts) in terms of classes, priorities, processing, latency, and determinism. Interrupts are disruptive to pipeline processing. RISC processors usually have excellent response to interrupts (a very low latency) due to the nature of the one-cycle instructions. Interrupts may follow a precise or imprecise model. In the imprecise model, it may not be possible to determine which instruction caused the interrupt. This model is usually the one found in high-end systems and supercomputer class machines.

4.4 SUMMARY

In the summary section, we will look at the RISC and non-RISC features of the architecture. As we saw in Chapter 1, RISC-like features usually include a large register set, a load/store format, single-cycle execution, a small instruction set, and hardwired instructions. Non-RISC features include multiple addressing modes, synthesized instructions, and other exceptions to the RISC features. Not all RISC machines have all of the features of "pure" RISC. Most RISC machines have some features we would classify as CISC. Each chip represents a set of tradeoffs, made by the chip architects and influenced by the market.

A bibliography of suggested further readings for each specific architecture is given at the end of each chapter. These include manufacturers' data books and data sheets, and third-party books. Key articles are also included.

4.5 BIBLIOGRAPHY

Abnous, Arthur and Christensen, Christopher, Gray, Jeffrey, "Design and Implementation of the 'Tiny RISC' microprocessor; Designed for Optimized Data Path Operation, Tiny RISC is a 16-bit RISC-Style Microprocessor," 1992, *Microprocessors and Microsystems,* 16(4), p. 187.

"ADA Environment Tailored to RISC Systems Development," July 1991, *Computer Design,* 30(10), p. 134.

Andrews, Kristy and Sand, Duane, "Migrating a CISC Computer Family onto RISC via Object Code Translation," Sept. 1992, *SIGPLAN Notices,* 27(9), p. 213.

"As RISC Wars Escalate, Simplicity May Be The First Casualty," Dec. 1990, *Computer Design,* 29(23), p. 27.

"The Battle Royal over RISC," Nov. 27, 1989, *Business Week,* (3135), p. 192.

Bernstein, D., Cohen, D., Lavon, Y., "Performance Evaluation of Instruction Scheduling on the IBM RISC System/6000," Dec. 1992, *SIGMICRO Newsletter,* 23(1/2), p. 226.

Bhandarkar, Dileep, "Performance from Architecture: Comparing a RISC and CISC with Similar Hardware Organization," Apr. 1991, *Sigplan Notices,* 26(4), p. 310.

Booker, Alan, McKeeman, John, "Design Considerations of RISC Microprocessors in Real-time Embedded Systems," Aug. 1993, *Computer Design,* 32(8), p. 71.

Bradlee, D.G., Eggers, S.J., Henry, R.R., "The Effect on RISC Performance of Register Set Size and Structure Versus Code Generation Strategy," May 1991, *Computer Architecture News,* 19(3), p. 330.

"Build A DMA Controller With RISC," Jan. 20, 1989, *Electronic Design,* 37(2), p. 61.

Bunnell, Mitchell, "Maximizing Performance Of Real-Time RISC Applications," Jan. 1994, *Dr. Dobb's Journal,* 19(1), p. 54.

Canny, John F., Goldberg, Kenneth Y., "A RISC Approach to Sensing and Manipulation," June 1995, *Journal of Robotic Systems,* 12(6), p. 351.

Chang, Joe, Song, S. Peter, Denman, Marvin, "The PowerPC 604 RISC 14 Microprocessor," Oct. 1994, *IEEE Micro,* 14(5), p. 8.

"CISC Speeds Close In On RISC," July 27, 1989, *Electronic Design,* 37(16), p. 41.

Cocke, John, Markstein, V., "The Evolution of RISC Technology at IBM," Jan. 1990, *IBM Journal Of Research And Development,* 34(1), p. 4.

Darley, Merrick, Kronlage, Bill, Bural, David, "The TMS390C602A Floating-Point Co-processor for Sparc Systems," Jun. 1990, *IEEE Micro,* 10(3), p. 36.

"Developments To Watch," Jan. 30, 1989, *Business Week,* (3089), p. 69.

"Developments To Watch," Dec. 4, 1989, *Business Week,* (3136), p. 123.

Diefendorff, Keith, Allen, Michael, "Organization of the Motorola 88110 Superscalar RISC Microprocessor," Apr. 1992, *IEEE Micro,* 12(2), p. 40.

Edmondson, John H., et al., "Superscalar Instruction Execution in the 21164 Alpha," April, 1995, *IEEE Micro,* 15(2).

Elliott, I.D., Sayers, I.L., "Implementation of 32-bit RISC Processor Incorporating Hardware Concurrent Error Detection And Correction," Jan. 1990, *IEE Proceedings,* 137(1), 88.

"Enhanced Instruction Set Processor," Nov. 1988, *Electronics & Wireless World,* 94(1633), p. 1111.

Evans, Joseph B. "Secondary Cache Performance in RISC Architectures," June 1993, *Computer Architecture News,* 21(3), p. 34.

"For RISC, Future May Lie In Integration," Nov. 1990, *Computer Design,* 29(2), p. 43.

Fountain, Dick, "A Different Kind of RISC," Aug. 1994, *BYTE,* 19(8), p. 185.

Francis, Bob, "What's Taking the Risk Out of RISC," Jan. 15, 1990, *Datamation,* 36(2), p. 61.

Frenger, Paul, "PIC 16C5x Series uP: The 8-Bit RISC Microcontroller," Fall 1992, *SIG FORTH,* 4(2), p. 27.

Fried, Stephen S., "Pentium Optimization And Numeric Performance," Jan. 1995, *Dr. Dobb's Journal,* 20(1), p. 18.

Gannes, Stuart, "IBM And DEC Take On The Little Guys," Oct. 10, 1988, *Fortune,* 118(8), p. 108.

Gerosa, G., Gary, S., Kahle, J., "A 2.2 W, 80 MHz, Superscalar RISC Microprocessor," Dec. 1994, *IEEE Journal of Solid-state Circuits,* 29(12), p. 1440.

Griffin, Glenn W., "The Ultimate Ultimate RISC," Dec. 1988, *Computer Architecture News,* 16(5), p. 26.

Halfhill, Tom R., "Intel's P6," April 1995, *BYTE,* 20(4), p. 42.

Hall, C. Brian, "Performance Characteristics of Architectural Features of the IBM RISC System/6000," Apr. 1991, *Sigplan Notices,* 26(4), p. 303.

Happel, L.P., Jayasumana, A.P., "Performance of a RISC Machine With Two Level Caches," May 1992, *IEE proceedings,* 139(3), p. 221.

Hayes, Frank, "Intel's Cray-on-a-Chip," May 1989, *BYTE,* 14(5), p. 113.

Hicks, Dave, "Implementing A Parallel Router With RISC," Mar. 1990, *High Performance Systems,* 11(3), p. 61.

Hokenek, E., Montoye, R.K., Cook, P.W., "Second-Generation RISC Floating Point with Multiply-Add Fused," Oct. 1990, *IEEE Journal Of Solid-State Circuits,* 25(5), p. 1207.

Huang, Victor K.L., "High-Performance Microprocessors-the RISC Dilemma," Aug. 1989, *IEEE Micro,* 9(4), p. 13.

Hwang, Kai, Cheng, Chien-Ming, "Stimulated Performance of a RISC-Based Multiprocessor Using Orthogonal-Access Memory," Sept. 1991, *Journal Of Parallel And Distributed Computing,* 13(1), p. 43.

Hwang, K., Dubois, M., Panda, D.K., "OMP: A RISC-based Multiprocessor using Orthogonal-Access Memories and Multiple Spanning Buses," Sept, 1990, *Computer Architecture News,* 18(3), p. 7.

"Integrated Circuits 80860 Blends Vector Processing Into A RISC-like Architecture," Apr. 1, 1989, *Computer Design,* 28(7), p. 25.

"Intergraph Aims High," Dec. 10, 1990, *Informationweek,* (299), p. 68.

"Japanese Chart Own Course In RISC," Aug. 1990, *Computer Design,* 29(15), p. 34.

Jimenez, G., Sevillano, J.L., Civit-Balcells, A., "RISC-Based Architectures For Multiple Robot Systems," 1992, *Microprocessors and Microsystems,* 16(4), p. 177.

Johnson, Jay, "Optimization in Ada and C++," Dec. 1992, *Embedded Systems Programming,* 5(12), p. 20.

Johnson, Stephen C., "Hot Chips and Soggy Software," Feb. 1990, *IEEE Micro.,* 10(1), p. 23.

Khazam, J., Mowery, D., "The Commercialization of RISC: Strategies for the Creation of Dominant Designs," Jan. 1994, *Research Policy,* 23(1), p. 89.

Lane, Alex, "Developing for RISC," *BYTE,* Apr. 1994 19(4), p. 139.

Lazzerini, Beatrice, "Effective VLSI Processor Architectures for HLL Computers: The RISC Approach," Feb. 1989, *IEEE Micro,* 9(1), p. 57.

Lee, D.D., Kong, S.I., Hill, M.D., "A VLSI Chip Set for a Multiprocessor Workstation—Part I: An RISC Microprocessor with Coprocessor Interface and Support for Symbolic Processing," Dec. 1989, *IEEE Journal Of Solid-State Circuits,* 24(6), p. 1668.

Lee, H.-C., Lai, F., Parng, T.-M., "Mar.S: a RISC Based Multiple Function Units Lisp Machine," Sept. 1992, *IEE Proceedings,* 139(5), p. 410.

Leibowitz, Michael R., "The New Generation of RISC," Aug. 1991, *UNIX/World,* 8(8), p. 70.

Li, Qiang, Rishe, Naphtali, Tal, Doron, "RISC Processors In A Massively Parallel Database Machine," July 1990, *Microprocessors and Microsystems,* 14(6), p. 351.

Lotz, J., Miller, B., Delano, E., "A CMOS RISC CPU Designed for Sustained High Performance on Large Applications," Oct. 1990, *IEEE Journal Of Solid-State Circuits,* 25(5), p. 1190.

Mallach, Efrem G. "RISC: Evaluation and Selection," Spring 1991, *The Journal Of Information Systems Management,* 8(2), p. 8.

Margulis, Neal, "i860 Microprocessor Internal Architecture," Mar. 1990, *Microprocessors and Microsystems,* 14(2), p. 89.

Margulis, Neal, "The Intel 80860: A Close Look At Intel's Newest RISC Design," Dec. 1989, *BYTE,* 14(13), p. 333.

Margulis, Neal, "Programming RISC Engines," Feb. 1990, *Dr. Dobb's Journal,* 15(2), p. 116.

"The MC88200—A Cache And Memory Management Unit For The M88000 RISC Processors," Mar. 1, 1989, *Electronic Engineering,* 61(747), p. 39.

Melear, Charles, "The Design of the 88000 RISC Family," Apr. 1989, *IEEE Micro,* 9(2), p. 26.

Mills, J.W., "A High-Performance Low Risc Machine for Logic Programming," Jan. 1989, *Journal of Logic Programming,* 6(1/2), p. 179.

Moore, David L., "Programming the 29050," Jan. 1992, *Dr. Dobb's Journal,* 17(1), p. 34.

Muller, Otto, "A Novel 32-bit RISC Microprocessor for Embedded Systems," Oct. 1992, *IEICE Transactions on Electronics,* 75(10), p. 1196.

"New Compilers Squeeze More Performance Out Of RISC Chips," Dec. 1990, *Computer Design,* 29(23), p. 30.

"New Long-Word Architecture Threatens To Outshine RISC," Sept. 1990, *Computer Design,* 29(17), p. 26.

Obaidat, M.S., Abu-Sawymeh, Dirar S., "Performance of RISC-based Multiprocessors," May 1993, *Computers & Electrical Engineering,* 19(3), p. 185.

Obaidat, M.S., "Performance Simulation Analysis of RISC-Based Multiprocessors Under Uniform and Nonuniform Traffic," Aug. 1993, *Information Sciences,* 72(1/2), p. 157.

Palem, Krishna V., Simons, Barbara B., "Scheduling Time-Critical Instructions on RISC Machines," Sept. 1993, *ACM Transactions On Programming Languages,* 15(4), p. 632.

Prarikh, V.N., Baraniecki, A.Z., "Comparison of RISC and DSP Processors For A Transform Domain Implementation Of The Discrete Wavelet Transform," Jan. 1993, *Journal of Microcomputer Applications,* 16(1), p. 19.

"Performance Pushes RISC Chips Into Real-Time Roles," Sept. 1991, *Computer Design,* 30(12), p. 79.

Perotto, J.-F., Lamothe, C., Arm, C., "An 8-Bit Multitask Micropower RISC Core," Aug. 1994, *IEEE Journal Of Solid-State Circuits,* 29(8), p. 986.

Piepho, Richard S., Wu, William S., "A Comparison of RISC Architectures," Aug. 1989, *IEEE Micro,* 9(4), p. 51.

Pountain, Dick, "Under the Hood: Pentium: More RISC Than CISC," Sept. 1993, *BYTE,* 18(10), p. 195.

"Prospect of RISC processors," Jun. 1993, *Australian Electronics Engineering,* 26(6), p. 34.

"RISC and DSP come together on LSI chip," July 13, 1992, *Electronics,* 65(7), p. 46.

"The RISC business: Reduced Instruction Set Computing (RISC) Is Now A Prime Factor In The Reshaping Of The Entire Computer Industry," Jan. 16, 1992, *The Engineer,* 274(7083), p. 18.

Roberts, Charles E., "A RISC Processor for Embedded Applications Within an ASIC," Oct. 1991, *IEEE Micro,* 11(5), p. 20.

"RISC Chip Accelerates Printers," Jun. 14, 1990, *Electronic Design,* 38(11), p. 103.

"RISC Chips Explore Parallelism For Boost In Speed," Jan. 1989, *Computer Design,* 28(1), p. 30.

"RISC Chips Head For The Mainstream," July 8, 1991, *Electronic Business,* 17(13), p. 43.

"RISC Increases Code Densities Without Processing Overhead," April 1995, *Computer Design,* 34(4), p. 114.

"RISC is Simple, But Benchmarking Isn't," Feb. 1992, *Computer Design,* 31(2), p. 67.

"RISC Power Moving Scientific Visualization Onto The Desktop," Oct. 1991, *Computer Design,* 30(13), p. 60.

"RISC Processors Dressed Up For Embedded Applications," Oct. 1991, *Computer Design,* 30(15), p. 34.

"RISC-y Business: Technophobia," Dec. 20, 1993, *Industry Week,* 242(24), p. 11.

"64 Bit RISC Processor Review," Oct. 11, 1994, *New Electronics,* 27(9), p. 21.

"Second-Generation RISC Chips: Intel Intros Family of i860s While Moto Goes Superscalar," July 1991, *Computer Design,* 30(10), p. 42.

Sproull, Robert F., Sutherland, Ivan E., Molnar, Charles E., "The Counterflow Pipeline Processor Architecture," Fall 1994, *IEEE Design & Test Of Computers,* 11(3), p. 48.

Steven, Gordon B., "A Novel Effective Address Calculation Mechanism for RISC Microprocessors," Sept. 1, 1988, *Computer Architecture News,* 16(4), p. 150.

Stoughton, C. and Summers, D.J., "Using Multiple RISC CPUs In Parallel To Study Charm Quarks," July 1992, *Computers in Physics,* 6(4), p. 371.

Suzuki, K., Yamashina, M., Yamada, H., "A 500 MHz, 32 bit, 0.4 mu m CMOS RISC Processor," Dec. 1994, *IEEE Journal of Solid-state Circuits,* 29(12), p. 1464.

Taylor, A., "High Performance Prolog on a RISC," 1991, *New Generation Computing,* 9(3/4), p. 221.

Trainis, S.A., Findlay, P.A., Steven, G.B., "iHARP: a Multiple Instruction Processor Chip Incorporating RISC and VLIW Design Features," Apr. 1992, *Microelectronics Journal,* 23(2), p. 115.

"Tron Joins The 32-Bit Processor Fray," Dec. 8, 1988, *Electronic Design,* 36(27), p. 41.

Tucker, Michael Jay, "The CISC-RISC Debate," Sept. 1989, *UNIX/world,* 6(9), p. 52.

Uchiyama, Kunio, Arakawa, Fumio, Narita, Susumu, "The Gmicro/500 Superscalar Microprocessor with Branch Buffers," Oct. 1993, *IEEE Micro,* 13(5), p. 12.

Wang, Chia-Jiu, Emnett, Frank, "Implementing Precise Interruptions in Pipelined RISC Processors," Aug. 1993, *IEEE Micro,* 13(4), p. 36.

Wayner, Peter, "VLIW Questions," Nov. 1994, *BYTE,* 19(11), p. 287.

Wayner, Peter, "VLIW: Heir to RISC?," Aug. 1989, *BYTE,* 14(8), p. 259.

Weiss, Ray, "Third-generation RISC processors," Mar. 30, 1992, *EDN,* 37(7), p. 96.

"Why It's a RISC Worth Taking," Oct. 10, 1988, *Fortune,* 118(8), p. 112.

Willenz, Avigdor, "Choosing The Right RISC Architecture," Mar. 1990, *High Performance Systems,* 11(3), p. 42.

Wilson, Dave, "Is RISC or DSP Best for your Application?," Apr. 1992, *Computer Design,* 31(4), p. 65.

Woehr, Jack J., "Writable Instruction Set Computers," Jan. 1992, *Dr. Dobb's Journal,* 17(1), p. 32.

Yano, K., Hiraki, M., Shukuri, S., "3.3-V BiCMOS Circuit Techniques for 250MHz RISC Arithmetic Modules," Mar. 1992, *IEEE Journal of Solid-State Circuits,* 27(3), p. 373.

York, George (Captain), "Architecture/Environment Evaluation," Oct. 1992, AD-A257-849, WL-TR-92-7015, Wright Laboratory, Armament Directorate, Eglin AFB, Florida.

Zachmann, William F., "RISC: The Time Has Passed," Nov. 10, 1992, *PC Magazine,* 11(19), p. 105.

CASE STUDIES

5

i80960

5.1 INTRODUCTION

The i80960 controller family from Intel presents a set of 32-bit processors for embedded control, with integrated features to support DMA and interrupts. Introduced in 1988, the i960s incorporate large register sets, with a RISC core of instructions and extensions provided by microcode. By 1994, ten members of the i960 family were in existence. In 1995, there were five major groupings of the 960 parts: K, S, J, C, and H. The first-generation parts include the KA and KB variants. The second generation adds the SA and SB. Third-generation parts, the CA and CF, are superscalar, executing more than one instruction per cycle. The MM, MC, and MX versions, with integral MMU and floating point unit (FPU), can sustain a rate of two instructions per clock. Military grade parts ("M" series) have found applications in avionics systems, and specialized versions for laser printer control have been produced. The popular Hewlett-Packard LaserJet 4 uses a 960 part, and they are found extensively in LAN bridges and routers. The J and H series parts continue the family into the later half of the 1990s.

5.2 BACKGROUND

The i960s address cost-sensitive volume markets and the military/aerospace embedded-control/fault tolerant arena. The i960 is not code compatible with the 80x86 family, nor with the i860 family. It was influenced by Intel's work on its iAPX432 micromainframe.

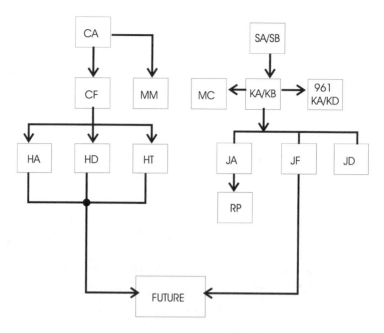

Figure 5.1 i960 family.

There are currently eleven major models of the i960 architecture and several minor variations. These include the KA/KB, the SA/SB, the CA/CF, XA, the MM/MX/MC, and the JF. Generally, the "A" versions do not have floating-point support. The "M" indicates a version addressing the military market. The discontinued models XA and MX are not discussed. The i960 family represents a 32-bit embedded controller family as a follow-on to Intel's 8- and 16-bit controller families. The RISC influence can be seen in the i960 architecture. Intel incorporated DSP features into the i960 line by 1995, resulting in the "H" series. The i960 is found in many volume applications, such as the popular Hewlett-Packard Laserjet-4 printer and numerous pieces of LAN switching gear. Figure 5.1 shows architectural characteristics of some of the i960 family members, along with their inter-relationships.

5.2.1 i80960KA/KB

The i80960KA processor features a high level of functional integration with an integral four-channel interrupt control and 512-byte instruction cache. All K-series 960s feature on-chip 512-byte instruction cache, and an on-chip cache for four sets of 16 registers. The i961KA and KD are special variations intended specifically for printers. K-series devices use a 32-bit-wide external bus. Speed ranges from 10 to 25 MHz. The KA has two hardware breakpoints, six trace modes, and implements a power-on self test.

The KB variant is the same as the KA, with added floating-point capability. It is pin compatible.

5.2.2 i80960SA/SB

The low-end SA variant has a 256-byte register cache, a 512-byte instruction cache, and an integral interrupt controller. The register unit, added to the S-series, automatically saves sixteen of the working registers upon subroutine call. The cache can hold four register sets. If more are needed due to nesting level, the oldest is copied to external memory, and restored as needed. S-series devices use a burst-mode transfer mode for external memory access. A write buffer, implemented as a three-deep first-in, first-out (FIFO), holds data waiting to be written to memory. S-series devices use a 16-bit-wide external bus, with 32-bit-wide internal buses. SA parts operate from 10 to 20 MHz. JTAG is not supported but the chip does have built-in debug features. There are two hardware breakpoint registers, software breakpoints, and instruction support for single-stepping and tracing. The i80960SA implements a power-on self test.

The SB variant is the same as the SA, with added floating point capability. It is a pin compatible part. Figure 5.2 shows the SA/SB architecture. The SB, because of the added floating point unit, has a more extensive power-on self test.

5.2.3 i80960CA

The i80960CA was the first commercial RISC microprocessor to achieve superscalar performance. The CA version of the processor is a high-performance, high-throughput model that features parallel instruction decoding, a two-way set-associative, one-kilobyte instruction cache, multiple execution units operating in parallel (superscalar), and a six-ported scoreboarded register file. The multiple internal data buses are wide for data transfer speed. The processor can sustain a rate of two instructions per clock. A four-channel DMA controller is integrated on-chip, as is an interrupt controller. The DMA controller supports demand mode or block mode transfers. Fly-by DMA, using single bus cycles, is also available. The CA has 1.5 kilobytes of SRAM on-chip with 128-bit-wide access. One kilobyte maps into the lower address space of the processor and effectively becomes a data cache. Five hundred and twelve locations are used for the local register cache. Figure 5.3 shows the CA architecture. Branch prediction is used in the CA, with hints provided from the compiler. Register bypassing is used to optimize pipeline operations in a read-after-write situation. The 32-bit multiply/divide unit (MDU) can perform a 32×32 multiply in four clock times.

5.2.4 i80960CF

The CF model is a follow-on to the CA. It is a low-cost part, available at a 40 MHz operating speed. It is pin and code compatible with the CA, but includes a four kilobyte I-cache, and a one kilobyte D-cache.

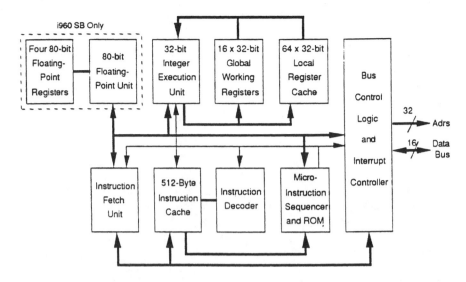

Figure 5.2 SA/SB architecture. Reprinted by permission of Intel Corporation, © 1994, Intel Corporation.

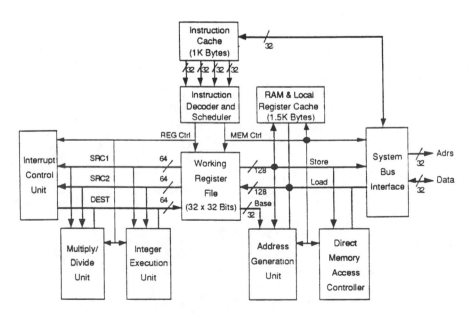

Figure 5.3 CA architecture. Reprinted by permission of Intel Corporation, © 1994, Intel Corporation.

5.2.5 i80960MM/MC

The MM series device builds upon the CA, and adds even more resources for a superscalar approach to throughput and performance. This chip has two integer execution units, and the floating-point unit is streamlined. Three instructions per clock can be issued. The MMU supports a 64-bit virtual address space, and has a 64-entry fully associative TLB. The on-chip instruction cache was expanded to two kilobytes, and is two-way set associative. A two-kilobyte directly mapped, write-through data cache is also used. Internal data paths are 256 bits wide. Eight interrupt inputs are supported. Figure 5.4 illustrates the MM architecture. Register and resource score boarding is used to allow instructions to execute in parallel. The MC version is derived from the K series parts. It adds memory protection and management features via an MMU, and ADA tasking support for military applications. Speed ranges from 16 to 25 MHz.

5.2.6 80960JA/JF/JD

The JF model is faster than older models (four times the KA speed), and has new features, including clock doubling. The JF has four kilobytes of two-way, set-associative I-cache, and two kilobytes of direct mapped D-cache. The JA has two kilobytes of I-cache, and one kilobyte of D-cache. The data codes are write-through. The JD features four kilobytes of I-cache and two kilobytes of D-cache. They also have one kilobyte of data RAM on-chip. They support big- and little-endian byte ordering. Two 32-bit timers and an interrupt controller are integrated on-chip. Full JTAG diagnostics are supported. These models include a halt mode for low power. A burst bus interface provides the ability to transfer four 32-bit words in six clocks. The J-series, code named Cobra, will drive future development in the 960 family.

5.2.7 H Series

The H-series was derived from the superscalar C-series, but has larger caches and clock multiplying, a trick derived from the i486 CISC family. The C-series' DMA controller is gone, but the H-series does have a 16-kilobyte four-way set-associative I-cache, and an 8-kilobyte, four-way set-associative, write-through D-cache. The chips include a power-down mode, and a byte-swap instruction for multi-endian applications. The models HA, HD, and HT feature operation at one, two, and three times the system clock, respectively. They operate at 3.3 volts, but tolerate 5 volt inputs. There is an on-chip interrupt controller, and two timers, as in the JA/JF. Full JTAG support is provided. On-chip data RAM is doubled from previous models.

5.2.8 RP Series

The RP variant was announced in the Spring of 1995, and is derived from the J series parts. It has a fully integrated PCI bus bridge, and is intended as an I/O server for Pentium class systems. As an intelligent I/O system, it offloads tasks from the

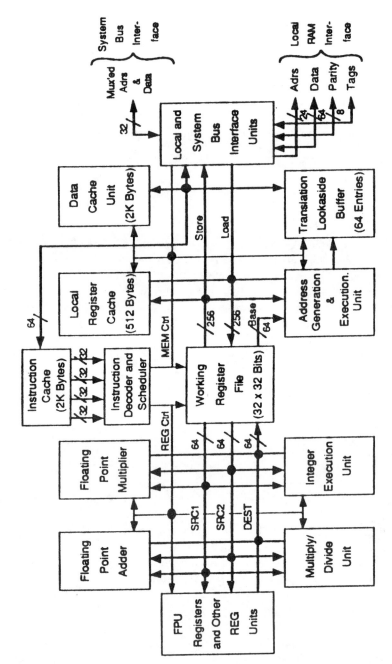

Figure 5.4 MM architecture. Reprinted by permission of Intel Corporation, © 1994, Intel Corporation.

90

main processor, allowing that device to concentrate on operating system and user application needs. The chip includes a four kilobyte two-way set associative I-cache, and a two kilobyte direct mapped data cache. There is one kilobyte of on-chip data RAM. An interrupt controller, and two 32-bit timers are built in. Compatibility with the KA processor external bus, including programmable bus width, is maintained. There is an integrated memory controller to support up to 256 megabytes of external DRAM, organized as 32 bit or 36 bit (with parity). There is a three channel DMA controller, optimized to PCI bus burst mode transfers. The PCI bus functionality includes two 64 byte posting buffers, PCI to PCI bridging, a primary bus interface and support for six secondary bus masters, and private PCI devices. The device has a JTAG interface.

The i800960RP shows a trend in embedded RISC devices. By integrating functionality, an application-specific processor can be spun off from an established family of chips to address specific market needs. By maintaining compatibility with an established family of chips, the development tools and experience base come along for free.

5.2.9 82961 KD

The 82961 KD is a printer coprocessor for the KA or KB. It interfaces to various laser and ink jet engines, such as those from Canon or Ricoh. It handles big- or little-endian font cartridges. It is optimized for the graphics and data compression needed to support the page description language (PDL) and printer control language (PCL).

5.3 ARCHITECTURE

Each of the i960 family members builds on the core architecture with features such as floating point and memory management that may be included for performance, or left out for lower cost. Architectural extensions for specific purposes have also been included in certain models.

The i960 core is a load/store architecture with 32 general registers, 16 global and 16 local, and 32 additional special function registers. Functions for these are undefined in the core architecture, and take on meanings for specific implementations. The registers are scoreboarded.

5.3.1 Hardware

The address space of the 960 family is flat, spanned by 32 address bits. The boot location is the first eight words of memory, and the last 16 megabytes of the memory space is reserved. The MMU extension, when provided, features a four-gigabyte virtual address space per process, with user/supervisor privilege modes. Memory mapped I/O is used in the 960 family parts.

The first-generation parts incorporated a five-stage pipeline. On the MM unit, four instructions can be dispatched from the decoder each clock cycle, if they are independent and don't require any of the same resources. Multimaster support is provided by a request/acknowledge handshake.

The CX series parts exhibit a high level of instruction parallelism by superscalar and pipelined techniques. The CA has four independent execution units, with up to three instructions dispatched each clock. The integer unit, a classical ALU, is augmented by the multiply/divide unit. The instruction decoder/scheduler and the address generation units operate in parallel. The decoder works on three instructions at a time. There are three independent pipelines of depth three each. Scoreboarded registers are used for internal communication. The CA cache can supply four new 32-bit instruction words per clock, ensuring that the pipelines will not be kept waiting for data. On-chip, the decoder classifies incoming instructions into one of three types, and groups instructions without conflicts. The decoder looks for combinations of three integer/memory/control instructions that can be executed simultaneously. Ideally, the optimizing compiler has arranged the code in this fashion. Control instructions are executed by the instruction scheduler itself. It also manages the pipelines and scoreboarded resources. The instruction fetch unit can supply up to four instructions per cycle, due to the wide bus interface to the caches.

The CX series has a multiply/divide unit that operates in parallel with the ALU. It can do a 32x32 multiply in five cycles, or a 64x32 division in thirty-four cycles.

There are four or eight interrupt lines and one acknowledge line. It is possible to use the i8259A interrupt priority controller chip from the i80x86 family with the i960 models, but it implements the opposite priority encoding. This can be corrected with added inverters.

An MMU is provided in certain i960 versions, with virtual memory support, protection, and paging. Task management is also provided. When a floating-point unit is present, it is IEEE standard.

The i960 uses a 32-bit multiplexed address and data bus that supports burst mode transfers. These allow the transfer of up to four words per address.

Upon reset initialization, the processor reads its configuration information from two input pins. This tells the processor whether it is the bus owner, and whether it should stop or continue after completing a self-test. Secondary cache support is provided by a cacheable bit. The 82965 BXU chip provides support for multiprocessors and fault-tolerant implementations.

The i960 family members operate from five volts. The KB draws less than 2 watts at 25 MHz. The CA draws about 4.5 watts, worst case. The JF and HX versions are offered in 3.3 volt operation.

Packaging for the i960 Family Members

Model	Chip Package
KA	132 PGA or PQFP
KB	132 PGA or PQFP
MC	132 CPGA or 164 CQFP

XA	132 CPGA or 164 CQFP
CA	168 PGA or 196 PQFP
CF	168 PGA or 196 PQFP
JF	132 PQFP or 132 PGA
SA	84 PLCC or 80 QFP
SB	84 PLCC or 80 QFP
MM	348 PGA
MX	348 PGA

5.3.2 Software

The instructions are all 32-bits in size, and three-operand, in the i960. They are word-aligned in memory. There are five instruction formats, with most instructions being triadic register, with a 12-bit opcode. Figure 5.5 shows the i960 instruction format. Multifunction one-word instructions serve to increase code density. In the core architecture, there is a user-supervisor model, and support for debug and trace. Instruction trace, branch trace, breakpoint trace, and call/return trace can be used. The memory model of the family is flat, with no segmentation. The stack may start at any memory address, and grows upward. Both a user and a supervisor mode are provided. In user mode, the lower 256 bytes of on-chip data RAM in the CX series are write-protected.

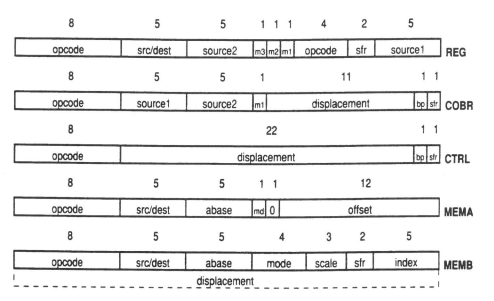

Figure 5.5 Instruction formats. Reprinted by permission of Intel Corporation, © 1994, Intel Corporation.

Integer math instructions include add, subtract, and multiply. Shift and bit manipulation instructions include AND, OR, XOR, bit set and clear, and scan for the first zero or one. Only compare instructions set the condition codes. This simplifies the checking of the possibility of simultaneous execution for instructions, with the penalty of requiring two instructions to be executed in some cases. (For example, an arithmetic operation must be followed by a compare instruction if the results are to be tested.) Instructions are provided to operate on extended data types, greater than 32 bits.

Branches are used for flow control. Instead of a delayed branch, the i960s use a branch-lookahead scheme. This involves branch prediction. The architecture defines two branch types: usually taken, and usually not taken, selectable by the programmer or compiler. Branches specify a signed displacement from the current instruction pointer.

Registers are scoreboarded. At any one time, the user program can see 32 general-purpose plus four floating-point registers. The general-purpose registers are divided into 16 global and 16 local. Upon a subroutine call, new local registers are allocated, but the globals remain the same. First-generation parts have four sets of local registers available. Second-generation parts include a local register cache that holds eight sets of registers, and can save or restore 16 local registers in two clocks. The register file is six-ported in the CX series. Result-forwarding is used to reduce dependencies.

In all members of the family, the 32 general-purpose registers, with globals and locals, map well to the C language. The register set of the i960 series is shown in Figure 5.6. Upon a context switch, all 16 of the local registers are saved in four clock cycles on the CX series.

New instructions on the JA/JF models include conditional moves, adds and subtracts, byte swap, and cache and interrupt control. The H series includes all the instructions of the J series, along with a new cache invalidate instruction.

The trace control register provides hardware support for single step and breakpoints. The arithmetic controls register holds condition codes and fault detection flags.

The i960 family has a very non-RISC-like eleven different data addressing modes. These include literal, register direct, register indirect, absolute, absolute displacement, register indirect with offset, with displacement, with index, or with index and displacement, index with displacement, and instruction pointer plus displacement. Byte ordering is little-endian. Big-endian support is provided at the compiler level. Supported data types range from single bits to 128 bits in width.

Intel claims that over 200 companies worldwide offer tools and applications for the 960s. Development and test tools include a cross-assembler and cross-compilers for ANSI C, hosted on the PC or on Unix systems. Evaluation boards are supplied, and a symbolic debugger is available. In-circuit emulation and debug tools are available in the GNU/960 toolset. The real time kernel iRMK is available from Intel as is a profiling compiler.

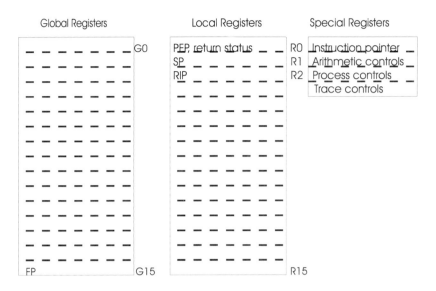

Global Registers   Local Registers   Special Registers

Figure 5.6 General-purpose register set. From Myers, The 80960 Microprocessor Architecture, © 1988. Reprinted by permission of John Wiley & Sons.

5.3.3 Floating Point

Floating point is available only on the KB, MC, SB, and MM versions. They provide full, single, double, and extended (80-bit) operands. Four 80-bit registers are included. Operations supported include the four basic math operations: square root; the transcendentals sin, cos, tan, and atan; log-e, exponents, conversion, and comparison. The square root operation can be aborted if an interrupt occurs. Exceptions include invalid operation, divide-by-zero, overflow, underflow, and inexact result.

The optimized floating-point unit in the MM version takes a worst-case 6 cycles to complete a single precision multiply, or 39 cycles for a divide.

5.3.4 Cache

On the SA, SB, KA, KB, XA and MC versions, a 512-byte instruction cache is included that is direct mapped, and has a 16-byte line size. On the CA, this is expanded to one kilobyte, and a register cache is added. The MM and MX models have a two kilobyte I-cache, and this goes to four kilobytes in the CF model. The CF also includes one kilobyte of D-cache. An LRU algorithm is used for line replacement. In the CX series, at reset time, the cache can be partitioned and locked. The H-series has 16 kilobytes of I-cache, and 8 kilobytes of D-cache. The D-cache is four-way set associative, and write-through. Cache bypass is used. This technique presents the fetched instruction to the decoder in parallel with the cache, after a cache miss.

5.3.5 Memory Management

Not all i960 family members support memory management features. Specifically, only the MC, XA, MM, and MX versions do. On the MC version, memory management support is included for a 32-bit virtual address space, with two levels of translations. Four-kilobyte pages are used, with a 48-entry TLB. User and supervisor modes are supported at the page level. The four access modes include supervisor-only, read-only; supervisor-only, read/write; read/write-any; and read-only-user, read/write-supervisor. At the page level, status bits are supported for accessed, altered, and cacheable. Out-of-order execution is supported.

5.3.6 Exceptions

There are 256 interrupt vector entries, with interrupts grouped into 31 priorities, eight vectors per priority. There are 248 possible external interrupts, and eight internal. The lowest address word is for the NMI. Some imprecise faults are included in the first-generation parts. Since some long instructions can cause excessive latencies, these instructions can be aborted if no processor state change has occurred. Otherwise, a long instruction can be suspended and resumed after the interrupt has been serviced.

The KA, KB, MC, XA, SA, and SB models have four direct interrupt inputs to the chip. The CA, CF, MM, and MX models double this to eight inputs.

5.4 SUMMARY

RISC Features

Large register set—yes, 112x32 in first generation

Load/store—yes

Three operand instruction format

Single-cycle execution—mostly

Pipelined

Hardwired instructions—mostly, but 3072x42-bit microcode for special cases and complex instructions

Non-RISC Features

Multiple data addressing modes

Synthesized instructions

BIBLIOGRAPHY

"80960CA User's Manual," 1989, Intel. ISBN 1-55512-099-7.

"80960kB Hardware Designer's Reference Manual," 1988, Intel order no. 270564.

i960CX Microprocessor Users Manual, Intel, 270710.

i960HA/HD/HT Super Scalar Microprocessor Overview, 1994, Intel Corp., 272591-001.

"i960KA/KB Programmer's Reference Manual," 1988, Intel order no. 270567-003.

"i960 Microprocessor Reference Manual," 1988, Intel. ISBN 1-55512-038-5. 271179.

"i960 Processors and Related Products," Intel Corp., 1995 272084-004, ISBN 1-55512-234-5.

"Big-Endian Byte Support in the i960(R) CA and CF Microprocessors," Nov. 1994. Intel White Paper.

"Big-Endian Programming Using i960(R) Processors," 1994. Intel White paper.

Brunner, R., Atallah, D., "The New i960 Processor that Offers More for Less, the i960JX Series," Aug. 14–16, 1994, *Hot Chips IV Symposium Record*, Stanford University, Palo Alto, California.

Case, Brian, "Intel Reveals Next-Generation 960 H-series," Oct. 3, 1994, *Microprocessor Report*, 8 (13): 11.

"Embedded I960 Offers 45 VAX Mips," July 11, 1994, *Electronic Design*, 42, p. 135.

"Faster i960 is still affordable," March 7, 1994, *Microprocessor Report*, 8 (3): 5.

Hinton, Glenn, "80960-Next Generation," 1989, *IEEE* (Paper) CH 2686-4.

"The Intel i960 Microprocessor Technology Story," 1990, Intel White Paper, 270925-002.

"Intel's Superscalar i960 CA Processor for Embedded Systems," Sept. 12, 1989, Intel order no. 270804-001.

McGeady, S. "A Programmer's View of the 80960 Architecture." 1989, *IEEE* CH2686-4/89.

Myers, Glenford, J., Budde, David L., *The 80960 Microprocessor Architecture*. New York: Wiley, 1988. ISBN 0-471-61857-8.

Ryan, Bob, "Intel's 80960: An Architecture Optimized for Embedded Control," June 1988, *IEEE Micro*, 8 (3): 63–76, Intel 270671-001.

"Software and Development Tools: Development Systems for i960 Tackles Complexities of Superscalar Code," June 1, 1991, *Computer Design*, 30 (9): 58.

"Understanding RISC Processors," 1993, *Microprocessor Report*, Chapter 2, Emeryville: Ziff-Davis. ISBN 1-56276-159-5.

6

MIPS

6.1 INTRODUCTION

This chapter discusses the architecture and implementation of the Stanford-derived MIPS machines. This includes the models R2000, R3000, R4000, and derivatives, available from at least six manufacturers. MIPS, meaning microprocessor without interlocking pipeline stages, is a multisourced architecture, built to an instruction set architecture (ISA) specification maintained by MIPS Computer Corporation. Kane's book [1], describing the R2000 is considered the definition of the base architecture. Originally addressing the workstation market, the family has expanded into special embedded versions.

MIPS, the company, does not build hardware, but designs chips and specifies architectures in conjunction with computer manufacturers. It was founded in 1984. The acquisition of MIPS by Silicon Graphics, Inc. (SGI), a workstation manufacturer, will probably guarantee that the chip emphasis will remain on the workstation market. MIPS Technology, Inc. became a wholly owned subsidiary of SGI, and still handles the architectural licensing to producing vendors. Ideally, SGI will allow MIPS to remain vendor neutral.

6.2 BACKGROUND

The MIPS design originated from John Hennessy's work at Stanford. The Stanford MIPS chip project was completed in 1984. The key output of the Stanford work was not the chip design as much as the instruction set architecture. The original MIPS processor was the R2000. It had an associated floating-point processor, the R2010. Second-generation devices follow the MIPS II architecture, and examples include the R3000 and R3010, along with a variety of specialized embedded controllers. The next generation includes the 64-bit MIPS-IV architecture, of which the first example is the R4000. Follow-ons include the R4400 series by the manufacturer Integrated Device Technology (IDT), and the R4200, R4600, R4700 and variants. Manufacturers of the MIPS chips include IDT, LSI Logic, Performance Semiconductor, NEC Electronics, Inc., Siemens, NKK America, Philips Semiconductor, and Toshiba. The R2000, R3000, and R4000 are, above all else, Unix engines.

Architecture	Examples
MIPS-I	R2000/2010
MIPS-III (32 bit)	R3000/3010
	R3001, R3500
	R3051/52/41/71/81
	R33000
	R6000
MIPS-IV (64 bit)	R4000
	R4400
	R4600, 4650, 4700
	R8000
	R10000

6.2.1 R2000

The original R2000 has two main functional units, the integer CPU and the MMU/TLB. This latter unit is referred to as *system control coprocessor.* The R2000 implementations have a five-stage pipeline, with thirty-two, 32-bit registers, and use 32-bit-wide byte addresses. The TLB is a 64-entry, fully associative element. Page size is four kilobytes, and pages are identified as to read/write access permission, cacheability, and process identifier. All instructions are 32 bits in length, and there are three different formats. The architecture relies on instruction synthesis by the compiler for complex instructions such as multiply and divide. This is essentially macro expansion at the assembler level. The R2000 was produced by Toshiba, and Sierra Semiconductor. Figure 6.1 shows a functional block diagram of the R2000 architecture.

6.2.2 R3000

The MIPS R3000 is a 32-bit architecture with a separate R3010 floating-point unit. Thirty-two 32-bit registers are included on-chip. The pipeline is five stages in depth. Branch latency is one clock time, and load/store latency is also one clock. The device averages 1.25 clocks per instruction. Several addressing modes are supported, including base register and 16-bit signed immediate offset. The Harvard ar-

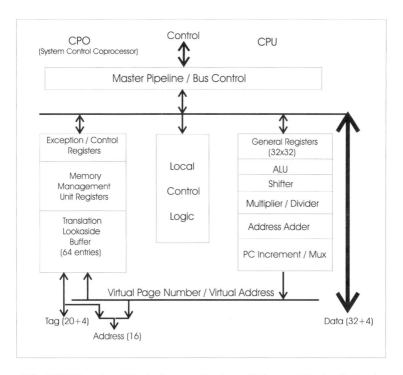

Figure 6.1 R2000 functional block diagram. Courtesy of Integrated Device Technology, Inc.

chitecture chip supports caching of from four to 256 kilobytes of instruction or data, and instruction streaming. On the main memory side of the cache, multiprocessor support is provided by provisions to ensure cache coherency. The R3000 architecture is shown in Figure 6.2. Integer multiply and divide hardware is included.

6.2.3 R3500

The R3500 RISCore processor from IDT is the result of combining the R3000 and R3010 units onto one chip, with the R3000 pinout. Essentially, this is the integer CPU plus coprocessors zero and one, analagous to the Intel i486™ incorporating a i386 and an i387 onto one chip. It is compatible with previous R3000 code and systems. The integer multiply and divide were streamlined. In addition, it is able to dynamically switch between little-endian and big-endian data access modes, not being locked into one or the other at reset time.

6.2.4 R3001

Numerous versions of the R3000 evolved for embedded systems application. Among these is IDT's R3001 "RISController," which has a synchronous memory

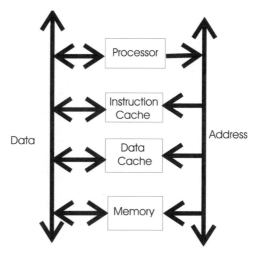

Figure 6.2 R3000 system with memory.

interface and an on-chip Direct Memory Access (DMA) interface. Several variations of the 30xx model with differing features have evolved.

The R3001 is R3000 compatible, but has been optimized for embedded control. A
synchronous memory interface has been added, as well as an integral DMA controller. Six interrupts are provided, although not individually vectorized. Interrupt
response is fast and predictable. The coprocessor model includes precise exceptions, which allow the complete specification of coprocessor state. Additional instructions have been added to the base set, but it retains compatibility with the
R3010 floating point coprocessor. DMA control is included. A cache isolation
mode forces cache hits, regardless of tags. The R3001 can execute R2000/R3000
code.

6.2.5 R3041/3051/3052

This series of embedded controllers from IDT address the cost sensitive embedded
control market. They are essentially the same design, with the -51 model having
four kilobytes of I-cache, and the -52 having eight kilobytes. Each has two kilobytes
of D-cache. The R3000 core processor is incorporated in each. Base versions of the
architecture use a simplified memory mapping. The 'E' versions of the device include full MMU and TLB functionality of CR0. The -41 model does not have an E
version. The devices are packaged in small footprint, plastic packaging for low cost
systems use. Table 6.1 shows the characteristics of the various models, for these
processors and the ones discussed in the next section.

Table 6.1 Characteristics of thirty-two-bit Pin-Compatible RISControllers. Courtesy of Integrated Device Technology, Inc.

Key Feature	R3041	R3051	R3052	R3071	R3081
32-bit MIPS R3000A Core	Yes	Yes	Yes	Yes	Yes
Instruction Cache	2KB	4KB	8KB	16KB	16KB
Data Cache	512B	2KB	2KB	4KB*	4KB*
Variable Bus Sizing (8-, 16-, 32-bit)	Yes	—	—	—	—
Floating-Point Accelerator	—	—	—	—	Yes**
Clock Speed (MHz)	16, 20, 25, 33	20, 25, 33, 40	20, 25, 33, 40	33, 40, 50	20, 25, 33, 40, 50
Performance (up to)	23.4 mips	38.7 mips	38.7 mips	56.3 mips	56.3 mips
Packages	100 TQFP, 84 PLCC	84 MQUAD, 84 PLCC	84 MQUAD, 84 PLCC	84 MQUAD	84 MQUAD, 100 TQFP

*User-configurable to 8KB I-Cache and 8KB D-Cache.
**Incorporates R3010A FPA hardware on-chip.

6.2.6 R3071/R3081

These processors, along with their 'E' variants, extend the embedded control capabilities of the -41, -51, and -52. The -71 and -81 use low cost, 84 pin plastic packaging. The -81 model includes on-chip 3010A floating point capability. A 32-bit-wide multiplexed address/data bus is used. There is a four deep on-chip write buffer, and a four deep read buffer. A DMA arbiter is also included on-chip. These models feature power down modes, and dynamic power management. The processor can operate at multiples of the system clock rate. The 3081 supports Adobe Postscript, and has found a home in many laser printers.

6.2.7 R33000

LSI Logic called the R33000 a self-embedding processor, because of the ease of designing it into systems. It included an R3000 core, eight kilobytes of I-cache and one kilobyte of data cache, DRAM control, bus interface, and three counter/timers. The chip did not support coprocessors, so the MMU/TLB functions of CR0 cannot be used. The chip could not use the R3010 floating-point unit. Two hardware breakpoint registers were added to the base architecture. The LR33020 model is targeted to the X-terminal market.

Families of support chips have evolved to complement the CPUs and allow the construction of full systems. One such family is LSI Logic's MipSET. This family includes an interrupt controller, a DRAM controller, a data buffer, a bus controller, and a DMA/Block Transfer controller. These functions will generally be integrated into the next-generation chip-level product. At the lower level, however, these chips reduce the overall system chip count by eliminating the need to implement the required functionality in discrete logic. The area of support chips is one in which individual vendors of the prescribed MIPS architecture can customize and show individuality and differentiation. Another such area is derived architectures for specific applications, such as embedded control.

6.2.8 R4000

Originally a 32-bit architecture, the MIPS specification has been expanded to include 64 bits. The R4000 is the first of the new 64-bit MIPS IV machines. This means that the address bus, the registers, the ALU, and all external and internal data paths are 64 bits in width. Compatibility has been maintained with the previous 32-bit members of the family at the source code level. Additional instructions are provided to optimize certain operations. The pipeline was expanded to an eight-stage superpipeline. The functional architecture of the R-4000 is shown in Figure 6.3.

The R4000 is available in three configurations to address three distinct market segments. The MC and SC variations include a 128-bit-wide secondary cache bus, with the MC version intended for multiprocessing. The PC variant does not include a secondary cache interface. This chip appears in desktop packages, in direct price competition with 80x86-based PCs. A multiplexed 64-bit address/data bus is used. The Windows-NT operating system was developed on and for the R4000.

6.2.9 VR4100

The VR4100 was announced by NEC in March 1995. It is a low-power version of the 64-bit R4000 design, intended for PDA and embedded usage. An initial 40 MHz version dissipates a low 120 mW at 3.3 volts, and the chip can operate on as low as 2.2 volts. Three power-down modes are included. On-chip cache is two kilobytes of I-cache and one kilobyte of D-cache. The external data bus is 32 bits in width. The chip can operate at four times the supplied clock rate. Power consumption is a low 120 milliwatts at 3.3 volts, 40 MHz. There are three low power modes: standby, suspend, and hibernate.

6.2.10 VR4200

This is a version of the R4000 that NEC is producing in conjunction with video game maker Nintendo, to support high-performance graphics at low cost. It uses a 208 pin package, and is generally compatible with other R4000 series parts. It becomes the basis of the Ultra 64 game set.

6.2.11 R4300i

The R4300i model is intended for low cost, low power embedded and consumer applications. It remains a 64-bit product, and is the first in an intended line of micro-

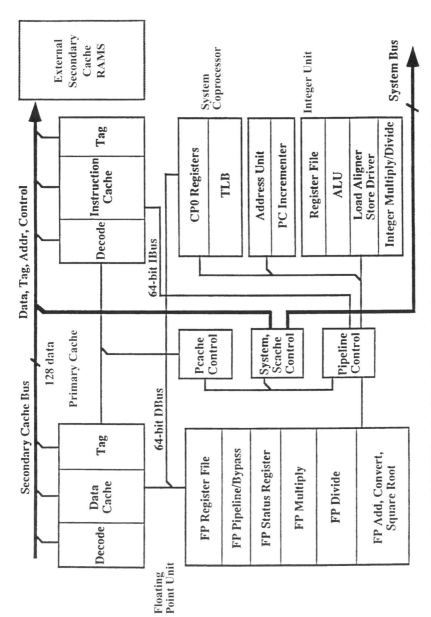

Figure 6.3 R4000 functional block diagram. Courtesy of Integrated Device Technology, Inc.

105

controllers. The R4300i has a power saving mode, and is packaged in an inexpensive 120 pin plastic housing. A five stage pipeline is used. It features 16 kilobytes of I-cache and 8 kilobytes of write-back D-cache on-chip. The TLB has 32 double entries, and accommodates various page sizes, from 4 kilobytes to 16 megabytes. At 3.3 volts, the device dissipates less than 1.8 watts at the maximum operating frequency of 50 MHz. The caches are partitioned into four banks, only one of which is powered at a given time. The TLB is implemented as an on-chip microTLB, in which entries are kept only for the two most recently used pages. In sleep mode, the processor operates at 1/4 of the clock speed. In power down mode, the internal state can be written to nonvolatile RAM (NVRAM), and later restored, allowing for an instant-on feature. The R4300i's system bus width is 32 bits for the multiplexed address/data. The address space is spanned by 32 bits, not the 36 bits of the R4000 series. The R4300i, in conjunction with a special Multi Media Accelerator (MMA) handles MPEG-2 video decompression and game quality 3D graphics.

6.2.12 R4400

The R4400 is a second generation R4000 part. It is available in the same three versions as the R4000: PC, SC, and MC. The R4400's feature dual instruction issue with no issue restrictions, and operation at a reduced 3.3 volts. There is an on-chip 16 kilobyte I-cache and 16 kilobyte D-cache, compared to the R4000's 8 kilobyte units. The SC model supports a direct mapped secondary cache with a 128-bit-wide data bus, and a 25-bit-wide tag interface. The secondary cache may be configured as unified or split, and can range to four megabytes in size. The MC version supports multiprocessing. The on-chip MMU has a fully associative TLB that supports variable page sizes. The floating point unit implements precise exceptions. A 36-bit physical address is used. There are six hardware interrupt inputs in the PC version, one hardware interrupt and an NMI in the MC. The R4400's are dynamically configurable to support little- or big-endian byte ordering. They have a series of new instructions beyond the baseline set. These include a series of doubleword shifts, doubleword multiply and divide, a set of new conditional branches, and doubleword support for the coprocessors. The R4400 series has the possibility of out-of-order execution due to its cache arrangement, as opposed to the strict execution order of the R4000.

The R4400 uses an eight stage superpipeline, which operates at twice the frequency of the system clock. There is a single uncached store buffer, that avoids seven nop's in the pipeline. A new cache error bit is added to the architecture. The R4400's implement the master/checker mode, and a JTAG interface. The PC part comes in a 179-pin PGA, and at 3.3 volts, it dissipates 6 watts at 75 MHz. Due to the secondary cache interface, the SC and MC versions require a 447 pin PGA package.

6.2.13 R4600/4650/4700

IDT's latest R4000 chip series, developed with Toshiba and Quantum Effect Devices, is the R4600, code-named "Orion." The R4600 is a full 64-bit design, and returns to a five-stage pipeline. The I-cache and D-cache are 16 kilobytes each, and two-way set associative. Power management features are used to reduce power consumption to 40 milliwatts in standby. The devices are fully static, and operate at 3.3 volts. The R4600 does not include the secondary cache nor multiprocessor support. The R4600 achieves a speed-up by doing virtual-to-physical address translation in parallel with the cache accesses.

The R4650 is targeted to cost-sensitive embedded applications. It adds a fast multiply-accumulate instruction to the R4600. It has improved real-time support because of faster interrupt processing and an improved integer multiply. The new hardware speeds up the multiple, multiply-accumulate, and the divide. This gives the R4650 a respectable performance on DSP-type tasks. The R4650 gives up double precision floating point capability, and there is no TLB. The address translation uses a simpler base/bound register pair. The address translation process consists of adding the base register to the virtual address, and comparing the result to the bound register. If the result is less than the bound register, the address is valid, else an exception is generated. The I-cache and D-cache are eight kilobytes each. Virtual and physical addresses are both 32 bits. The R4650 has new exception conditions defined, including a double precision floating point exception. The R4650 is packaged in a 208-pin PQFP or MQUAD.

The R4700 is an R4600 optimized for high-end graphics applications, with an improved floating point multiply. The latency for double precision is now six pc clocks, and floating point multiply is now pipelined. The 4700 is pin compatible with the R4600, R4000pc and R4400pc, using a 179-pin PGA. Table 6.2 shows the

Table 6.2   Orion Family Features. Courtesy of Integrated Device Technology, Inc.

Key Feature	Orion R4600	Orion R4650	Orion R4700
64-bit MIPS Core	Yes	Yes	Yes
DSP Features	—	Fast Multiply-Add Instr.	—
FPU Performance	50 MFLOPS	44 MFLOPS	87 MFLOPS
MMU	R4400-compatible	Base-bounds	R4400-compatible
Instruction Cache*	16KB	8KB	16KB
Data Cache*	16KB	8KB**	16KB
External Bus Interface	64-bit	32-/64-bit	64-bit
Peak Power @ 3.3V	21mW/MHz	16mW/MHz	21mW/MHz
Clock Speed (MHz)	100, 133, 150	80, 100, 133	100, 133, 150, 175
Performance	199 Dhry, mips @ 150 MHz	175 Dhry, mips @ 133 MHz	227 Dhry, mips @ 175 MHz
Packages	179 PGA, 208 MQUAD	208 PQFP, 208 MQUAD	179 PGA, 208 MQUAD

*Two-way set-associative caches.
**Cache-Locking support.

various models in the R4600 Orion family.

6.2.14 R6000

The R6000 was a high-speed, high-power emitter coupled logic (ECL) version of the R3000. The circa-1989 chip set consisted of the R6000 CPU, the R6010 FPU, and a 6020 bus interface. It was built by Bipolar Integrated Technology (BIT). The ECL yields were a problem, and ECL technology has since been surpassed by Bipolar-CMOS (BiCMOS) as the choice for high-speed design.

6.2.15 R8000/R10000

These chips are discussed in the appendix to this chapter.

6.3 ARCHITECTURE

This section discusses the hardware architecture of the MIPS machines, including the standard R3000 pipeline and the superpipeline of the R4000 series. The MIPS-IV architecture is discussed in the R8000/R10000 appendix to this chapter.

6.3.1 Hardware

The MIPS standard five-stage instruction pipeline consists of these steps:

1. Fetch instruction from cache.
2. Decode instruction and read operands.
3. Perform ALU operations.
4. Access memory if required.
5. Write results to register file.

Each pipeline step takes one clock or less. After the pipeline fill latency, instructions proceed at one per clock. Instruction interference is minimized. Delayed loads and delayed branches are used to eliminate the latency inherent in these operations.

The MIPS architecture is Load/Store, with all ALU operations occurring between registers. The hardware is configurable at reset time to operate in a little-endian or big-endian mode. There are thirty-two registers, of which R0 is defined as zero on a read, and R31 contains the return address for a subroutine call. The other registers are general purpose. There are two special registers to provide a 64-bit holding area for multiply and divide operations. The R3000 five-stage pipeline architecture is shown in Figure 6.4.

The MIPS machines are designed to operate with one to four tightly coupled coprocessors, of which one is the integral CP0 system control coprocessor. The sys-

Instruction Execution:

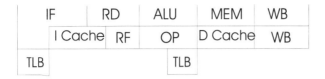

IF	RD	ALU	MEM	WB
	I Cache	RF	OP	D Cache	WB
TLB			TLB	

Five Stage Pipeline:

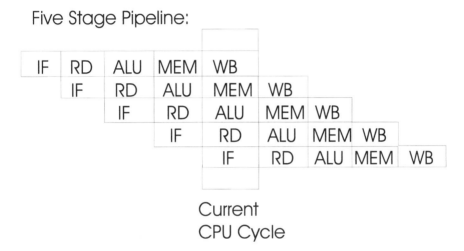

IF	RD	ALU	MEM	WB			
	IF	RD	ALU	MEM	WB		
		IF	RD	ALU	MEM	WB	
			IF	RD	ALU	MEM	WB
				IF	RD	ALU	MEM	WB

Current
CPU Cycle

Figure 6.4   R3000 pipeline architecture Courtesy of Integrated Device Technology, Inc..

tem control coprocessor handles the tasks of memory management, exceptions, and diagnostics. Coprocessor 1 is the floating-point unit. The other units are implementation unique. The functional units may be implemented in separate chips or may share the same chip. In user mode, half of the virtual address space is available for up to 64 user processes. In kernel (or supervisor) mode, three distinct virtual address spaces are available.

The baseline R2010 floating-point unit has its own six-stage pipeline. The R4000 integral floating-point unit has three overlapped execution units. The multiplier is also pipelined. Figure 6.5 shows the superpipeline of the R4000.

The R4000 architecture includes a dual-issue superpipeline and integral floating-point unit to increase integer and floating performance beyond that gained by the increase in clock speed. It decouples instruction-level parallelism from the compiler, and removes some previous issue restrictions. In essence, the R4000 superpipeline can issue two instructions to the R3000's one. Both the integer and the integral floating-point unit are superpipelined. An eight-stage pipeline is used, with each stage completing in one-half clock time. Both leading and trailing clock edges are used to synchronize operations in the pipeline.

The on-chip data and instruction caches of the R4000 can feed two instructions and two data words every pipeline cycle. The ALU supports single-cycle execution. No restrictions are placed on instruction issue, such that any two arbitrary instructions can be issued each cycle. The integer unit uses the floating-point unit (coprocessor) for multiply and divide on the 4600.

In the 4000 architecture, an upgrade path to 64-bit-wide ALUs and 64-bit addressing is also defined. The MMU provides a choice of selectable hardware cache coherency policies for different applications. The TLB refill is under software control for flexibility.

The R3000 defines two privilege levels, user and kernel. The R4000 defines a third intermediate level—the supervisor level.

Smooth pipeline operation can be upset by several conditions. These include cache misses, data dependencies, and exceptions. If the entire pipeline must stop, we have a pipeline stall. If certain portions can continue, we have a pipeline slip. Upon exception detection, the affected instruction and subsequent pipeline contents are invalidated. Stalls for canceled instructions are themselves canceled. Execution resumes with a new instruction stream, defined by the exception vector.

Upon stall, all eight stages of the R4000 superpipeline are frozen. If necessary, incorrect results from previous erroneous steps are corrected before resumption of the pipeline operation (an operation called *correction of pipeline overrun*). Upon pipeline slip, certain stages must advance to resolve data dependencies. The R4400 unit reverts a simpler five-stage pipeline, like the R3000.

The memory bus interface of the MIPS is internally Harvard, going to a unified (von Neumann) format off-chip. Bus width is 32 bits in the R3000 series and 64 bits in the R4000. From the processor, multiplexed address/data lines are provided. In the R3000, a six-element-deep write buffer allows for up to six pending writes in a row. The R3071 and 3081 use a four deep write buffer.

Upon reset, the R4000 processor reads a 256-bit serial data stream at a low rate (clock divided by 256) to set fundamental operating modes. A bit in the status register dictates whether 32- or 64-bit addressing will be used.

JTAG boundary scan support is provided in the R4000 series. In addition, the 4400 implements a master/checker mode, in which two units may be used in parallel, and outputs of the active unit are checked for equality. If a discrepancy occurs, the fault signal is asserted. One unit is chosen to drive the output lines, but each can sample the other's outputs, and either one can assert a fault condition.

The R3000 draws 650 milliamps (ma.) at 25 MHz, with the floating-point coprocessor R3010 drawing 600 ma. at 20 MHz. The R4000 draws 1800 milliamps at 75 MHz, for a total of 9 watts. The R3071 and R3081 include advanced power management features to selectively reduce power consumption. The R4300i dissipates a low 1.8 watts at 3.3 volts.

Through the R4000 model, MIPS chips operate at 5 volts. The 4400 and 4600 were introduced at 5 volts, and have transitioned to 3.3 volts. The 4000 dissipates

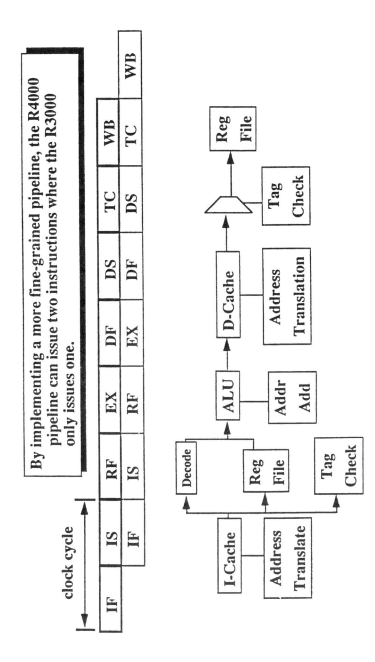

By implementing a more fine-grained pipeline, the R4000 pipeline can issue two instructions where the R3000 only issues one.

clock cycle								
IF	IS	RF	EX	DF	DS	TC	WB
IF	IS	RF	EX	DF	DS	TC	WB

Figure 6.5 R4000 superpipeline. Courtesy of Integrated Device Technology, Inc.

111

2.1 watts at 100 MHz and 3.3 volts, and has a standby mode to reduce power consumption to 40 milliwatts. The 4400 uses 20 watts at 150 MHz and 5 volts. The R3000 is available in a 175-pin PGA format, with the R3010 in an 84-pin PGA. The R4000 MC and SC are both packaged in a 447-pin PGA format. The PC version is packaged in a smaller, lower-cost package of 179 pins. The 4600 is packaged pin-compatibly to the R4000PC's 179-pin PGA. The 4100, designed as a low-power part, uses 120 mW at 3.3 volts and 40 MHz. The 4650 uses a 208-pin PQFP, not compatible with the 4600.

6.3.2 Software

All MIPS instructions prior to the R4000 model are 32 bits in size. There are three instruction formats: immediate, jump, and register.

The load/store instructions are the only ones that reference memory, and only a single addressing mode of base register plus offset is supported. Load instructions have an inherent latency of one cycle before data are available to subsequent instructions. This can cause a load delay in the pipeline. However, the pipeline always executes the instruction following the load. It is the job of the compiler to ensure that the instruction following the load does not depend on the data to be loaded. If the compiler cannot rearrange the code properly, a no-op is inserted as a last resort. A SYNC instruction is provided to force completion of pending loads and stores before any new loads or stores are initiated. Delayed branches are handled in the same fashion. The base instruction set is shown in Figure 6.6.

As with the R2000 architecture, four coprocessors are supported on the R3000 and R4000. These are closely coupled, synchronous units, sharing the data bus and bus transactions with the main processor. Usually, two are included. By convention, in the MIPS system, coprocessor 0 is the system control coprocessor, and coprocessor 1 is the floating-point unit. In the R3000, coprocessor 0 (MMU) is implemented on the same chip as the main CPU. For a coprocessor load or store operation involving memory, the main CPU handles the addressing and control and ignores the data. Data transfers between units use the data bus. The coprocessor can initiate a stall of the main processor, if a data dependency needs to be resolved.

Integer math instructions for the MIPS architecture include add, subtract, multiply, and divide. The floating-point instructions, implemented in coprocessor 1, include add, subtract, multiply, divide, conversion, comparison, square root, and conditional branches. Bit manipulation instructions include AND, OR, XOR, and NOR, and various shifts are provided. For flow control, both jumps and branches are used. The difference is that jumps are to an absolute address, and branches are relative to the program counter, with a 16-bit offset. Processor state control is provided by systems calls, breakpoints, and traps.

The MIPS architecture includes 32 registers, which are 32 bits wide in the 3000 series, and 64 bits wide in the R4000. Register zero is defined to be zero, and register 31 is the link for branch and link instructions. The other registers are general purpose. A program counter is provided, as are two registers used for multiply and

OP	Description	OP	Description
	Load/Store Instructions		**Multiply/Divide Instructions**
LB	Load Byte	MULT	Multiply
LBU	Load Byte Unsigned	MULTU	Multiply Unsigned
LH	Load Halfword	DIV	Divide
LHU	Load Halfword Unsigned	DIVU	Divide Unsigned
LW	Load Word		
LWL	Load Word Left	MFHI	Move From HI
LWR	Load Word Right	MTHI	Move To HI
SB	Store Byte	MFLO	Move From LO
SH	Store Halfword	MTLO	Move To LO
SW	Store Word		**Jump and Branch Instructions**
SWL	Store Word Left	J	Jump
SWR	Store Word Right	JAL	Jump And Link
	Arithmetic Instructions (ALU Immediate)	JR	Jump to Register
		JALR	Jump And Link Register
ADDI	Add Immediate	BEQ	Branch on Equal
ADDIU	Add Immediate Unsigned	BNE	Branch on Not Equal
SLTI	Set on Less Than Immediate	BLEZ	Branch on Less than or Equal to Zero
SLTIU	Set on Less Than Immediate Unsigned	BGTZ	Branch on Greater Than Zero
		BLTZ	Branch on Less Than Zero
ANDI	AND Immediate	BGEZ	Branch on Greater than or Equal to Zero
ORI	OR Immediate		
XORI	Exclusive OR Immediate	BLTZAL	Branch on Less Than Zero And Link
LUI	Load Upper Immediate	BGEZAL	Branch on Greater than or Equal to Zero And Link
	Arithmetic Instructions (3-operand, register-type)		**Coprocessor Instructions**
ADD	Add	LWCz	Load Word from Coprocessor
ADDU	Add Unsigned	SWCz	Store Word to Coprocessor
SUB	Subtract	MTCz	Move To Coprocessor
SUBU	Subtract Unsigned	MFCz	Move From Coprocessor
SLT	Set on Less Than	CTCz	Move Control to Coprocessor
SLTU	Set on Less Than Unsigned	CFCz	Move Control From Coprocessor
AND	AND	COPz	Coprocessor Operation
OR	OR	BCzT	Branch on Coprocessor z True
XOR	Exclusive OR	BCzF	Branch on Coprocessor z False
NOR	NOR		**System Control Coprocessor (CP0) Instructions**
	Shift Instructions		
SLL	Shift Left Logical	MTC0	Move To CP0
SRL	Shift Right Logical	MFC0	Move From CP0
SRA	Shift Right Arithmetic		
SLLV	Shift Left Logical Variable	TLBR	Read indexed TLB entry
SRLV	Shift Right Logical Variable	TLBWI	Write Indexed TLB entry
SRAV	Shift Right Arithmetic Variable	TLBWR	Write Random TLB entry
	Special Instructions	TLBP	Probe TLB for matching entry
SYSCALL	System Call	RFE	Restore From Exception
BREAK	Break		

Figure 6.6 Base MIPS instruction set. Courtesy of Integrated Device Technology, Inc.

divide. Floating-point registers are defined in coprocessor 1, and include thirty-two 32-bit registers that can be configured as sixteen 64-bit registers. The floating-point unit also has a 32-bit status/control register.

Byte ordering is configurable at reset time to little- or big-endian mode. Supported data types include bytes, half words, words, and double words. The R4000 adds a bit to enable 64-bit features, which include all of the 32-bit functions as a subset. New instructions and new bits in the status register are also included. The new instructions implement the 64-bit features of the processor, and provide for long word loads and stores, and operations on 64-bit data structures.

A complete set of development and test tools are available from the chip manufacturers, and third-party vendors. These tools include assemblers and disassemblers, evaluation boards, simulators and hardware and software simulation models. Compilers for C, C++, FORTRAN, Pascal, Ada, COBOL, and PL/1 are available. Tools are hosted on the MIPS machines and the MAC or PC. A ROM-able kernel for debugging is available, as are several real-time operating systems (RTOS) including C-executive and VxWorks. The R4000 series is supported by the operating systems Windows-NT and Unisoft Unix.

6.3.3 Floating Point

Floating-point operation in the MIPS architecture is handled by coprocessor 1. This is a separate chip in the early models, being fully integrated in the 3500 and 4000 series. The R2010 and R3010 floating-point chips implement 32- and 64-bit arithmetic, with a simple coprocessor interface to the processor to allow concurrent operation. The FPU, coprocessor 1, has a simple load/store architecture with sixteen 64-bit on-chip registers. Three internal execution units allow the device to expedite the operation of traditionally time-intensive floating-point operations. These include the add/subtract unit, the multiply unit, and the divide unit. IEEE-754 format math is supported. The unit does the four basic math operations plus format conversion. The floating-point unit has a six-stage pipeline. Instructions require from one to nineteen cycles to complete in this unit, so pipeline stalls are more frequent. Instructions that don't contend for the same resources can be overlapped, but only one multiply and one divide can be running at a given time. However, an add/subtract operation can be started and completed during a multiply. Figure 6.7 shows the architecture of the R3010 floating point unit.

The R4000 integral floating-point unit has three overlapped execution units. The multiplier is pipelined, with a new start possible every four cycles. Add, subtract, multiply, divide, square root, and conversion and comparison operations are supported. Sixteen 64-bit registers are included, and a double word load or store every cycle is possible using the 64-bit-wide cache. Four IEEE standard rounding modes are supported. The R3010, R4000, and R4600 support precise floating-point exceptions. The floating-point-optimized R8000 unit is discussed in the appendix to this chapter.

6.3.4 Cache

In the R2000 and R3000, cache is external. IDT's R30xx embedded controllers incorporate on-chip cache. Separate data and instruction caches are provided in the

Cache
Data

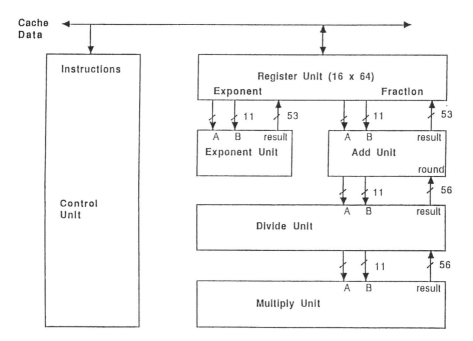

Figure 6.7 R3010 floating-point architecture. Courtesy of Integrated Device Technology, Inc.

R3000. A write-through policy is used for the data cache. A write buffer allows for multiple pending writes to be queued.

Direct mapped external cache is used, with a line size of four words for instruction, and one or four words for data. Physical tags are kept, so that a context switch does not require a cache flush. The data and instruction caches share the same implementation. A write-through policy is used for the data cache. A cache parity error is treated as a cache miss. Since DMA as well as multiprocessing can invalidate cache contents in a system, coherent DMA is used. The R4000 uses eight kilobytes each of direct-mapped I-cache and D-cache. The 4400 and 4600 double these, and they are two-way set associative. The 4600 series D-cache can be enabled for write-back or write-through operation on a per-page basis. The replacement algorithm is random. A selectable number of mappings can be locked. There is a four-entry TLB for data. No hardware coherency mechanism for multiprocessing is provided, but included features allow the mechanism to be constructed in external hardware.

6.3.4.1 Cache Swapping For cache flushing and diagnostics, there is a provision to swap the I- and D-caches. This is controlled by a bit in the status register. A load or a store cannot be executing at the time of the swap. In addition, execution must be proceeding from a noncacheable region of memory.

On the R4000, instruction and data caches are eight kilobytes in size, with parity protection. On the 4400 and 4600 by IDT, these cache sizes are doubled to sixteen kilobytes each. Provision for up to four megabytes of secondary cache is included. The system control coprocessor, or CP0, of the R4000 is a superset of that of the R3000. Three modes of virtual addressing are supported: kernel, supervisor, and user. Page size is configurable on a per-entry basis, from four kilobytes to sixteen megabytes. The on-chip I-cache and D-cache are directly mapped, virtually indexed, and physically tagged. The D-cache uses a write-back policy, with a two-entry store buffer, and a write buffer of line size. A 36-bit physical address is used. On the 4600 product, the internal I-cache and D-cache are two-way set associative. Figure 6.8 illustrates the cache architecture of the R4000.

The secondary cache on 4000MC and SC models can be configured as either unified or separate data and instruction. ECC protection is used, whereas on-chip cache uses parity. The secondary cache interface uses a 128-bit data bus, a 25-bit tag bus, and an 18-bit address bus. Secondary cache is physically tagged and physically indexed.

6.3.5 Memory Management

The virtual-physical address translation in the MIPS architecture is handled by coprocessor zero, integrated on-chip. Three modes of virtual addressing are provided for user, supervisor, and kernel modes.

The MIPS processors were designed with multiprocessing in mind, using such features as physical cache and a mode for externally generated stall and the ability to invalidate cache status inputs. Memory management functions are provided by coprocessor zero. Multiprocessing depends on interprocessor communication, synchronization between processes, and data coherence. A mix of hardware and software is used to address these issues.

The MMU divides the memory space into a two-gigabyte user space, and a two-gigabyte kernel/systems space. The MMU uses a 64-entry fully associative translation lookaside buffer. Externally implemented write buffers provide decoupling of write-latency from CPU operations. Both big- and little-endian data formats are supported, with the mode selected during reset. The 4600 write buffer holds four sets of 64-bit addresses and 64-bit data.

In a simplistic multiprocessor system, duplicate tags for the D-cache can be provided. Note that I-cache issues are much simpler, since the I-cache is only filled from the memory (except for self-modifying code, which is frowned upon). With write-through D-cache, the main memory is always consistent with the cache, and the two caches either match or they don't. During a write operation, if the second unit is snooping on the bus and sees a write to a location it has cached, it invalidates that location in its own cache. However, write-through caches generate much redundant bus traffic, because not all writes to cache need be written to main memory.

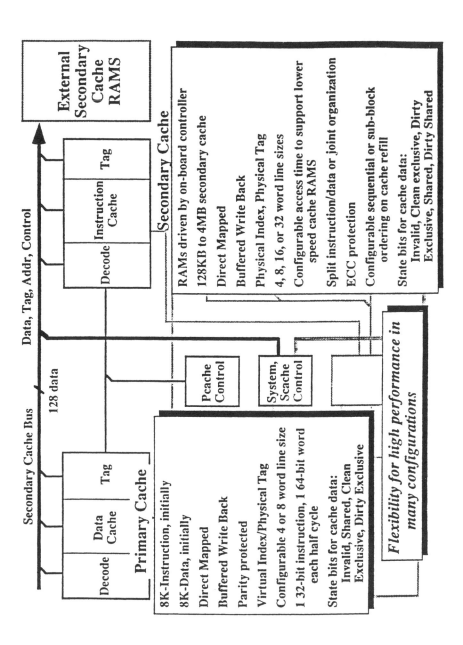

Figure 6.8 R4000 cache architecture. Courtesy of Integrated Device Technology, Inc.

External Secondary Cache RAMS

Data, Tag, Addr, Control

Secondary Cache Bus

128 data

Instruction Cache — Decode / Tag

Secondary Cache

- RAMs driven by on-board controller
- 128KB to 4MB secondary cache
- Direct Mapped
- Buffered Write Back
- Physical Index, Physical Tag
- 4, 8, 16, or 32 word line sizes
- Configurable access time to support lower speed cache RAMS
- Split instruction/data or joint organization
- ECC protection
- Configurable sequential or sub-block ordering on cache refill
- State bits for cache data:
  Invalid, Clean exclusive, Dirty
  Exclusive, Shared, Dirty Shared

Pcache Control

System, Scache Control

Flexibility for high performance in many configurations

Data Cache — Decode / Tag

Primary Cache

- 8K-Instruction, initially
- 8K-Data, initially
- Direct Mapped
- Buffered Write Back
- Parity protected
- Virtual Index/Physical Tag
- Configurable 4 or 8 word line size
- 1 32-bit instruction, 1 64-bit word each half cycle
- State bits for cache data:
  Invalid, Shared, Clean
  Exclusive, Dirty Exclusive

117

With a write buffer, the situation gets more complicated, because the write buffer may need to be flushed to main memory to maintain coherency among caches.

A more sophisticated scheme uses a secondary cache with a write-back policy. Not only does the secondary cache function as a write buffer from primary cache to main memory, but it does the tag comparison and coherency transactions. Again, note that this level of complexity is required only for the D-cache, and not the I-cache.

With physically addressed primary and secondary caches, the on-chip primary cache is a subset of the secondary cache, which is, in turn, a subset of the main memory. In the 4000 series, the 64-bit virtual address space is mapped to a 32-bit physical space. The 4600 does address translation in parallel with cache accesses. It provides a two-entry instruction TLB, each entry mapping one four-kilobyte page. A large, fully associative TLB maps 96 virtual pages to the 64-Gbyte physical address space. The page size is selectable from four kilobytes to sixteen megabytes. The physical address of the 4000 series is provided by 36 addresses. The 4650 does not include a TLB but has a base/bound register pair to support a much simpler address mapping. The 4700 has a two-entry instruction TLB and a four-entry data TLB.

6.3.6 Exceptions

Exception handling in the MIPS architecture is handled by coprocessor zero. The external interrupt capability of the chip is provided by six hardware pins that are sampled only during the ALU step. There are two software interrupts. Interrupt response has a one-cycle latency. There are no hardware interrupt vectors, and only one general exception vector. Other vectors are used for reset and TLB miss. All exception cases force the processor into kernel mode. The system control coprocessor handles all exception conditions and processing.

Sources of exception in the R-3000

- Reset
- Interrupt (6 inputs) (These are maskable in the status reg)
- Coprocessor unusable
- Reserved or undefined instruction execution
- System (trap) call (maskable in status reg)
- Breakpoint instruction
- Overflow
- Address error (misaligned, or illegal address in user mode)
- Bus error
- TLB modified or TLB miss
- UTLB miss

Upon an exception case, the current instruction and all subsequent instructions in the pipeline are aborted. The exception program counter is loaded with the restart address, which may be an instruction address or the address of a branch following a delay slot. Extensions to the instruction set may be provided by the reserved instruction exception and associated handler.

Although the machine state is saved, certain conditions or fragments of incomplete instruction execution may remain. For example, a multiply or divide may be in progress. The contents of the I-cache may have been updated in response to a bus error. Thus, certain conditions, called reorganization constraints, are imprecise after an interrupt. The alternative to this is to disallow exceptions or interrupts, or to save a massive amount of state information for each exception. The 4600 has a nonmaskable interrupt (NMI), timer interrupt, and two software interrupts, and supports precise exceptions.

6.4 SUMMARY

RISC Features

Large register set—yes
Load/store—yes
Single-cycle execution—yes
Small instruction set—yes
Hardwired instructions—yes

Non-RISC Features

Multiple addressing modes

6.5 REFERENCES

[1] Kane, Gerry, *MIPS RISC Architecture.* Englewood Cliffs, NJ: Prentice Hall, 1988. ISBN 0-13-584293-X.

6.6 BIBLIOGRAPHY

Bourekas, Philip, "IDT 79R3001 Simplifies Design of High-Performance Control Systems," IDT.

Bruess, R. J., *RISC—The MIPS-R3000 Family: Architecture, System Components, Compilers, Tools, Applications.* New York: VCH Publications, 1991. ISBN 3-8009-4103-1.

Bruss, Rolf-Jurgen, *RISC: The MIPS-R3000 Family.* Berlin: Siemens Aktiengesellschaft, 1991.

Bursky, Dave, "ECL-Based RISC Chip Set Delivers Top Throughput," June 8, 1989, *Electronic Design*, pp. 42–45.

Chow, Paul [ed], "The MIPS-X RISC Microprocessor," Boston: Kluwer Academic, 1989.

Cmelik, Robert F., Ditzel, David R., Kelly, Edmund, J., "An Analysis of SPARC and MIPS Instruction Set Utilization on the SPEC Benchmarks," Apr. 1 1991, *Sigplan Notices,* 26 (4): 290.

"CW33000 MIPS Embedded Processor User's Manual," 1991, LSI Logic, MV72-000103-99A.

"Development Products Catalog for R3000, R3001, R3051/52/81, and R3500 Systems," April 1992, IDT.

"First of the Red-Hot R4000s: SGI Crimson Lights the Flame for the R4000 Processor from MIPS," July 1, 1992, *Byte*, 17 (7): 46.

"Fourth Generation 64-bit RISC Microprocessor," March 1994, IDT.

Freitas, Dan, "32-bit RISC Processor Achieves Sustained Performance of 20 Mips," IDT White paper, undated.

Goodman, James L., "A Programmer's View of Computer Architecture: with examples from the MIPS RISC architecture," Fort Worth, TX: Saunders College, 1993.

Hudson, Edwin et al., "A 10 MIPS 32-bit RISC Processor with 128 Mbytes/sec Bandwidth," *MIPS Computer Systems, Inc.*, White Paper, undated.

"IDT 79R3051 Family-Hardware User's Manual," 1991, IDT.

"The IDT 79R3071 IDT79R3081 RISController Hardware User's Manual," April 4, 1994, IDT Rev. 2nd ed.

"IDT 79R3081, Advance Information," Jan. 1992, IDT.

"IDT 79R4000 Family, Preliminary," Jan. 1991, IDT.

"IDT 79R4600 Orion Processor Hardware User's Manual," Oct. 1993, IDT, ver. 1.0.

"IDT 79R4600 Processor Hardware User Manual," 1994, IDT.

"IDT 7RS357 R3000 Family Cross Assembler, User Guide," IDT.

"IDT 7RS382 RISC Evaluation Board, Hardware User Guide," IDT.

"IDT 7RS382 Theory of Operation," undated, IDT.

"IDT Data Book Supplement," 1989, IDT, section 9.

"IDTR3051/R3081 Application Guide," 1992, IDT.

"IDT RISC IDT79R3081/3081E Integrated RISController," IDT.

"IDT RISC, New Directions for MIPS RISC," 1990, IDT.

"IDT RISC R3001 RISController Handbook," 1990, IDT.

"Inferfacing DMA Controllers to the LR33000 MIPS Embedded Processor," 1991, Applications note, LSI Logic.

"Interrupt Handlers and Interrupt Latency Calculations for the LR33000 Self-Embedding Processor," 1991, LSI Logic, *1991 User's Manual.*

"Introduction to the LR4000 MIPS Microprocessor," 1991, LSI Logic.

"LR3000/LR3000A MIPS RISC Microprocessor User's Manual," 1990, LSI Logic.

"LR3010/LR3010A MIPS Floating-Point Accelerator User's Manual," August 12, 1991, LSI Logic.

"LR33000 Self-Embedding Processor, User's Manual," 1991, LSI Logic, MD70-000120-99B.

"LR33020 GraphX Processor, User's Manual," 1992, LSI Logic, MM71-000103-99-A.

"LR33050 MIPS IFX Processor User's Manual," 1992, LSI Logic, MM72-000111-99A.

Malone, Michael S., "Going Public: MIPS Computer and the Entrepreneurial Dream," New York: E. Burlingame Books, 1991.

Miller, Michael J., "Designing Embedded Control Applications with the R3001 RISController," IDT.

"MIPS R4000 Chip-Set PC Runs Windows NT," Mar. 18, 1993, *EDN*, 38 (6): 142.

"MIPS R4000 Microprocessor Introduction," 1991, IDT, M8-00041.

"MIPS R4000/R4400 Microprocessor User Manual," Jan. 1995, 2nd ed. MIPS Technologies, Inc.

"MIPS R4000 User's Manual," 1991, IDT, M8-00040.

"MIPS R4300i Microprocessor Technical Background", 1991, MIPS Technologies, Inc.

"MipSET Technical Manual," 1991, LSI Logic, MM71-000101-99A.

Mirapuri, Sunil, Woodacre, Michael, Vasseghi, Nader, "The Mips R4000 Processor," Apr. 1, 1992, *IEEE Micro*, 12 (2): 10.

"Orion IDT 79R4650 Preliminary Data Sheet," Oct. 1994, IDT.

"Orion IDT 79R4700 Preliminary Data Sheet," Oct. 1994, IDT.

"PACEMIPS R3400A, 32-Bit RISC Processor with Floating Point Accelerator," 1990, *Performance Semiconductor.*

"R3000 Family Assembly Language Programmer's Guide," Aug. 1988, IDT, 02-00036-001 (A).

"R3000 Family System Programmer's Guide," Aug. 1988, IDT, 02-00037B.

"R3000 Family System Programmer's Package Reference," Aug. 1988, IDT.

"R3000/R3001—Designers Guide," 1990, IDT.

"R3001 RISController Performance Comparison Report," 1990, IDT.

"RISC Data Book," 1991, IDT.

"RISC Microprocessor Computer and Subsystems 1992/1993 Data Book," 1992, IDT.

"RISC Microprocessor Data Book," 1994, IDT.

"RISC R3000 Family Development Support Guide," 1991, IDT.

"RISC Technology Seminar Workbook," 1989, 1990, IDT.

"Rowen, Chris, Johnson, Mike, Ries, Paul, "The MIPS R3010 Floating Point Coprocessor," June 1988, *IEEE Micro*, 53–62.

"System Design Using the MIPS R3000/3010 RISC Chipset," 1989, MIPS, *IEEE Micro.*

"Understanding RISC Processors," 1993, *Microprocessor Report*, Chapter 6, Ziff-Davis. ISBN 1-5627159-5.

"Under The Hood: The MIPS R4000," Dec. 1, 1991, *Byte*, 16 (13): 271.

"Vr3000, Advanced, High-Performance RISC Microprocessor," Sept. 1989, NEC.

"Vr3000 Series, Benchmark," Oct. 1989, NEC.

"Vr3000 Series, RISC Microprocessor, Electrical Specifications," NEC.

"Vr4400MC (uPO30412) 64-bit RISC Microprocessor," Nov. 1993, NEC Electronics, Inc.

"Vr4400PC (uPO30410) 64-bit RISC Microprocessor," Nov. 1993, NEC Electronics, Inc.

"Vr4400SC (uPD30411) 64-bit RISC Microprocessor," Nov. 1993, NEC Electronics, Inc.

Weiss, Ray, "Third-Generation RISC Processors," Mar. 30, 1992, *EDN*, 37 (7): 96.

Willenz, Avigdor, "A High Performance Deterministic 79R3000-based Embedded System," Sept. 1989, IDT Applications note.

Yoshida, Junko, "MIPS' Magic Carpet takes Set-top-box Ride," May 1, 1985, *EE Times*, 846, p. 1.

APPENDIX TO CHAPTER 6: R8000 AND R10000

A.6.1 Introduction

The R8000 and R10000 are both high-end MIPS products, but are addressed to different applications, and use different techniques for performance. The R8000 is a 64-bit, superscalar instantiation of the MIPS IV 64-bit architecture, by MIPS Technologies, NEC, and Toshiba. The emphasis of the R8000 is floating-point-intensive operations, where it achieves levels of performance comparable to a Cray Y-MP supercomputer. The chip is also designed to support symmetric multiprocessing. The R10000, called the VR10000 by NEC, is more of an evolutionary product in the R4000 line. It was announced in late 1994, and will ship at the end of 1995. The R10000 is expected to set the direction of MIPS processors for the next few years. It is also an implementation of the MIPS IV architecture.

A.6.2 Background

The R8000 project started in 1991 as " TFP," with a goal of bringing down the cost of supercomputing levels of performance to workstation levels. The approach was to gain an order of magnitude improvement in throughput from the symmetric multiprocessor (SMP) architecture and organization, and another order of magnitude from multiprocessing. R8000 is an extension to the R4000 design, and is binary compatible with that unit.

The R10000, previously code-named T5, uses a superscalar approach with out-of-order execution. These latest chips from MIPS utilize a technique called ANDES—architecture with nonsequential dynamic execution scheduling. The R10000 implements the 64-bit MIPS-IV instruction set architecture.

A.6.3 Architecture

The R8000 and R10000 can each dispatch up to four instructions per clock cycle.

There are two floating-point units, two load/store memory interface units, and two integer units. Out-of-order execution is supported for floating point, but not in the integer pipeline. Floating-point instructions are issued in-order with respect to other floating point instructions in the stream, but may execute out-of-order with respect to integer instructions in the input stream. In essence, the floating and integer pipes are decoupled. The R10000 introduces dynamic instruction scheduling, which is essentially instruction reordering in real time. This design is an "aggressive," out-of-order, superscalar design. Decoded instructions go to one of three 16 entry queues. Dynamic scheduling takes place within each queue. It is possible to have up to 32 instructions in varying levels of completeness. Register renaming is used, as is branch prediction.

A.6.3.1 Hardware Initial R8000 silicon operates at 75 MHz. With four-issue, this translates to 300 MIPS. Two of the four issued instructions can be double-precision floating point. Simultaneously, two double-precision loads or stores can be conducted. The integer ALUs and the shifter unit operate in one cycle. Double-precision multiply can be accomplished in 6 cycles in the nonpipelined unit, but divide can take up to 73 cycles.

The translation lookaside buffer of the R8000 is a dual-ported, three-way set-associative cache of 384 entries. A random replacement algorithm is used.

The R8000's integer pipeline consists of five stages. ALU operations can occur in parallel with data cache access. A delay is incurred in the pipeline when an address from an ALU operation calculation is used as a base address for the following load or store. This is in contrast to the normal "load shadow" of a delayed load, whereby an instruction following a load cannot use the result of that load. The complexity of the two-chip R8000 design requires a costly multichip module (MCM) package. Both R8000 units require a 591 pin chip.

The R8000's floating-point unit is implemented as an associated, tightly coupled R8010 chip. Dual floating-point execution units are included. The integer unit includes two ALUs and an integer multiply/divide unit. The instruction queue of the R8000 is six elements deep.

The R10000 has five independent execution units. There are two integer ALUs, and two floating point ALUs. Only one of the floating point units does divide and square root.

The R10000 requires a 527-pin ceramic PGA package. It operates from 3.3 volts, and supports JTAG. It operates at 200 MHz.

A6.3.2 Software and Programmer's View The architecture of these machines is 64-bit, with data structures and addresses being of this size. The R8000 is MIPS instruction set compatible, and implements a superset of the R4000 64-bit instruction set. New instructions include the fused multiply-add, register to register addressing for performance enhancement on arrays with arbitrary strides, and conditional moves on both integer and floating conditions. An 8-bit floating condition code set was added. Simple if-then-else constructs can compile directly to linear code. The R8000 register file has nine read and four write ports. The R10000 has 64 integer and floating point physical registers, and 32 logical registers.

Alignment-free instruction dispatching is provided by a queue that decouples the fetch pipeline from the dispatch logic. An issue rate of four instructions per cycle for the R8000 implies an instruction fetch rate of four per cycle. Although this is feasible for linear code, it requires clever branch prediction logic to avoid costly branch penalties. The chosen scheme has a low prediction accuracy countered with a large branch target cache size. All predicted branch targets are assumed to be in the cache, which usually works, but does provide a substantial penalty if incorrect. There is a single prediction possible per four instructions, which can cause cache thrashing when there is more than one branch per group of four instructions. More than two branch instructions are precluded by the nature of MIPS instruction architecture. The chosen branch prediction schema matches the requirements for the object-oriented programming paradigm, according to SGI. The R8000 and R10000 are R4000 code compatible, but code for them must be optimized differently. The R4000 is superpipelined, whereas the R8000 and R10000 are superscalar. Third-generation MIPS compilers support code development in C, C++, or Fortran-77 for R8000. Tools for porting Cray code are also available. Windows-NT and Unix (IRIX-6) run on these processors. The indexed data addressing mode provides for enhanced array addressing.

A.6.3.3 Floating Point The R8000 includes dual floating point units, in the R8010 chip. Full 64-bit IEEE floating point is supported. Each FPU unit can do adds and subtracts, multiplies, divides, square roots, and type conversions. A multiply-accumulate operation is also included. A fully bypassed 12-port (8 read, 4 write) register file is used. Full pipelining allows four-cycle multiplies and adds. An aggregate rate of two floating-point operations per cycle can be achieved in the R8000. Imprecise interrupts are supported in the floating-point unit. In the R10000, the integral floating point units accomplish addition, subtraction, or multiply with a two-cycle latency, and a one-cycle repeat rate. A floating point double precision divide has a latency of 18 cycles. The square root has a latency of 32 cycles.

A.6.3.4 Cache The cache in the R8000 is split in an interesting way. Data references go to a 16-kilobyte, dual-ported, on-chip cache, but floating-point references bypass this to an off-chip cache that can be up to 16 megabytes. This external cache is two-way interleaved, and four-way set associative. The D-cache is virtually addressed, physically tagged. MESI coherency is enforced in hardware, and the D-cache is always a proper subset of the external cache. No write buffer is required, because the bandwidth of the external cache is such that it can accept full write-through from the internal cache. The external cache is write-back, and the controller is included on-chip.

An on-chip, 16-kilobyte direct-mapped instruction cache is also used. It is refilled from external cache. The I-cache is virtually indexed and tagged. This is the result of extensive trades in favor of minimizing complexity from the instruction fetch path. On-chip cache is filled from external cache over a 128-bit-wide data path, in seven cycles for data, eleven cycles for instruction. There is a one kilobyte branch prediction cache, which is direct mapped, and virtually indexed.

The R10000 uses a 32-kilobyte two-way set-associative I-cache and D-cache, and has on-chip secondary cache control. The data cache is two-way interleaved, and uses an LRU algorithm. An on-chip one kilobyte branch target cache is also provided. This minimizes the branch misprediction penalty to three cycles. The data cache is virtually indexed, and physically tagged. Secondary cache is external, and interfaced by means of a 128-bit-wide bus. Up to 16 megabytes may be used. 26 tag lines are used. The external cache is two-way set associative.

A.6.3.5 MMU In the R8000, virtual addresses are 48 bits and physical addresses are 40 bits. Dual TLBs are provided, which are 384-entry and three-way set associative. The R8000 MMU is R4000 compatible. The R10000 uses a 64 entry TLB on-chip. It supports page sizes from 4 kilobytes to 16 megabytes.

A.6.3.6 Exceptions Precise exceptions are used for conditions from the integer pipe, such as illegal op-code or invalid memory address conditions. Exceptions from the floating-point pipe are imprecisely handled, with a precise model available. The precise mode stalls the integer pipeline when a floating-point instruction is being executed.

A.6.4 Summary

RISC Features

Pipelined execution
Fixed-length instructions
Load/store architecture
Large register file

Non-RISC Features

Base register plus index register addressing

A.6.5 Bibliography

Gwennap, Linley, "MIPS R10000 uses Decoupled architecture; High-performance Core will Drive MIPS High-End for Years," *Microprocessor Report*, Oct. 24, 1994, V8 NH 18–22.

Hsu, Peter Yan-Tek, "Design of the R8000 Microprocessor," 1993, *IEEE Micro.*

McCornack, Richard, "The Silicon Graphics Supercomputing Story," June 30, 1994, *High Performance Computing and Communications Week*, HPC 3 (26).

"Performance Optimizations, Implementation, and Verification of the SGI Challenger Multi-processor," 1994, SGI.

"POWER CHALLENGE and POWER ONYX Preliminary Performance Report," June 6, 1994, Silicon Graphics.

"PowerChallenge Technical Report," 1994, SGI.

R10000 Microprocessor Product Overview, Oct. 1994, MIPS Technologies, Inc.

"'Super' Chip Due on Desktop by Year End," June 27, 1994, *PC Week*, 11 (25): 49.

"TFP Designed for Tremendous Floating Point," August 23, 1993, *Microprocessor Report*, 7 (11): 9.

7

TRANSPUTER

7.1 INTRODUCTION

The Inmos Transputer architecture, introduced in 1985, is a single-chip RISC microcomputer architecture, optimized for parallel use in multiple instruction, multiple data (MIMD) configurations. It provides excellent and balanced interprocessor communications as well as computational ability. Transputers provide the capability to implement scalable systems.

7.2 BACKGROUND

The architecture of the Transputer from Inmos Corporation can best be understood by looking at the origins of the device. The Transputer family is a British design, like the Acorn machine discussed in Chapter 11. However, it couldn't be more different. In essence, the Transputer implements in hardware the parallel language *Occam*. Emphasis is placed on communicating among processes as well as on computational ability. To understand the Transputer architecture you have to understand Occam and communicating parallel processes. However, to use the Transputer, you can program in C, Pascal, FORTRAN, or several other familiar languages. The Occam language proved a barrier to widespread acceptance of the Transputer, but it remains the most efficient software tool that matches the hardware. Most working system designers prefer to use the most familiar tools and accept the suboptimum solution.

Since the introduction of the Transputer in 1985, the unit went on to be the world leader in number of units shipped for any RISC processor in 1989 and 1990. By the end of 1990, over one-half-million Transputer units had been shipped, which translates into a large installed base for RISC chips, even considering that a large number of units went into embedded applications.

Inmos, now owned by SGS-Thompson, a major semiconductor manufacturer and systems developer in Europe, also manufactures graphics chips and memories. Fabrication and manufacturing facilities are located in Europe and the United States. A military products line provides Transputer family parts in compliance with MIL-STD-883. As single-chip microcontrollers, Transputers have flown on space missions, as described in Appendix 3.

As embedded controllers, Transputers provide an excellent approach, as they include CPU, memory, and I/O in one package. A minimum of external components is required for systems. Using their unique interprocessor communication architecture, Transputers are the ideal building block for parallel systems. The Transputer family was derived as the instantiation of the Occam language, developed at Oxford University.

The Transputer processor family consists of the 16-bit T222 and T225 and the 32-bit T400, T414, T800, T801, and T805. All are microcomputers, with ALU, memory, and I/O integrated in one package. The early T200 devices were 16-bit architectures, with subsequent models being true 32 bit. The T400 series of Transputers included 32-bit integer processors, four kilobytes of internal memory, and two high-speed serial links (four links on the T414). The T800 family added an integral 64-bit concurrent floating-point processor in 1987. If the T414 is compared to a i80386, then the T800 is a i80486. The T9000 series, announced in April 1991, seeks to expand the capabilities of the device by a factor of 10 in terms of computation and communication, and is discussed as an appendix to this section.

The T801 Transputer is a variation of the T800 with a nonmultiplexed address/data bus. Thus, the package size (i.e., pin count) is larger than the standard T800, but it is easier to interface directly with external static memory than is the T800. The T805 is a T800 with some additional debug instructions, and with several additional control signals to ease the design of dynamic memory systems in a DMA environment. In addition, the T805 has support for 2D graphics through a new set of instructions, and provides CRC calculations on arbitrary-length data streams. Multiplexed data and address lines are used.

The Transputer features high-speed interconnect by means of full-duplex asynchronous serial communications. Associated communication interface devices include the C011 and C012, which interface parallel data transfers to the Transputer's two-wire link protocol. The C004 device is a 32x32 crossbar switch for links. The C004 is fully programmable, dynamically switchable, and controlled by a link interface.

In addition to the general-purpose T-800 series, Inmos manufactures a series of special-purpose processor units. These include the A100 Cascadable signal processor, the A-110 image and signal processing subsystem, the A121 2D discrete cosine transform image processor, and the STI3220 motion estimation processor. The M212 is a special-purpose Transputer device for peripheral control. It is a derivative of the T2xx 16-bit architecture, with specific interface logic for disk drives. It allows disk drives to become a node on a network of link-connected Transputers.

7.3 ARCHITECTURE

The Transputer is a fast single-chip microcomputer requiring a minimum of external support chips. This low-cost unit performs fast, on-chip, 64-bit floating-point processing and has built-in support for parallelism. The key to understanding the architecture is the Occam language. The Occam language is discussed in Section 7.3.2.1.

7.3.1 Hardware

The Transputer itself is a small (one square inch) 84-pin chip that has a high degree of functional integration. External support requirements are minimal. The Transputer even has four kilobytes of fast RAM on-chip so that practical systems can be built with no external memory. The Transputer supports very fast on-chip floating point and has four bidirectional serial links built into the chip that operate at a DMA rate of 20 Mbps each. These links allow the Transputer to be connected as building blocks into arrays of arbitrary size and complexity. The advantage of the Transputer architecture lies not only in its computation speed, but also in its I/O capacity. A reasonable balance of processing to I/O can be configured for a wide range of applications. The architecture of the Transputer is shown in Figure 7.1.

The Transputer's four-kilobyte on-chip SRAM may be allocated for cache, data, or instructions. Simple programs executing entirely from on-chip SRAM are very fast. Four kilobytes may not seem like much space, but recall that Transputer instructions are one byte. On-chip SRAM provides single-cycle access, while external memory is a minimum of three-cycle access.

Instead of having a large number of registers on the chip, the Transputer is actually a stack machine. This provides for a very fast task context switch for interrupt response and task switching. The three-deep operand stack corresponds to the three-address instruction format of other processors. The transistors, or silicon real estate, normally used for scoreboarded registers were devoted to on-chip fast static SRAM, which can be used for code, data, or stack space. The external memory space is spanned by 32 address bits, and is addressed in a flat model. The internal memory provides a fast access workspace. Only workspace and instruction pointers are saved in a context switch. For interrupts, the three stack registers also need to be saved.

A Transputer has a number of simple operating system functions built into the hardware. These include hardware multitasking with foreground and background priority levels, hardware timers, and hardware time-slicing of background tasks. I/O setup is extremely simple with this device typically requiring three instructions to initiate DMA read or write across a link with automatic task disabling until I/O completion or timer expiration. Interrupt context switching is also very fast, typical-

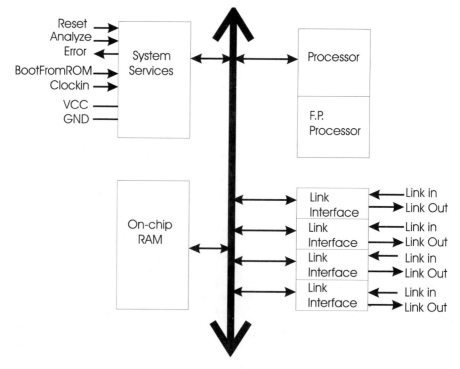

Figure 7.1 Architecture of the Transputer. © Copyright Inmos Limited.

ly less than one microsecond. In addition, generated code is extremely compact, the most commonly used instructions being only one byte long.

A Transputer represents a computing resource with both integer and floating-point calculation capability and with I/O resources of four links of 20 megabits/second input and output simultaneously. Transputers can be connected in a variety of network topologies. The links may be hardwired, jumpered, or connected through the Inmos C002 32x32 programmable crossbar switch.

Few processors provide the same level of connectivity and processing–I/O balance as the Transputer. The closest candidate is Texas Instruments' C080 Parallel DSP, which is marketed as a DSP, not a general-purpose computer. The communication architecture of the TI chip uses parallel ports with DMA engines, and is necessarily distance limited. No other current architecture provides the Transputer's inherent communication capability and connectivity, without extensive glue-logic. Many emerging board-level systems use the Transputer as a communication element for fast RISC or DSP processors such as Intel's i860 or Motorola's 96000 series. The communication bandwidth of a system using Transputer links tends to increase linearly with the number of Transputers. These links, are, however, point to point, but operate without CPU involvement and with little overhead. Connectivity is four nodes per Transputer. Hardware support for Virtual Channels is introduced with the T-9000 model.

A microcoded scheduler maintains time sharing between processes running on the hardware. Two priorities are provided. Besides the internal execution units, memory, and link I/O, several integrated functions are provided. Support for external DRAM memory is provided by 17 different selectable timing configurations. DMA handshaking is implemented, and an interrupt request and acknowledge are provided.

The Transputer has two on-chip 32-bit timers. The high-priority process timer is incremented every microsecond. The low-priority process timer is incremented every 64 microseconds. The timers are used for process scheduling, and the current value can be read onto the stack with a load timer instruction.

A Transputer's external memory interface is von Neumann, using 32-bit-wide address and data paths. No memory management or virtual memory features are included.

Upon reset, the Transputer can boot from a ROM or from one of the serial links. This feature is selected by the state of an input pin on the processor. When booting from ROM, one Transputer can initialize a whole network of Transputers by transferring the initial program serially over the links. In the case of a boot ROM, control is passed to the top two bytes in the address space.

Transputer processors and I/O chips all use a simple five-Megahertz system clock, which is then phase-locked within the chip to the proper operating frequency. Processor speed is selectable by three hardware pins on the T800 series.

No JTAG support is included. Support for debugging includes the analyze and error pins and a breakpoint instruction. When the "analyze" signal is asserted, the Transputer will halt after high-priority processes complete. State is saved, and memory refresh continues. A Transputer will assert the "error" signal upon detection of an internal error state, such as overflow or division by zero. The associated error flag must be specifically cleared by an instruction. An error input pin is also provided, which is OR-ed with the internal error flag. Thus, arrays of Transputers can pass error information along to the master unit.

The four independent serial links on each Transputer support bidirectional asynchronous communication at TTL levels, and operate concurrently with the integer and floating-point engines. Internal to the Transputer chip, the links terminate at DMA engines, which operate concurrently with calculations. Thus, it is possible for a Transputer to be executing an integer and a floating-point operation, and simultaneously sending and receiving on four channels. Transputer links are shown schematically in Figure 7.2.

The Transputer links implement a point-to-point protocol, with a separate 32x32 crossbar switch chip (C004) available. Virtual channel architecture can be implemented in software on the T800 series, with hardware support in the T9000 series. T800 links support 20 Mbps bidirectional communication on a three-wire medium. Messages are transferred as a series of bytes, with a byte acknowledge. There is a 3-bit-per-byte overhead on transmission, and the acknowledge packet is two bits in length.

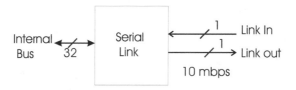

Figure 7.2 Transputer links. © Copyright Inmos Limited.

The link adapter allows the interface of 8-bit bidirectional data to the Transputer link protocol, and thus serves as a custom Universal Asynchronous Receiver/ Transmitter (UART). It is applicable when interfacing to other communication standards such as MIL-STD-1553 or FDDI is desired. The crossbar switch allows the connection among Transputers to be configurable instead of hardwired. It serves as essentially a telephone exchange between Transputers. Power dissipation and packaging for the various Transputer models is shown below.

Power Dissipation (all Transputer parts operate at five volts)

Processor	Power, mW
T80x	525 @ 20MHz
T4xx	450 @ 20MHz
T222	350 @ 20MHz

Packaging

Processor	Package
T805	84-pin PGA or PLCC
T801	100-pin PGA
T800	84-pin PGA
T425	84-pin PGA or PLCC
T414	84-pin PGA or PLCC
T222	68-pin PGA or PLCC
T225	68-pin PGA or PLCC
T400	84-pin PGA or PLCC; 100-pin PQFP

7.3.2 Software

All transputer instructions are one byte in size, with an operate instruction used to expand the repertoire to 145 instructions. The subset of 31 single-byte instructions is used about 70 percent of the time. An on-chip instruction queue handles four byte-sized instructions fetched simultaneously from memory over the 32-bit bus. As a direct RISC counterexample, microcoding is used to decode instructions. The instruction format is a 4-bit operation code, followed by a 4-bit data value. In this scheme, 13 of the 4-bit codes are assigned to important functions such as load, store, add, and jump. Two more codes are used in conjunction with the operand register. The last op code is an "operate" instruction, which specifies 16 operations on the top of the stack. Up to 70 percent of encoded instructions are single-byte in this scheme, and most require just one cycle to execute.

The integer unit implements the four basic math operations, as well as left and right arithmetic shifts and rotates. The instruction set also includes load and store, conditional jump, the logical 'AND', 'OR', 'XOR', and 'NOT', bit-reversal and extension, and the stack operations push and pop.

Floating-point instructions include floating load and store and "operate" instructions, implicitly referencing the top of the floating-point stack. I/O instructions are organized as link commands to input or output a byte, a word, or an arbitrary-length message.

In the T805, block-move instructions are included to address high-speed graphics applications. Also, CRC calculation instructions are included, as well as bit-count features.

The CPU of the Transputer has three registers, organized as a stack. Similarly, the floating point unit has its own three-register stack. The three values on the stack provide a triadic operand for the op code. It is up to the compiler to ensure that no more than three elements are on the stack at any given time. The integer stack is used for operand address generation for the floating-point unit as well as integer operands. The floating-point stack is duplicated, allowing fast context switching because it does not need to be saved and restored. Besides the stack registers, the CPU includes a workspace pointer to local variable memory, an instruction pointer (program counter), and an operand register.

The Transputer references memory with a 32-bit address. The four-kilobyte internal memory is located at address 8000 0000, and can be accessed in one machine cycle. External memory accesses require three or more cycles. The byte ordering mode is little-endian.

The Transputer has been available in a commercial chipset long enough for an installed base of applications and software to emerge. Available software compilers include Ada, ANSI C/C++, FORTRAN, Pascal, Modula-2, Prolog, Occam, Forth, and others. A cross-assembler is available, but rarely used. Specialized profiling and debug tools for the parallel environment are emerging from companies such as Inmos and Logical Systems Corporation. Tools are available in the PC and Unix environments. Inmos's integrated development environment includes a folding editor, a compiler, and a debugger. It is hosted on PC- based systems.

7.3.2.1 The Occam Language A full discussion of the theory and implementation of the Occam language is beyond the scope of this section. To gain a full understanding of the Transputer, you have to understand the background of Occam, and this is given in references [1], [2], [3], and [4]. To use the Transputer, such an in-depth understanding is not necessary.

Occam provides the conceptual framework, and the tools for programming parallelism. A discussion of the degrees of parallelism is in order. Superscalar machines exploit independent execution of multiple execution units to achieve a low level parallelism, and break the one-instruction-per-clock limit per package. Certain classes of problems decompose easily into autonomous subtasks for simultaneous execution on vector machines. Vectorizing compilers ferret out this latent parallelism from inherently sequential process. Occam forces us to program in parallel, a mindset switch that does not come easily, but is worth the effort. Explicit parallelism in the instantiation of the program leads to the best results, but existing languages such as Pascal and C may be extended with parallel constructs to ease the programmer transition to this new paradigm. Granularity of the process refers to the size or level into which we decompose the parent process. The level of granularity affects the computation-to-communication ratio. A ten-person-year task is done by one person in ten years, but can't necessarily be done by ten people in one year, or by a staff of 3,650 in one day. Coarse-grained parallelism (an example is the computationally intensive fractal calculations of the Mandelbrot set) refers to processes that are computationally independent, and require little or no communication. Fine-grained decomposition results in more and smaller portions in greater level of detail, with correspondingly higher need for communication. For example, attempting to decompose the Mandelbrot set calculation below the one processor-per-pixel limit would have separate processors for the real and imaginary parts of the equation, with a need for communication bandwidth sufficient to transmit the absolute value of the complex number for comparison against a limit.

Problems have a certain intrinsic granularity that maps best to a given processor topology. Then the communication and interaction between processes must be considered. Generally, as the granularity is increased, the need for communication is increased. In Occam, a channel is the communication mechanism between processes. Among processes on one Transputer, the number of channels is unlimited. Between Transputers, the channels are mapped to the four available hardware links. Using virtual channels, the aggregate bandwidth of the physical channels is again available to an unlimited number of virtual channels.

The origin of the name Occam is traced to the fourteenth century. Sir William of Occam's principle of Occam's razor, literally translated from the Latin, says "entities must not be multiplied beyond what is necessary," or, in the vernacular, "keep it simple, stupid." Sir William was essentially saying: Of two or more solutions or approaches, always choose the simplest. In the Occam language, an independent task is a collection of simple or atomic tasks and events, linked to other tasks. A process is mapped to one or more processors (Transputers), as shown in Figure 7.3.

The strength of the Transputer lies in its computation/communication balance, and its inherent parallel ability. Networks of Transputers, connected by their links, can be used in parallel processor fashion to tackle computationally imposing problems.

The Occam language implements a simple syntax for parallel processes, and for communication between processes. Multiple processes can be implemented on one Transputer or on multiple Transputers; the communication method at the software level is the same. On one Transputer there is virtual concurrency, and on multiple

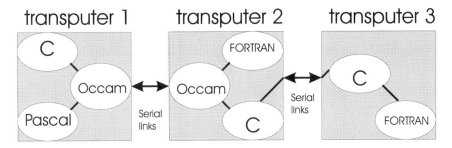

Figure 7.3 Mapping processes onto one or several Transputer processors. © Copyright Inmos Limited.

Transputers there is real concurrency of processes. The Transputer does have an assembly language, but its use is discouraged by Inmos, which takes the view that the Transputer hardware directly implements Occam.

Concurrent processes are executed using a linked-list approach. A process can be active or inactive. An active process can be executing or awaiting execution. An inactive process, which consumes no processor time, may be waiting for I/O resources, or for a particular time to execute. Task switching is implemented in the processor hardware.

7.3.3 Floating Point

The T2 and T4 series do not support floating point in hardware. The integral floating-point unit of the T80x series uses the IEEE 754 format, and provides operations on 32- or 64-bit data. These functions include add, subtract, multiply, divide, format conversion, comparison, and square root. All rounding modes of the IEEE standard are supported. Operation of the unit is microcoded and redundant sets of three registers organized as stacks are included. An error flag can be set by the unit, and read by the integer processor.

7.3.4 Cache

The Transputer does not make use of cache, having memory on-chip as part of the normal memory space. The T9000 allows for some of its internal memory to be considered cache.

7.3.5 Memory Management

The Transputer does not use virtual memory management techniques.

7.3.6 Exceptions

Interrupts or exceptions are termed *events* in the Transputer, and a single set of request and acknowledge pins are available. Associated with an event is a process (handler) that is scheduled when the event happens. Latency is typically 19 cycles, and a maximum of 78 cycles (58 cycles for no floating-point operations). This assumes no high-priority task is active at the time of the event. Otherwise, the event, a high-priority task, must await the completion of the current high-priority task.

7.4 SUMMARY

RISC Features

Load/store—yes, stack architecture
Single-cycle execution
Small instruction set—145

Non-RISC Features

Microcoded instruction decoding
No registers—stack orientation
Variable instruction length

7.5 REFERENCES

[1] Roscoe, A. W. & Hoare, C. A. R., "Laws of Occam Programming," Feb. 1986, Oxford University Computation Lab. Technical Monograph PRG-53.

[2] *Communicating Process Architecture.* London: Prentice-Hall, 1988. Inmos, Ltd. ISBN 0-13-629320-4.

[3] Pountain, "A Tutorial Introduction to OCCAM Programming," Inmos.

[4] Ellison, D., "Understanding Occam and the Transputer: Through Complete, Working Programs," 1991, UK: Sigma.

7.6 BIBLIOGRAPHY

Cok, Ronald, S., *Parallel Programs for the Transputer.* Englewood Cliffs, NJ: Prentice Hall, 1991.

Hinton, Jeremy, Pinder, Alan, *Transputer Hardware and System Design.* Englewood Cliffs, NJ: Prentice Hall, 1993. TK7895. T73H56.

"Image Processing Databook, 1st. edition," Oct. 1990, SGS-Thompson Inmos.

IMS T400 32-bit Transputer, Feb. 1995, Inmos Corporation.

"Inmos Digital Signal Processing Handbook," July 1989, Inmos Corporation.

Japp, "Inmos Technical Note 62: The Design of a High Resolution Graphics System Using the IMS G300 Colour Video Controller," Inmos Corporation.

Kim, Jong Hyun, O'Grady, E. Pearse, "Effect of the Interprocessor Communication Mechanism on Performance of a Parallel Processor System," 1989, IEEE, *RISC Management*, issue 28, January 1991.

Mattos, "The Transputer Based Navigation System—An Example of Testing Embedded Systems," Inmos Technical Note 2, Inmos Corporation.

McLean, Mick, Rowland, Tom, *The Inmos Saga*. London: Frances Pinter, Ltd., 1985. ISBN 0-86187-559-1.

"The Military and Space Transputer Databook," 1990, Inmos.

Mitchell, David A. P., *Inside the Transputer*. UK: Blackwell Scientific Publications, 1990.

Nussbaum, Daniel, Agarwal, Anant, "Scalability of Parallel Machines," March 1991, *CACM*, 34 (3).

Pool, "Inmos Technical Note 56: Example Programs in the TDS," Inmos Corporation.

Ragsdale, Susan, *Parallel Programming*. New York: McGraw-Hill, 1991. ISBN 0-07-051186-1.

Roberts, John, "Transputer Assembly Language Programming," New York: Van Nostrand Reinhold, 1992.

"SGS Details Strategy for Transputer," Mar. 29, 1993, *Electronic Engineering Times*, 739 p. 1.

"The T9000 Transputer Products Overview Manual," 1991, SGS-Thompson Inmos.

"The Transputer Applications Notebook, Architecture and Software," 1989, Inmos Corporation.

"The Transputer Applications Notebook, Systems and Performance," 1988, Inmos Corporation.

Theoharis, "Exploiting Parallelism in the Graphics Pipeline," 1985, Oxford University Computation Lab White Paper.

"Transputer Claims Single-Chip Speed Record," May 13, 1993, *Electronic Design*, 41 (10): 95.

"Transputer Databook, 2nd. edition," 1989, Inmos Corporation.

Transputer Instruction Set: A Compiler Writer's Guide. Englewood Cliffs, NJ: Prentice Hall, 1988. ISBN 0-13-929100-8.

"Transputer's Modularity Lets Designers Insert Specific Modules for an Application," May 13, 1993, *Electronic Design*, 42 (10): 32.

Transputer Reference Manual. Inmos. Englewood Cliffs, NJ: Prentice Hall, 1988. ISBN 0-13-929001-X.

"Transputer: The Transputer and the Toolset," Training Guide, Inmos.

Turner, "Inmos Technical Note 53: Some Issues in Scientific-Language Application Porting and Farming Using Transputers," Inmos Corporation.

"Understanding RISC Processors," 1993, *Microprocessor Report*, Chapter 13, Ziff-Davis. ISBN 1-56276-159-5.

"Under the Hood the Transputer Strikes Back: A Look at Inmos's Amazing New T9000 Transputer Chip," Aug. 1, 1991, *BYTE*, 16 (8): 265.

APPENDIX TO CHAPTER 7: T-9000

This section discusses the T-9000 Transputer from Inmos Corporation.

A.7.1 Background

The T-9000 transputer is an extension of the earlier T-800 model, with both computation and communication scaled upward. It uses the same clock and boot from link features, but the link physical design has been changed to accommodate higher speeds. An interface chip is available to bridge the old and new link architectures. In addition, the T-9000 implements the concept of virtual channels, such that any number of processes can share a physical link. A Virtual Channel Processor (VCP) provides packet distribution and routing, and is implemented in hardware. Packets are up to 32 bytes in length. No software overhead is incurred in the transference of packets by the VCP.

A.7.2 Architecture

The T-9000 has a 32-bit integer engine and a 64-bit floating point engine, as well as four high-speed serial links, and cache memory on one chip. The integer unit is multiple-issue superscalar, and has a five stage pipeline. Up to four instructions per cycle can be executed. Figure 7.4 shows the architecture of the T-9000.

Along with the T-9000 processor, Inmos released a series of new communications products. These include the C104 packet routing switch, the C100 Protocol converter, and the C101 link adapter.

The C101 interfaces between the T-9000 links and external devices. The C100 interfaces T-800 transputer link devices to the T-9000. The C104 is a 32 by 32 non-blocking crossbar switch with submicrosecond latency. It handles the link configuration of the T-9000, and is expandable. The C104 uses wormhole routing, in which a connection through the switch is set up when the header is read, and closes after the message is delivered.

A.7.2.1 Hardware The T-9000 uses a five-stage pipeline, of which the fourth step involves the ALU or FPU operation. Before being issued to the pipeline, instructions are grouped by the processor, to achieve maximum pipeline utilization. This grouping is above and beyond any done by the optimizing compiler, and represents real-time instruction scheduling and optimizing. A 32 byte instruction buffer is also included.

A hardware scheduler allows a process to be active or inactive (pending), and provides functionality usually requiring a real-time executive kernel software.

The memory interface is designed to utilize 8-, 16-, 32-, or 64-bit-wide memory devices. The memory interface is programmable for flexibility in using different DRAM types. Four banks of memory with different timing and decoding can be used. The T-9000 also has two 32-bit interval timers, one with a period of one microsecond, and the other with a period of 64 microseconds.

As with the T-800 device, the T-9000 includes high speed communication channels on-chip. These are capable of 20 megabytes/second, full-duplex, and use a DMA engine to allow communication concurrently with operation of the integer and floating point units.

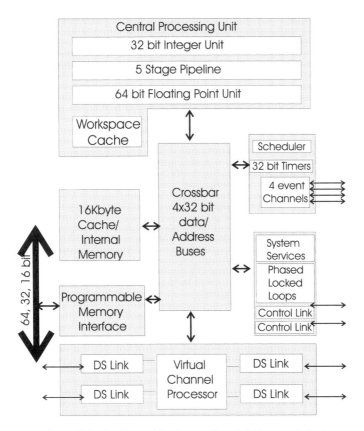

Figure 7.4 T-9000 architecture. © Copyright Inmos Limited.

The T-9000 may boot from ROM or a communication link, and has on-chip pow-er-on-reset features. As with the T-800, single 5 MHz clock is all that is required for operation. The clock rate is derived from the 5 MHz clock by a phase-locked loop circuitry, and is selectable by three input lines to the processor. It can be selected as six, seven, eight, nine, or ten times the base clock frequency. A control link is pro-vided for processor commands and status. Multiple T-9000's can be configured into a network arrangement, with separate control and data networks. Control links are used for monitoring, diagnostics, debugging, and code downloading.

The T-9000 operates with a 5 volt supply, and power dissipation is on the order of seven watts. The T-9000 is housed in a 208-pin ceramic leaded chip carrier (CLCC) package. The processor contains a 16-bit read-only device identification register, and a similar device revision register.

A.7.2.2 Software The Transputer architecture includes three registers, arranged as a stack. The floating point unit has a similar stack. Most instructions are coded in one byte, with a prefix indicator to allow extension. The instruction set is an extension to that of the T-800.

The T-9000 is supported by a C and a C++ compiler, as well as an Occam-2 toolset. Tools are hosted on Sun-4 or IBM PC systems. The Occam language is discussed in Section 7.3.21. Debugging and profiling tools are provided by Inmos' IN-QUEST software development environment.

A.7.2.3 Floating Point The floating point unit of the T-9000 supports IEEE-754 double precision floating point operations. Hardware support for floating add, subtract, multiply, divide, and square root is provided. Four IEEE rounding modes are also supported.

A.7.2.4 Cache The T-9000 features 16 kilobytes of unified cache memory on-chip. It is organized as four independent banks of 256 lines each. It is 256-way set associative, and uses a write-back feature. An access can be made to each of the banks on each cycle. Each cache line is 16 bytes in size. The caches are multiported. The cache may be organized as 16 kilobytes of on-chip memory, for a minimum system. The on-chip memory can also be configured as half cache and half RAM.

In addition, a workspace cache has an on-chip copy of the first 32 words of the procedure stack and workspace. Two reads and a write may occur to this unit simultaneously. The workspace cache supports zero-cycle access to current data items.

A.7.2.5 Memory Management The T-9000 follows the T-800 in using 32-bit linear addressing, with limited memory management functions. However, a protected mode is provided, in which an MMU function checks privileges of addressing before allowing references. This mode also allows a simple virtual to physical address translation using size and base registers for four regions of memory. Paged virtual memory is not supported.

A.7.2.6 Exceptions Interrupt response for the T-9000 has been optimized into the sub-microsecond area. This is partially the result of the limited context that must be saved upon interrupt. The processor has four input pins, or event channels, to be used as interrupt inputs.

A.7.3 Summary

RISC Features
Superscalar, pipelined
Non-RISC Features
Small register set (3 element stack)

A.7.4 Bibliography

"T9000 Transputer Begins Sampling, Complexity Causes Schedule Delays, Increased Transistor Count," April 19, 1993, *Microprocessor Report*, 7 (5): 18.

"The T-9000 Transputer Instruction Set Manual," 1993, Inmos Corporation, 1st edition.

"The T-9000 Transputer Hardware Reference Manual," 1993, Inmos Corporation, 1st edition.

8

29k

8.1 INTRODUCTION

This chapter discusses the architecture of Advanced Micro Devices' (AMD) Am29000 series processors. Development of the 29k family began in 1985, with specifications published in early 1987. Chips have been available since 1988. The 29k achieves its level of performance by pipelining, a Harvard architecture, a large number of registers on-chip, a branch target cache, and a three-address format for instructions. Each of these techniques will be discussed in this section. The 32-bit 29k family has 100% binary software compatibility across all family members. A user organization, Fusion29k, links third-party developers and toolset providers.

8.2 BACKGROUND

AMD is a merchant chip manufacturing company that produces processors, memory, and associated logic chips. AMD is a U.S. company, with worldwide manufacturing facilities. It entered the Intel-dominated 80x86 market with competitive processors. The 29k family addresses the advanced embedded market. This includes the laser printer, the networking, and the telecommunications segments. 29k family members are also found in X-terminals.

The 29k family currently includes six microprocessors and six microcontrollers. The microprocessors include the three-bus 29000, 29005, and 29050 and the two-bus 29030, 29040, and 29035. The microcontrollers, addressed specifically to the embedded market incorporate more integrated features such as DRAM and ROM control, on-chip DMA and I/O, counter/timer, serial port, and JTAG. These models include the 29200, 29202, 29205, 29240, 29243, and 29245. A new processor family member for 1995 incorporates superscalar techniques and clock-multiplying, along with speculative and out-of-order execution. It can dispatch up to four instructions to six execution units, and has a 10 entry reorder buffer.

The 29000, the original family member, defines the core 32-bit architecture. The 29005 and 050 share the 29000's three-bus architecture (address, instruction, data). The 29050 adds on-chip floating point, the equivalent of incorporating the previous 29027 floating-point unit onto the base 29000. In addition, the BTC is expanded to 1024 bytes. All of the microprocessor units feature on-chip interrupt control, with six interrupt pins and an on-chip timer, and can operate in either endian mode. All but the 005 model feature on-chip memory management functions. Figure 8.1 shows the Am29000 architecture. The 29000 has a 512 byte BTC on-chip and a 64-entry MMU.

The 29000 family influenced AMD's K5 project, which is the follow-up to AMD's i486 and intended as a direct competitor to the Pentium. In essence, the K5 translates 80x86 instructions to 29k instructions on the fly, and reorganizes the results at the end. Lessons learned on the K5 (discussed in section 19.7.1) were then applied to the latest 29k family members.

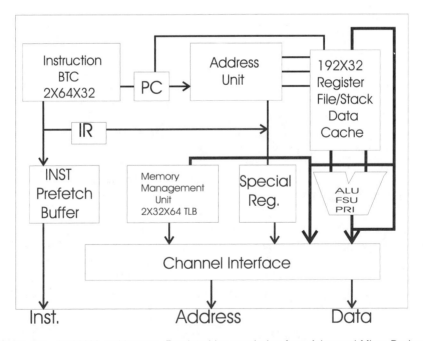

Figure 8.1 Am29000 architecture. Reprinted by permission from Advanced Micro Devices, Inc., 29K Family 1990 Databook © 1989.

8.2.1 29030 and 035

The Am29030 and 035 are members of the 29k family intended for embedded applications. Code compatible, the 030 has an 8-kilobyte, two-way set-associative cache, while the 035 has a 4-kilobyte direct-mapped cache. Both have relaxed and simplified external clock timing requirements, allowing for eased restrictions on memory delays, hold times, and setups. The 030 and 035 use a two-bus architecture. These family members support scalable clocking and programmable bus sizing. The 030 and 035 address the imaging and page printer markets. Neither model includes floating-point capability on-chip. Figure 8.2 shows the block diagram of the 29030 and 035 models. The 29030 and 035 are pin compatible with other family members. Both feature JTAG support.

8.2.2 29040

The 29040 family member features an eight-kilobyte I-cache, a four-kilobyte D-cache, and a 32x32 multiplier. The hardware integer multiplier is two-cycle. There is also an on-chip MMU with dual TLBs. It operates from 3.3 to 5 volts, and features JTAG support, as well as a power saving mode. It is a two-bus product.

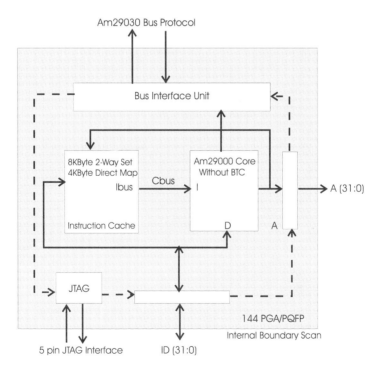

Figure 8.2 29030 and 035 architecture. Reprinted by permission from Advanced Micro Devices, Inc., Am29030/Am29035 User's Manual and Data Sheet © 1993.

8.2.3 29200

The 29200 series is designed as highly integrated microcontrollers that are code compatible with the 29k architecture. The 29200 has on-chip programmable DRAM and ROM control, as well as two-channel DMA. It features 16 programmable digital I/O lines, and four interrupt inputs. It includes a wait-state generator, a 24-bit counter, and a programmable serial and parallel port. It also features a JTAG 1149.1 boundary scan test interface. All of the microcontrollers feature a DRAM and ROM interface, on-chip DMA support, parallel ports, serial ports, and interrupt controllers. The 29200 uses a 24-bit address bus, and video DRAM is supported, as well as burst-mode ROM access. The 29200 family targets the low-cost laser printer market. The architecture is shown in Figure 8.3.

8.2.4 29202

AMD introduced the 29202 model in the Spring of 1995. It is a variation of the 29200, implemented to support the IEEE-1284 Advanced Parallel Interface (API)

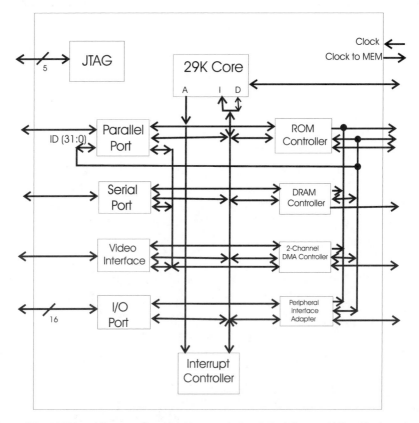

Figure 8.3 29200 architecture. Reprinted by permission from Advanced Micro Devices, Inc., Am29200 RISC Microcontroller User's Manual and Data Sheet.

for laser printers with the Windows Printing System (WPS) standard from Microsoft Corp. It is a low cost device, packaged in a 132-pin plastic package. It supports 600 dots-per-inch (dpi) Postcript and PCL printing, as compared to the 29205's 300 dots-per-inch. It was released in 12, 16, and 20 MHz versions. It has a 22-bit address bus, two channels of DMA, and the video interface.

8.2.5 29205

The 29205 is a low-cost unit that has on-chip programmable DRAM and ROM control, and single-channel DMA. It is basically a 29000, less the BTC and MMU. It has the 29000 three-bus architecture. It features eight programmable I/O lines and a serial port. It has a 16-bit external data bus and a 22-bit address bus. Two external interrupt pins are provided. No JTAG test support is included, however. Figure 8.4 shows the 29202 architecture.

8.2.6 29240

The 240 is a high-end embedded controller, addressing the digital video applications area. All of the 2924x models feature four kilobytes of I-cache, while the 240

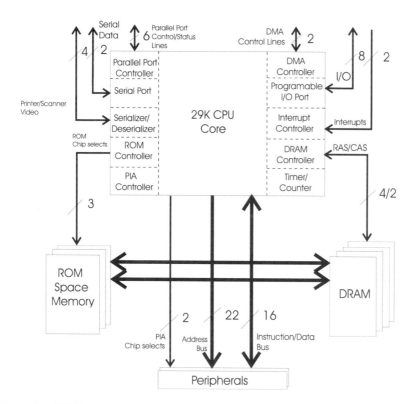

Figure 8.4 29205 architecture. Reprinted by permission from Advanced Micro Devices, Inc., AMD publication 17198. Rev. A, Sept. 1992.

and 243 have in addition two kbytes of D-cache. The 240 and 243 also feature 32x32 hardware multiply, and the 240 and 245 have a single translation lookaside buffer of 16 entries. All 2924x models have a 24-bit address bus, and all support video DRAM. Four external interrupt pins are provided. The 2924x models can operate at 3.3 or 5 volts. Figure 8.5 shows the 29240 architecture. The 29240 supports the fly-by DMA mode for burst transfers, using page mode DRAM. The DMA uses four channels.

8.2.7 29243

The 243 processor includes a parity feature, which is important to telecommunications switching applications. It can handle fly-by DMA at 100 megabits per second, and incorporates the DSP multiply-and-accumulate (MAC) primitive. It features dual translation look aside buffers, a 32-entry MMU, and two serial ports. Figure 8.6 shows the 29243 architecture. The part is targeted to telecommunications switching, and embedded applications requiring communications signal processing.

8.2.8 29245

The 245 microcontroller is a low-cost part similar to the 240, but with a 16-bit ex-

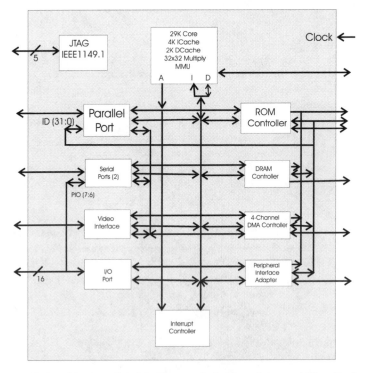

Figure 8.5 29240 architecture. Reprinted by permission from Advanced Micro Devices, Inc., "Announcing the Am29249 Series," May 1993.

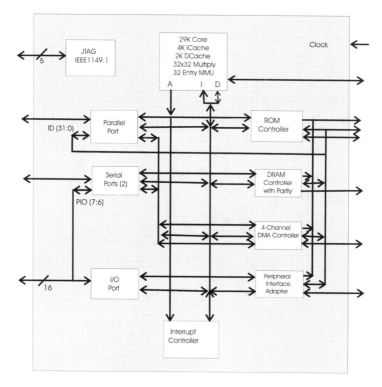

Figure 8.6 29243 architecture. Reprinted by permission from Advanced Micro Devices, Inc., "Announcing the Am29249 Series," May 1993.

ternal data bus interface, no cache, and no multiplier. It interfaces only to 16-bit-wide ROMs, where the other microcontrollers handle 8-, 16-, or 32-bit-wide parts. It does not support burst-mode access. A single serial port is included. Figure 8.7 shows the 29245 architecture. It does have a two channel DMA interface, one serial port, and a single TLB with a 16 entry MMU.

8.2.9 29005 and 29050

Both of these processors have the three bus architecture. The 29005 is the 29000 minus the Branch Target Cache and the MMU. The 29050 is the 29000 with integral floating point; essentially, a 29027 integrated on-chip. It does integer multiply and divide, sharing the floating-point hardware. It has a one kilobyte BTC on-chip.

8.3 ARCHITECTURE

The Am29000 architecture features a Harvard architecture, 192 on-chip registers, a 512 byte branch target cache (BTC), and an on-chip MMU. This section will focus on the common features of the core architecture. Specific features of particular family members will be discussed where relevant.

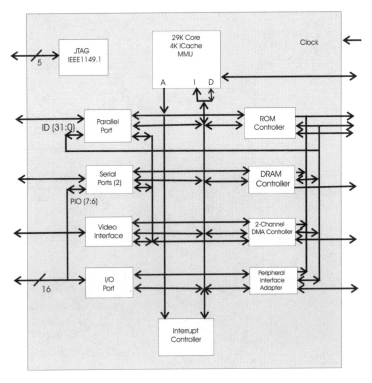

Figure 8.7 29245 architecture. Reprinted by permission from Advanced Micro Devices, Inc., "Announcing the Am29249 Series," May 1993.

8.3.1 Hardware

The Am29k uses a four-stage instruction pipeline, with the stages being fetch, decode, execute, and write-back. This allows for a maximum execution rate of one instruction per cycle, with a latency of four cycles. Loads and stores are overlapped, meaning that they are performed concurrently with execution of other instructions that are not data dependent on the load or store. The optimizing compiler rearranges the code to take advantage of this feature. Hardware interlocks are provided for data dependencies. Figure 8.8 illustrates overlapping and forwarding in the 29k pipeline.

The problem with a pipeline architecture is that it is very fast and efficient as long as sequentially accessed, nondependent instructions are being issued. Efficiency problems stem from disruptive operations such as branches or exceptions, or the need to access external memory. According to AMD's analysis, on the average, one of every five or six instructions is a branch, and one of every five is a load or store. Of course, the compiler has some control over this mix and relative ratio. With a branch every five or six instructions, the pipeline must be flushed every five or six cycles. This says a pipeline depth greater than five doesn't make sense. It also implies that system-level performance is heavily dependent on instruction and operand access. Figure 8.9 shows the 29000 pipeline during a branch.

The instruction fetch process is optimized by use of an on-chip branch target cache

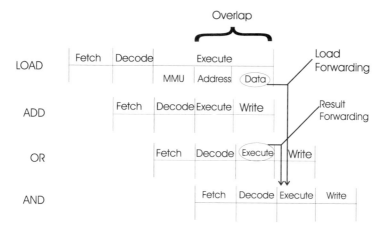

- Complier re-organizes code to use overlapping
- Hardware interlocks for data dependencies
- One cycle per instruction maintained through load

Figure 8.8 Overlapping and forwarding in the 29K pipeline. Reprinted by permission from Advanced Micro Devices, Inc., Am29000 Architecture Summary.

(BTC), with a latency of two cycles. The BTC operates on virtual addresses, before the translation lookaside buffer gets to see them. According to AMD, the BTC results in a 20 percent average increase in overall system performance. Single-cycle branching can be maintained within the pipeline, operating with three-cycle external memory. The BTC is of size 32 blocks, and is two-way set-associative. The BTC holds enough instructions to cover the latency of the external memory fetches for the new op-code locations. According to AMD's analysis, a BTC is more efficient in use of silicon, because a 0.5 kilobyte BTC provides the same system-level performance as a 4 kilobyte instruction cache, with one-wait-state memory. Figure 8.10 illustrates the 29000 instruction fetch process. An instruction prefetch buffer ensures that instructions are available from memory before they are needed.

The pipeline has the effect of hiding the instruction-fetch latency for sequential

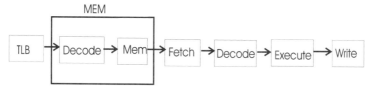

Figure 8.9 Pipeline during branch. Advantage—once filled, the pipeline executes one instruction per clock. Disadvantage—latency of first instruction is six cycles to reach execute stage. Reprinted by permission from Advanced Micro Devices, Inc., Am29000 Architecture Summary.

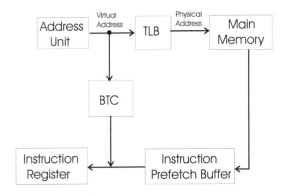

- BTC hits have latencies of two cycles
- BTC compares virtual addresses
- Average of 20% increase in system performance

Figure 8.10 Instruction fetch—BTC. Reprinted by permission from Advanced Micro Devices, Inc., Am29000 Architecture Summary.

code. The BTC hides the instruction-fetch latency for nonsequential code. Since only the branches are cached, a BTC can make more optimal use of available silicon than a straight instruction cache. The sequential instructions in the instruction cache waste space that could be used for the more disruptive branches.

Various integrated functions are provided on the 29k microcontrollers. Standard support for DMA includes request and acknowledge pins for bus master handoff. Interrupts are supported by four external pins, and the integral counter may also be used as a source of interrupts. The timer operates at the CPU clock frequency, and consists of two registers. A 64-entry TLB is provided for memory management functions, and will be described later. DRAM control is provided with a Row Address Strobe/Column Address Strobe (RAS/CAS) generator and address multiplexer. DRAM organization can be by 4 or by 16 bits, and from 1 to 16 megabytes per bank. Support for page-mode or static-column SRAM is provided, as is CAS-before-RAS timing.

The serial ports on the microcontrollers (two on the 29240 and 243; one on the others) are RS-232 logical signal compatible, and have a programmable baud rate generator. The serial port can be configured to be a DMA channel, with the maximum baud rate in excess of 1 megabit per second. The parallel ports (two on the 205; six on the others) allow programmable 8-bit transfers, and can make use of DMA or interrupts. Parallel I/Os can also be used as edge- or level-sensitive interrupts.

Memory parity is provided on the 29243 on a byte basis for reads and writes. Invalid parity results in a parity error trap to vector four. Fly-by DMA mode on the 2924x series allows for 100-megabytes-per-second transfer between external peripherals and the DRAM, in both directions.

There are three types of memory accesses used by the processor: simple, pipelined, and burst. Instructions are always fetched in burst mode, and load/store multiples use burst mode. Data and address bus width is 32 bits. ROM can be accessed during DRAM refresh. On-chip mapping registers provide a simple relocation mechanism with 64-kilobyte segments.

Some of the 29k family members (29000, 005, 050) use a three-bus architecture out of the processor chip to provide high data bandwidth. These buses include address-out, instruction-(op code)-in, and data-in/out. There is a single address bus but Harvard-style data buses. The other models use a standard two-bus architecture (for address and data, non-Harvard style).

On-chip DMA control allows for a configurable width of 8 or 16 bits for the transfer, and can be configured to the serial port, parallel port, or to a laser printer engine interface in certain models for a raster-style configuration. A serializer/deserializer for 32-bit data is provided for the laser printer engine interfaces.

JTAG support is provided on the 030, 035, 040, 29200, and 2924x variants. In addition, there is hardware support for testing and debugging. The test mode puts all processor outputs in a high-impedance state. There is also hardware support for single-step, halt, and forced load of an instruction from the bus. Tracing of the instruction stream through the cache is possible with the JTAG interface.

There is a master-slave mode in the 29k, in which two processors can be coupled for diagnostic purposes. The processor designated as slave does not output signals, but compares its computed outputs with the master's. Discrepancies are signaled.

The 29k microprocessor family is designed to operate from 5 volts, with the 2924x series and 29040 operating from 3.3 volts. A 2x clock is used. In "turbo mode" (2924x), the processor can run at twice the external bus clock rate.

All of the devices are available in PQFP packaging, with the exception of the 050, which comes in a PGA format. Pin counts are as follows:

Chip	Pins	Chip	Pins
29205	100*	29005	168
29200	168	29000	168
*same as 386sx			
29245	196**	29050	169
29240	196**	29035	144
29243	196**	29030	144
29202	132	29040	144
**same as 486			

8.3.2 Software

The single-instruction size and format and the single-addressing mode of the Am29k facilitate optimization at the compiler level. The large register set can be allocated optimally, and parameters passed between procedures can be handled within registers.

The load- and store-multiple instructions transfer multiple registers to or from external memory in burst mode within a single instruction, providing a sort of "software DMA" function. It is interruptible, so that interrupt latency is not adversely affected. These transfers can occur at the rate of one register per cycle up to 100 megabytes per second.

The Am29k instruction format is a uniform 32 bits wide, and includes an op-code field and three operand fields. This three-address format reduces the instructions/task term of the performance equation when used by the optimizing compiler. In the best case, one instruction can replace a load, operate, store sequence of two-operand instructions. All instructions are inherently single cycle, except load/store multiple, interrupt return, and floating point. The instruction format of the 29000 is shown in Figure 8.11.

The instruction is a three-operand format, with two sources and one destination register specified by the instruction word. In addition, a load/store-multiple scheme is used, with three buses for address, data, and instruction. There is capability for burst-mode access to fill the on-chip instruction prefetch buffer. An on-chip cache for branch targets provides optimization of this inherently disruptive operation.

Integer math operations include add, subtract, multiply, and divide on 32-bit words. The multiply and divide are not provided by hardware, but trap to emulation routines. The 240 and 243 models provide a hardware multiplier. Floating point is not included in the basic processor. Load and store operations are provided and the load/store multiples are interruptable. The shift/bit manipulation instructions include compares, shifts, and bit extracts. Jumps and calls allow for flow control. An instruction is provided to determine the number of leading zeros in a word.

The Am29k provides 192 general registers, each of width 32 bits. These are divided into 64 global and 128 local registers. On the 29050, of the 64 global registers, 32 are reserved for operating system and interrupt usage, 4 for user-defined static variables, 4 for stack management, and 24 for temporaries and returned parameters. The stack cache, using the remaining registers, provides variable-sized stack frames. The general purpose register organization of the 29000 can be seen in Figure 8.12. The register file can perform two read and one write access per clock.

This approach was chosen by AMD because of a tradeoff with a traditional register file architecture. Too few registers in the register file force excessive memory references. On the other hand, too many registers cannot be effectively used within a

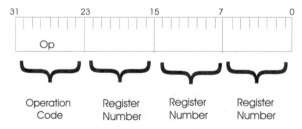

Figure 8.11 Instruction format. Reprinted by permission from Advanced Micro Devices, Inc., Am29000 Architecture Summary.

Absolute REG#	GENERAL-PURPOSE REGISTER
0	Indirect Pointer Access
1	Stack Pointer

2 THRU 63	not Implemented

64	GLOBAL REGISTER 64
65	GLOBAL REGISTER 65
66	GLOBAL REGISTER 66
. . .	. . .
126	GLOBAL REGISTER 126
127	GLOBAL REGISTER 127

128	LOCAL REGISTER 125
129	LOCAL REGISTER 126
130	LOCAL REGISTER 127
131	LOCAL REGISTER 0
132	LOCAL REGISTER 1
. . .	. . .
254	GLOBAL REGISTER 123
255	GLOBAL REGISTER 124

Figure 8.12 Register diagram. Reprinted by permission from Advanced Micro Devices, Inc., Programming the 29K RISC Family © 1995.

procedure, and excessive registers lead to time-consuming save and restore operations upon procedure calls and returns. The register file architecture of the Am29k allows for dynamic allocation of only the number of registers needed by a procedure, rather than a fixed number. The optimizing compiler will allocate enough registers for all of the scalar data. AMD claims this approach is better than an on-chip data cache. Figure 8.13 shows the 29000 register file, with its 192 general registers.

In addition the stack cache is kept in registers. The stack-cache speeds linkage to and from procedures. It has the additional benefit of eliminating special address

192 GENERAL REGISTERS

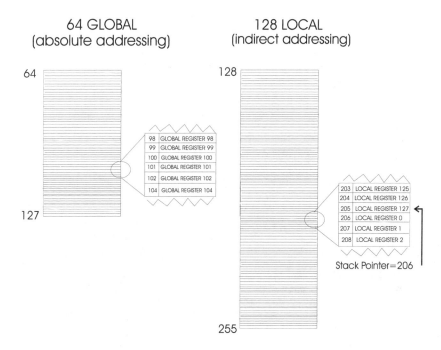

Figure 8.13 General register file. Reprinted by permission from Advanced Micro Devices, Inc., Am29000 Architecture Summary.

modes for operating on local variables or procedure arguments. The stack-cache is shown in Figure 8.14.

The register file, used in this format, increases overall system performance by keeping frequently accessed variables immediately available in the global registers, and eliminating multiple memory accesses. The 29k architecture provides for up to 256 special-purpose registers that may be protected or unprotected. In the 29000, 23 are implemented. The special purpose registers are shown in Figure 8.15.

All operand memory accesses are through a load or store, and there is only one addressing mode. The operand address computation is completed before the load or store, and is contained in a register. Byte ordering is selectable by a bit in the configuration register. Supported data types include bytes, half words, and words (32 bit).

29K development and test tools include a full package of cross-development software hosted on VAX, PC, or Unix. There is a macro-assembler, with linker, loader, librarian, and IEEE floating-point emulation. Optimizing compilers for C, C++, FORTRAN, and Pascal are available. The ROM-based Mon29k includes an interface for source-level debugging, breakpoints, and inline assembly/disassembly. An instruction set simulator is available and provides useful insight into the interaction

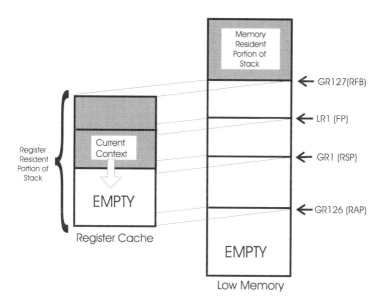

- RFB--- Register Free Bound

- RAB--- Register Allocate Bound

Figure 8.14 Stack-cache. Reprinted by permission from Advanced Micro Devices, Inc., Am29000 Architecture Summary.

of hardware features and instruction execution rate. The software development environment VxWorks by Wind River Systems is ported to the 29k family. This allows the development and debugging of real-time and embedded applications in a Unix environment. C-executive, a realtime multitasking ROM-able kernel, is also available for the 29k, as is VRTX from Microtec.

8.3.3 Floating Point

The associated Am29027 chip (no longer available) provided IEEE standard floating-point support for the Am29000. This device was optimized for scalar operations by a flow-through, fully combinatorial design. Single- and double-precision (32 and 64-bit) formats were supported. In pipeline mode, vector operations were optimized. Coprocessor handshaking protocols were used between the 29k main processor and the 027. The functionality of the 29000 and the 29027 floating point unit was combined on one piece of silicon as the 29050. Other 29k microprocessor members do not include floating-point support. If the 29000 is analagous to the 80286, and the 29027 is like the 80387, then the 29050 is like a 80486.

Most single-precision operations can be issued at a rate of one per clock, with a

Special Purpose
Number   Protected Registers

Number	Protected Registers
0	Vector Area Base Address
1	Old Processor Status
2	Current Processor Status
3	Configuration
4	Channel Address
5	Channel Data
6	Channel Control
7	Register Bank Protect
8	Time Counter
9	Timer Reload
10	Program Counter 0
11	Program Counter 1
12	Program Counter 2
13	MMU Configuration
14	LRU Recommendation

Unprotected Registers

Number	Unprotected Registers
128	Indirect Pointer C
129	Indirect Pointer A
130	Indirect Pointer B
131	Q
132	ALU Status
133	Byte Pointer
134	Funnel Shift Count
135	Load/Store Count Remaining

Figure 8.15 Special-purpose registers. Reprinted by permission from Advanced Micro Devices, Inc., Am29000 Architecture Summary.

three- to four-cycle operation latency. The floating point unit includes hardware multiply, with a three-cycle latency, as well as support for divide and square root. Conversions from integer to floating point take four cycles. Floating point operations supported include addition, subtraction, multiplication, division, square root, comparison, and format conversion.

8.3.4 Cache

Various cache organizations are used in different 29k family units. For the base 29000, the cache organization is only for branch targets. Because the BTC caches only branches, it has a higher hit rate than traditional instruction caches. It allows a higher instruction rate with lower-cost, slower memories. It provides its best performance on repetitive tasks, the ones that characterize embedded systems. The 512-byte branch target cache of the 29000 is expanded to one kilobyte on the 29050. The one kilobyte BTC caches the first four instructions of 64 different branch targets, as shown in Figure 8.16. Caching the first four instructions gives the processor time to catch up and fill the pipeline in the case of a taken branch.

The 29005 has no instruction cache; the 29035 includes four kilobytes of I-cache, doubled to eight kilobytes on the 29030. The 29200 and 205 have no I- or D-cache, but the 2924x units have four kilobytes of I-cache, with an additional two kilobytes of D-cache on the 240 and 243. The 29040 provides eight kilobytes of I-cache and four kilobytes of D-cache that is two-way set associative. The data caches use a copy-back protocol.

The instruction cache in the 2924x models is physically tagged and allows prefetching. Block checking is done for taken branches. The data cache on the 29240 and 243 is two-kilobyte, two-way set associative with write-through and physical tags. A two-entry write buffer is also included.

8.3.5 Memory Management

The Am29k on-chip memory management unit (MMU) provides the traditional resolution of 32-bit virtual to 32-bit physical addresses, as well as access control for multitasking. The purpose of the MMU is partition, allocation, and protection of

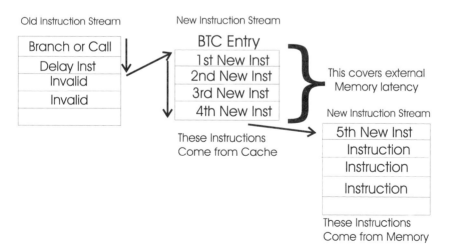

Figure 8.16 Branch target cache. Reprinted by permission from Advanced Micro Devices, Inc., 29K Family 1990 Databook.

memory resources. This MMU provides two operating modes, user and supervisor. Each mode of operation can mark its own memory as read-only, read/write, or execute-only. The MMU is a 64-entry, two-way translation lookaside buffer. Address translation is pipelined, and a user-selectable page size of 1, 2, 4, or 8 kilobytes is provided. Up to 256 unique tasks can be tracked in the 8-bit task identifier field. The replacement algorithm is least recently used (LRU). The address translation is done in parallel with cache accesses. The 29040 uses a 32-entry MMU with dual TLBs on-chip. The address translation process of the 29000 is shown in Figure 8.17.

Support for multiprocessors is provided in the 29k family. The TLB supports 6 partition bits for user or supervisor; read, write, or execute-only segments. Overlapped loads and stores are provided, and operand forwarding is used to provide results to subsequent pipeline steps without requiring a memory-write followed by a memory-read. There is a separate I/O space in these processors.

8.3.6 Exceptions

Interrupt handling in the 29k family is focused on minimizing latency, and providing a known, deterministic response. Interrupts are user definable, and the proces-

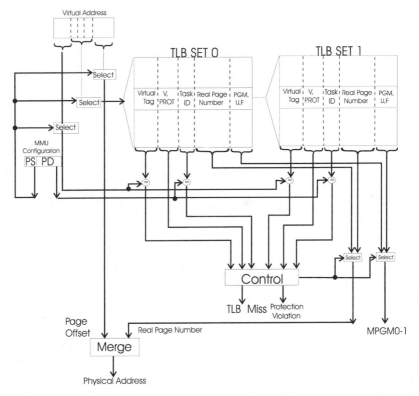

Figure 8.17 MMU. Reprinted by permission from Advanced Micro Devices, Inc., 29K Family 1990 Databook.

sor state is not automatically saved upon interrupt. Thus, each interrupt routine can be customized and streamlined to save and restore only those variables directly affected. Only the necessary portions of the processor state are preserved, increasing performance for simple, "lightweight" interrupts. A fast interrupt response, with a frozen process state, can be completed in as few as 13 cycles. Nested interrupts, which allow other interrupts or for process switching, involve an overhead of 38 cycles. A 256-entry vector table is maintained. All but interrupt zero can be disabled in the software. There are two inputs for TRAPS on program conditions. These can include instruction- or data-access violation, coprocessor exception, or illegal op code.

8.4 SUMMARY

RISC Features

Large register set—192
Load/store
Single-cycle execution
Small instruction set—112
Hardwired instructions

Non-RISC Features

Multiplication, division by emulation

8.5 BIBLIOGRAPHY

"29k Family 1990 Data Book," 1989, AMD, #12175.

"29k Family 1993 International Press Coverage Update," 1993, AMD, pub. 16695.

"29k Ups CPU Throughput, Cuts Power Dissipation," July 1994, *Computer Design*, 33, pp. 111.

"Am29000 Microprocessor, Memory Design Handbook," AMD, 10623.

"Am29000 Streamlined Instruction Processor User Manual," 1988, AMD, #10620.

"Am29027 Handbook," Oct. 1988, AMD, #11852.

"Am29030 and Am29035 Microprocessor User's Manual and Data Sheet," 1994, AMD, #15723.

"Am29040 Data Sheet," June 1994, AMD, pub. 18459, rev. A.

"Am29050 Microprocessor Data Sheet," AMD, #15039.

"Am29050 Microprocessor User's Manual," 1992, AMD, #14788.

"Am29205 RISC Microcontroller Data Sheet," Sept. 1992, AMD, #17198.

"Am29200 RISC Microcontroller User's Manual and Data Sheet," 1991, AMD, #16362.

"Am29205 RISC Microcontroller Data Sheet," Sept. 1992, AMD, #17198.

"Architectural Support for Optimizing Compilers in the AM29000 Microprocessor," AMD, White Paper, undated.

"Fusion 29K Catalog," 1992, AMD.

Johnson, Mike, "System Considerations in the Design of the Am29000," Nov. 1987, *IEEE Micro*, pp. 28–41.

"Maintaining Referenced and Modified Bits with the Am29000 MMU," AMD, White Paper, undated.

Mann, Daniel, "29K Family Context Switching," Nov. 1991, *Embedded System Programming*, 4, pp. 55–62.

Mann, Daniel, "Evaluating and Programming the 29K RISC Family," May 1995, AMD Corporation, 2nd ed.

Mann, Daniel, *Programming for the 29k RISC Family.* Englewood Cliffs, NJ: Prentice Hall, 1994.

Mann, Daniel, "RISC Performance Depends on Compiler," Dec. 1991, *Computer Technology Review.*

Mann, Daniel, "Speed System Operation by Matching CPU to Need," Nov. 1992, *Electronic Design*, 40, pp. 44–58.

Mann, Daniel, Stewart, Brett, "Registereinsatz bei C-Compilern für RISC/CISC," Nov. 1991, *Design & Electronik*, 24 vom 19.11.1991, pp. 40–48.

Mann, Daniel, Stewart, Brett, "Register Usage Strategies," Nov. 1991, *The C Users Journal*, p. 66.

Mann, Daniel, "UNIX and the Am29000 Microprocessor," Feb. 1992, *IEEE Micro*, pp. 27–31.

Mann, Daniel, "Working with GDB," Dec. 1992, *Embedded Systems Programming*, 5 (12).

Olson, Tim, "Programming the Am29000," Sept. 1990, *Embedded Systems Conference.*

Relph, Richard, "From RESET to Main: Getting the 29k Family Started," Oct. 1994, *Fusion News*, AMD, 19, pp. 4–6.

Relph, Richard, "Programming the Am29000 Family," Sept. 1991, *Embedded Systems Conference.*

Smith, Michael R., "How RISCy is DSP," Dec. 1992, *IEEE Micro*, pp. 10–23.

Smith, Michael R., "To DSP or Not to DSP," Aug. 1992, *Computer Applications Journal*, 28, pp. 14–25.

"The Stack Cache Explained," AMD, White Paper, undated.

"Understanding RISC Processors," 1993, *Microprocessor Report*, Chapter 5, Ziff-Davis. ISBN 1-56276-159-5.

"The Universal Debugger Interface," Sept. 1992, *Dr. Dobb's Journal*, 17, pp. 58–68.

9

INTEL'S MEGAPROCESSOR i80860

9.1 INTRODUCTION

This chapter will discuss Intel's i860 chip—known as "a Cray on a chip." The chip is optimized for floating-point performance and is often used as an arithmetic accelerator. Development of the i860 architecture was phased out in 1993–1994, with no apparent successor.

9.2 BACKGROUND

The i860 addresses the high-end graphics and computation enhancement markets. System-level products based on the i860 address simulation and modeling, animation, virtual reality, image processing, and other high-end, computationally intensive applications.

9.3 ARCHITECTURE

There are two members of the i860 family, the XR and the XP. The i860 processor achieves high levels of integer, floating-point, and 3D graphics performance simultaneously. The i860XR is a pure 64-bit RISC design at the one million transistor level, using one-micron, double-metal processes in CHMOS. The i860XR achieves the same scalar performance and one-fourth to one-half of the vector performance of the first-generation Cray machine, which is, of course, now in the Smithsonian.

The era of the desktop supercomputer is truly here. By using a superscalar architecture, up to three instructions per clock can be executed. The on-chip eight-kilobyte data and four-kilobyte instruction caches have very high bandwidth due to wide internal data paths. The caches are two-way set associative, and use a write-back scheme. The instruction cache's data path is 64 bits, while the data cache's is 128 bits. The chip's external data bus is 64 bits in width, but secondary cache is not supported. The chip is internally of a Harvard architecture but externally has a unified memory architecture. Dual instruction mode, in which a 64-bit-wide integer and floating-point pair is fetched and executed, is a variation of the long instruction word format. The chip uses a load/store architecture, with on-chip transfers taking advantage of the wide internal data paths.

Intel's second-generation i860, the XP variant, extends the performance envelope a considerable distance using 0.8-micron, triple-level CHMOS to achieve a density of 2.5 million transistors. The new chip is binary compatible with the previous, but doubles the performance figures by adding support for second-level cache, faster busses, and larger on-chip caches, as well as upping the clock speed. Multiprocessing support is added in the form of hardware support for bus snooping for cache consistency and bus arbitration features. The i860XP architecture and data paths are shown in Figure 9.1.

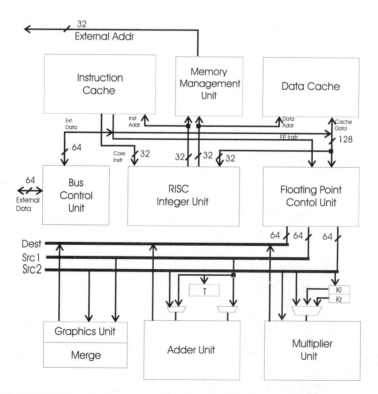

Figure 9.1 860XP acrhitecture and data paths. Reprinted by permission of Intel Corporation, copyright 1992 Intel Corporation.

9.3.1 Hardware

The integer unit of the XR achieves the one-instruction-per-clock goal. Integer register bypassing is available, where the result of an operation is available as an input to the next stage in the pipeline without a register write/read. A single-cycle loop instruction is included. The integer unit can handle loads, stores, and loop control, while the floating-point unit does multiplys and adds.

The floating-point unit uses dedicated three-stage pipelines for the add and multiply units. The unit supports the data types, operations, and exceptions defined in the IEEE 754 standard format.

The built-in 3D graphics unit also uses pipelined techniques to speed up operations, such as management of 16- and 32-bit Z-buffers and color shading. These techniques are used in shading and hidden line removal algorithms for high-performance graphics. Display techniques such as pixel interpolation and Gouraud shading are supported by hardware graphics primitives, high-speed floating-point multiply, and vectorization of operations. In addition, the graphics unit can add and subtract 64-bit integers.

DMA handshake protocols also provide for multiprocessor busmastership handoff. A single interrupt pin is provided, and the external interrupt can be masked in software. The i860 MMU design is borrowed from the 386 family. The XR includes hardware support for cache consistency, bus snooping, and arbitration.

The i860 bus architecture is internally Harvard, externally unified. Bus width is 64 bits. On-chip write buffers are used. Upon reset, execution begins at the high memory address. Control registers must be initialized by the program, and the caches must be flushed, although they are marked as invalidated. Execution begins at the supervisor level. A one-times clock is used, 25–40 MHz for the XR, 40–50 MHz for the XP.

Hardware support for testing is provided in the i860 parts, with a compliance with the IEEE P1149.1/D6 specification, and a test access port (tap). Second-level (external) cache for the XP part is supplied by the companion 82495XP cache controller in conjunction with the 82490XP cache RAM. The secondary cache is unified, with cache write-through supported.

9.3.2 Electrical/Packaging

All the i860 parts operate at a 5-volt level. Power dissipation is 2.7 watts for the XR at 40 MHz and 6 watts for the XP at 50 MHz. The XR comes in a 168-pin PGA package, extending to a 262 pin PGA for the XP.

9.3.3 Software

In the i860 instruction set, all instructions are 32 bits in size, and in either a register or a control format. The integer math instructions include add and subtract on up to 32-bit entities. No add-with-carry or subtract-with-borrow are included. Integer multiply is done in the floating-point unit. Sixty-four-bit integers are handled in the graphics unit. Floating-point instructions include add, subtract, multiply, approximations to reciprocal and square root, compares, and some conversions. Pipelined floating operations, possible because the adder and multiplier are separate, include add/multiply, subtract/multiply, multiply/add, and multiply/subtract. Load/store operations operate on integer, floating, or pixel items. Left and right shifts are provided, as are the AND, OR, and XOR logical operations. Flow control instructions include call subroutine, branch conditional and unconditional, and a software trap instruction. Breakpoint support is provided by the trap. Special graphics instructions support Z-buffer and pixel operations. The XP provides additional operations for load and store I/O and cache flush.

Thirty-two 32-bit integer registers and thirty-two 32-bit floating-point registers are found on the i860 chips. R0 is read as zero, as are F0 and F1. There are 12 control registers, including the processor status register (PSR), the floating-point status register (FSR), the extended PSR (EPSR), the data breakpoint register (DBR), the directory base register, the fault instruction register, the bus error address register, the concurrency control register, and four privilege registers P0–P4. The registers of the i860 are illustrated in Figure 9.2.

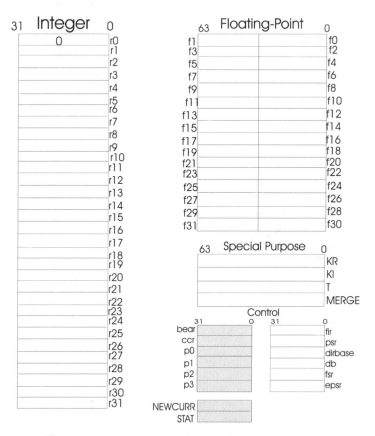

Figure 9.2 Register set diagram. Reprinted by permission of Intel Corporation, copyright 1991 Intel Corporation.

The PSR contains current state information, including condition codes, the loop condition code, a shift count, a pixel size indicator, bits for data access trapping, indicators of interrupt mode and previous interrupt mode, and user/supervisor mode and previous user/supervisor mode. In addition, five trap flags are included. The other fields are delayed switch, dual instruction mode, and kill next floating-point instruction. The PSR fields are diagrammed in Figure 9.3.

The EPSR contains more information about the state, including the processor type and stepping number (manufacturing variation), endian setting, on-chip data-cache size, the bus error flag, the overflow flag, trap indicators for delayed instruction, auto increment, pipeline usage, a write-protect bit for the directory and page-table entries, and an interlock bit for trap sequences. The extended processor status register fields are shown in Figure 9.4.

The floating-point status register contains information about the current state of the floating-point processor, including rounding modes, trap status, overflow and underflow from the adder or multiplier, and trap enables. The data breakpoint register stores the breakpoint address if a trap is taken. The Directory base register is

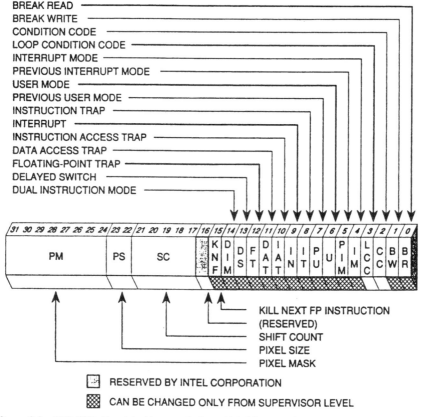

Figure 9.3 i860 PSR. Reprinted by permission of Intel Corporation, copyright 1992 Intel Corporation.

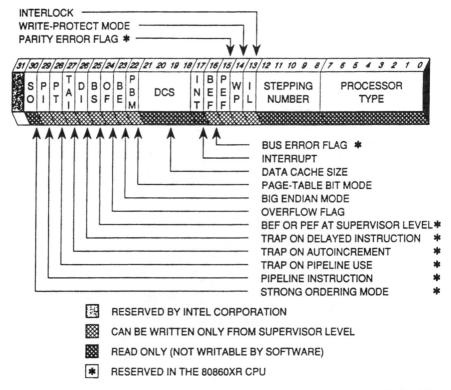

Figure 9.4 i860 EPSR. Reprinted by permission of Intel Corporation, copyright 1992 Intel Corporation.

used to control caching, address translation and bus options. It contains the 20 high-order bits of the page directory, the fields for the cache replacement and flushing control, a bus-lock bit, a virtual-address enable, a DRAM page-size indicator, and a code size bit, to allow bootstrapping from 8-bit-wide devices. The fault-instruction register is used to hold the address of the instruction causing a trap. Similarly, the bus-error address register holds the address for the bus cycle during which a bus-error or parity error was detected. The concurrency control register is used to enable or disable the concurrency control feature for multiprocessing, and to specify the controlled address space.

Byte ordering is selectable in software, with the normal mode being little-endian. The controlling bit is contained in the extended PSR register.

In the i860, most data types are compatible with those of the 80x86 family. Data types include 8- to 64-bit integers, and 32-, 64-, or 128-bit floating-point operands. The i860XP pixel processor operates on 8-, 16-, or 32-bit data items. In a 16-bit-wide pixel, there are 6 bits of intensity for red and green, and 5 bits for blue. The 32-bit format has 8 bits for each color plus 8 bits for general use.

Unix and OSF/1 are available on the i860 platform with a full suite of compilers and software tools. The early i860s met with little acceptance in the marketplace until adequate software toolsets were provided for code development. The software tools and development environments are now mature for the i860. Toolsets include the C language, FORTRAN-77, a vectorizer, associated graphics and math libraries, Ada, the assembler, linker, loader, and librarian, and are available from Intel and various third-party vendors. MASS860 is the vendor organization.

9.3.4 Floating Point

Floating point is the i860 architecture's strong point, with double-precision adds taking three cycles, and double-precision multiplys taking four cycles. A pipelined mode for vectorized operations allows one result per cycle (after latency). The adder and multiplier can operate simultaneously. Hardware support for square root and reciprocal are provided. The floating-point unit has its own set of 32 registers. IEEE format is supported. All four rounding modes of the IEEE standard are supported. There is no divide operation per se, but a reciprocal and a square root are calculated by Newton-Raphson techniques. An add/subtract and a multiply can be done in parallel.

9.3.5 Cache

The i860XR cache is two-way set associative, and includes 4 kilobytes for instruction, and 8 kilobytes for data. This maps well to operations on double-precision data. Caches are virtually mapped, and use a copy-back mode. There is no explicit support for multiprocessing snooping.

The i860XP uses four-way set-associative 16-kilobyte internal instruction and data caches. Both virtual and physical tags are kept. The MESI protocol is supported for multiprocessor cache consistency. The cache can operate in copy-back, write-through, or write-once mode. The i860XP MMU has been extended to add a 4-megabyte page size. Compatibility with paged 32-bit addressing based on the 386/486 model is maintained. The external data path remains 64 bits in width with posted-writes, three-stage read pipelines, and a one-clock burst bus. New control registers are added to support multiprocessing and other operating system functions. Write-back and write-through policies are selectable for the on-chip I- and D-caches. The MESI protocol for cache coherency is supported by the XP.

9.3.6 Memory Management

The on-chip MMU is based on the i80386 design, and provides two-level paging, and 4-kilobyte page size. User and supervisor mode protection are provided. The MMU uses a 64-entry TLB that is four-way set associative. Hardware support is provided for TLB-miss exceptions. On the XP, there is an additional 4-megabyte page size, dynamically selectable. Address translation can be enabled or disabled, and I/O occupies a separate space. The page table includes bits for present, writable, user/supervisor, write-through, cacheable, accessed, and dirty.

9.3.7 Exceptions

Exception processing in the i860 is very complex, due to the complications of the pipeline status. In the i860, there are eight types of exceptions defined by bits in the PSR and EPSR. These include instruction fault, floating-point fault (according to the IEEE model), instruction or data-access fault, parity or bus error, reset, or external interrupt. Interrupt vectors are used. Result exception includes overflow, underflow, and inexact result. There are lock and unlock instructions to allow indivisible read-modify-write via an interrupt call. Reset causes the processor to begin executing at address 0xFFFFFF00. This is the same address for all traps, and the condition must be resolved by the processor examining the trap bits.

9.4 SUMMARY

RISC Features

Large register set—32 + 32
Load/store—yes
Single-cycle execution—yes
Small instruction set—yes, 88 (xp)
Hardwired instructions—yes

Non-RISC Features

Multiply-accumulate

9.5 BIBLIOGRAPHY

"i750, i860, i960 Processors and Related Products," 1993, Intel, order 272084-002.

"i860 64-bit Microprocessor," 1992, Intel, order 240296-006.

"i860 64-bit Microprocessor Hardware Reference Manual," 1990, Intel, Order 240330-002.

"i860XP 64-bit Microprocessor Hardware Reference Manual," 1992, Intel, Order 241304-001.

"i860 64-bit Microprocessor Programmer's Reference Manual," 1989, Intel, order 24032003. ISBN 1-55512-080-6.

"i860 Microprocessor Family Programmers Reference," 1992, Intel, order 240875-002.

"i860 Microprocessor Performance Brief," Aug. 1989, Intel, Release 1.1, order 240588-001.

"i860 XP Microprocessor Data book," 1991, Intel, order 240874-002.

Atkins, Mark, "Performance and the i860 Microprocessor," Oct. 1, 1991, *IEEE Micro*, 11 (5): 24.

Barrenechea, Mark J., "Numeric Exception Handling," May 1, 1991, *Programmer's Journal*, 9 (3): 40.

Cohen, Debra, "The i860 as a Graphics Controller," July 1, 1992, *Dr. Dobb's Journal*, 17 (7): 62.

Fried, Stephen S., "i860 Software Performance Considerations," Microway, White Paper, undated.

Grimes, Jack, "The Intel i860 64-Bit Processor: A General-Purpose CPU with 3D Graphics Capabilities," July 1, 1989, *IEEE Computer Graphics and Applications*, 9 (4).

Hayes, Frank, "Intel's Cray on a Chip," May 1989, *BYTE*, 14 (5), p. 113.

Ido, S., Hikosawa, S., "Parallel Programming in MIMD Type Parallel Systems Using Transputer and i860 in Physical Situations," 1992, *Computational Mechanics*, 10 (3/4): 151.

Kohn, Les, Margulis, Neal, "Introducing the Intel i860 64-Bit Microprocessor," Aug. 1, 1989, *IEEE Micro*, 9 (4): 15.

Margulis, Neal, *i860 Microprocessor Architecture.* New York: McGraw-Hill, 1990. ISBN 0-07-881645-9.

Margulis, Neal, "i860 Microprocessor Internal Architecture," Mar. 1, 1990, *Microprocessors and Microsystems*, 14 (2): 89.

Margulis, Neal, "Programming RISC Engines," Feb. 1, 1990, *Dr. Dobb's Journal*, 15 (2): 116.

"Newborn RISC Systems with i860 Microprocessors," July 13, 1992, *Electronics*, 65 (7): 8.

"Overview of the i860xp Supercomputing Microprocessor," 1991, Intel, order 241088-001.

Stock, Rodney, "The Super Chip," July 1, 1990, *Computer Graphics World*, 13 (7): 85.

"Understanding RISC Processors," 1993, *Microprocessor Report*, Chapter 7, Emeryville, CA: Ziff-Davis. ISBN 1-56276-159-5.

"Under the Hood: Personal Supercomputing with the Intel i860," Jan. 1, 1991, *BYTE*, 16 (1): 347.

"Who Will Wear the i860 Crown?" Aug. 1994, *SunExpert Magazine*, 5 (8): 8.

10

SPARC

10.1 INTRODUCTION

The *s*calable *p*rocessor *ar*chitecture (SPARC) is an open architecture, based on the Berkeley RISC. In contrast to the specification level of the MIPS processor, SPARC processors are instruction-set compatible and may be hardware compatible. In addition, the MBus specification and the reference MMU specifications are usually adhered to by implementers. Multiple vendors support SPARC in different technologies. By early 1991, over 36 SPARC implementations were in existence, from at least eight different vendors. A 200 MHz, gallium arsenide implementation of the SPARC architecture was demonstrated by Bipolar Integrated Technology. Its 80-watt peak power consumption at 80 MHz convinced most designers to wait for BiCMOS versions.

The SPARC architecture is into its fourth generation. It was announced in 1987. Version 7 of the architecture, circa 1989, had no multiply, divide, or MMU functions. The SPARC version 8 architecture, announced in March 1991, was implemented by 1993, and the 64-bit version 9 architecture was revealed in 1994. Version 8 (V8) brings integer multiply and divide, 128-bit floating-point support, and a multiprocessor memory model. Version 9 (V9) of the SPARC reference architecture is the 64-bit extension to the 32-bit version 8. It includes support for 64-bit addresses and data types. V9 is upwardly compatible with V8.

The version 8 architecture has two memory models: total store ordering and partial store ordering. Version 9 adds a relaxed memory ordering. This is accessed by a bit in the processor state register. Relaxed memory ordering allows the processor to reorder the memory references but keep memory consistency. Store-barrier and memory-barrier instructions are provided to enforce strong memory ordering when necessary.

In V9, all registers are 64 bits, plus there are new condition codes. There is a new static branch prediction bit. The privileged registers are updated and redefined. The register windows and CWP are unchanged. The V9 adds 32 single-precision floating-point registers, which can also be sixteen, 64 bit, or eight, 128 bit. There are new instructions for the 64-bit functions, including loads, stores, shifts, and conditional branches. Superscalar is supported. Both big- and little-endian modes are defined. New instructions include conditional moves (checking against zero, if the value is in a register), and a population count, useful for compression, encryption, and finding the first "one" bit. One implementation of the version 9 architecture was the UltraSPARC chip from Texas Instruments. SPARC-64, from Fujitsu, is also a SPARC V9 design. Both companies claim to have had the first instantiation of the SPARC V9 architecture.

10.2 BACKGROUND

The specification for the commercial SPARC processors, their bus structure, and memory management was developed and is maintained by SPARC International. SPARC processors address the high-end workstation and the embedded markets. Sun Microsystems integrates SPARC chips into systems, and is the largest customer for the chip vendors. Sun, derived from the Stanford University Network workstation, was originally implemented with Motorola's 68k line of processors. SPARC International is the keeper of the SPARC binary interface, and includes Fujitsu, LSI Logic, Ross Technology, Texas Instruments, and Sun, among others. They are responsible for compliance and direction. Cypress Semiconductor, a longtime chip vendor, sold its Ross HyperSPARC unit to Fujitsu in 1993. LSI Logic, having been in a position of supplying both MIPS and SPARC architectures, refocused on the MIPS only by 1992. Texas Instruments is a major SPARC player, with its Super-SPARC and MicroSPARC products. New entry Intergraph has given up a major effort in its own "Clipper" architecture (see section 19.1) to address new SPARC systems. Fujitsu, with its own efforts and the acquisition of the HyperSPARC from Cypress, has become a major player. Fujitsu's SPARClite product features integrated functions for the embedded controller market. Weitek announced a clock-doubled version of the SPARC in 1993.

10.2.1 HyperSPARC

The superscalar, superpipelined HyperSPARC version of the SPARC version 8 architecture was developed by Ross Technology. On-chip is a 16-kilobyte two-way set-associative instruction cache with provision for a 128-kilobyte or 256-kilobyte unified external cache. Up to two instructions per clock may be issued. Both integers and floating-point paths are six-stage pipelines. In the integer pipeline, results of operations are made available to succeeding instructions, a process called *data*

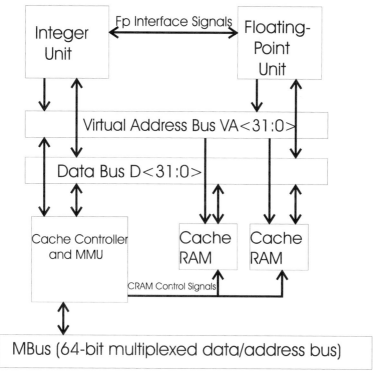

Figure 10.1 HyperSPARC. Reprinted from the ROSS SPARC RISC User's Guide (Hyper-SPARC Edition), 1993.

forwarding. This eliminates the need to store the result in a register, and then re-trieve it immediately. There are five execution units on-chip, for load/store, branch/call, integer, floating add, and floating multiply. The architecture is shown in Figure 10.1.

The original HyperSPARC chipset consisted of the 7C620 processor, the 7C625 cache controller/MMU, and two or four 7C627 SRAMs. It was available on a module and supported the Level 2 M-bus. The integer adds and divides were slower than those of the SuperSPARC.

10.2.2 SuperSPARC

Texas Instruments' approach to a third-generation version 8 SPARC Architecture is the TMS390Z50 SuperSPARC. Truly an impressive machine, this 0.8-micron BiC-MOS implementation is capable of issuing three instructions per clock (one floating, and two integer). It incorporates 3.1 million transistors, does all loads and stores in 64-bit-wide mode, and can optimize most branches to operate without delays, whether taken or not. It incorporates a high-performance floating point unit, and has two on-chip caches for instructions and memory. The instruction cache is

20 kilobytes in extent, and accessed by a 128-bit-wide internal data bus. The instruction cache is five-way set-associative. The data cache is 16-kilobytes in extent, four-way set associative, and is accessed by a 64-bit-wide path. The SuperSPARC supports the level-2 interface of the M-bus. The integer multiply and divide use the floating-point hardware, and take four and five cycles, respectively. The Super-SPARC implements a JTAG test feature, and has a built-in self-test (BIST). The part is packaged in a 313 pin PGA.

10.2.3 MicroSPARC, MicroSPARC-II

At the other end of the spectrum, the TMS390S10 MicroSPARC from Texas Instruments addresses the desktop market with a highly integrated SPARC-architecture-compatible unit for low cost. Incorporating I-cache, D-cache, and a floating-point unit, the MicroSPARC can be interfaced easily to the S-bus architecture. Memory management and DRAM control are included on-chip. A data-bus width of 32 or 64 bits is provided, and up to 128 megabytes of system memory can be addressed. MicroSPARC has a four-kilobyte I-cache, two-kilobyte D-cache, and a 32-entry, fully-associative TLB. It uses a five-stage pipeline, and is version-8-architecture compatible, with multiply and divide. It supports seven register windows. It includes JTAG support, and has a static design that can allow the processor clock to be stopped with no loss of state.

The MicroSPARC-II is also a version 8 architecture, and includes the MMU, 64-bit wide DRAM controller, SBUS controller, JTAG support, and power management features. It implements eight register windows, and has a 16 kilobyte fully-associative, virtually-indexed and tagged I-cache and eight kilobyte direct mapped D-cache. It is packaged in a 321-pin PGA package. There is a four entry write buffer, and a 64 entry fully-associative TLB in the MMU. The MicroSPARC-II uses 32-bit virtual and 31-bit physical addresses, and eight address spaces.

10.2.4 SPARClite

SPARClite describes a family of 0.8-micron CMOS embedded devices from Fujitsu. The five-stage pipeline is maintained, but an eighth register window was added, for a total of 136 32-bit registers. A static CMOS design, the device's power consumption at idle is minimal. The clock can be stopped to conserve power, without losing state. Two kilobytes of instruction- and data-cache were included in the initial product, the MB86930. These caches are two-way set associative. The architecture is internally Harvard, unified at the chip boundary. It has fast 32 by 32 multiply, and 64 by 32 divide. Figure 10.2 shows the architecture of the SPARClite.

The interrupt latency of the SPARClite has been kept to four cycles. DRAM timing support is built onto the chip. The architecture was enhanced by the addition of a 32-bit multiplier on-chip as well. A new SCAN instruction checks how many leading bits are the same. No floating-point hardware is included. Hardware breakpoint registers are included, and JTAG boundary scan is supported. Hardware debugging features in the 930 model cost an additional five percent of the silicon area, and ten

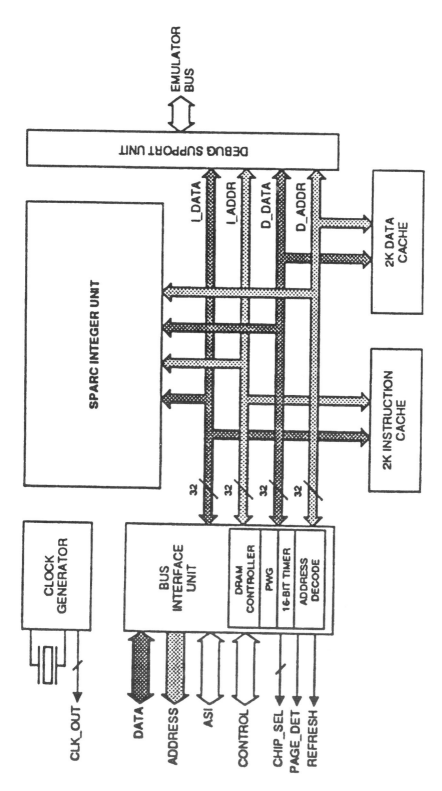

Figure 10.2 SPARClite. Copyright Fujitsu Microelectronics, Inc. 1992. Reprinted with permission of Fujitsu Microelectronics, Inc.

177

percent additional chip pins. This is a reasonable price to pay for these useful features. The MB86931 resembles the 86930, and has an integral 15 channel interrupt controller, four 16-bit timers, and dual synchronous/asynchronous data ports.

The 86933 model has a one kilobyte, directly mapped I-cache, and six register windows. It supports external memory with minimum interface logic. The 933 provides a DRAM controller, programmable chip selects and wait states, and can use 8-, 16-, or 32-bit-wide memory. It is a fully static design, with JTAG. The hardware multiplier operates in five clocks for 32-bit data. There is a one word instruction prefetch buffer, and a one word write buffer. An on-chip interrupt controller handles the four interrupt pins.

The 86934 operates to 60 MHz, and includes full IEEE floating point support. It has eight kilobytes of I-cache and two kilobytes of D-cache, both two-way set associative. There is a dual channel DMA controller, and full JTAG support. The caches can be filled in burst mode. There are eight register windows.

The MB86932 product expands the on-chip I-cache of SPARClite to eight kilobytes. Burst-mode cache fills are also supported. There is a 16-entry TLB, and writes are buffered. There is an on-chip, two-channel DMA controller. Added features include programmable wait states, and chip-selects. Although virtual memory is usually not used in embedded applications, the protection mechanisms provided by the MMU can come in handy. Cache policy is write-through, but cache lines can be locked. The low-cost MB86933 unit only has six windows, for a total of 104 registers. It is designed to interface directly to memory with few or no additional logic chips required. A companion chip, the MB86940 provides 15-interrupt prioritization, four 16-bit counter/timer functions, and two 8251 USART ports.

10.2.5 SPARC POWERuP

The Weitek clock-doubled version of the SPARC architecture uses a 40 MHz clock to achieve 80 MHz operation. It includes 24 Kbytes of cache on-chip, and is directly pin compatible with previous versions.

10.2.6 UltraSPARC

UltraSPARC refers to the 64-bit high end of the SPARC line, starting with the UltraSPARC-1 from Texas Instruments in 1994. These are developed according to the SPARC V9 architecture. The SPARC road map specifies enhanced multiprocessing capability and faster clock speed for future models. The UltraSPARC includes a nine-stage pipeline, and a speculative superscalar design that can issue up to four instructions per cycle. Up to 18 instructions may be executed speculatively before branch resolution. The integer unit has two ALUs, and the floating-point unit has three floating-point and two graphics functional units. Graphics operations are provided for image scaling, rotating, and smoothing. Dynamic branch prediction is used, and a power-down mode is included, reducing current consumption to 20 milliwatts. There is a 16 kilobyte I-cache, with secondary cache support. The Ultra-

SPARC requires a 521-pin BGA package. The MMU contains 64 entry I-TLB and D-TLBs. Forty-four-bit virtual and 41-bit physical addresses are used.

10.2.7 SPARC-64

SPARC-64 is a 64-bit version 9 implementation, from Fujitsu and Hal Computer Systems, Inc., using a seven-chip multichip module. Approximately 22 million transistors are employed. Register renaming and speculative execution are used for performance enhancement. The chip was announced in February 1995. Up to 64 instructions may be in various states of execution on the chip.

10.3 ARCHITECTURE

A classic RISC design, the SPARC provides fixed-length instructions, a load/store model, hardwired decoding of instructions, and single-clock execution achieved by pipelining. The integer, floating-point, and memory management units may be separate or integrated. A four-stage pipeline is used, with 6 to 32 overlapping register windows. A single-length load is a two-cycle instruction, while a single store is a three-cycle instruction. A branch is a one- or two-cycle instruction. An "annul" bit is used for conditional branches.

10.3.1 Hardware

The SPARC architecture defines a pipelined integer unit. The four stages of the SPARC integer pipeline are: op-code fetch, decode/operand read, execute, and write-back.

Register windows are the key differentiator of the SPARC architecture. Each window features 8 global and 24 local 32-bit-wide registers, with 6 control registers. The register window concept is discussed in section 10.3.2.

Various implementations of the SPARC architecture employ the reference model differently. Recent designs have used superscalar techniques within the envelope of the reference architecture to provide enhanced performance. The four pipelines of the HyperSPARC are load/store, branch/call, integer, and floating point. There is also a floating-point adder, and a floating-point multiplier, fed by a floating-point queue. The floating-point section has its own 32 separate registers.

External interrupts are provided by four pins and include an NMI unit. Separate chips provide for prioritization. DMA handshake is provided for multimaster operation. Integrated memory management functions, including I/O mapping, are as defined in the SPARC reference architecture.

10.3.1.1 M-bus The M-bus specification was developed by Sun Microsystems, and defines the interconnect among the CPU(s) and memory modules in a SPARC system. It is best described as a cache-to-memory interface, because most CPU modules have integral cache. M-bus specifies a 64-bit multiplexed address/data

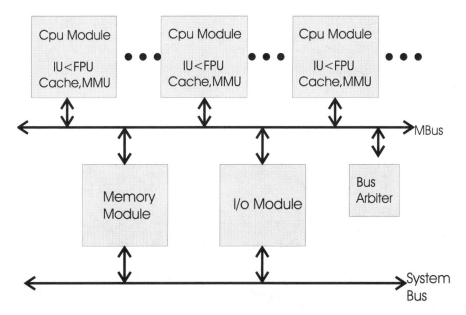

Figure 10.3 M-bus. Reprinted from the ROSS SPARC RISC User's Guide (HyperSPARC Edition), 1993.

scheme, with synchronous operation, and burst transfer capability. It operates at 40 MHz. The data path is 64 bits wide, and a 36-bit address is supported in a 105-pin configuration. Support for multimaster and multiprocessors is included. Various manufacturers supply interface chips to go between CPUs and the M-bus. The M-bus supports multimasters, as well as 32-byte burst transfers. The M-bus specification is a pin-level spec. Two levels are defined: Level 1 covers uniprocessors, and level 2 extends this to multiprocessor systems, with the associated problems of cache coherency policy. M-bus uses a MOESI cache coherency protocol for shared memory systems. The S-bus is a lower-speed bus, used for I/O devices. Figure 10.3 illustrates the architecture of the M-bus.

Internally, the SPARC uses a Harvard architecture, with separate I- and D-cache, with an externally unified data bus. Write buffering is used to minimize memory latency. Read-before-write is implemented in some versions.

SPARC chips generally use a 1x clock, where the processor operates at the incoming clock frequency. The exception is the Weitek clock-doubled chip, which operates at twice the clock frequency. Support for JTAG is provided in the latest implementations, such as SuperSPARC, MicroSPARC, and SPARClite.

Different support chips are available from different manufacturers of the family. They include features like bus arbitration, secondary cache support, peripheral/control, USART functions, interrupt prioritization, counter/timers, and so on. SPARCs intended for embedded control applications usually integrate these functions onto a single chip.

10.3.1.2 Electrical/Packaging The original integer SPARC unit occupied a 160-pin QPFP, with the associated floating-point unit requiring a 144-pin package. Integer power draw was about 3 watts. The Fujitsu unit is typical, and draws 570 mA at 40 MHz and 5 volts. It is packaged in a 179-pin PGA or 208-pin QFP package. The SuperSPARC is housed in a 293-pin PGA, and is also available on modules. The MicroSPARC is available in a unique 288-pin TAB (tape automated bonding) package. Ross's HyperSPARC is available in Multidie packaging.

The trend with SPARC chips, as with all CMOS processors, is toward 3.3-volt (and lower) operation.

10.3.2 Software

SPARC is designed as a Unix engine. The basic SPARC instruction set architecture includes 84 integer and control instructions, plus 57 floating-point instructions, all being 32 bits in size. The most common instruction format specifies three registers. The SPARC instruction format is shown in Figure 10.4.

Integer math instructions include add, subtract, and multiply. The floating-point set includes add, subtract, multiply, divide, load/store, convert, compare, and square

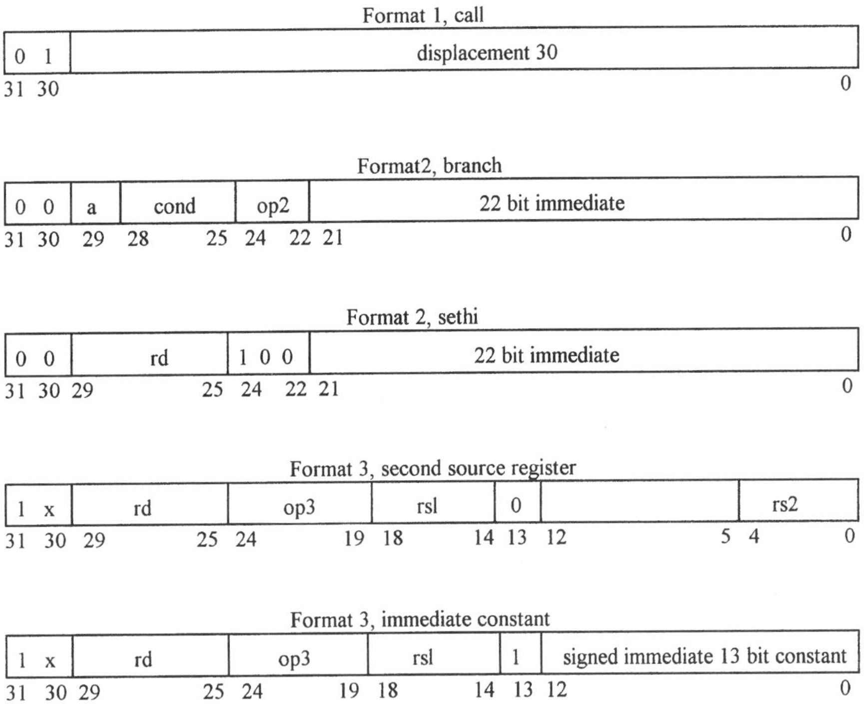

Figure 10.4 SPARC instruction format. Reprinted from the ROSS SPARC RISC User's Guide (HyperSPARC Edition), 1993.

root. The load/store instructions for the integer unit operate on bytes, half-words, and words. The shift/bit manipulation instructions include AND, OR, XOR, XNOR, left and right shift logical, and right shift arithmetic. Flow control includes conditional and unconditional branches, conditional and unconditional traps, calls, and jumps. Instructions are provided to save and restore register windows. Version 9 of the SPARC architecture defines new 64-bit operations and data types, and backward compatability with the 32-bit versions.

The SPARC architecture relies on the register window architecture, which provides a hardware mechanism for procedure calling, reduces access to memory, and is configurable for fast context switching. Each windows contains a number of registers. The alternative to register windowing is a flat register file.

In a flat register file model, all of the registers are visible at once and each has a unique address or identifier. In the SPARC windowing scheme, the processor state register has a current window pointer (CWP) entry. If the CWP is changed by one, the register addressing changes by 16. The CWP partitions the register file into separate sets, called windows. Only one window is visible at a time. For context switching, a new set of windows is available by changing the contents of the cwp, which occurs in one cycle. The register window concept is illustrated in Figure 10.5.

The register window concept came from the Berkeley RISC design, and was an attempt to reduce register allocation burden on compilers while reducing loads and stores to memory. The register window set is a circular buffer of overlapping registers.

Register windows resemble a stack. They are, however, implemented in on-chip

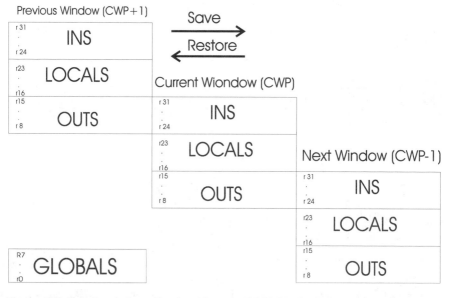

Figure 10.5 Register windows. Reprinted from the ROSS SPARC RISC User's Guide (Hyper-SPARC Edition), 1993.

RAM, not defined in system memory. The size is fixed. The structure of the window, those registers visible to the program at any given time, is made up of three parts: ins, outs, and locals. Multiple (1–32) windows are possible, and the actual number provided is implementation dependent. A SPARC register window has 24 registers. Besides these, there are 8 global registers visible at any given time, for a total of 32.

SPARC maintains a CWP register, which is analogous to a stack pointer. The SAVE instruction decrements the CWP, and the RESTORE instruction increments it.

Registers are 32 bits in size, and there are 32 of these in a window. V9 specifies 64-bit registers, and a "clean window" mode, where registers contain zeros initially. Registers are classified as ins, outs, globals, and locals. The windows are overlapped in the sense that in a call operation to a subprogram, the caller's "outs" are the called routine's "ins." Thus, according to a basic tenet of software engineering, we do not move information, only pointers. The architecture supports up to 32 windows or sets of registers. Various implementations have different numbers of windows. In a window are eight unmapped, eight out, eight in, and eight local-registers. In a new window, the old "out" become the new "in," and eight new locals are provided, along with eight new "out" registers.

Register windowing has some advantages for procedural languages such as C++ or Smalltalk, where the number of registers used is not known at compile time, but only at runtime. Here, the low overhead of context switching has performance advantages.

Special-purpose registers include the processor state register (PSR), a window invalid mask, a trap base register, the program (PC) and nPC, and a Y register, used in multiply and divide. Up to 32 auxiliary state registers are defined in the architecture, and various numbers of these are implemented by different manufacturers.

Byte ordering in the SPARC through V8 of the architectural specification is big-endian. Supported data types are the byte half word, word (32 bits), and double word. V9 introduces bi-endian operators. V9 also includes specific support for multiprocessing, including a memory barrier instruction.

SPARC development and test tools are generally hosted on Unix (Solaris), and include assemblers and compilers for C. A real-time operating system VxWorks is available. Emulation/simulation tools are available, as is in-circuit emulation (ICE) support. A debugger is available for assembler or higher-order language code.

10.3.3 Floating Point

The SPARC architecture defines a floating-point unit that adds single- and double-precision floating-point performance to the integer processor. It features its own register set, and internal 64-bit data paths. There are 32 floating-point registers, not in a window format. It is synchronous with the integer processor, which does the data fetches. The floating-point unit is IEEE compatible, and operates on single- and double-precision data. Operations include add, subtract, multiply, divide, square root, absolute value, format conversions, and comparisons. Version 8 of the SPARC architecture allows for 128-bit floating point. The Fujitsu MB86934 implements the SPARC Version 8 FPU architecture.

Texas Instruments' first implementation of a SPARC FPU was the 74ACT8847 chip. It was a generic part that required a gate array chip for the interface to the main processor. Weitek and Cypress/Ross also made FPU chips. The Texas Instruments' TMS390C602A was a SPARC-compatible FPU. The LSI FPU unit was the L64814, and Weitek's was the 3171, identical to the Cypress 7C602. Meiko, a parallel processor manufacturer utilizing SPARC chips, also influenced SPARC floating point design. Extra floating point registers are defined in the V9 architecture. Floating point divide and square root in the UltraSPARC may be completed out of order.

10.3.4 Cache

Different implementations of the SPARC architecture include different amounts and styles of on-board cache. The SPARClite has two kilobytes of instruction and two kilobytes of data-cache, both two-way set associative. The HyperSPARC on-chip I-cache is two-way set associative, and holds 16 kilobytes, with no D-cache provided. Texas Instruments' SuperSPARC has a 20-kilobyte five-way set-associative I-cache, and a 16-kilobyte, four-way set-associative D-cache. The I-cache is accessed over a 128-bit-wide data path, and the D-cache over a 64-bit-wide path. The caches in the Texas Instruments unit are physically addressed. Support for secondary cache of up to a megabyte is provided by a separate chip. The Texas Instruments MicroSPARC has a 4-kilobyte instruction cache, and a 2-kilobyte data cache.

The UltraSPARC has a 16-kilobyte, two-way set-associative I-cache, and a 16-kilobyte, direct-mapped, write-through data cache. A 128-bit-wide path to external secondary cache, with an associated on-chip controller, is also provided. The MOESI+ protocol for cache coherency in multiprocessors is supported.

10.3.5 Memory Management

The SPARC memory management scheme includes an address space identifier bit field, which identifies the memory access types as user or supervisor, instruction or data fetches (four types).

The SPARC reference MMU (V8) specifies a 32-bit virtual to 36-bit physical address space translation, with support for multiple contexts, and page-level protection mechanisms, and virtual cache. Each manufacturer implements the reference MMU and some additional special or custom functions. Figure 10.6 shows the SPARC reference MMU.

Cypress's implementation was the 7C604 CMU, which implements the reference MMU plus cache tag and control and M-bus control into one device. It features a 4-kilobyte page size and 64 fully associative, lockable TLB entries. It implements memory address protection checking, and 4096 different contexts. The cache controller handles 2 kilobytes of direct-mapped virtual-cache-tag entries, and has a write-through and a copy-back mode. The 32-byte cache size allows for eight in-

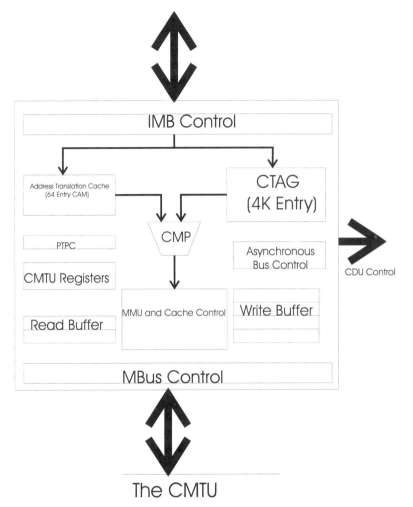

Figure 10.6   SPARC MMU. Reprinted from the ROSS SPARC RISC User's Guide (Hyper-SPARC Edition), 1993.

structions to be cached. It can be locked, and features alias detection in hardware. It uses burst-mode access to main memory. Multiple CMUs may be used in a system, which expands the cache size and the number of TLB entries.

The HyperSPARC MMU translates 32-bit virtual addresses to 36-bit physical addresses. A 64-entry, fully associative TLB is used. In addition to translation, access-level protection is supplied. Multiprocessor support with bus-snooping is also provided. Both write-through and copy-back protocols are supported. It supports burst mode, and has a 32-byte read, and 64-byte write buffer. It features lockable TLB entries. The controller conforms to the MOESI cache consistency model. Architecture V9 allows for 64-bit virtual addresses.

10.3.6 Multiprocessing

SPARC system multiprocessing involves the issue of cache coherency. The MOESI cache coherency model is used, along with bus snooping. Figure 10.7 illustrates a multiprocessor system built in the SPARC architecture.

10.3.7 Exceptions

Support is provided for 128 different hardware and software exceptions. Another set of 128 exceptions is reserved for software interrupts. Exception handling depends on whether an internal or external event is occurring. An internal event is synchronous, and response is immediate, where the currently executing instruction is aborted before the processor changes state. An external event, occurring asynchronously, allows the currently executing instruction to complete. Interrupt latency ranges from three to seven cycles. For traps, an 8-bit trap number provides an index to the vector table. Hardware features in the UltraSPARC provide a fixed interrupt stack for fast processing. V9 adds support for multiple levels of nested traps. UltraSPARC supports five trap levels.

10.4 SUMMARY

RISC Features

Large register set—register windows, 32x32 defined
Load/store—yes
Single-cycle execution—yes
Small instruction set—yes , 50
Hardwired instructions—yes

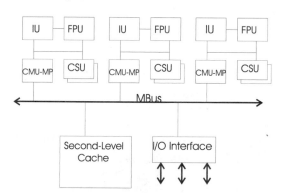

Figure 10.7 SPARC multiprocessing. Reprinted from the ROSS SPARC RISC User's Guide (HyperSPARC Edition), 1993.

Non-RISC Features

Multiple addressing modes

10.5 BIBLIOGRAPHY

Agrawal, A., Garner, R. B., "SPARC: A Scalable Processor Architecture," April 1, 1992, *Future Generations Computer Systems: FGCS*, 7 (2/3): 303.

"Applications Handbook," Aug. 1991, Cypress Semiconductor, section 8.

"Bipolar Integrated Technology SPARC Overview, B5000, B5100, B5110/B5120, B5210," Bipolar Integrated Technology, 1989.

"CY7C600 SPARC Program Update," Cypress/Ross Technology, 1991.

"CYM6226k HyperSPARC Superscalar Dual-CPU Module," March 1992, Cypress Semiconductor.

"Cypress (SPARC) RISC Seminar Notes, RISC 7C600," 1989, Cypress Semiconductor.

"The Future of SPARC," March 1990, *Personal Workstation*.

Gutierrez, "Raising the Parallel Bar," 1992, *Electronic Engineering Times*, 1992 Systems Design Guide.

"HyperSPARC Fact Sheet," March, 1992, Cypress Semiconductor.

"HyperSPARC Modules," October, 1992, Cypress Semiconductor.

Lightner, Bruce, D., "The THUNDER SPARC Processor," 1994, *Hot Chips VI Conference*, Stanford University, Palo Alto, California.

"MB86930 SPARClite 32-bit embedded processor," May 25, 1994, Fujitsu.

"MB86931 SPARClite 32-bit RISC embedded processor," May 24, 1995, Fujitsu.

"MB86932 SPARClite 32-bit RISC embedded processor," May 25, 1995, Fujitsu.

"MB86933H 930 Series 32-bit RISC embedded processor," Nov. 7, 1994, Fujitsu.

"MB86934 MB8693x 32-bit RISC embedded processor," Sept. 21, 1994, Fujitsu.

McKeever, Bruce, "On-chip Support Eases RISC Debugging," Sept. 19, 1994, *Embedded Systems*, 815, p. 51.

"MicroSPARC-II, STP1012A," June 1995, SPARC Technology Business.

"NASA Gets a Glimpse of 200 MHz SPARC," Feb. 22, 1993, *Electronic Engineering Times*, 4.

Paul, Richard F., *SPARC Architecture, Assembly Language Programming, and C*. Englewood Cliffs, NJ: Prentice Hall, 1994. ISBN 0-13-876889-7.

"Ross Returns with Beefed Up HyperSPARC," May 9, 1994, *Electronic Engineering Times*, p. 4.

Russell, Dan, Peterson, Jim, "SPARC Takes Off," June 1989, *High Performance Systems,* p. 72.

Slater, Michael, "SPARC at the Heart of the New Machine," Fall 1992, *SunWorld*, pp. 21–29.

"SPARC Architecture Manual (version 7)," 1990, LSI Logic.

The SPARC Architecture Manual, Version 8, SPARC International. Englewood Cliffs, NJ: Prentice-Hall, 1992. ISBN 0-13-825001-4.

The SPARC Architecture Manual, Version 9, SPARC International. Englewood Cliffs, NJ: Prentice-Hall, 1994. ISBN 0-13-099227-5.

"SPARC Architecture," ROSS Technologies, *Cypress White Paper.*

"SPARC as a Real-Time Controller," *Cypress White Paper.*

"SPARCore Superscalar, CPU Module, CYM6221K," April 1992, Cypress Semiconductor.

"SPARC CPU Roadmap," Oct. 1993, Sun Microsystems.

"SPARC Gets Smaller Still," Sept. 1, 1991, *Computer Design*, 30 (12): 136.

"SPARC Mbus Interface Specification, Rev. 1.2 Draft," Jan. 31, 1991, Sun Microsystems.

"SPARC Module Targets Real-Time Applications," Dec. 1, 1988, *Computer Design*, 27 (22): 100.

"SPARC RISC User's Guide," Feb. 1990, Cypress Semiconductor, 2nd ed.

"SPARC RISC User's Guide, HyperSPARC Edition," Sept. 1993, Ross Technology, Inc.

"SPARCset, System Specification," May 1992, Cypress Semiconductor.

"Superscalar SPARC Chips Offer Performance Gains, Compatibility," July 1, 1992, *Computer Design*, 31 (7): 32.

"SuperSPARC II, STP1021," June 1995, SPARC Technology Business.

"TMS390C602A SPARC Floating-Point-Unit," Jan. 1991, Texas Instruments.

"UltraSPARC-I, STP1030," May 1995, SPARC Technology Business.

"Understanding RISC Processors," 1993, *Microprocessor Report*, Chapter 4, Emeryville, CA: Ziff-Davis. ISBN 1-56276-159-5.

11

THE ADVANCED
RISC MACHINE*

11.1 INTRODUCTION

This chapter discusses the Advanced RISC Machine (ARM—née Acorn RISC Machine). ARM claims the distinction of having introduced the first commercial RISC microprocessor, circa 1985. It is, in the United States, not a well known or popular design, but that may change shortly. ARM processors represent a nontraditional RISC design, optimized for low power consumption. Their high-power efficiency gives them a serious edge in battery-powered portable equipment. ARM currently has one of the best MIPS watt ratings in the industry.

11.2 BACKGROUND

The ARM RISC processor project was started by Acorn Computer of Cambridge, England in 1983. It was intended as a replacement for the 6502 processor, then used in the Apple-II. Early models used a 26-bit address, and were dynamic designs. The current 32-bit ARM line is the result of a design effort by Advanced RISC Machine, Ltd., a joint venture of Acorn Computers (UK), Apple, and VLSI Technology. ARM, Ltd. does not build chips, but rather licenses the design. The actual fabrication of the devices is done by various manufacturers, including VLSI Logic, Plessey, Cirrus, Texas Instruments, Samsung, and Sharp. The major applications for the device

*All figures in this chapter were reprinted by permission from VLSI Logic, Inc., Acorn RISC Machine Family Data Manual © 1990. Figure 11.3 from the VY86C600 and VY86C610 Presentation Material, Feb., 1993.

are in 32-bit embedded control, and the portable computing market, including Apple's Newton palmtop product. The ARM was also used in the Teenage Mutant Ninja Turtle animated puppets.

Acorn has experience with RISC designs going back to 1983, and markets its RISC-based Archimedes computers in Europe. Originally a dynamic logic design for minimal silicon area, the complexities of this approach convinced the designers that the core should be fully static. In late 1994, ARM, Ltd. bought the rights to Steve Furber's work at Manchester University on asynchronous computing. Whether this signals a return to its roots for ARM remains to be seen.

ARM describes a family of processors, 32 bits in word size. There are only ten basic instruction types. On-chip will be found a 16-element register set, a barrel shifter, and a hardware multiplier. According to the designers, the ARM is easier to program in assembly language than most other RISC processors. The ARM is designed as a static device, meaning that the clock may be arbitrarily slowed or stopped, with no loss of internal state. This also affects power consumption, which is specified at 1.5 ma per MHz for the processor core, currently one of the lowest in the industry. The ARM is also available as an application specific integrated circuit (ASIC) macrocell, allowing integration into systems at the chip level. The ARM6 core has 37,000 transistors. The T-series ARM7 machines implement a subset of regular ARM7 instructions. The ARM8 is the defined follow-on. The "StrongARM" project, in conjunction with Digital Equipment Corporation, is targeted at the embedded market of games, interactive TV set-top boxes, and PDA's. A variation on the ARM7 core is called the "Thumb."

11.2.1 ARM6

The low-end member of the family, the ARM2 (86C010, or LH74610) implements the core architecture, with no cache or MMU. The ARM3 (86C020) has the core plus a 4-kilobyte combined cache, a coprocessor interface, and semaphore support for multiprocessing. The ARM600 (86C600) adds an MMU and a write buffer. Other members of the family include the 86C060, the 26-bit bus 86C061, which provides compatibility with earlier products, and the ARM 610. The P700 and 710 ARMs from Plessey do not have an on-chip floating-point unit, but do include a memory management unit, and a four-way, set-associative cache. JTAG is supported. The ARM7 family also includes DSP extensions to the architecture. Figure 11.1 shows the architecture of the 86C010 unit. Figure 11.2 shows the internal architecture of the 86C020. Figure 11.3 shows the ARM 610 unit.

11.2.2 ARM7

The ARM7 family is derived from the ARM6, with more features and more performance, at lower power consumption. The ARM7 features a reference RISC core, and is implemented in three volt versions. Each instantiation of the ARM7 consists of the core CPU plus integrated peripherals or architectural extensions. The basic ARM7 core consists of just over 35,500 transistors, and is a fully static design. It has a 32-bit-wide ALU, thirty-one 32-bit registers, a 32-bit barrel shifter, and a 32

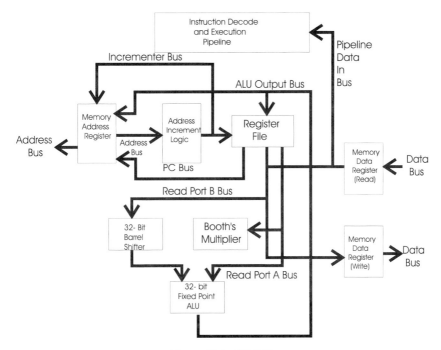

Figure 11.1 86C010.

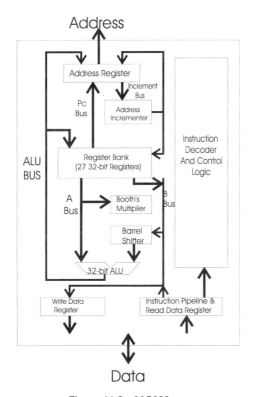

Figure 11.2 86C020.

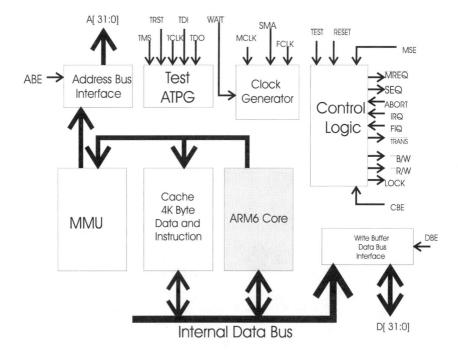

Figure 11.3   ARM610 architecture.

by 8 multiplier. This approach provides performance without the size impact of a full 32 × 32 multiplier. The ARM7D adds hardware support for in-circuit emulation (ICE) and JTAG to the ARM7 core. The ARM7DM adds DSP extensions such as a 32- and 64-bit multiply-accumulate operation, and support for unsigned arithmetic.

The ARM710 from Plessey, VLSI, or Sharp implements an eight kilobyte unified cache, MMU, write buffer, and coprocessor interface. It supports little- or big-endian data structures, and has full JTAG functionality. It operates at three volts. The ARM7500 has an ARM7 core with three DMA channels, and dual stereo sound ports (four D/A units). There is also an on-chip video controller to drive CRT or LCD controllers. The 7500 uses a four kilobyte cache.

11.2.3 Thumb

The Thumb (ARM7TDMI) is a low end version of the ARM7, designed to use a 16-bit interface. A compressed version of 36 of the 32-bit instructions of the ARM7 is defined with 16-bit-wide instructions for the Thumb. The 16-bit instruction tokens are expanded via on-chip decompressor hardware into 32-bit form, and presented to the integral ARM7 core for execution. The result is a better operating speed than a 32-bit-wide ARM7 executing from 16-bit-wide memory, according to ARM, Ltd. In Thumb mode, registers 8 to 15 of the 16 register system and user set have limited access for the programmer. The Thumb maintains the embedded ICE interface.

There is a status bit in the Current Program Status Register that controls whether it operates as a 16-bit access Thumb, or a dual 16-bit access native ARM7. In any case, the core is executing 32-bit instructions. Thumb instructions are a subset of the ARM7 set, and do not include system control, MMU, or coprocessor functions. They do not include the conditional execution feature of the traditional ARM instructions. The Thumb may be said to implement a reduced-reduced instruction set, and could be the first RRISC processor.

11.2.4 StrongARM

StrongARM is a collaboration between ARM, Ltd. and DEC's Digital Semiconductor group. It hopes to achieve a high performance model, with a five times performance improvement over the ARM7 models.

11.2.5 ARM8

ARM8 is the designated follow-on to the ARM7 series. Some of the concepts from the asynchronous design Amulet1, itself a derivative of the ARM60, will appear in the ARM810 model.

11.3 ARCHITECTURE

The architecture of the ARM600 processor was driven in part by Apple's requirements. It has a 32-bit address bus, and supports virtual memory. The hardware is optimized for applications that are price and power sensitive. The processor supports both a user and a supervisor mode. Not a Harvard design, the ARM caches data and instructions together on-chip. However, it has a 64-way set-associative cache with 256 lines of four words each. The cache is virtual, and the MMU must be enabled for caching to become effective. A cacheable bit allows the I/O space to be marked as not cacheable. The ARM's heritage in RISC and embedded applications gives a fast interrupt response and good code density. It has a small die size, leading to both low power consumption and low cost of production. The implementation, at just over 11 square millimeters, is roughly a quarter the size of other popular 32-bit processors. Current devices are fully static, which allows power-down with no loss of state. This is a critical factor for battery-powered equipment.

11.3.1 Hardware

The architecture of the ARM is load/store with no memory reference instructions. The load/store operand is a register (32 bit) or immediate. These operations may specify operand increment or decrement, pre- or post-operation. There is a load/store multiple feature, essentially a block data transfer, but it affects interrupt response because it is not interruptible. A three-operand instruction format is used. The hardware includes a barrel shifter that one operand always goes through. A barrel shifter is a combinatorial circuit that takes no clock cycles for its operation. The instruction execution process is pipelined to a depth of three. A Booth algorithm hardware multiplier is used.

Multiply and Multiply/accumulate operations take up to 16 cycles. Although the instruction encoding only allows 16 registers to be addressed, the instruction format allows a complete orthogonal encoding of ALU operations. The instruction encoding, which is very "microcode"-like, gives a very large number of possible instruction cases, with the conditional execution feature. Floating-point operations are not supported in the core, nor is out-of-order execution.

The processor provides a complete coprocessor interface for up to 16 devices. Request lines for two interrupt lines are included. A floating-point coprocessor has been designed by ARM, Ltd., and is being produced by Plessey.

The ARM chips use a von Neumann architecture, with only one address space. Width is 32 bits for data, with a 26-bit address on the 610 and earlier processors, expanding to a 32-bit address on the 620 and subsequent. A write buffer is included, with room for two pending writes of up to eight words. Used with the write-through cache, this feature allows the processor to avoid waiting for external memory writes to complete.

Reset initialization provides for the execution of no-operations (NOPs) when activated, and going to the reset vector address when deactivated. The 610 uses a maximum 12 MHz clock, extended to 20 MHz on the 620. JTAG support is provided in the ARM60, the ARM610, and subsequent models.

The ARM60 is a CMOS macrocell, available as a VHDL model. It can be designed into custom applications. The ARM60 macrocell comes in a 100-pin PQFP, and features JTAG support, and both big- and little-endian operating modes. It is fully static, and achieves a 1μs interrupt response. It operates at 5 volts, and is available from Plessey or VLSI. Several support chips for the ARM family processors are also available. These include the 410 I/O controller, the 110 memory controller, and the 310 video controller.

The 110 memory controller provides control signals for DRAM, DMA arbitration, and MMU functions. Three levels of protection are provided to separate regions of supervisor, operating system and user. Support for slow ROM is also provided. Up to 4 megabytes of DRAM can be controlled by the chip. For the memory mapping, a default page size of 4 kilobytes is used, but this can be changed to 8, 16, or 32 kilobytes under program control. Multiple 110 units may be used in a system. Figure 11.4 shows the architecture of the 86C110 memory controller.

The 310 video controller accesses video RAM, and outputs data through a color lookup table to a CRT device. It includes three 4-bit DACs, and can serialize to 8 bits per pixel. It also includes stereo sound generation capability.

The architecture of the 86C410 I/O controller is interesting. This device includes four timers, an interrupt controller, a clock generator, a serial port, and six programmable I/O pins. Combined with the processor, this peripheral forms the basis for many embedded control applications. The support chip is compatible with all members of the processor family. Two of the timers can function as baud rate generators. There is a bidirectional serial keyboard interface, interrupt mask, request, and status for the two interrupt lines of the processor, with 14 level- and two edge-triggered in-

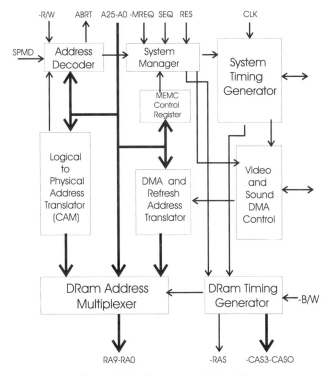

Figure 11.4   Memory controller 110.

terrupts. The 410 provides interface for a wide variety of external peripherals to the ARM. Figure 11.5 shows the 86C410 I/O controller.

The complete ARM600 chip draws 5mA per MHz, or about 0.5 watt at 5 volts, 20 MHz. The devices are designed to operate at 5 volts. The ARM610 is available in 84-pin PLCC or 144-pin TQFP or PGA. The 710 comes in a 144-pin TQFP. The FPA10 is available in a 68-pin PLCC. The 620 uses a 160-pin PGA. The ARM 7500 dissipates 0.5 watt at 5 volts, and comes in a 240-pin PQFP. The 710 comes in three or five volt versions.

11.3.2 Software

All instructions are 32 bits in size. An interesting feature is that all instructions are conditionally executable—not just the branches! This means that the programmer does not need to conditionally branch over or around instructions—the instruction itself is conditional. This feature is under program control through setting of the S-bit. Conditions for execution include the cases "always" and "never." Instructions have three operand references—two source and one destination. Integer math operations include add, subtract, and multiply. No floating-point instructions are provided. Load/Store operations provide memory access, and a block transfer is provided,

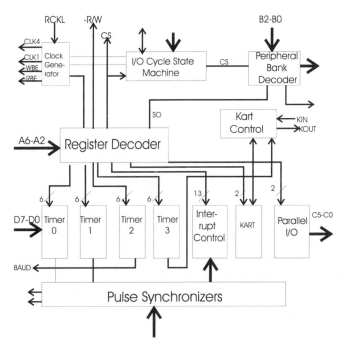

Figure 11.5 I/O controller 410.

which can be aborted. There are AND and XOR operations, as well as bit clears and compares. Flow control is accomplished by branch, and branch-and-link. A software interrupt mechanism provides for supervisor service calls. The ARM7 adds DSP support in the form of new instructions, including 32 by 32 unsigned and signed multiply, and multiply-accumulate. A special 16-bit version of the 32-bit ARM instruction is used for the Thumb processor. These instructions are then expanded via hardware on-chip into 32-bit form, for execution by the ARM7 core. The Thumb can switch between native mode and ARM7 mode by means of a special branch instruction that flushes the pipeline also.

The ARM architecture provides visibility and use of twenty-seven 32-bit registers. The ARM620 has thirty-seven 32-bit registers in six overlapping sets, and six modes of operation. Although the registers are general-purpose, register 15 is used for the program counter. This has some advantages and disadvantages. If we use R15 as the destination of an ALU operation, we get a type of indirect branch for free. However, this approach doesn't support delayed branches, which requires two program counters for a short while. The ARM7 has six banks of 32-bit-wide registers, and six status registers.

Register 14 holds the return address for calls, and is shadowed in all cases. The stack pointer is generally held in register 13, with register 12 being used for the stack frame pointer. Interrupts and the supervisor mode have private stack pointers and link registers. When the Thumb is operating in its native mode, the PC becomes R10, R9 is the link register, and R8 is the stack pointer.

In terms of byte ordering, the 610 is little endian, but the 620 and ARM7 models can operate in little- or big-endian mode. Supported data types include bytes and 32-bit words.

Development support includes C and C++ compilers, an assembler with linker and librarian, a floating-point emulator package, symbolic debugger, and emulator. Third-party offerings include compilers for FORTRAN 77, Pascal, LISP, ANSI C, Modula-2, and an RTX real-time kernel. For the Thumb model, the programmer can direct the compiler to produce either 32-bit ARM7 code, or 16-bit Thumb instructions. Hardware evaluation and prototyping cards are available for the PC bus, and as a standalone platform-independent unit. A bootstrap ROM code and resident monitor are available, with a machine-level debugger. Host environments include the PC and the Sun. Numerous real time operating systems are available for the ARM family, including nucleus from Accelerated Technology, Inc., Perihelion's Helios, the TAOS operating system from TAO Systems, the public domain uC/OS, and Jump Start from VLSI Technology.

11.3.3 Floating Point

The FPA10 from Plessey has its own register set (8x81 bits), a four-stage arithmetic pipeline, and an integral load/store unit that can do type conversions.

11.3.4 Cache

The cache is a 4-kilobyte unified organization in the ARM620. It is a 64-way set-associative unit, with a line size of 16 bytes. Multiprocessor support is provided by semaphores. Write-through policy is used. Memory can be marked as not-cacheable in control register 3, allowing for a memory mapped I/O region. A random replacement algorithm is used. The ARM 710 includes an eight kilobyte unified cache.

11.3.5 Memory Management

MMU support is provided on the ARM610 and 710. The ARM MMU architecture implements facilities for object-oriented programming, including memory protection strategies, and features for real-time concurrent garbage collection. The MMU controls memory access permissions, with tables in main memory, and a 32-element translation lookaside buffer on-chip. Pages can be a fixed one megabyte, or selectable to 64 kilobytes in size. Access permissions are mapped separately and manipulated independently of addresses. Address faults are handled separately from permission faults. Semaphore operations for multiprocessing are implemented by means of indivisible read-lock-write bus cycles. There are two levels of access permission maintained. The first is straightforward, but the domain level access permission is a differentiator for the ARM MMU. Domain access, maintained in a register, is defined as the four cases: no access, client, reserved, or manager. For the client case, access permission checking is traditional and straightforward. For the manager case, an override of the encoded permission allows unrestricted access to the section. This facilitates the task of a garbage collector. The domain concept allows the privilege bits in the access control register to override both levels of protection encoded in the descriptor fields. Access to the control register is a restricted operation. Figure 11.6 shows the layout of the ARM register.

11.3.6 Exceptions

There are two interrupt pins, regular and fast, and two corresponding interrupt modes. In fast mode, there is a 2.5 clock interrupt latency, best case. Exception vectors are used. A software-interrupt instruction is included, and execution of an undefined or unsupported instruction causes an exception (abort mode) that may be used for software emulation. Exceptions can also occur due to internal events, such as undefined instruction. An abort pin provides the MMU with a signal to the processor to indicate a memory access problem. Worst-case latency in the fast interrupt case is 25 cycles.

11.4 SUMMARY

RISC Features

Load/store—yes

Single-cycle execution—yes

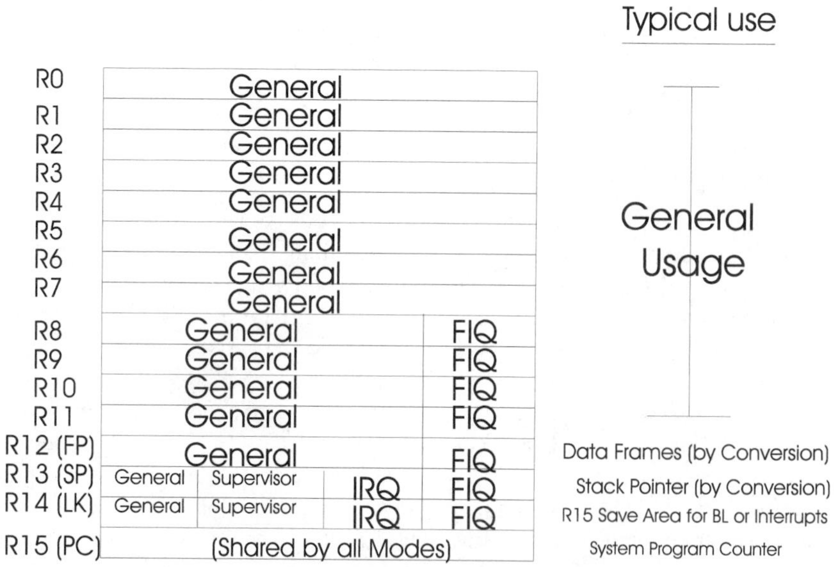

Typical use

R0	General			
R1	General			
R2	General			
R3	General			
R4	General			
R5	General			
R6	General			
R7	General			
R8	General		FIQ	
R9	General		FIQ	
R10	General		FIQ	
R11	General		FIQ	
R12 (FP)	General		FIQ	
R13 (SP)	General	Supervisor	IRQ	FIQ
R14 (LK)	General	Supervisor	IRQ	FIQ
R15 (PC)	(Shared by all Modes)			

General Usage

Data Frames (by Conversion)
Stack Pointer (by Conversion)
R15 Save Area for BL or Interrupts
System Program Counter

Figure 11.6 Register organization.

Small instruction set—yes

Hardwired instructions—yes

Non-RISC Features

Small register set (16)

11.5 BIBLIOGRAPHY

Acorn RISC Machine Data Manual, VLSI Technology. Englewood Cliffs, NJ: Prentice Hall, 1990. ISBN 0-13-781618-9.

"ARM600 Data Booklet," June 1992, VLSI Technology.

"ARM Product Family ARM60," March 1993, GEC Plessey, DS3553.

"ARM Product Family ARM610," March 1993, GEC Plessey, DS3554.

Bursky, Dave, "Software-Efficient RISC Core Trims System-Memory Needs," March 20, 1995, *Electronic Design,* 43.

Case, Brian, "ARM-600 Targets Low Power Applications," Dec. 18, 1991, *Microprocessor Report*, 5 (23).

Case, Brian, "ARM Architecture Offers High Code Density," Dec. 18, 1991, *Microprocessor Report*, 5 (23).

Clarke, Peter, "ARM Gains Rights to 'ASYNC' Research," Dec. 19, 1994, *EETimes*, 828 p. 22.

Lammers, David, "Sharp Aims to Enter the ARMs Race," Feb. 8, 1993, *Electronic Engineering Times,* p. 1.

Magowan, Peter and Muller, Mike, "DSP Operations Extend RISC Architecture," March 1994, *EPD.*

Pountain, Dick, "The Archimedes A310," product review, Oct. 1987, *BYTE*, 12 (10).

Pountain, Dick, "ARM600: RISC Goes OOP," Dec. 1991, *BYTE.*

Pountain, Dick, "Under the Hood: A Call to ARM," Nov. 1, 1992, *BYTE*, 17 (12): 293.

Turley, James L., "Thumb Squeezes ARM Code Size," March 27, 1995, *Microprocessor Report*, 9 (4).

"Understanding RISC Processors," 1993, *Microprocessor Report*, Chapter 8, Emeryville, CA: Ziff-Davis. ISBN 1-56276-159-5.

Van Someren, Alex, Ata, Carol, *The ARM RISC Chip: A Programmer's Guide.* Reading, MA: Addison-Wesley, 1994. ISBN 0201544393.

VL86C010 32-bit RISC CPU and Peripherals User's Manual, VLSI Technologies, Inc. Englewood Cliffs, NJ: Prentice-Hall, 1989. ISBN 0-13-944968-X.

12

DIGITAL EQUIPMENT CORPORATION: ALPHA

12.1. INTRODUCTION

This chapter describes the architecture of Digital Equipment Corporation's (DEC) Alpha RISC architecture. According to DEC, the Alpha architecture is designed for a 25-year life, which represents eons in the RISC world, where the design life of a part may be only 18 months. The Alpha is a 64-bit superscalar, superpipelined architecture that was designed to provide viability into the next century. Besides longevity and high performance, the architecture is designed to support easy migration from existing architectures and multiple operating systems, including Unix (OSF-64-bit) and Windows/NT. Several single-chip implementations of the Alpha architecture have been produced.

12.2 BACKGROUND

The Alpha project was initiated in 1988, and by 1992 resulted in silicon. Mitsubishi is a second source manufacturer of the Alpha. An Alpha-based PC has appeared, and Alpha chips are used in the Cray MPP machine. The architecture has evolved with shorter latencies, larger caches, and wider instruction issues. Digital Equipment Corporation is also actively pursuing research into compiler-hardware interactions.

Digital Equipment Corporation is predominantly a minicomputer company that has built up an understanding of software, users, systems, and networks over the years. It has a large installed base of machines in many different application areas, and a loyal cadre of users. Digital understands the computer business, not just the chip business. The company can build world-class chips, integrate those chips into systems, add software and connectivity, and provide solutions to end users. Digital Equipment Corporation chips are made on submicron assembly lines in Massachusetts and Scotland. Digital maintains design centers in Massachusetts, California, Texas, and Israel. The Alpha effort was made possible in part by DEC's earlier efforts in reducing the VAX architecture to a single chip [1,2]. Notably, the I-box and E-box of the Alpha appear in the NVAX.

The Alpha machines are targeted to the engineer's desktop and the enterprise's server. By supporting industry standard multiplatform operating environments such as Windows/NT, Digital Equipment Corporation broadens the appeal of the product line, and opens up access to existing software. At the same time, Digital provides support to the Unix and VAX worlds. Support of the VAX line is architectural baggage, but necessary for Digital so as not to alienate the large base of installed customers. Digital Equipment Corporation also hopes to build up a merchant chip business with Alpha chips. At the other end of the spectrum, the massively parallel Cray T3D, announced in Fall 1993, uses 32 of the 150 MHz Alpha chips. The Alpha 21064 chip is listed in the *Guinness Book of Records* (Oct. 1992) as the world's fastest single-chip microprocessor.

12.3 ARCHITECTURE

The Alpha's pedigree dates back to the PRISM architecture, circa 1986 [3]. Alpha was designed as a 64-bit device; all registers are 64 bits in width. The part uses a load/store architecture, with all ALU operations performed on or between registers. All instructions are 32 bits in width. There are 32 integer and 32 floating-point registers. The first implementation of Alpha issues two instructions per cycle, and the superscalar architecture is expandable to higher order multiple issues. Load and branch delays are not used; static and dynamic branch predictions being incorporated instead. The global state has been kept to a minimum, to facilitate context switching. A scoreboarded global register file is located on-chip. Result bypassing is implemented. This means that results of an operation are available as inputs to subsequent instructions in the pipeline, without requiring a write followed by a read. Condition codes are avoided in the interests of instruction execution streamlining. Similarly, byte reads and writes are not supported due to their impact on memory accesses.

Both a kernel and a user mode are provided. The Alpha can operate at up to 200 MHz internally, which is a five-nanosecond cycle. Forty-three-bit virtual and 34-bit real addresses are implemented. Most operations are single cycle, with a load operation being three cycles. Swap predict is provided. Multiprocessing support is included, and built-in performance monitoring is provided. This performance monitoring, implemented as a combination of hardware and PALcode, provides access to statistics such as cache misses, stall causes, and cycle counts. Figure 12.1 shows a block diagram of the 21064 chip.

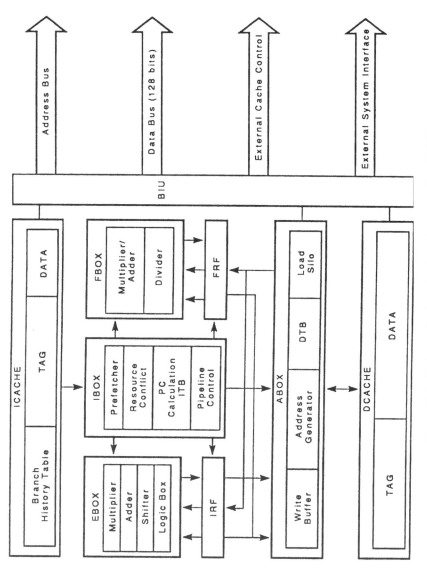

Figure 12.1 Alpha architecture. Reprinted by permission of DEC.

203

12.3.1 Hardware

Although the first-generation part, the 21064, has a seven-deep integer pipeline, the architecture can support up to a 10-deep pipeline. The floating pipeline is 10 stages. The first Alpha implementations are two-issue, but the architecture is easily extendible to higher-order multi-issue. Pipelining is enhanced by other architectural features, such as the lack of condition codes. Alpha avoids implementation-specific hazards to pipelining operation such as load-delay or branch delay slots. The load/store unit uses a three-stage pipeline. The architecture includes four basic operation units: load/store, integer, floating point, and branch.

The integer unit, the "E-box," contains the ALU plus a barrel shifter and integer multiplier. The register file is also part of the E-box. Figure 12.2 illustrates the internal architecture of an Alpha chip.

There are currently several major variations on the basic Alpha architecture: the 21064, 21066, and 21068. Integral MMU support is provided on all family members. All of the current chips are EV4 series. The EV5 series, the first member of which is the 21164, was announced in the fourth quarter of 1994, and is four-issue superscalar. It operates at 300 MHz. The EV6 series is planned for 1996/1997.

The 21066 model has the basic Alpha architecture with more integrated functions, such as a graphics accelerator, PCI-bus I/O control, and DRAM control. The graphics accelerator works with VRAM to provide fast graphics operation on 1- to 32-plane frame buffers. The PCI I/O controller provides direct PCI bus connectivity without external components. The DRAM control allows direct connection of DRAM, VRAM, or SRAM in up to four banks. The 21066 has most of the features

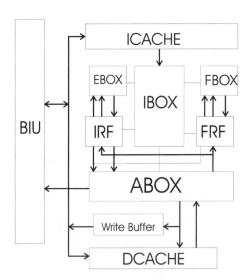

Figure 12.2 Chip block diagram. From Alpha Architecture Handbook, 1992, Butterworth Heinemann. Reprinted with permission.

required for low cost desktop computers. The 21066 is second sourced by Mitsubishi.

The 21068 is pin compatible with the 21066, and uses a much slower external clock but achieves a comparable performance. Its memory controller allows for the use of industry-standard SIMMs. It is targeted to the embedded controller market.

The 21164 model was introduced in September 1994 for the server and workstation markets. It operates at 300 MHz initially, and implements 9.3 million transistors. It has a two-level cache on-chip, and eliminates the need for external cache. The level 1 cache is 8 kilobytes, and the level 2 cache is 96 kilobytes. A companion five piece chipset, the 21171, provides PCI bus functionality and connectivity, and a 256-bit-wide data path to memory. The 21164 can issue two integer and two floating point instructions in one cycle to the four functional units.

The Alpha architecture is of a von Neumann design, with 128- or 64-bit-wide data paths and a 34-bit address path. The data path width is chosen at reset time. A 4x32-byte write buffer is provided.

The actual read/write instruction ordering may differ from that specified in the program. The ordering can be forced by a memory barrier instruction. This isn't necessary for uniprocessor configurations, but may be for multiprocessors. Figure 12.3 shows the Alpha integer pipeline.

Upon reset, the I-cache can be filled from a serial ROM. This allows for easy configuration and diagnostics. Secondary cache support is provided for off-chip 128k to 8 megabytes in the EV4 series. Cache accesses are synchronized to multiples of the system clock. The secondary cache is accessed through a 128- or 64-bit-wide path, and longword parity or ECC is available.

The first-generation Alpha chip, the 21064, implements about 1.68 million tran-

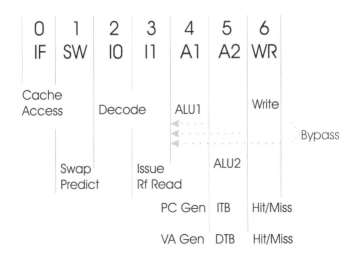

Figure 12.3 Integer pipeline.

sistors in 0.75-micron CMOS, with three-layer metal, and uses 3.3 volts to reduce power consumption. At 150 MHz, power dissipation is 22 watts for the chip, going to 27 watts at 200 MHz. The 21066 draws a maximum of 21 watts at 166 MHz. The 21068 draws 9 watts at 66 MHz, and the 21164 draws 50 watts at 300 MHz. The 21064 chip is housed in a 431-pin PGA package, while the 21066 and 21068 use a 287-pin PGA. The 21164 uses a 499-pin PGA. External memory is run synchronously to the main processor. The width of the data bus, 32 or 64 bits, is chosen at reset time. TTL or ECL interface levels are supported. A 1x clock is used on the 21064, with a phase-locked loop being incorporated in the 21066 and subsequent units to allow synthesis of the processor clock from lower input frequencies. JTAG support is included for the 21066, 21068, and 21164.

12.3.2 Software

The Alpha can support VAX/VMS mode and other operating systems through a hardware abstraction layer called *PALcode*. PALcode is a derivative of a similar feature in the earlier (1986) PRISM RISC design, but is not implemented as a hardware compatibility mode. PAL stands for *privileged architecture library*, and functions as extensions to the basic instruction set. It is downloaded into ROM on the system board. Specific PALcode is available for Windows/NT, VMS, and OSF/1. Migration from VAX and other architectures is accomplished by binary translation. Usually, a total of less than 32 kilobytes of PALcode is required.

PALcode serves to allow customization of hardware features. It sits between the hardware and the operating system software, and allows customization without hardware changes. PALcode is software, but it runs in a special privileged, noninterruptible mode to read and set control and status registers.

Several specialized instructions are included in the Alpha to support common features. These include a scaled add to support FORTRAN subscripting, and a compare-8-bytes to support string operations. Interinstruction dependencies have been removed in the interest of pipeline efficiency. Arithmetic exceptions are imprecise in the interest of multiple issue. Preciseness can be enforced at the cost of operation speed.

Branch prediction has had considerable emphasis in the Alpha architecture. For example, in a conditional branch, the sign of the displacement is used as an initial guess of the taken branch. The compiler provides hints to the hardware and subroutine returns are also predicted. Short branches are removed through conditional moves.

There are five basic instruction formats in the Alpha. All instructions are 32 bits long. Operation codes are six bits, and there are four major classes of instructions, using 0-, 1-, 2-, or 3-register operand fields, as shown below.

Instruction Classes of the Alpha

Class 1: PALcode—complex instructions.

Class 2: conditional branch—tests a register, and specifies a 21-bit target displacement, relative to the PC.

Class 3: load/store—long or quad words between registers and memory.

Class 4: operate/floating—integer and floating operations between registers. Integer operations are triadic register.

The Alpha instruction set of 164 instructions includes the integer math operations add, subtract, multiply, and compare, signed and unsigned. There is no integer divide. Floating-point operations include add, subtract, multiply, and divide on single-precision and double-precision IEEE and DEC formats, and format conversions. The shift/bit manipulation instructions include AND, OR, XOR, NAND, NOR, NXOR, shift-left-logical, and shift-right-arithmetic or logical. The extract instruction extracts part of a 1-to-8-byte field from a quad word. Figure 12.4 shows the instruction formats of the Alpha.

In program flow control on the Alpha, there are no condition codes. The processor uses a calculated jump, with a target hint from the compiler. Both conditional and unconditional branches are used. You can branch or jump to a subroutine, where a branch is +/– one million instructions, relative to the program counter. A jump is anywhere in the address space. The compiler provides hints for the branch predict logic. Forward conditional branches are predicted to fall through. Backward conditional branches are predicted to be taken.

In the 21164, instructions are always issued in order, although they may complete out of order. The slotting function in the I-box functional unit examines instructions

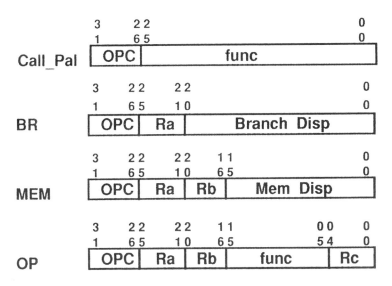

Figure 12.4 Instruction formats.

for static functional resource conflicts, and issues instructions accordingly. Resource conflicts can occur in the availability of registers, the multiplier, the divide unit, or read or write operations. Register bypassing in the pipeline is used to expedite read-after-write dependencies, but the multiplier in the 21164 cannot access bypass data.

Miscellaneous instructions include CallPAL, a prefetch data (hint) of 512 bytes, and an instruction for memory barrier. For the memory barrier instruction, subsequent loads and stores will not access memory until all pending loads/stores have completed.

In the Alpha, there are 32 general-purpose 64-bit integer registers, and 32 floating point. R31 as well as F31 are always read as zero.

The control register set includes a program counter, lock registers, and, in some implementations, a memory prefetch register and a VAX compatibility register. The program counter is 64 bits. The lock_flag and locked_physical_address registers are used in a test-and-set mode for multiprocessor coordination. Some versions of the Alpha implement unique VAX compatibility registers.

Addresses in Alpha are 64-bit virtual little-endian byte addresses. Only aligned quad words or long words may be accessed. Big-endian addresses are supported at the compiler level. Data are byte addressable. The basic data type in the Alpha is the 64-bit quad word, but bytes, words, and long words are also addressable.

Numerous code development and test tools are available under Windows/NT, OpenVMS, and OSF/1 (Unix) on the Alpha. A full line of compilers, an assembler/linker/loader/librarian, and debuggers are provided. In addition, performance monitoring is provided by a combination of hardware and PALcode. This gives the programmer insight into instruction cycle counts, cache misses, and pipeline stalls. Tools to produce customized PALcode using a Gnu assembler and loader are also available under OSF/1. A parallel C toolset for the Alpha is available from 3L, Ltd., which supports message passing, a network loader and file I/O.

12.3.3 Floating Point

The integral floating-point unit of the Alpha has its own 32 registers. It supports both VAX and IEEE floating-point format. The floating-point pipeline is ten deep, with most operations requiring six cycles. Underflow to zero was chosen as the preferred approach, in place of exceptions, for denormals. The floating point unit is capable of issuing a 64-bit result every cycle after the pipeline is filled, except for divide instructions. Included in the floating point unit are such features as a 64-bit adder, two exponent adders, a pipelined Booth multiplier, a 64-bit shifter, and a divide unit. Clearly, attention has been paid to optimizing floating-point performance in this architecture. Both the integer and the floating-point 64-bit adders feature single-cycle latency. Figure 12.5 shows the floating point pipeline of the Alpha.

The floating point unit provides the basic four math operations and arithmetic comparison, on single- and double-precision IEEE and DEC VAX F, G, and some D formats. It implements conversion instructions between the various formats and integer representation.

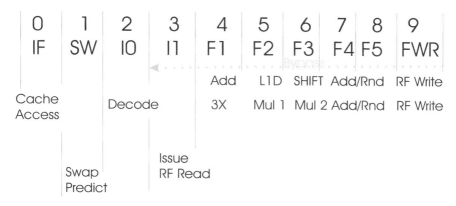

Figure 12.5   Floating-point pipeline. Reprinted by permission of DEC.

12.3.4 Cache

The on-chip instruction and data caches of the 21064 and 21066 are each 8 kbytes direct mapped, with support for up to 16 Megabytes of off-chip secondary cache. There is a 12-entry, fully associative instruction TLB and a 32-entry data TLB on-chip, in addition to a 4x32-byte write buffer. The D-cache is write-through. Both the I-cache and D-cache are directly mapped. Cache misses are handled by PALcode sequences.

At the system level, there is a translation buffer, a virtual I-cache, and a virtual D-cache. A problem with write-back caches in multiprocessors occurs when one processor detects a later write from another processor and the cache must be invalidated.

The 21164 model implements both a primary and a secondary cache on-chip. The primary I-cache and D-cache are eight kilobytes in size. The I-cache is dual ported. The data cache uses a write-through policy. The level 2 cache is 96 kilobytes, is 3-way set associative, and uses a write-back policy. A third level cache may be added externally if desired.

12.3.5 Memory Management

The on-chip memory management scheme is demand-paged, with a 12-entry instruction translation buffer, and a 32-entry data translation buffer. The instruction address page size is either 8 kilobytes or 4 megabytes. The data page is 8 kilobytes, 64 kilobytes, 512 kilobytes, or 4096 kilobytes.

The physical address space is 2^{34} bytes, with a 2^{43}-byte virtual address being output. A full 64-bit virtual byte address is generated, but truncated. There are four defined memory regions. These can be individually designated as not-cacheable, write-through, or write-back. The 21064 can address a physical address space of 64 gigabytes.

Out-of-order execution is normally done in Alpha. There is normally no guarantee of ordering in Alpha multiprocessors. Explicit ordering can be forced by an instruction.

Alpha has a multiprocessor atomic update primitive interlock mechanism, and a method to branch back and retry interrupted instructions. Reflective memory, a technique originally developed by Encore Computer, is used by DEC for multiprocessing.

The 21066 and 21068 allow loading of the I-cache from a serial ROM upon reset.

12.3.6 Exceptions

Exceptions in Alpha are generally imprecise. They can occur an arbitrary number of instructions after the cause. Virtual memory exceptions are precise. When required, a trap barrier instruction can be inserted to guarantee precise ordering. This model is adopted from the Cray-1 architecture. Interrupts are handled by PALcode routines.

12.4 SUMMARY

RISC Features

Large register set—32x64 and 32x64 fp
The Alpha is a load/store architecture
Single-cycle execution
Small instruction set—164
Hardwired instructions

Non-RISC Features

Synthesized instructions by means of PALcode

12.5 REFERENCES

[1] Uhler, G. Michael, et al., "The NVAX and NVAX+ High-Performance VAX Microprocessors," Summer, 1992, *Digital Technical Journal* 4 (3), p. 11.

[2] Donchin, Dale R. et al., "The NVAX CPU Chip: Design Challenges, Methods, and CAD Tools," Summer, 1992, *Digital Technical Journal*, 4 (3), p. 24.

[3] Conrad, R. et al., "A 50 MIPS (Peak) 32/64-bit Microprocessor," Feb. 1989, *ISSCC Digital Technology Papers*.

12.6 BIBLIOGRAPHY

"Alpha AXP and its 64-bit Architecture," August 1994, DEC White paper.

"Alpha AXP: A Technology Foundation for the 21st Century," Feb. 1992, Digital Equipment Corporation White paper.

"Alpha Bet," May 4, 1992, *Business Week*, (3264): 33.

Commerford, Richard, "How Digital Equipment Corp. Developed Alpha," July, 1992, *IEEE Spectrum*, 29 (7): 26.

"DEC Alpha Architecture Handbook," 1992, Digital Equipment Corporation.

"DECchip 21064-AA Microprocessor Hardware Reference Manual," Oct. 1992, Digital Equipment Corporation, EC-N0079-72.

"DECchip 21064-AA RISC Microprocessor Preliminary Data Sheet," April 20, 1992, Digital Equipment Corporation.

"DECchip 21064 Alpha AXP Microprocessor Product Brief," Oct. 1993, Digital Equipment Corporation.

"DECchip 21064 PALcode System Design Guide," Digital Equipment Corporation, EC-N0543-72.

"DECchip 21066 Alpha AXP Microprocessor Product Brief," May 1994, Digital Equipment Corporation.

"DECchip 21068 Alpha AXP Microprocessor Product Brief," Sept. 1993, Digital Equipment Corporation.

"DEC Gets 'Alpha-Ready'," July 13, 1992, *Informationweek*, (382): 14.

"DEC Hopes its New Alpha Microprocessor Will Take it into the Next 25 Years of Computing," May 1, 1992, *BYTE*, 17 (5): 23.

"DEC in Alpha Mode, VAX 9000 Users Await Word on Digital's Plans to Migrate to New CMOS-Based Technology," Jan. 6, 1992, *Informationweek*, (354): 39.

"Digital 21064-AA Microprocessor," Feb. 1992, Digital Equipment Corporation.

Digital News, May 11, 1992, Digital Equipment Corporation.

Dobberpuhl, Daniel et al., "A 200 MHz 64-bit Dual Issue CMOS Microprocessor," 1992, *DEC Technical Journal*, 4(4), special issue, p. 35.

Edmondson, John, Rubinfeld, Paul, "An Overview of the Alpha AXP 21164 Micro Architecture," Aug. 14–16, 1994, *Hot Chips VI Symposium Record*, Stanford University, Palo Alto, CA.

"Introducing the 'World's Fastest' 64-bit Microprocessor," March 1992, Digital Equipment Corporation.

"Introduction to Designing a System with the DECchip 21064 Microprocessor," 1992, Digital Equipment Corporation.

McLellan, Edward, "The Alpha AXP Architecture and 21064 Processor," June 1, 1993, *IEEE Micro*, 13 (3): 36.

"Mitsubishi to Build Faster 21066 Alpha CPU . . . ," Oct. 3, 1994, *Microprocessor Report*, 8 (13): 5.

Rubinfeld, Paul, "The Next-Generation Implementation of Alpha AXP," Oct. 1994, DEC White paper.

"Scheduling and Issuing Rules for the Alpha 21164," DEC White paper, Nov. 1994.

Sites, Richard L., "Alpha AXP Architecture," 1992, *Digital Technical Journal*, 4 (4): 19–34, special issue.

Taylor, Allen G., "What Are Customers Saying About Alpha?" Jan. 1, 1993, *UNIX/world*, 10 (1): 67.

"Understanding RISC Processors," 1993, *Microprocessor Report*, Chapter 11, Emeryville, CA: Ziff-Davis. ISBN 1-56276-159-5.

13

HEWLETT-PACKARD'S PRECISION ARCHITECTURE

13.1 INTRODUCTION

This chapter discusses the architecture of Hewlett-Packard's (HP) Precision Architecture (PA) approach to RISC design. PA goes beyond the definition of a processor architecture into the system-level definitions of how the processor/memory/I/O play together, the bus structures and interfaces, and transactions. Several defined levels of the architecture exist (1.0, 1.1, and 2.0), with increasing features and complexity. PA is technology independent, and predates RISC. The first PA machines were fashioned in 1986 from TTL parts. Current chip parts include the 7100, 7150, 7100LC, 7200, and 8000.

13.2 BACKGROUND

HP is an instrument company, a measurement and control company, a printer company and a real-time computer company. Perhaps it is best not to view HP as one company with diverse interests, but rather as a loose collection of specialty companies. HP is globally renowned in calculators, laser printers, disk and tape drives, minicomputers, laboratory automation, and other fields. The PA definition was an attempt to set an overall architecture to bring together its diverse product lines. The PA machines find applications as workstations and controllers, and replace traditional minicomputers. PA machines excel at graphics and transaction processing.

Although the current line of HP9000 computers uses the PA chips, not all HP products do. For example, HP chose Intel's i960 chip for use in its Laserprinter line.

HP's incorporation of the PRISM technology from Apollo in 1989 brought advances in high-throughput, floating-point-intensive processors. This technology supported compound instructions of up to five operands. In the PRISM, up to two floating-point and one integer operation could be launched simultaneously.

HP's direction with the PA chips may be influenced by its collaboration with Intel, announced in June of 1994. This joint project covers 64-bit chips such as the PA 8000, and Intel's Pentium Pro Processor. This collaboration will probably define HP's next generation, having aspects of VLIW (see Section 3.5.6 in Chapter 3).

Hitachi is building PA laptop machines with its own 50 MHz chips, as well as massively parallel machines with several thousand of the HP-PA chipset. Convex Computer also builds very large parallel machines out of collections of PAs. Taiwan-based Winbond is doing embedded controllers with PA, and OKI uses its own fabricated chips for printers and controllers. Samsung, Hitachi, and OKI, also build PA chips.

The first PA7 part chipset appeared in 1989, and operated at a clock rate of 50 MHz. This was followed in 1991 by a two-chip set, operating at 66 MHz. The 7100 version is a single-chip instantiation introduced in 1992, and operating at 99 MHz. The model 7150 chips operate at 125 MHZ. A note on naming conventions: HP uses the "7xxx" designation to indicate the seventh implementation of PA, operating at xxx MHz. Thus, the 7100 is the seventh implementation and is specified to operate at 100 MHz. The 7200 is a higher-speed model. The 8000 family appeared in 1995, after an announcement at the Fall 1994 Microprocessor Forum.

13.2.1 PA7100 and 7150

The PA7100 chip is the microprocessor instantiation of the PA RISC 1.1 architecture and a follow-on to the PA7000. It is a 100-MHz chip, implemented in 0.8-micron CMOS processes, and incorporates 850,000 transistors. The single-chip device includes the floating-point unit, but no on-chip cache is included, in favor of large external caches. The I-cache can range to one megabyte, and the D-cache can grow to two megabytes. It is a superscalar design with a six-stage pipeline, capable of issuing a floating-point and an integer instruction each clock. Bus snooping supports multiprocessor systems. There is floating point multiplier hardware, and support the square root operation. The PA-RISC architecture is licensed and multisourced, with Samsung, OKI, and Hitachi, among others, manufacturing the chips. The 7150 is the faster version of the 7100, initially released at 125 MHz, later upgraded for 150-MHz operation. It is two-way superscalar. Figure 13.1 shows the architecture of the PA7100 model.

13.2.2 PA7100LC

The PA7100LC is the designated low-cost, low power variant of the 7100. The LC version sacrifices the multiprocessor support, but was made two-way superscalar

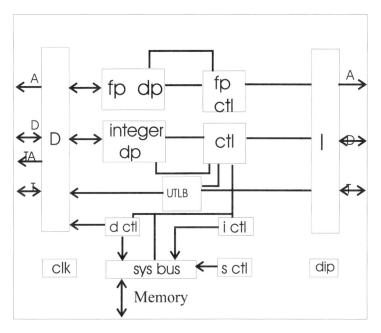

Figure 13.1   PA architecture.

with the addition of a second ALU. It also has added instructions to facilitate MPEG and JPEG decoding, and includes support for little-endian data structures. The 7100LC has an integrated, on-chip one kilobyte instruction cache, and a JTAG diagnostics interface. An off-chip unified cache can be used, and can range from four kilobytes to two megabytes. This serves as a primary data cache, and a secondary instruction cache. The chip includes an MMU, and a memory controller for up to four gigabytes of standard SIMMs. Both big- and little-endian data structures are supported.

13.2.3 PA7200

The 7200 chip, released in late 1994, is similar to the 7100LC, but has relaxed most of the integer dual-issue restrictions of that chip and is optimized for symmetric multiprocessing. It includes a two-kilobyte assist-cache on-chip for speculative fetch support. Little-endian support is included. The chip can now support up to four outstanding memory fetches. The previous Harvard-style caches of the 7000 and 7100 were combined into a unified cache in the interests of saving pins on the chip. The 7200 was tuned to a new HP backplane bus, that is used without any required transceivers or interface chips. The "runway" bus uses a 64-bit multiplexed data/address, and supports four-way symmetric multiprocessing. It can be run at submultiples of the CPU clock. A 7200LC version is planned.

13.2.4 PA-8000

The PA-8000, announced in March of 1995, is the first PA 2.0 64-bit architecture. It retains compatibility with the previous 32-bit members of the PA family. The chip is superscalar, and features out-of-order and speculative execution. The PA-8000 has 10 functional units, including dual integer ALUs, shift/merge units, floating point multiply/accumulate units, divide/square root units, and load/store units. There is a 56 entry instruction reorder buffer, divided into an integer half, and a floating unit half. The instruction scheduler has a horizon of 56 instructions to examine for multiple issue to the various functional units. Four instructions can be issued at once, and instruction scheduling is done in hardware. A dual port data cache is also used, and the instruction cache remains off-chip. The PA-8000 directly interfaces with the 960 megabyte/second "runway" bus. The physical address space supported on the bus is spanned by 40 address bits. A 64-bit-wide multiplexed data/address interface is used. The PA-8000 implements a 32 entry branch target address cache, that is fully associative, and uses a "round-robin" replacement algorithm. Either static or dynamic branch prediction is used. Statically, backward branches are predicted taken, and forward branches not taken. Compiler hints, from profiling, are encoded into branches as well. For dynamic branch prediction, there is a 256 entry branch history table. The branch prediction mode is on a page by page basis, controlled by a bit in the TLB.

The issue rate of instructions is not as important as the retirement rate, and the PA-8000 can complete up to four instructions per cycle. This means that the instructions have completed their desired operation, and no traps resulted. Upon instruction retirement, the rename buffer resolves final register results, and data to be stored are held in a queue of 11 doublewords. Cache writes from the queue are deferred to otherwise idle bus cycles. A 96 entry, dual ported TLB is used. Each entry in the TLB corresponds to a segment of 4 kilobytes to 16 megabytes, in power-of-four ranges. Translations for loads and stores have precedence over instruction address translations. Bus snooping is implemented for multiprocessor support.

13.3 ARCHITECTURE

13.3.1 Hardware

In the PA design, all instructions are a fixed 32 bits in width, and instruction decode is hardwired. There are 70 basic instructions in the basic set, expanded to 140 with the options considered. The memory accessing mechanism is load/store, with three addressing modes. Most computational instructions can inherently specify skipping of the next sequential instruction, eliminating the need for some branches. The instruction set includes BCD arithmetic to support COBOL transaction processing, a large part of HP's customer base. Another non-RISC feature, support for unaligned strings, is also included. Figure 13.2 shows the architecture of the PA, with support for SFUs.

The system level of the PA design allows processors to include eight special function units (SFUs), called *assist processors*, and eight coprocessors. The distinction is that a coprocessor has its own registers, whereas an SFU uses the CPU's registers. To date, a floating-point coprocessor for PA has been implemented by Texas Instruments. It supports single- and double-precision IEEE floating point, and has 16 internal registers, expanded to 32 registers with PA 1.1. The compiler can issue a load into register zero that is a functional no-operation, but serves as a cache hint to preload the cache. Figure 13.3 shows the connection of assist processors in the PA architecture.

The 7100 is dual issue, as an integer and compound floating-point operation may be issued on the same clock. The 7100LC version includes two integer ALUs, and two integer instructions, with certain restrictions, can be issued in conjunction with the compound floating-point operation. Only one shift, for example, can execute per cycle. Data dependencies are checked dynamically. In the 7200, data dependencies and chip resource conflicts are checked earlier, as the instructions are fetched from memory into cache. Certain issue restrictions of the 7100LC can be relaxed. Instructions can be considered in three groups: integer, load/store, and floating point. Either two integer, or two instructions from different groups: can be issued. The compiler stores information in six predecode bits for the instruction issue and steering logic.

The instruction address queues hold the address of the currently executing instruction and the next one to be executed. These queues are the instruction address

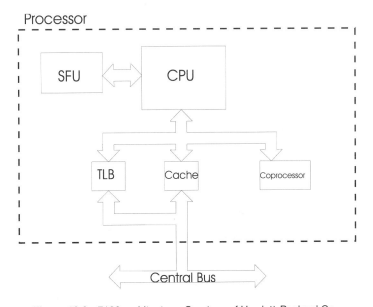

Figure 13.2 7100 architecture. Courtesy of Hewlett-Packard Co.

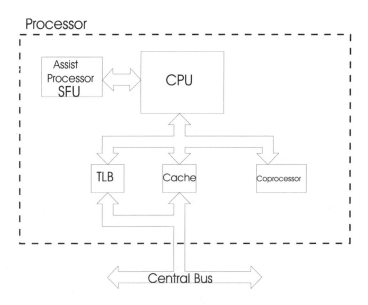

Figure 13.3 Assist processors.

offset queue and the instruction address space queue. All I/O in the PA is memory mapped and uses load/store techniques.

Multiprocessing support has been provided in the PA design since 1986. Bus-snooping features in hardware allow for cache consistency to be maintained in multiprocessor systems. For each cache line, private, dirty, and valid bits are maintained. The data cache policy is write back. A low-cost, dual CPU configuration is possible with a minimum of external chips. The 7200 is designed for the symmetrical multiprocessing environment, with interface to a 768 megabytes/second interprocessor bus. Figure 13.4 illustrates multiprocessing in the PA family.

The PA integer pipeline includes six stages: I-cache read, operand read, execute/D-cache read, D-cache read-complete, register write, and D-cache write. In the floating-point section, all instructions except divide and square root are pipelined. The floating-point execution units provide separate circuitry for multiplication, add/subtract, divide, and square root.

The memory bus interface is Harvard, with a 64-bit data path to the caches. PA7100 packaging is in a 504-pin PGA. The 7100LC uses a 432-pin PGA. The 7150 unit is packaged in a 504-pin PGA. The 7200 uses a 540-pin PGA. The 7100LC, 7150 and 7200 support full JTAG (IEEE 1149.1) boundary scan testing. The Winbond W89K uses a 208-pin flatpack. The 7150 can operate at 3.3 or 5 volts. The 7200 operates at 4.4 or 3.3 volts. The 8000 uses 3.3 volts.

13.3.2 Software

All instructions are 32 bits wide, with a 6-bit major op-code field first. Special in-

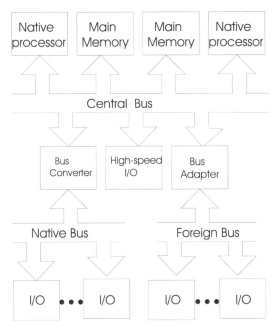

Figure 13.4 PA multiprocessing.

structions are provided for graphics support, including block move, Z-buffering support, and color interpolation. The 7100LC variation brings little-endian support, set by a bit in the PSW. The default is still big-endian. The 7100LC also provides instructions to support JPEG/MPEG multimedia applications. These provide independent add and subtract operations on each 16-bit half of a 32-bit register using modulo arithmetic with the overflow ignored. A halfword average takes the average of each 16-bit pair in a 32-bit register. These special instructions address choke points in the MPEG decoding.

The processor contains 32 general-purpose registers, 25 control registers, 8 space- and 7 shadow registers. General register zero always contains zero. GR1 and GR31 have special functions, GR1 being the target for the add immediate left instruction, and GR31 for the branch and link external. All other registers are truly general purpose. The shadow registers capture GR1, -8, -9, -16, -17, -24, and -25 upon interrupt. The space registers hold space identifiers for virtual addressing. The 32-bit processor status word is copied to the interruption processor status word upon interrupt. The control registers are numbered CR0, and CR 8–31. They provide protection mode bits on a per-page basis. CR11 is the shift amount register, and CR16 is the interval timer. Figure 13.5 illustrates the various registers in the PA architecture.

In the floating-point unit, the register file is organized as 28x64 or 56x32, and is eight ported. Five read- and three write-ports are supported. Byte ordering is big-endian. Data types range from 8- to 64-bit integer, and 32-, 64-, or 128-bit floating. Packed and unpacked BCD format is also supported.

	0	31	
CR 0	Recovery Counter		(32 bits)
	reserved		
CR 8	reserved	PID 1	WD	(16 bits)
CR 9	reserved	PID 2	WD	(16 bits)
CR 10	reserved	CCR	(8 bits)
CR 11	nonexistent	SAR	(5 bits)
CR 12	reserved	PID 3	WD	(16 bits)
CR 13	reserved	PID 4	WD	(16 bits)
CR 14	Interruption Vector Address		(32 bits)
CR 15	External Interrupt Enable Mask		(32 bits)
CR 16	Interval Timer		(32 bits)
CR 17	Interruption Instruction Address Space Queue		(16, 24, or 32 bits)
CR 18	Interruption Instruction Address Offset Queue		(32 bits)
CR 19	Interruption Instruction Register		(32 bits)
CR 20	Interruption Space Register		(16, 24, or 32 bits)
CR 21	Interruption Offset Register		(32 bits)
CR 22	Interruption Processor Status Word		(32 bits)
CR 23	External Interrupt Request Register		(32 bits)
CR 24	Temporary Register		(32 bits)
	. . .		
CR 31	Temporary Register		(32 bits)

Figure 13.5 PA registers. Courtesy of Hewlitt-Packard Co.

Since HP has software capability in-house, hardware and software design for PA started simultaneously. The PA architecture was to be compiler visible from the start. The in-house compiler group continues to optimize the compiler performance in parallel with advances in the silicon. Improvements in the efficiency of the compiler are just as valuable (maybe more so) than improvements in the chip instruction rate.

13.3.3 Floating Point

A highly optimized IEEE floating-point unit is included on the 7100 chip, with a Booth algorithm double-precision multiplier, and specialized SRT algorithm divide/square root circuitry operating at two times the processor clock frequency. The floating-point register file is eight ported, and has 28 64-bit registers. All operations

```
         0                                              31
GR 0  | Permanent zero                                     |
GR 1  | Target for ADDIL or General use                    |
GR 2  | General use                                        |
       :              •
       :              •
       :              •
GR 30 | General use                                         |
GR 31 | Link register for BLE or General use               |
```

General Registers.

```
SR 0  | Link code space ID                                      |
SR 1  | General use                                             |
SR 2  | General use                                             |
SR 3  | General use                                             |
SR 4  | Tracks IA space                                         |
SR 5  | Process private data                                    |
SR 6  | Shared data                                             |
SR 7  | Operating system's public code, literals and data       |
```

Space Registers.

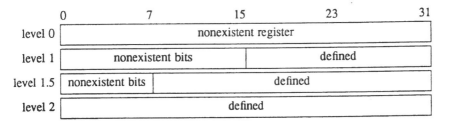

SRs, IASQ and IIASQ elements, and the ISR in Different Levels.

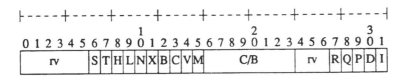

Figure 13.5 *(continued)*

except divide and square root have a two-cycle latency. Divides and square roots need 8 cycles single and 15 cycles double precision. Emphasis on floating-point performance was driven by the requirements for high-performance graphics calculations, which are a feature of HP's workstations. The 7200 floating point unit is carried over from the 7100 model.

The 7100LC is optimized for single-precision floating point at the expense of double precision, to save power and chip area. Double-precision multiply requires two passes through the multiplier, giving a three-cycle latency compared to the 7100's two-cycle latency. Divide and square root are not affected; however, other operations are not allowed in the latencies of these operations.

The PA-8000 has dual floating-point units, each with their own multiply/accumulate and divide/square root hardware. The pipelined multiply/accumulate units have a latency of three cycles, while the divide/square root units have single/double precision latencies of 17/31 cycles.

13.3.4 Cache

PA processors use external cache, with the exception of the 7100LC, which has an on-chip I-cache. Various data cache optimizations were used in the 7100 to minimize the cache-miss penalty. For example, in the hit-under-miss scheme, for a load miss, execution continues until the target register is needed for another instruction. Knowing this, the compiler can use this feature to prefetch data into the cache. For a store miss, execution continues until a load occurs to the line causing the miss. Other techniques used are streaming, store cache hint, and semaphore operations performed in cache.

The external cache of the 7100 uses a 64-bit data path to I-cache and D-cache, which are direct mapped. The tradeoff in putting the caches off-chip was decided in favor of having very large caches capable of operating at processor speed. The processor operates at a multiple of the external, synchronous bus. A unified, fully associative TLB supports 120 fixed and 16 variable entries. The variable entries can be used to map large memory areas, such as a graphics frame buffer. The load latency is one cycle, except when the subsequent instruction uses the destination register of the load. Single-cycle execution for branches is almost always achieved by predicting forward branches untaken and backward branches taken. Stores require two clocks.

The LC version implements a combined cache for instructions and data. The 7100LC adds bits to specify uncacheable pages, and support for little-endian processes. The LC model also has an on-chip 1 kilobyte instruction buffer. The Winbond W89K has a 2-kilobyte cache.

The 7200 adds a special on-chip assist-cache. This has 64 fully associative lines. On each cache access, 65 entries are checked in parallel: the 64 entries of the assist-cache, and one from off-chip cache. Data are moved to the assist-cache, and replace existing data in a first-in, first-out fashion. In effect, the assist-cache adds dynamic associativity to the main cache. The 7200 allows for up to four data prefetches to be outstanding.

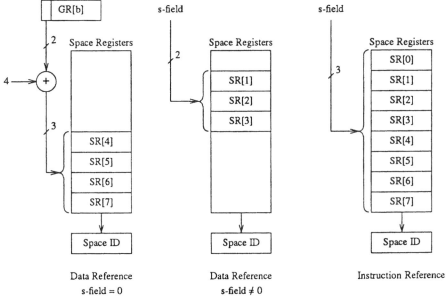

Space Identifier Selection

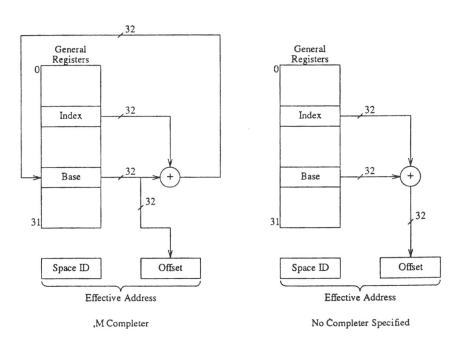

Effective Address Computation

Figure 13.6 PA MMU. Courtesy of Hewlitt-Packard Co.

13.3.5 Memory Management

The MMU in the 7100 supports three levels of virtual addressing, and 48-, 56-, or 64-bit virtual addresses, with a TLB and provision for cache. Address translations are done at the page level. Level zero is the 32-bit physical address. Virtual memory support was introduced at level 1. Four-kilobyte pages are supported, with a 16-, 24-, or 32-bit space identifier concatenated with a 32-bit offset address. The translation lookaside buffer maintains access rights on a per-page basis, and the architecture was designed with the Unix operating system in mind. The Block TLB feature can maintain one entry for the operating system and one for the graphics buffer. All I/O is memory mapped in the PA architecture. Level 1, implemented now in the 7100, uses a 48-bit virtual address. Level 2 supports a full 64-bit physical address. Figures 13.6 illustrates the details of space identifier selection and effective address calculation in the PA architecture.

The unified TLB of the 7100 has 120 fixed size, fully associative entries, and 16 variable entries. The 7100LC has a 1 kilobyte direct-mapped instruction buffer, and a 64 entry TLB. The 7200 provides increased memory page protection ID size, as well as a 120-entry, fully associative TLB. The PA8000 has a dual ported, 96 entry TLB.

13.3.6 Exceptions

Exceptions in the PA use a vector table. Classes of exceptions on the 7100 include traps, faults, checks, and external interrupts. The PA8000, although aggressively superscalar and implementing out-of-order execution, maintains a precise exception model.

13.4 SUMMARY

RISC Features

Large register set—yes
Load/store—no
Single-cycle execution
Small instruction set—70
Hardwired instructions—yes

Non-RISC Features

Addressing modes—3
Other:
    BCD support for COBOL
    Unaligned strings
    JPEG/MPEG (model 7100LC)

13.5 BIBLIOGRAPHY

"The Advantages of the PA-RISC Architecture," Hewlett-Packard draft white paper.

Asprey, T., et al., "Performance Features of the PA7100 Microprocessor," June 1993, *IEEE Micro*, 13 (3): 22–35.

Ban, Mike, et al., "Design Methodologies for the PA7100LC Microprocessor," April 1995, *HP Journal*, 46 (2): 23–35.

Burroughs, Gregory D., Gore, Audrey B., "Design Verification of the HP 9000 Series 700 PA-RISC Workstation," Aug. 1, 1992, *Hewlett-Packard Journal*, 43 (4): 34.

Delano E., et al., "Hewlett-Packard's 7100: A High-speed Superscalar PA-RISC Processor," Feb. 1992, Compcon Digest of Papers, IEEE, pp. 116–121.

DeLano, Walker, Yetter, Forsyth, "A High Speed Superscalar PA-RISC Processor," 1992, *IEEE Compcon 92 Proceedings*, Feb. 24–28, 1992, San Francisco.

Hewlett-Packard Journal, Sept. 1987, Vol. 38, No. 9 (five articles on PA).

"Hewlett-Packard Precision Architecture, A New Perspective," 1986, Hewlett-Packard.

"HP 3000 Series 955 System, Hewlett-Packard, Technical Data," 1988, 1989, Hewlett-Packard.

"HP 9000 Series 800 Model 815S, Technical Data," 1989, Hewlett-Packard.

"HP 9000 Series 800 Models 825SRX/835SRX, Hewlett-Packard Technical Data," Sept. 1988, Hewlett-Packard.

"HP 9000 Series 800 Models 835S & 835SE, Hewlett-Packard Technical Data," 1988, Hewlett-Packard.

"HP 9000 Series 800 Model 850S, Hewlett-Packard Hardware Technical Data," 1988, Hewlett-Packard.

"HP Adds Little-Endian Addressing so PA-RISC Supports Windows NT," Dec. 20, 1993, *Digital News & Review*, 10 (24): 3.

"HP Describes Plan to Regain Performance Lead," Dec. 27, 1993, *Microprocessor Report*, 7 (17): 4.

"HP PA-RISC Compiler Optimization Technology, Technical White Paper, version 1.0," August 1992, Hewlett-Packard.

"HP Precision Architecture," Hewlett-Packard seminar notes.

"HP Precision Architecture Handbook," 2nd ed., June 1987, Hewlett-Packard.

"HP-UX 9.0 Operating System Technical Data," 1992, Hewlett-Packard.

Hunt, Doug, "Advanced Performance Features of the 64-bit PA-8000," March 1995. *IEEE Compcon Digest of Papers.*

Knebel, Patrick et al., "HP's PA7100LC: A Low-Cost Superscalar PA-RISC Processor," Feb. 1993, Compcon Digest of Papers, IEEE, pp. 441–447.

Kurpanek, Gordon et al., "PA-7200: A PA-RISC Processor with Integrated High Performance MP Bus Interface," 1994, IEEE paper 1063-6390/94.

Lee, R. B., "Precision Architecture," Jan. 1989, *IEEE Computer*, 22: pp. 78–91.

Lee, Ruby, Mahon, Michael, Morris, Dale, "Pathlength Reduction Features in the PA-RISC Architecture," 1992, *IEEE Compcon Spring 92 Digest of Papers*, IEEE Computer Society.

Lee, Ruby, "Multimedia Enhancements for PA-RISC Processors," 1994, *Hot Chips VI Conference*, Stanford University, Palo Alto, CA.

Mahon, M. J. et al., "HP Precision Architecture: The Processor," August 1986, *Hewlett-Packard Journal*, 37(8), pp. 4–21.

McGrory II, John J. et al., "Transaction Processing Performance on PA-RISC Commercial Unix Systems," Feb. 1992, *IEEE Compcon Digest of Papers*, IEEE Computer Society.

McLachlan, Gordon, "Why Not RISC It?" Aug. 1994, *HP Professional*, 8 (8): 72.

"PA-RISC 1.1 Architecture and Instruction Set Reference Manual," Nov. 1990, Hewlett-Packard, part 09740-90039.

"PA-RISC Strategy: HP Unveils Low-end Computing Strategy with PA-7100LC RISC Microprocessor," Dec. 27, 1993, *EDGE: Work-Group Computing Report*, 4 (188): 2.

"PowerOpen, HP Boost RISC Futures," Dec. 20, 1993, *Digital News & Review*, 10 (24): 1.

"Understanding RISC Processors," 1993, *Microprocessor Report*, Chapter 10, Emeryville, CA: Ziff-Davis. ISBN 1-56276-159-5.

14

IMS 3250

14.1 INTRODUCTION

This chapter discusses the architecture of the IMS 3250 RISC chip, which is unique in having hardware emulation modes for both 80x86 and 680x0 architectures. The chip features both low cost and low power. The emulation part of the technology, now the subject of a pending patent, could be applied to any RISC core. IMS claims a 5 percent increase in silicon to implement the emulation features. The emulation technique relies on decoding and executing register-register operations in one clock cycle. Implementing these on superscalar systems means a superscalar core could execute some CISC instructions in less than one clock. This is the basis for the Intel Pentium Pro Processor.

14.2 BACKGROUND

International Meta Systems, Inc. (IMS) of Torrance, California is a small research and development firm with roots in the aerospace industry. It was founded in 1986. An early product was a PC add-in board with a special microcoded Smalltalk engine. The IMS 3250 chip was manufactured by Sharp and SGS Thompson. First prototypes operated at 60 MHz.

14.3 ARCHITECTURE

The unique feature of the IMS 3250 is its emulation mode, in which 80x86 instructions are executed at 80486 levels of performance, and the chip can operate in 80486 protected mode. The chip also has a RISC native mode. In RISC mode, the performance is comparable to a Pentium. DSP functionality is also built in. The chip has an impressive mips-per-watt rating. Figure 14.1 shows the architecture of the IMS 3250.

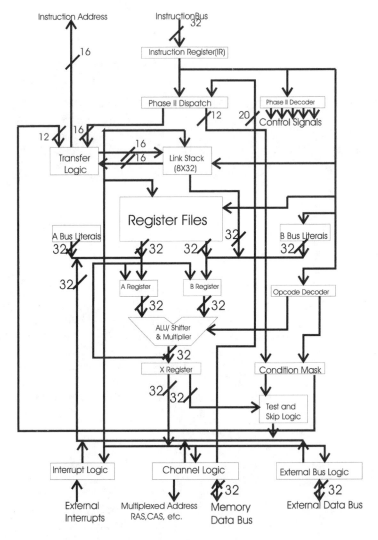

Figure 14.1 IMS 3250 architecture. Reprinted by permission from IMS, Microcode Engine Offers Enhanced Emulation, Sept. 1994.

14.3.1 Hardware

The RISC core is two-issue superscalar. For emulation of another (CISC) processor, a 6-kiloword x 32-bit PROM is required, with integral decoding logic. The external data bus is 32 bits wide. The CPU uses a four-stage pipeline. Clock scaling is provided for power management.

14.3.2 Software and Programmer's View

The on-chip register file includes eight 32-bit general-purpose registers, thirty-two 32-bit emulation registers, a total of 32 memory registers, and eight 80-bit floating-point registers.

The native instruction set is three-operand format. All instructions are 32 bits in length. All execute in one cycle, except the 32-bit multiply/accumulate, which takes two. Besides the usual ALU operations, there is a variable-width bit flip for DSP-type butterfly operations.

Emulation of foreign binary instruction sets is nontrivial, particularly in terms of proper setting of condition codes, and if the code is self-modifying. These cases are handled by the IMS 3250.

The development environment is hosted on a PC, and includes a full set of development and debug tools. The debugger provides step, trace, breakpoints, and disassembly of the microcode and the emulated machine.

14.3.3 Floating Point

There is currently no floating-point hardware; floating-point operations are emulated.

14.3.4 Cache

The IMS 3250 chip has 2 kilobytes of on-chip cache, organized as 1 kilobyte of instruction and 1 kilobyte of data. A 32-bit-wide, 2 kilobytes of SRAM is provided for user-defined microcode.

14.3.5 Memory Management

Memory management functions are included on-chip, with a 32-entry MMU servicing a 32-bit virtual address space.

14.4 SUMMARY

RISC Features

Regular, 32-bit instructions
Single-cycle execution

Non-RISC Features

Microcode

14.5 BIBLIOGRAPHY

"'Chameleon' Chip Due," April 11, 1994, *PC WEEK*, 11.

"IMS' 3250 RISC Chip Emulates both PC, Macintosh CPUs," May 2, 1994, *PC WEEK*, 11.

"IMS Demonstrates x86 Emulation Chip," May 9, 1994, *Microprocessor Report.*

"IMS to Develop Hardware-Assisted Emulators," April 11, 1994, *Infoworld*, 16, p. 33.

"Microcode Engine Offers Enhanced Emulation," July 1994, IMS white paper.

"Microcoded Emulation Puts New Processor in x86 PC Fray," June 1994, *Electronic Products.*

"On-chip RISC Module Emulates X86 Apps," April 4, 1994, *PC WEEK*, 11.

"RISC + Microcode = Fast CISC Emulation," May 12, 1994, *EDN.*

Speckhard, Arthur E., Bryan, G. Edward, "Max-2: A WISC Architecture Supporting High Level Languages," March 4, 1988, IMS.

15

PowerPC

15.1 INTRODUCTION

The PowerPC family results from a joint effort between IBM, Apple, and Motorola to design and manufacture a family of RISC processors scalable from palmtop to mainframe. The alliance was formed in October 1991 to develop an open computing platform, in competition with the Intel 80x86 architecture that dominates the desktop. The first in the series, the Motorola-produced MC98601, is a 32-bit implementation of the 64-bit family architecture. First silicon appeared in 1992. The PowerPC design is a blend of IBM's RIOS processor architecture and Motorola's 88100 internal bussing structure. IBM and Apple laid out the basic architecture of the device in 1991. IBM and Motorola do joint development on the mainstream chips and independently develop their own unique versions for embedded and other applications. PowerPC defines an instruction set architecture that is adhered to by the various family members. The Somerset Design Center in Austin, Texas, drives the development of the PowerPC family. The center is staffed at the level of 300 microprocessor designers.

15.2 BACKGROUND

The PowerPC family currently includes the 601, 602, 603, 604, 615, and 620 processors, and the 630 has been announced. The PowerPC design was influenced by the previous IBM ROMPS (RT) architecture. It traces its heritage back to IBM's pioneering work in defining RISC in the mid-1970s at the Watson Research Center. This architecture was extended to address multiprocessing in the PowerPC family. The PowerPC represents a refocusing of the IBM POWER architecture, as used in the RS/6000 series of computers. The RS/6000 line now uses the PowerPC chip, as does IBM's AS/400 midrange computer line. A proprietary version of the PowerPC is used in the AS/400. Apple has also switched its Macintosh line to the PowerPC. Embedded versions of the PowerPC from Motorola will be used in Ford's EEC-V powertrain controller.

15.2.1 601

The 32-bit 601, first in the series, is a subset of the IBM-unique RIOS/POWER architecture. The IBM POWER architecture is discussed in Section 19.5.4. It is a pipelined and superscalar unit, with a 32-kilobyte, eight-way set-associative unified cache. The 601 is three-issue superscalar, the execution units being branch, integer, and floating point. Static branch prediction is used. Any POWER features can be trapped and emulated. This allows the PowerPC 601 to address the existing family of RS/6000-AIX applications, and gives IBM an upgrade path for those machines. A 32-bit address bus and a 64-bit data bus interface derived from the Motorola 88k line are used. Units first shipped in April 1993, in 50 and 66 MHz speed grades. The 601 model is supposed to be a bridge between the existing POWER architectures, and a new family of user-driven processors. The 601 part is closest to the original POWER architecture, and the PowerPC family is expected to diverge more from the POWER architecture with subsequent models. Motorola uses the MPC prefix for the parts, and IBM uses a PPC prefix. Otherwise, parts with the same numbers should perform in the same way. Figure 15.1 illustrates the architecture of the PowerPC 601. There is a 32 kilobyte combined cache on-chip, as well as a 256 entry TLB. The 601 has an eight entry prefetched instruction queue, and does out-of-order dispatch. Register renaming is used.

15.2.2 602

The 602 is designed as a minimum configuration, low power unit for applications such as PDAs. It includes a power management unit that implements power saving modes. The 602 can operate at multiples of the bus clock by means of a clock multiplier. The instruction unit dispatches and retires up to one instruction per cycle, but multiple instructions may be in varying stages of completion in the different execution units. The load/store unit supports one cycle cache accesses, and speculative cache loads. The integer unit supports single cycle add, subtract, shift, rotate, and compare. There is hardware support for integer multiply and divide. The 602 has a 32 entry I-TLB and a 32 entry D-TLB on chip. The caches are separate, and are each four kilobytes and two-way set-associative. The data cache uses a copy back scheme. JTAG support is included.

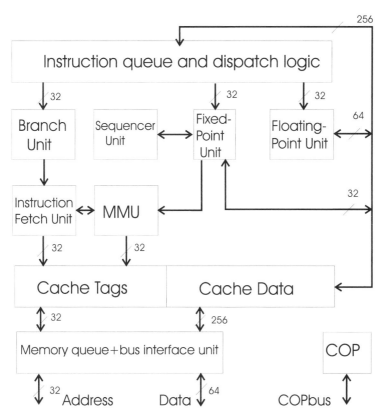

Figure 15.1 Power PC 601 microprocessor block diagram. From Chakravarty and Cannon, Power PC Concepts, Architecture and Design, © 1994. Reproduced by permission of McGraw-Hill, Inc.

15.2.3 603 and 603e

This second-generation part is a lower-cost, lower-power, but faster family member, targeted to the notebook and low-end systems markets. The 603 has five execution units and is dual-issue superscalar. The unit went from concept to silicon in 18 months at the Somerset Design Center. A four stage instruction prefetch queue is included. The 603 dispatches two instructions per cycle, and the 603e can issue three, into five execution units.

The 603 has 8 kilobytes of D-cache and 8 kilobytes of I-cache. Intelligent power management features are included for battery-powered applications. This has four basic power management modes: on, doze, snooze, and sleep. The enhanced 603e version doubles the cache size of the 603 to 16 kilobytes. The 603e can select a 32- or 64-bit-wide data bus width.

15.2.4 604

First silicon of the superscalar 604 model was announced in early 1994. Four instructions may be simultaneously issued. The unit has six execution units. These include three integer units, a floating-point unit, a load/store unit, and a branch unit. Load and store queues are included. Dynamic branch prediction is supported. The 604 ignores the hint bit in the branch instructions, and relies on a 512-entry, directly mapped branch history table (BHT). On the basis of recent execution history, the branch is classified as strong or weak, taken or not taken. The BHT then feeds a 64 entry branch-target-address-cache, which is fully associative. The 604 is produced by both IBM and Motorola. The 604 is designed as a replacement for the 601, and supports multiprocessing as well as 64-bit addressing and data types. The I- and D-caches are each 16 kilobytes, and four-way set associative. The I- and D-TLBs are each 128 entry, and two-way set associative. JTAG support is included. The 604e model is reported to have a hardware/software approach to supporting 80x86 instructions, instead of the pure hardware approach of the 615.

15.2.5 615

The existence of the 615 model has been both confirmed and denied by IBM. The bimodal PowerPC 615 is expected to contain both PowerPC and i486 cores. The i486 core will open up the world of 80x86 applications to the PowerPC. Whether a full i80486 core or an emulator that executes 80x86 instructions in RISC will be included is not yet revealed, as the 615 model has not yet appeared. This version of the chip is being developed by IBM outside of the PowerPC partnership. The chip may be designed to be pin compatible with the "overdrive" socket on Pentium-based PCs, which would position the 615 head to head against the Pentium. Whatever the final approach, the ability to execute the large installed base of 80x86 code on the PowerPC models would be a major marketing advantage. The Motorola PowerPC 615 program was killed in September, 1995.

15.2.6 620

The high-performance 620 is a full 64-bit architecture, with quad dispatch into six execution units. It has a five stage integer pipeline, and three integer execution units. It includes speculative and out-of-order execution, dynamic branch prediction, and register renaming for both integer and floating point. Integral secondary cache control is included. One hundred MHz parts were initially produced, with upgrades to 133 MHz by the end of 1994. Although out of order dispatch and execution are used, in-order completion is enforced. Speculative execution through four unresolved branches is supported. There is a 256-entry branch target address cache, and a 2048 entry branch history table.

15.2.7 630

The 630 is IBM's follow-on to the 620, and is expected by 1997. It will be available with a large external cache and a cache controller in an MCM format. The 630 will replace the POWER-3 (or RIOS-3) architecture that had been planned, resulting in a complete merge of the POWER and the PowerPC architectures.

15.2.8 MPC505

This derivative chip by Motorola combines a PowerPC core with the 32-bit Motorola 68300 embedded controller peripherals. It features four kilobytes each of I-cache and D-cache. The MPC53x series, and the enhanced MPC8xx models also build on the PowerPC core.

15.2.9 PPC403GA/GB

These IBM-produced models are addressed to the embedded control market. The GA part includes on-chip DRAM/SRAM/ROM control, a four-channel DMA controller, and an integral serial port. The GB has two DMA channels, and no serial port. They have two kilobytes of I-cache and one kilobyte of D-cache, and are dual-issue. They have a JTAG interface. No floating-point support is included. The user can select 8-, 16-, or 32-bit-wide data paths for memory. Variations on the 403 are expected, as well as a stripped down 401 model. The goal is to produce a part under $10. This opens the door to price sensitive markets such as low end printers, set top boxes, and X-terminals.

15.3 ARCHITECTURE

The PowerPC features superscalar architecture, which allows simultaneous dispatching of multiple instructions into multiple independent execution units. The 601 and 603 have three execution units, while the 604 and 620 have six. These execution units include integer, floating point, load/store, and the branch processing unit. Multiple integer units are added on later models. Simultaneous instructions can execute in parallel, and complete out of order, while the hardware ensures program correctness. The on-chip branch processing unit does hardware branch prediction, with reversal. Thirty-two 32-bit registers are provided, and two modes of operation (supervisor and user) are implemented.

15.3.1 Hardware

Motorola's version of the 601, the MC98601, includes an internal memory management unit, instruction and data cache, and a pipelined internal floating-point execution unit. The MMU is 256-entry, two-way set associative, and translates 52-bit virtual addresses into 32-bit real addresses. Access privileges are maintained at the block and page level. The on-chip cache is 32 kilobytes in size, and is eight-way set associative. The cache is unified; that is, it holds both instructions and data. Second-generation parts use split caches.

The 601 and 604 use a 32-bit address bus and a separate 64-bit data bus. Multiple processors can be handled on one bus system by means of external arbitration circuitry and bus snooping is used for cache consistency. The cache is designed to use a write-back policy. The MESI coherency model is followed.

The instruction unit contains the instruction queue, and a branch prediction unit. Unconditional branches are folded, and conditional branches result in prefetches from a predicted target instruction stream. The instruction queue of the 601 holds up to eight instructions. The instruction decoding in the PowerPC architecture is hardwired.

The three execution units of the 601 are the integer, floating point, and branch. If the branch processor can resolve a branch early, a zero-cycle branch will result. The branch processing unit has its own adder to compute target addresses, and its own registers. The instruction unit handles memory access as well as integer ALU operations. It includes a hardware multiplier and divider. Instructions issued beyond a predicted branch are not allowed to complete execution until the branch is resolved. Loads and stores can be issued back to back. They are issued in program order, but the memory accesses may occur in a different order. A SYNC instruction is provided to force strict memory-access ordering. The floating-point unit contains a multiply/adder and a divider. This unit is IEEE 754 compliant, and pipelined.

The processor can dynamically order the load/store memory traffic at runtime, to optimize performance. The PowerPC 601 is compatible with the previous IBM POWER architecture. Thus, extensions to the reference PowerPC definition to address specific POWER features from previous architectures are included. However, this is expected to provide only a temporary bridge to existing applications, as subsequent PowerPC designs will follow their own plan.

The 604 and 620 include six execution units, three of which are integer. Of these, two are single cycle, and the third handles multicycle operations such as 32-bit multiply and divide. The single-cycle units handle adds, logical operations, shifts, and rotates. There is also a floating-point unit, the load/store unit, and a branch unit. A branch history table of size 512 entries is maintained and has four levels of dynamic branch prediction. These are strongly taken, taken, not taken, and strongly not taken. There is no penalty for a wrong guess, but there is a benefit for a correct guess. The decode/dispatch unit checks for interinstruction dependencies in the input queue. Thirty-two rename registers are provided to assist in reducing register contention for out-of-order execution. The load/store unit has its own adder for effective address calculations.

Three integer pipelines are included in the 604 model. Two of the pipelines handle simple register-to-register operations, but the third has a three-stage pipeline and does integer multiply and divide units. Four instructions per cycle are fetched into an eight-entry prefetch buffer. After decode, up to four instructions can be dis-

patched. Register renaming is used to minimize contention and to support speculative execution. Twelve rename buffers are provided for the 32 integer registers. The
register file is 12-ported. A 16-deep reorder buffer is used to support speculative execution as well. The 603 and 604 do out-of-order execution, but in-order completion
is guaranteed. The 601 does out-of-order dispatch. Figure 15.2 shows the construction of the 601 pipeline.

Various integrated functions are included in embedded versions of the PowerPC.
No specific DRAM control is provided in the 601 and there is a single-interrupt
line. There is a real-time clock in the 601 chip consisting of two registers, with resolution to one nanosecond, and a range in excess of 136 years. The real-time clock requires a 7.8125 MHz clock source.

An MMU is provided in the PowerPC architecture. The memory/bus interface is
Harvard, with a width of 32 address, 64 data, and 52 control lines on the 601. Be-
tween the cache and the memory is a two-entry read, and a three-entry write queue.
An entry is eight words. Read-before-write is supported, with data coherency main-

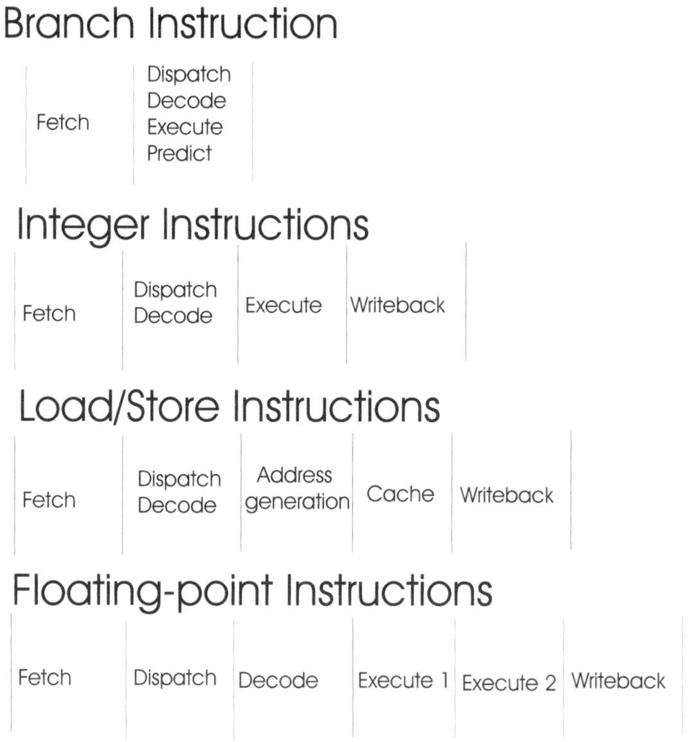

Branch Instruction

| Fetch | Dispatch Decode Execute Predict |

Integer Instructions

| Fetch | Dispatch Decode | Execute | Writeback |

Load/Store Instructions

| Fetch | Dispatch Decode | Address generation | Cache | Writeback |

Floating-point Instructions

| Fetch | Dispatch | Decode | Execute 1 | Execute 2 | Writeback |

Figure 15.2 601 pipeline structure. From Chakravarty and Cannon, Power PC Concepts, Architecture and Design, © 1994. Reproduced by permission of McGraw-Hill, Inc.

tained. There is dynamic optimization and runtime ordering of the load/store memory traffic on the bus. Except for dependencies, reads always precede stores. Secondary cache support is provided.

Initial silicon of the 601 operates at 50 and 66 MHz, at 3.6 volts. Later versions, such as the 603, 604, and 620, use 3.3 volts. The 601 chip was initially fabricated in 0.6-micron technology, and incorporated a level of 2.8 million transistors. Power dissipation of the 601 is approximately 5.6 watts at 50 MHz. The 603 power dissipation is 3 watts at 80 MHz. The 600 dissipates 30 watts at 133 MHz. The 601 is packaged as a 304-pin QFP. The 603 and 603e use a 240-pin CQFP. JTAG support is provided in the 603 and subsequent models. The JTAG interface of the PowerPC is shown in Figure 15.3.

15.3.2 Software and Programmer's View

The PowerPC has two levels of privilege defined: user and supervisor. Some registers are reserved for the supervisor mode access.

The instruction set operates entirely on registers, except for the load/store. Integer math instructions include the four basic math operations on bytes, half-words, and words. Compares are also provided. Floating-point operations support single- and double-precision format, and include the four basic math operations, rounding, conversion, and compare.

Load/store supports integer or floating operands. Addressing modes are register indirect, with the options of immediate index, or indexed. Register-indirect-with-immediate-index mode uses a 16-bit immediate operand from the instruction word.

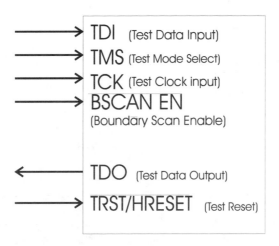

Figure 15.3   JTAG interface of the PowerPC.

Register-indirect-indexed mode involves the contents of two general-purpose registers that are added to form the address of the operand. There are load/store multiple instructions, and move-strings, which can function as a software DMA. These instructions are interruptible. Logic operations include AND, OR, XOR, NAND, NOR, extract and insert (bits), and various rotates and shifts. Flow control includes an unconditional branch and numerous conditional branches. Processor state control instructions allow moving data to and from the special-purpose registers.

Move string instructions are provided in the instruction set. System calls are used to generate exceptions that are used to communicate with the operating system. The 601 can do byte-reversal access with no delay penalty. There is an instruction to enforce in-order execution, by delaying subsequent executes until all previous instructions have completed to the point where no exceptions are possible. The 601 includes certain POWER instructions not implemented in other PowerPC family members.

The PowerPC has 32 general-purpose registers, and thirty-two 64-bit-wide floating-point registers. There is a processor ID register, with a 4-bit tag for use in multiprocessing. The tag is cleared upon reset. There are condition registers, floating point status and control, a machine state register, and sixteen 32-bit segment registers (in the 32-bit implementations; the 64-bit implementations use a segment table). The PowerPC architecture allows implementation-unique special-purpose-registers. The 601 has 3 user-level and 28 supervisor-level special-purpose registers.

There is a conditional code register in the PowerPC, and the 604 implementation has eight condition-code-rename registers. The byte-ordering format is little- or big-endian, with big-endian as the default. The mode is switchable by a bit in a register (in the 601) at reset time. In the PowerPC, two bits are used for the endianess of the separate supervisor and user modes. Data types supported include bytes to 64-bit double words.

Supervisor-level instructions are provided for cache management and for segment and TLB management. User-level cache management instructions are also supported. Access to external I/O devices can be either memory mapped or I/O mapped. Memory-mapped I/O involves issues of noncacheability.

For new instructions that are not included in the POWER architecture, the designers used op codes that were typically illegal in the POWER. A few supervisor level instructions in POWER became user level in PowerPC. Some POWER instructions were dropped in PowerPC. Minor differences in the definition and usage of status bits are also present. Refer to Appendices B and C of reference [1].

PowerPC runs AIX, Apple System-7, Microsoft Windows/NT, and OS-2 Warp. A version of Solaris will also be released, as will Novell Netware. A full range of development tools under these operating systems is available, including compilers for C, C++, Basic, Pascal, ADA and FORTRAN. A command-line option tells the compiler which processor is being used, so the proper optimization can be applied. A PowerPC architectural simulator is also available, as is a version of OS-9 Real Time Operating System. VxWorks from Wind River Systems and LynxOS from Lynx Real Time Systems are also ported to the PowerPC.

15.3.3 Floating Point

The integral floating-point unit of the PowerPC handles IEEE single- and double-precision operations. The unit is pipelined, although an executing instruction may make multiple use of these stages. It includes a single-precision multiply/add unit, a divider, and its own registers. The floating-point unit has its own dual-instruction queues. These buffer instructions from the main instruction issuer, allowing other integer instructions to proceed. The unit supports the IEEE data formats, exception models, and rounding modes. The *floating-point status and control register* is 32 bits wide, and contains flag-bits and enable-bits. The floating-point register set consists of thirty-two 64-bit-wide registers. All floating-point operations occur between floating-point registers. The load and store operations allow for format conversion, and are performed by the integer unit. Operations supported include add, subtract, multiply, divide, multiply-add, multiply-subtract, and compare. Figure 15.4 shows the data and instruction flow in the PowerPC 604 microprocessor.

15.3.4 Cache

Different members of the PowerPC family use different cache schemes. The internal cache of the PowerPC 601 is a 32-kilobyte, unified, eight-way set-associative unit, with a line size of 64 bytes. Write-back policy is used, although the cacheability and write policy can be changed at the page or block level. The cache is physically addressed, and physically tagged. LRU is used for line replacement. Snooping is supported for multiprocessor concurrency. The MESI coherency protocol is used. Because of the on-chip cache, most external bus operations are burst reads followed by burst writes. Secondary cache and multiprocessing support are provided. Dynamic optimization of load/store traffic at runtime is done by the processor.

The cache scheme was changed to split (separate I-cache and D-cache) in the second-generation products. The 602 has dual four kilobyte caches. The 603 has two caches of 8 kilobytes each, which are two-way set-associative and physically addressed. A least-recently-used replacement algorithm is still used. There is an MEI cache policy in the 603, since the chip does not explicitly target multiprocessing. The 603e and 604 models have dual 16 kilobyte, four-way set-associative caches. The 604 has physically indexed cache with a MESI consistency model. Cache write-back or write-through is selectable at the page or block level. Software disabling of the caches is also provided, and the caches can be locked against updates. The 604 includes a controller for a direct-mapped, unified, external secondary cache of up to 128 megabytes. The 620 uses a 32 kilobyte eight-way, set-associative data cache, with selectable write-back or write-through. The MESI protocol is used. The 620 supports the use of an external cache to 128 Mbytes. The external cache is direct mapped, physically indexed and tagged.

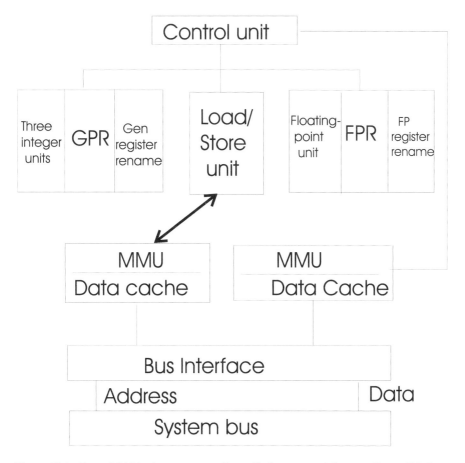

Figure 15.4 PowerPC604 microprocessor. From Chakravarty and Cannon, Power PC Concepts, Architecture and Design, © 1994. Reproduced by permission of McGraw-Hill, Inc.

15.3.5 Memory Management

The MMU of the PowerPC architecture provides support for demand-paged virtual memory. The virtual address space is 2^{52} bytes in extent, mapped to a 2^{32}-bit real address space. The memory bus width is 64 bits in the low-end units, going to 128 bits in the higher-end units. Access control of the virtual space is provided at the block and page levels. An eight-way set-associative tag array is used in the translation. Block size is 128 kbytes to 8 megabytes, selectable in software. Supervisor and user-privilege levels are provided. A segment is a 256-megabyte region of virtual space. There are 16 of these segments defined. A page is the smallest region of virtual space, at four kilobytes. Figure 15.5 shows the address translation process in the memory management unit.

The 601 has a single MMU with three TLBs. There is a 256-entry, two-way set-associative TLB that is unified; a four-entry, fully associative first-level instruction TLB; and a four-entry, block address translation (BAT) array. They use an LRU replacement algorithm. The 604 has two MMUs, as well as dual 128-entry two-way set-associative TLBs for data and instructions. Address translation is provided for four-kilobyte pages, variable-sized blocks, and 256-megabyte segments. There are sixteen 32-bit segment registers in the architecture. The 603e also includes dual MMUs, with 64-entry TLBs. The 620 uses 80-bit virtual, 64-bit real addresses. It makes use of a 128 entry, two-way set associative shared TLB.

15.3.6 Exceptions

Instructions can be issued out of order, but are guaranteed to produce results in program order. Exceptions are particularly tricky on a machine with out-of-order in-

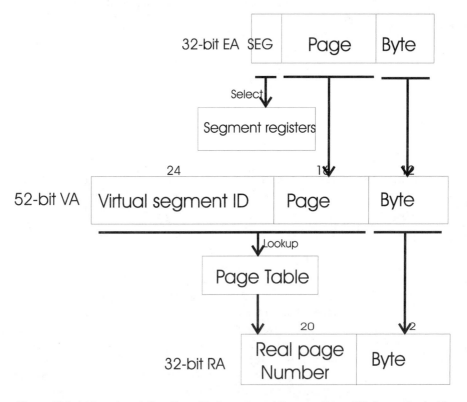

Figure 15.5 Address translation. From Chakravarty and Cannon, Power PC Concepts, Architecture and Design, © 1994. Reproduced by permission of McGraw-Hill, Inc.

struction dispatch. On the PowerPC, exceptions may be recognized out of order, but will be handled in order. Exceptions may be precise or imprecise and synchronous or asynchronous. A synchronous, precise exception will be caused by an instruction. The synchronous-imprecise exceptions include two imprecise floating-point nonrecoverable modes. There are two types of asynchronous exceptions defined: maskable and nonmaskable. The external interrupt and the system management interrupt are maskable. The nonmaskable interrupts include system reset and machine check. Figure 15.6 illustrates the types of exceptions in the PowerPC. Upon recognition of an exception, instructions in the stream are allowed to complete. A vector address table is maintained. Only one exception is handled at a time, and multiple exceptions are handled in order. Two bits in the machine state register define how floating point exceptions are to be handled. The options are ignore, handle precisely, and handle imprecisely. In the 604, there is a performance-monitoring interrupt that can be programmed to occur when a value in one of the performance-monitoring counter registers triggers. There is also an instruction address breakpoint interrupt.

15.4 SUMMARY

RISC Features

Single-cycle execution, or superscalar
Large register set

Types of Interrupts in PowerPCs
- System reset
- Machine check
- Data storage
- Instruction storage
- External
- Alignment
- Program
- Decrementer
- System call
- Trace
- Floating-point assist
  Floating-point unavailable

Figure 15.6 Types of interrupts.

Load/store architecture

Hardwired instruction decoding

Non-RISC Features

Multiple memory addressing modes

15.5 REFERENCES

[1] "PowerPC 601 RISC Microprocessor User's Manual," 1993, Rev. 1, Motorola, MPC601UM/AD.

15.6 BIBLIOGRAPHY

Allen, Michael S., Becker, Michael C., "Multiprocessing Aspects of the PowerPC 601 Microprocessor," 1993, *Proceedings of IEEE COMPCON*, pp. 117–126.

Alvarez, J. et al., "A Wide-Bandwidth Low-Voltage PLL for PowerPC Microprocessors," *Proceedings of 1994 IEEE Symposium on VLSI Circuits*, pp. 37–38.

Anderson, William, "An Overview of Motorola's PowerPC Simulator Family," *Communications of the ACM*, 37 (6): 64(6).

"Apple and IBM Demonstrate 120-MHz 601 (PowerPC 601 chip)," June 20, 1994, *Microprocessor Report*, 8 (8): 4(2).

Becker, Michael C. et al., "The PowerPC 601 Microprocessor," Oct. 1993, *IEEE Micro*, pp. 54–68.

Bertsch, J. et al., "Experimental 2.0 V Power/Performance Optimization of a 3.6 V-design CMOS Microprocessor-PowerPC 601," *Proceedings of 1994 VLSI Technology Symposium*, pp. 83–84.

Biedny, David, "PowerPC: The Era of RISC Begins," *Windows Sources*, 2 (6): 140(7).

Bortman, Henry, "PowerPC: Where No Mac Has Gone Before," Sept. 1, 1992, *MacUser*, 8 (9): 142.

Burgess, Brad et al., "The PowerPC 603 Microprocessor: A High Performance, Low Power, Superscalar RISC Microprocessor," *Proceedings of COMPCON 1994*, pp. 300–306.

Burgess, Brad et al., "The PowerPC 603 Microprocessor," June 1994, *Communications of the ACM*, 37 (6): 34.

Bursky, Dave, "RISC Microcontrollers Start with PowerPC Roots but Grow in Different Directions: IBM's PowerPC 403GA Embedded Processor and Motorola's RMCU505 Microcontroller," 1994, *Electronic Design*, 42 (10): 38(2).

Chakravarty, Dipto, Cannon, Casey, *PowerPC Concepts, Architecture, and Design.* New York: McGraw-Hill, 1994. ISBN 0-07-011192-8.

Dawson, B., "PowerPC Hits the Road," *BYTE*, 19 (7): 141–142.

Denman, Marvin, "PowerPC 604 RISC Microprocessor," 1994, *Hot Chips IV Conference Notes*, Stanford University, Palo Alto, CA.

Diefendorff, Keith, "History of the PowerPC Architecture," June 1994, *Communications of the ACM*, 37 (6): 28(6).

Duntemann, Jeff, Pronk, Ron, *Inside the PowerPC Revolution*. Scottsdale, AZ: Coriolis Group Books; April 30, 1994. ISBN 1-883577-04-7.

Evolution of PowerPC Architecture (Video), IEEE, 1992, ISBN: HS05553 pin.

"Floating-Point Bottleneck: Comparing Performance of Motorola PowerPC and Intel CPUs," 1994, editorial, *MacWEEK*, 8 (21): 44(1).

Foley, Mary Jo, "IBM to Push OS/2 for PowerPC Over Windows NT, AIX Ports," 1994, *PC Week*, 11 (24): 23(1).

Ford, Ric, "Hacking PPC Enabler Plus Other Updates," July 4, 1994, *MacWEEK*, 8 (27): 28(1).

Gwennap, Linley, "Prep Standardizes PowerPC Systems," Dec. 27, 1993, *Microprocessor Report*.

Heath, Steve, *NEWNES PowerPC Programming Pocket Book*. Newton, MA: Butterworth-Heinemann, Nov. 1994. ISBN 0-7506-2111-7.

Hoskins, Jim, *The PowerPC Revolution MaxFacts Special Report*. Gulfbreeze, FL: Maximum Press, Aug. 1994. ISBN 0-9633214-9-8.

Houts, Ean, "Lower Priced Power Macs Offer Different Strengths," May 2, 1994, *InfoWorld*, 16 (18): 128(1).

Huang, Wayne et al., "CBGA Package Design for C4 PowerPC Microprocessor Chips: Trade-off Between Substrate Routability and Performance," *Proceedings of the 1994 IEEE 44th Electronic Components & Technology Conference*, pp. 88–93.

"IBM Announces New Embedded Part," April 21, 1995, *PowerPC News*.

"IBM Chip to Serve as Pentium Upgrade; PowerPC Chip Fits in OverDrive Slot," July 4, 1994, *Infoworld*, 16 (27): 1.

"IBM Confirms Work on PowerPC 630 Chip," June 6, 1994, *PC Week*, 11 (22): 14.

"IBM Could Pre-empt Intel-HP; PowerPC 615 Chip Ahead of Joint Effort in X86 Compatibility," June 20, 1994, *PC Week*, 11 (24): 10.

"IBM PowerPC 615 to Run X86 Apps; On-Chip Interpreter Is Expected to Wring Pentium-Level Performance From Software," Feb. 14, 1994, *PC Week*, 11 (6): 1.

"IBM, PowerPC Architecture," Oct. 1993, IBM book number SR28-5124-00.

"IBM Unveils 64-bit PowerPC Variant," June 19, 1995, *PowerPC News*.

Kass, E. M., "PowerPC Surprise," *InformationWEEK*, (474): 12–14.

Lawrence, Andrew, "PowerPC—A New Desktop Standard?" May 1994, *IBM System User*, 15 (5): 43(2).

Marris, J., "PowerPC—An Analysis," 1994, *Desktop Publishing Commentary*, 9 (9): 6–9.

May, Cathy et al. (eds.), *PowerPC Architecture, Specification for a New Family of RISC Processors*. San Francisco, CA: Morgan Kaufmann, 1994. ISBN 1558603166.

"Microsoft, Apple Make Nice. But the prospect of Windows NT on the PowerPC Could Divide Them," July 20, 1992, *Informationweek*, 383, p. 14.

Moore, Charles R. et al., "The PowerPC Alliance," June 1994, *Communications of the ACM*, 37 (6): 25(3).

Moore, Charles R., "The PowerPC 601 Microprocessor," *Proceedings of IEEE COMPCON*, 1993, pp. 109–116.

Nass, Richard, "VME Boards Combine PCI Bus and PowerPC CPUs," July 11, 1994, *Electronic Design*, 42 (14): 129(3).

Paap, George, "PowerPC(™): A Performance Architecture," *Proceedings of IEEE COMPCON*, Spring, 1993, pp. 104–108.

"Parsytec Produces TRAM Module that Combines PowerPC with T425 Transputer for Industrial Applications," June 20, 1994, *Computergram International*.

Poursepanj, Ali, "The PowerPC: Performance Modeling Methodology," June 1994, *Communications of the ACM*, 37 (6): 47(9).

"PowerPC 601 RISC Microprocessor Hardware Specifications," 1993, Motorola, MPC601EC/D.

"PowerPC 603 Technical Summary," Motorola, 1994, MPC603/D.

"PowerPC 603 User's Manual," 1994, Motorola, MPC603UM/AD.

"PowerPC 604 First Silicon," May 1994, *RS/Magazine*, p. 10.

"PowerPC 604 RISC Microprocessor Technical Summary," 1994, Motorola, MPC604/D.

"PowerPC 604 Technical Summary," 1994, Motorola, MPC604/D.

"PowerPC 604 Weighs In," June 1994, *BYTE*, 19 (6): 265.

"PowerPC Architecture," IBM, 1994, 52G7487.

"PowerPC Goes After X86 PCs and Embedded Systems," June 1994, *Computer Design*, 33, p. 32.

"PowerPC Microprocessor Family: the Programming Environments," 1994, Motorola, MPC FPE/AD.

"PowerPC Special Issue," Oct. 1994, *IEEE Micro 14(5)*.

"PowerPC: The New Generation of Computing," Dec. 1993, *Datapro Reports.*

"PowerPC Tools, Development Tools for PowerPC Processor," 3rd ed., Nov. 1994, IBM/Motorola.

"PowerPC Will Manage Ford Engines," Nov. 1, 1993, *Design News*, p. 43.

"PowerPC: Your Next CPU?" Feb. 22, 1994, *PC Magazine*, 13 (4): 181.

"PPC '615' Intel Emulation Hit by Slow Mode-Switch," Sept. 23, 1994, *PowerPC News*.

Rahmel, Ron and Rahael, Dan, "Interfacing to the PowerPC Microprocessor," 1995, Indianapolis: Sans Publishing. ISBN 0672365488.

Rose, Chris, "Abstracting the Meat of the PowerPC Reference Platform Beta Version—Part One," May 27, 1994, *Computergram International*.

Rose, Chris, "Abstracting the Meat of the PowerPC Reference Platform Beta Version—Part Two," June 6, 1994, *Computergram International*.

Ryan, Bob, and Thompson, Tom, "PowerPC 604 Weighs In," June 1994, *BYTE*, 19 (6), pp. 265–266.

Seltzer, Larry J., "OS/2 for PowerPC: Microkernel for the Masses?" June 6, 1994, *PC Week*, 11 (22): 81(2).

Shipnes, Julie et al., "A Modular Approach to Motorola PowerPC Compilers," June 1994, *Communications of the ACM*, 37 (6): 56(8).

Silha, E. et al., "PowerPC: A Performance Architecture," *Proceedings of IEEE COMPCON*, 1993, pp. 104–108.

Slater, Michael, "Motorola and IBM Unveil PowerPC 603," Oct. 25, 1993, *Microprocessor Report,* 7.

Smith, J. E. et al., "PowerPC 601 and Alpha 21064: A Tale of Two RISCs," *Computer*, 27 (6): 46–58.

"Software-based Emulation 604e for Windows on Tap," June 26, 1995, *Infoworld*.

Suessmith, Brad W. et al., "PowerPC 603 Microprocessor: Power Management," June 1994, *Communications of the ACM*, 37 (6): 43(4).

Sydow, Dan, *Programming the PowerPC*. San Mateo, CA: M&T Books, Aug. 1994. ISBN 1-55851-400-7.

"Technical Summary PowerPC 601 RISC Microprocessor," April 1993, Motorola.

"The Making of the PowerPC," June 1994, special issue, *CACM,* 37(6).

Ullah, Nasr et al., "The Making of the PowerPC," June 1994, *Communications of the ACM*, 37 (6): 22(2).

"Understanding RISC Processors," 1993, *Microprocessor Report*, Chapter 9, Ziff-Davis. ISBN 1-56276-159-5.

Vizard, Michael, "The Tower of PowerPC: Untapped Potential in Search of a Killer Application," 1994, *PC Week*, 11 (24): 22(2).

Weiss, Shlomo, Smith, James E., *IBM Power and PowerPC: Architecture and Implementation*. San Francisco, CA: Morgan Kaufmann, May 1994. ISBN 1-55860-279-8.

"'What 615?' Hester Lays Out IBM's Emulation Options," March 10, 1995, *PowerPC News*.

"Windows NT to Run on IBM's PowerPC," May 3, 1993, *Electronic Engineering Times*, issue 744.

Young, Jerry, "Insider's Guide to PowerPC Computing," 1994. Indianapolis, IN: Que. ISBN 1-56529-625-7.

16

V800

16.1 INTRODUCTION

The V800 architecture by NEC was introduced in 1992 and began shipping in 1993. It has features of both RISC and non-RISC designs. The V800 family is targeted at the handheld consumer electronics market, meaning PDAs and games, and the embedded-control arena. This market is power- and cost sensitive. The V800 can be found in Nintendo's CD-ROM player. NEC plans a 100 mips version.

16.2 BACKGROUND

NEC manufactures the MIPS R3000 and 4200 RISC chips. Its V-series processors were originally designed to substitute for the Intel 80x86 family of chips. The V20 was essentially an 8-bit 8085 and a 16-bit 8088 in one package, switchable under software control. The 800 series does not attempt to be instruction-set compatible with previous chips. Models currently available include the 805, 810, and 820. The 805 uses a 16-bit external data bus, with a 32-bit bus internally. The 810 and 820 have 32-bit-wide external buses. The 820 includes dynamic memory control; a 16-bit timer with three compare registers; a four-channel; 32-bit-wide DMA control; a phase-locked loop; and dual synchronous/asynchronous serial I/O channels integrated on-chip. Current offerings run at 25 MHz. Figure 16.1 shows the architecture of the V800.

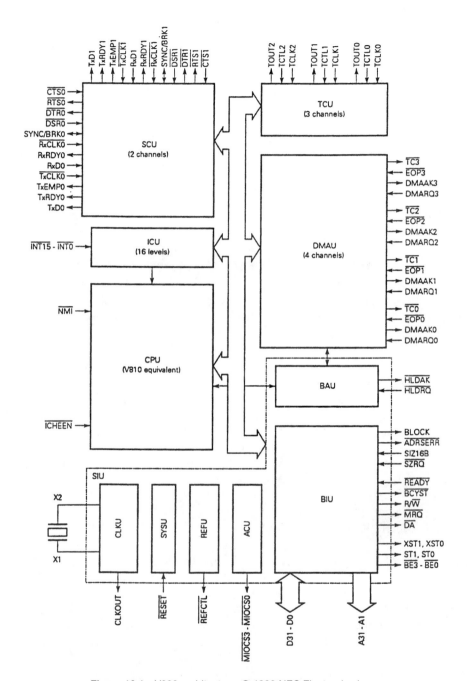

Figure 16.1 V800 architecture. © 1993 NEC Electronics Inc.

16.3 ARCHITECTURE

The V800 series is a 16-bit architecture, which is load/store, and register oriented. Most instructions execute in one cycle. A fully static design allows the clock to be stopped in the 810 without corrupting internal state. In the 32-bit versions, dynamic bus sizing allows the use of 16- or 32-bit-wide transfers.

16.3.1 Hardware

A pipeline approach to instructions is used. A register file of thirty-two 32-bit general-purpose registers is included, although register zero is defined as zero. Some of the registers have special uses with specific instructions: R31 is the link pointer, R2 is the interrupt stack pointer, and R3 is the program stack pointer. R4 and R5 as well as R26 through R30 have special uses. A hardware processor ID register holds a unique code for each family member. There is a processor status register, and two register pairs for state. The "task control word" holds the floating-point exception status information. A hardware breakpoint is included in the ADTRE register.

Five-volt operation is the standard, but transition to a lower-voltage model is provided by the 810, which operates at 3.3 and 2.2 volts. Power dissipation is 750 mW. The 805 is available in a 100-pin QFP. The 810 uses a 120-pin QFP or a 176-pin PGA. The 820 comes in a 208-pin PQFP or 280-pin PGA, and is manufactured in a 0.8-micron CMOS, with three metal layers.

16.3.2 Software

The V800 has two different instruction lengths, 16 bits or 32 bits. Most instructions are encoded as 16 bits, which provides a good code density. The instruction formats were designed to be regular, consistent, and thus easy to decode. Eighty-nine total instructions are included, of which 59 are 16-bit types, and 30 are 32-bit types. There are no triadic register instructions. Addressing format is little-endian.

The logical instructions AND, OR, XOR, and NOT are included. Integer add, subtract, multiply, and divide are provided. A set of I/O instructions is provided, accessing a separate address space with different bus cycles. Conditional and unconditional branches are included. Bit-string instructions can specify these structures anywhere in memory, and can specify strings to four gigabits in length. The capability to search for the first "one" or first "zero" in a string is provided. Bit-string instructions are very RISC-pathological, causing pipeline problems and requiring microcode. An uninterruptible multiprocessor synchronization instruction, called CAXI, is also provided.

The V800 has run TRON, the Industrial Real Time Operational Network, which is favored by the Japanese.

16.3.3 Floating Point

Floating-point support is included, although no separate floating-point registers are included. Only single precision is supported, for the basic operations add, subtract, multiply, and divide. Compare and convert are provided.

16.3.4 Cache

On-chip instruction cache is included. Some or all of the cache can be dumped or restored to and from memory under explicit program control. Interrupts are held during these operations. The 800 series implements one kilobyte of on-chip cache.

16.3.5 Memory Management

The V800 family does not provide for an MMU, which is a design tradeoff based on the desire to reduce power consumption. Besides address mapping, an MMU can provide protection and isolation. Up to four different independent address spaces can be defined in the 820's access control unit.

16.3.6 Exceptions

Sixteen levels of maskable interrupt and a nonmaskable interrupt are accommodated.

16.4 SUMMARY

RISC Features

Pipelined execution
One-cycle instructions
Large register file
One addressing mode (register + displacement) for loads/stores

Non-RISC features

Bit string instructions
No triadic address operations
Mixed instruction lengths

16.5 BIBLIOGRAPHY

"NEC Joins Embedded Processor Plethora: High-End V800 Architecture Takes Yet Another RISC-like Approach," Oct. 25, 1993, *Microprocessor Report*, 7 (14): 25.

"Three in Mini-RISC Race," Feb. 7, 1994, *Electronic Engineering Times*, (783) p. 10.

"V805 Preliminary Data Sheet," Nov. 1993, NEC.

"V810 Preliminary Data Sheet," Nov. 1993, NEC.

"V820 Preliminary Data Sheet," Nov. 1993, NEC.

17

SH7000

17.1 INTRODUCTION

The SH7000 RISC chip family from Hitachi features an integrated CPU and peripheral functions in one chip. The SH7000 architecture by Hitachi is being used in the SEGA Genesis 32X game system. The SH7000 models 7032 and 7034 are targeted to embedded control and PDA markets, which are power- and cost sensitive. More members of the family are due soon, with enhanced features such as on-chip cache, hardware multiply, faster clock rate, and new instructions. Third-generation parts are expected to include an MMU, and fourth-generation parts are expected to be superscalar, according to Hitachi's architecture road map. Both on-chip ROM and ROMless versions are offered.

17.2 BACKGROUND

Hitachi, a $71 billion company, manufactures everything from computer chips to mainframes. Their 63xx series of embedded controllers paralleled and expanded the 8-bit Motorola 68xx line. On the high end, Hitachi manufactures IBM plug-compatible mainframes, and is expanding into massively parallel machines using HP's PA RISC architecture. Several other projects are also ongoing at Hitachi, one of which involves large numbers of the PowerPC chip, linked on the PCI bus. Hitachi also makes the H8 series, a RISC-influenced 32-bit microcontroller. The SH series will initially appear in four groups. The SH1 includes models 7020, 21, 32 and 34. The SH2 is represented by the model 7604, and the SH3 by the models 7702 and 7708.

TABLE 17.1 SH Series. Courtesy of Hitachi, Ltd.

SH1 Series	SH7032	SH7034	SH7020	SH7021	SH2:SH7604
CPU SH7000CPU	32-bit RISC SH7000CPU	32-bit RISC SH7000CPU	32-bit RISC SH7000CPU	32-bit RISC	32-bit RISC SH7000CPU
DSP functions	Multiply: $16 \times 16 \rightarrow 32$ MAC* $16 \times 16 + 42 \rightarrow 42$	Multiply: $16 \times 16 \rightarrow 32$ MAC* $16 \times 16 + 42 \rightarrow 42$	Multiply: $16 \times 16 \rightarrow 32$ MAC* $16 \times 16 + 42 \rightarrow 42$	Multiply: $16 \times 16 \rightarrow 32$ MAC* $16 \times 16 + 42 \rightarrow 42$	Multiply: $16 \times 16 \rightarrow 32$ MAC* $32 \times 32 + 64 \rightarrow 64$
Interrupts	9 external, 31 internal	9 external, 31 internal	9 external, 30 internal	9 external, 30 internal	5 external, 11 internal
On-chip Memory	ROM: none RAM: 8 kbytes	ROM: 64 kbytes (ZTAT/mask) RAM: 4 kbytes	ROM: 16 kbytes (mask) RAM: 1 kbyte	ROM: 32 kbytes (mask) RAM: 1 kbyte	Cache: 4 kbytes 4 way set associative LRU replace algorithm
Bus state controller	Direct interface to SRAM or DRAM	Direct interface to SRAM or DRAM	Direct interface to SRAM or DRAM	Direct interface to SRAM or DRAM	Direct interface to SRAM, DRAM or SDRAM
DMAC	4 ch	4 ch	4 ch	4 ch	2 ch
Timers	5 ch	5 ch	5 ch	5 ch	1 ch
Watchdog timer	yes	yes	yes	yes	yes
SCI	2 ch	2 ch	2 ch	2 ch	none
A/D converter	10-bit, 8 ch	10-bit, 8 ch	none	none	none
I/O ports	I/O: 40 (input: 8)	I/O: 40 (input: 8)	I/O: 32	I/O: 32	none
Operating voltage/ frequency	5.0 V/20 MHz 3.3 V/12.5 MHz	5.0 V/20 MHz 3.3 V/12.5 MHz	5.0 V/20 MHz 3.3 V/12.5 MHz	5.0 V/20 MHz 3.3 V/12.5 MHz	5.0 V/28.7 MHz 3.3 V/16.6 MHz
Other functions	User break controller	User break controller	User break controller	User break controller	Divider $64 + 32 \rightarrow 32 \ldots 32$ $32 + 32 \rightarrow 32 \ldots 32$ User break controller
Packages	QFP112/TQFP120	QFP112/TQFP120	TQFP100	TQFP100	QFP144

*Multiply and accumulate

The SH4 models to appear later will be superscalar. These chips are targeted to the video-game market, with applications in personal digital assistants (PDAs) as well. Table 17.1 shows the characteristics of the various SH models.

17.3 ARCHITECTURE

The Hitachi SH7000 series uses a 16-bit instruction length and most instructions execute in a single cycle. Short, fixed-length instructions serve to increase code density, a key component of system cost. A 16-bit instruction length limits the number of variations allowed for register specification and for branch offsets, as well as immediate fields. Sixteen general-purpose registers are provided, in additional to seven CPU registers. These are the three 32-bit control registers, and four 32-bit system registers. R0 is not defined as zero as in most architectures, and is available as a general register. It does have some special uses in conjunction with the MOV instruction, for longword offsets. R15 is the stack pointer to the exception frame in main memory. The seven CPU registers include the status register, the global base register, the vector base register (for exception handler vectors), a PR register for return addresses from subroutine calls, and two registers for the multiply-accumulate instruction (MACL and MACH). A block diagram of the SH series is shown in Figure 17.1.

17.3.1 Hardware

Instruction execution on the SH7000 is pipelined, and the internal data path is 32 bits wide. An on-chip multiplier is used for fast 16×16 multiply in one to three cycles, and for the multiply/accumulate. The SH3 series features a five-stage instruction pipeline, delayed branches, and introduces power management features. The SH-1 and SH-2 have a watchdog timer feature. The 5 channel, 16 bit integrated timer unit can be used to generate and output waveforms, as a pulse-width modulated (PWM) source, or to capture input waveforms. The units have 32 I/O lines.

A sleep mode is provided for low power consumption during periods of planned nonactivity. The memory access logical operations present special problems to the pipeline. In a tradeoff, conditional branches are nondelayed but unconditional branches are delayed. Branches are not allowed in the delay slot of another branch. Also, interrupts are suspended between a delayed branch and its inserted instruction. The four-channel DMA controller can operate in cycle-steal or burst mode, with selectable channel priority. The packaging of the various units is shown in Table 17.1.

17.3.2 Software

Although the SH7000 is a load/store architecture, there are no explicit load and store instructions, variations of the MOV being used instead. Byte versions of AND,

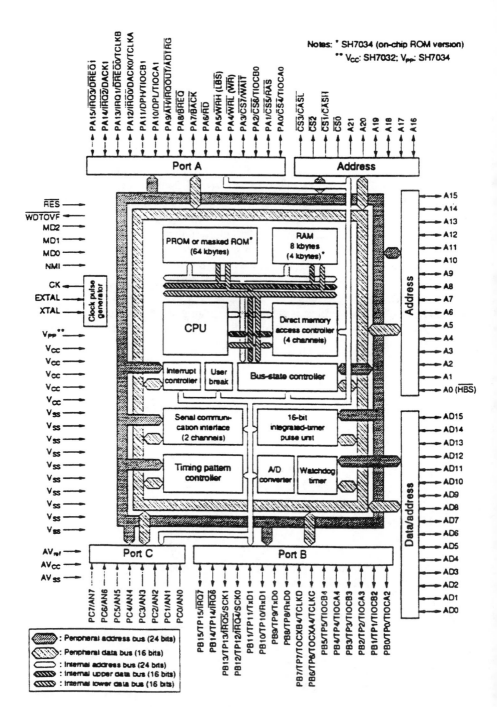

Figure 17.1 SH7000 architecture. Courtesy of Hitachi, Ltd.

258

OR, and XOR use a read-modify-write memory format. Five different memory addressing modes are provided, including preincrement and postdisplacement. Most operate on byte, word, and longword sizes.

Ten shift and four rotate instructions are provided, but the general case of shift by a variable number of places is not supported, probably due to the lack of a barrel shifter.

Multiply is implemented by 16×16 multiplier hardware, and division primitives allow a divide in less than 72 clocks, although the remainder is not saved. A multiply/accumulate instruction reads two of three operands from memory. The special registers can be loaded from and stored to main memory. A conditional code bit (the "T" bit in the PSR) is set by explicit compare instructions and used as the basis of conditional branches.

No supervisor mode is provided. A delayed unconditional branch provides minimal pipeline disruption.

Development tools include compilers for GNU-C and C++, the CMX-RTX real-time multitasking operating system, ICE units, Green Hills C and C++, FORTRAN, Pascal, and Ada. Tools are hosted on PC, Unix, and Vax platforms. A fuzzy-logic development system is also available. C-executive and VxWorks real-time operating systems are also available for the SH.

17.3.3 Floating Point

No hardware floating-point support is currently provided.

17.3.4 Cache

The early series of chips (703x) have 8 kilobytes of on-chip memory, which is not configured as a cache. The SH3 has 8 kilobytes of four-way set-associative write-back cache.

17.3.5 Memory Management

The initial 703x series chips do not include an MMU function. DRAM support and bus sizing are supported. DRAM burst access is supported. The SH3 has a 128-entry MMU, and supports selectable big- and little-endian data accesses. A one stage write-buffer is included.

17.3.6 Exceptions

The SH7000 provides for nine external interrupts, including an NMI. There are 31 possible internal interrupt sources, and 16 programmable priority levels. Debugging is supported by a programmable interrupt upon match of specified bus cycle conditions. The SH3 has four external interrupts, plus NMI.

17.4 SUMMARY

RISC Features

Pipelined execution
Fixed-length instructions
Load/store architecture
Register file (16)

Non-RISC Features

Memory stack frame on exceptions
Registers not really general
Read-modify-write memory operations
Multiple memory addressing modes

17.5 BIBLIOGRAPHY

"32-bit RISC Minimizes Power, Size," March 1995, *Computer Design*, p. 114.

"8/32-bit Microcontroller Combines RISC and Traditional Design," March 17, 1994, *EDN*, p. 86.

"E7000 SH7032, SH7034 Emulator User's Manual," Sept. 1993, Hitachi.

"Hitachi Outlines Roadmap for SH7000," Oct. 25, 1993, *Microprocessor Report*, 7 (14): 16.

Kawasaki, S., "SH2: A Low Power RISC Microprocessor for Consumer Applications," 1994, *Hot Chips IV Symposium*, Stanford University, Palo Alto, CA.

"SH7000 Architecture Bends RISC Rules," Aug. 23, 1993, *Microprocessor Report*, 7 (11): 14.

"SH7000 Series Overview," 1993, Hitachi, Rev. 1.0.

"SH7020/SH7021 SH-1 (SH7000) Embedded 32-bit RISC Controller," Dec. 16, 1994, Hitachi product brief.

"SH7032/SH7034 SH-1 (SH7000) Embedded 32-bit RISC Controller," Dec. 9, 1994, Hitachi product brief.

"SH7604 SH-2 (SH7600) Embedded 32-bit RISC Controller," Dec. 16, 1994, Hitachi product brief.

"Three in Mini-RISC Race," Feb. 7, 1994, *Electronic Engineering Times*, p. 10.

Wilson, Ron, Lammers, David, "Hitachi Spins 'Cool RISC'," March 6, 1995, *EE Times*, p. 61.

18

MICROCHIP PIC—
A MINIMALIST APPROACH

18.1 INTRODUCTION

The Microchip PIC series is certainly different from what is commonly thought of as RISC, but it does fit most of the definitions. Where others have concentrated on the 32- and 64-bit workstation and high-end embedded control markets, Microchip Technology, Inc. presents a family of low-cost CMOS 8-bit RISC controllers. Different family members include features to address specific application areas, and there is commonality across the various flavors of PIC.

18.2 BACKGROUND

Microchip Technology, Inc. is a specialty chip manufacturer with multiple fabrication and R&D facilities in Arizona. The company addresses the embedded microcontroller market with processor, memory, and support chips. The PIC line is an attempt to present single-chip solutions for small, well-defined, cost-sensitive control tasks. The company claims to ship over one million units a week.

18.3 ARCHITECTURE

The PIC family (see Table 18.1) includes devices with onboard ROM, EPROM, or EEPROM program memory. One-time programmable devices are also available. The 16C5X series are classic microcontrollers, with data and instruction memory.

TABLE 18.1 PIC Family Members

	Clock Maximum Frequency of Operation	Program Memory (words) EPROM	ROM	EEPROM	RAM Data Memory (bytes)	EEPROM Data Memory (bytes)	Timer Modules	Capture Compare/ PWM Module
High-End								
PIC17C42	25	2K	—	—	232	—	4 + WDT[1]	2[5]
Mid-Range								
PIC16C61	20	1K	—	—	36	—	1 + WDT	—
PIC16C64	20	4K	—	—	128	—	3 + WDT	1
PIC16C5[6]	20	4K	—	—	192	—		
PIC16C71	20	1K	—	—	36	—	1 + WDT	—
PIC16C73[6]	20	4K	—	—	192	—		
PIC16C74	20	4K	—	—	192	—	3 + WDT	2
PIC16C84	10	—	—	1K	36	64	1 + WDT	—
Base-Line								
PIC16C54	20	512	—	—	35	—	1 + WDT	—
PIC16C54A	20	512	—	—	25	—	1 + WDT	—
PIC16CR54	20	—	512	—	25	—	1 + WDT	—
PIC16C55	20	512	—	—	25	—	1 + WDT	—
PIC16C56	20	1K	—	—	25	—	1 + WDT	—
PIC16C57	20	2K	—	—	72	—	1 + WDT	—
PIC16CR57A	20	—	2K	—	72	—	1 + WDT	—
PIC16C58A	20	2K	—	—	72	—	1 + WDT	—

(1) PIC17C42 can concatenate Timer1 and Timer2 to form a 16-bit Timer. Timer 0 is a 16-bit prescaler.
(2) All PIC16/17 Family devices have Power-on Reset, fuse selectable Watchdog Timer and fuse selectable code protect. (3) All PIC16/17 devices offer 20-25mA source/sink current per pin. (4) SCI (US-

TABLE 18.1 *(continued)*

Peripherals			Features[2]					
Serial Port(s) (SPI/I²C, SCI)	Parallel Slave Port	Analog to Digital Converter (8-bit)	External Interrupts	Interrupt Sources	I/O[3]	Voltage Range (Volts)	Number of Instructions	Packages
SCI[4]	—	—	Yes	11	33	4.5–5.5	55	40-pin DIP 44-pin PLCC, QFP
—	—	—	Yes	3	13	3.0–6.0	35	18-pin DIP, 18-pin SOIC
SPI/I²C	Yes	—	Yes	8	33	2.5–6.0	35	40-pin DIP 44-pin PLCC, QFP
In Development								40-pin DIP 44-pin PLCC, QFP
—	—	4 ch	Yes	4	13	3.0–6.0	35	18-pin DIP, 18-pin SOIC
In Development								28-pin DIP, 28-pin SOIC
SPI/I²C, SCI[4]	Yes	8 ch	Yes	12	33	3.0–6.0	35	40-pin DIP 44-pin PLCC, QFP
—	—	—	Yes	4	13	2.0–6.0	35	18-pin DIP, 18-pin SOIC
—	—	—	—	—	12	2.5–6.25	33	18-pin DIP, 18-pin SOIC, 20-pin SSOP
—	—	—	—	—	12	2.5–6.25	33	18-pin DIP, 18-pin SOIC, 20-pin SSOP
—	—	—	—	—	12	2.5–6.25	33	18-pin DIP, 18-pin SOIC, 20-pin SSOP
—	—	—	—	—	20	2.5–6.25	33	28-pin DIP, 28-pin SOIC, 28-pin SSOP
—	—	—	—	—	12	2.5–6.25	33	18-pin DIP, 18-pin SOIC, 20-pin SSOP
—	—	—	—	—	20	2.5–6.25	33	28-pin DIP, 28-pin SOIC, 28-pin SSOP
—	—	—	—	—	20	2.5–6.25	33	28-pin DIP, 28-pin SOIC, 22-pin SSOP
—	—	—	—	—	12	2.5–6.25	33	18-pin DIP, 18-pin SOIC

ART) includes dedicated Baud Rate Generator. (5) The PIC17C42 has two 16-bit Capture Inputs and two high-speed PWM outputs. (6) In development. Please contact your local Microchip Sales Office for more information.

The 16C71 adds an integral A/D. The 17C42 model adds dual channel pulse width modulation (PWM) for motor control, and a USART function.

18.3.1 Hardware

The PIC 16C71 is an 8-bit CMOS part with EPROM and four analog inputs to an integral A/D converter. The device has only 35 instructions, and all are single cycle except for the branch, which is two cycles. It is a fully static CMOS part with a Harvard architecture, using 12-bit-wide instructions, and 8-bit data. Instructions may be stored in a 1024 location EPROM memory on-chip. There are 35 general-purpose registers in a register file configuration. Three addressing modes are included: direct, indirect, and relative. As a controller, the device has 13 digital I/O pins and a clock/counter. The analog/digital converter features four analog inputs multiplexed to one 8-bit converter. The device has on-chip power-on-reset, a watchdog timer, and four interrupt sources. An instruction can be used to put the device into a very low power sleep mode, from which it can be awakened by interrupt or a defined state change on an I/O pin. This is a small, low-pin-count device (18-pin package) for specialized applications. Figure 18.1 shows the architecture of the PIC 16C5x models. Figure 18.2 illustrates the architecture of the PIC 16C71 model. Figure 18.3 shows a block diagram of the 17C42 model.

Instruction execution in the PIC device is pipelined and takes two steps. Fetch takes one step, and decode/execute another. Instructions are 12 bits in width (for the 16C5X; 14 for the 16C71; 16 for the 17C42), and on-chip memory ranges from 512 to 4096 words of EPROM, or to 2048 words of ROM in the mask programmed version. Data memory, 8 bits wide in all units, ranges from 32 to 232 locations, organized as registers. There are 454 general purpose RAM locations on the PIC 17C44. Figure 18.4 shows the data memory layout of the 16C5x models.

All instructions are single word, and all execute in a single cycle except for branches, which take two cycles. The instruction set is orthogonal, meaning that each instruction can operate on any register and use any addressing mode. Special cases are avoided. No floating-point hardware is included. Math accumulator hardware is available on the PIC 17C44.

The PIC processors incorporate numerous integrated functions that differ by processor type. At least one watchdog timer is included, which forces a reset unless reset periodically in software. The timer cannot be disabled from software. The 17C42 version of the family does not have the A/D features, but includes three 16-bit counter/timers, two pulse-width-modulated outputs for motor control applications, and a serial port. Microchip can pick and choose a large number of options to include along with the base architecture of the PIC.

No support for DRAM in the PIC is included. Most devices can operate solely from internal memory. External SRAM is easily interfaced to the 17C42 to expand the program memory to 64kx16. DMA to the internal memory is not supported. MMU support is not needed, due to the small address space.

No interrupts are supported on the 16C5x models, but polled I/O can be used to examine external events. On the 16C6x, 7x, and 8x models, there are external inter-

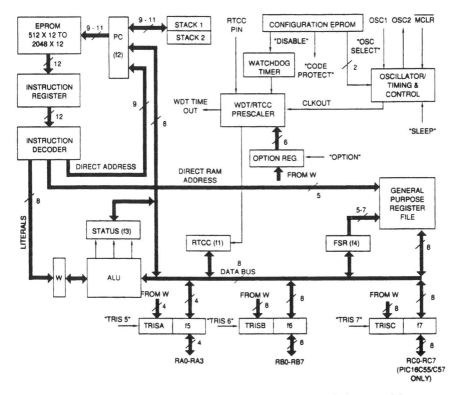

Figure 18.1 16C5x architecture. (Reprinted with permission of the copyright owner, Microchip Technology Inc. 1995.)

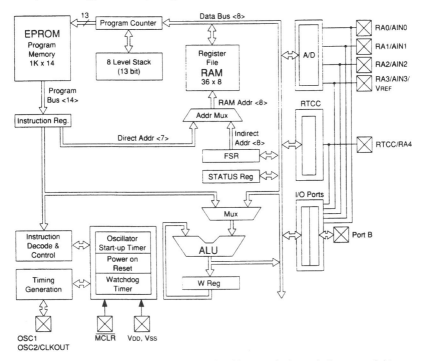

Figure 18.2 16C71 architecture. (Reprinted with permission of the copyright owner, Microchip Technology Inc. 1995.)

266

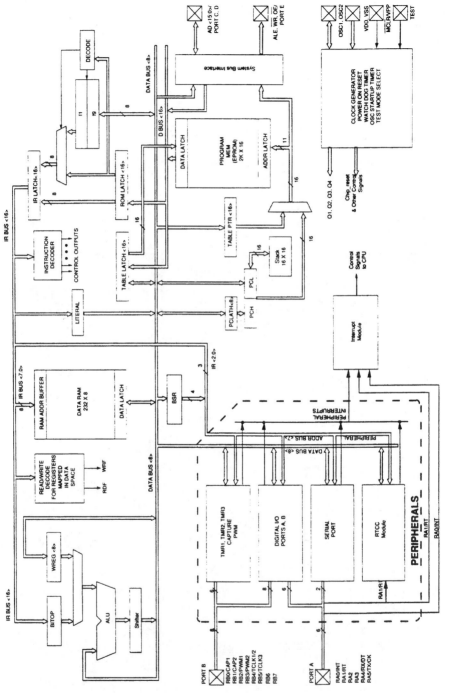

Figure 18.3 17C42 architecture. (Reprinted with permission of the copyright owner, Microchip Technology Inc. 1995.) All rights reserved.

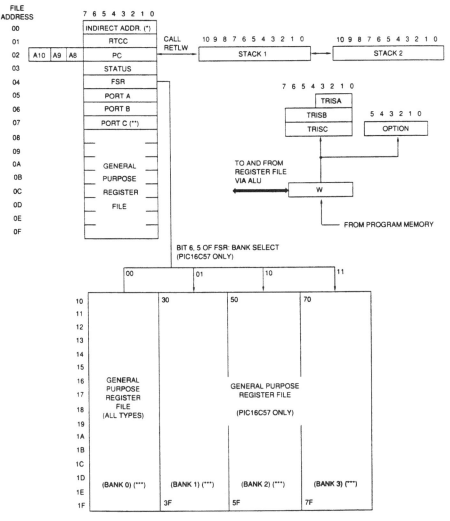

Figure 18.4 Data memory map. (Reprinted with permission of the copyright owner, Microchip Technology Inc. 1995.) All rights reserved.

rupt pins, and interrupts can also be generated by the real-time clock overflow, end-of-conversion by the A/D converter, and a change in state on one of four input pins. The 17C42 supports 11 interrupts with four vectors. Interrupt sources are external pins, real-time clock overflow, one of the counter/timers, serial port transmit or receive, and change on input port pins.

An 8-bit real-time clock/counter with an 8-bit programmable prescaler is available on the 16C5X family. A watchdog timer with its own clock is also provided. The watchdog can be set to provide a wakeup from sleep mode or a reset.

Each member of the PIC family has unique features to support specific applications. Some of these are summarized here:

A/D—16C71 has a multiplexed, four input, 8-bit A/D. 16C74 has 8 inputs.
PWM—17C42 has a dual-channel PWM register, as does 16C74.
USART—17C42 has a USART function.

The pulse width modulator in the 17C42, useful in digital motor control, is a two-channel unit that can operate with 8- or 10-bit resolution. In 8-bit resolution, an external clock to 97 KHz may be used. In 10-bit resolution, one of the internal counter/timers is used and supports an output frequency in excess of 24 KHz. The duty-cycle registers are double buffered.

The 17C42's USART can operate as a full-duplex asynchronous or half-duplex synchronous interface. An 8-bit baud rate generator is included, which supports data rates in excess of 300 kbaud.

The PIC is a classical Harvard architecture, with 12-bit-wide (14 on the 16C71) instructions, and 8-bit-wide data. Separate memory spaces are provided for each. Memory is internal, with ROM/EPROM for instructions and a register file for data.

A power-on-reset function can also be activated by the watchdog timer timeout. DC to 20 MHz operation is possible with the fully-static CMOS design. No JTAG support is included. PICs generally don't need any support chips, being designed for single-chip microcontroller applications.

18.3.2 Software

The 16C5X has thirty-three 12-bit instructions, the 16C71 has thirty-five 14-bit instructions, and the 17C42 has fifty-five 16-bit-wide instructions. All instructions in all models are one word, and operate on a selected register and the working register, W. Integer math operations include add, subtract, increment, and decrement. No floating-point operations are included. Logical operations include AND, OR, and XOR. Data may be moved between registers and the working register, and literals may be loaded. Program control includes a CALL and RETURN, a GOTO, and forms for increment/decrement and skip-if-zero/not zero. Rotate left or right, either through the carry or not, are included. Individual bits may be set, tested, or cleared. A special instruction puts the processor into a low-power sleep mode. Figure 18.5 shows the instruction set of the 16C5x models.

A register file format is used. W is the working register, or accumulator. A total of 80 addressable 8-bit registers are included, with data, control, status, and I/O functions. Operational registers include the program counter, real-time clock, status, and I/O. General-purpose registers include the real-time clock/counter register, the program counter, status registers, and I/O ports, mapped as registers. Registers may be

BYTE -ORIENTED FILE REGISTER OPERATIONS

	(11-6)	(5)	(4 - 0)
	OPCODE	d	f(FILE #)

d = 0 for destination W
d = 1 for destination f

Instruction-Binary (Hex)	Name	Mnemonic, Operands	Operation	Status Affected	Notes
0001 11df ffff 1Cf	Add W and f	**ADDWF** f, d	W + f → d	C,DC,Z	1,2,4
0001 01df ffff 14f	AND W and f	**ANDWF** f, d	W & f → d	Z	2,4
0000 011f ffff 06f	Clear f	**CLRF** f	0 → f	Z	4
0000 0100 0000 040	Clear W	**CLRW** -	0 → W	Z	
0010 01df ffff 24f	Complement f	**COMF** f, d	f̄ → d	Z	2,4
0000 11df ffff 0Cf	Decrement f	**DECF** f, d	f -1 → d	Z	2,4
0010 11df ffff 2Cf	Decrement f,Skip if Zero	**DECFSZ** f, d	f - 1 → d. skip if zero	None	2,4
0010 10df ffff 28f	Increment f	**INCF** f, d	f + 1 → d	Z	2,4
0011 11df ffff 3Cf	Increment f,Skip if zero	**INCFSZ** f, d	f + 1 → d. skip if zero	None	2,4
0001 00df ffff 10f	Inclusive OR W and f	**IORWF** f, d	W v f → d	Z	2,4
0010 00df ffff 20f	Move f	**MOVF** f, d	f → d	Z	2,4
0000 001f ffff 02f	Move W to f	**MOVWF** f	W → f	None	1,4
0000 0000 0000 000	No Operation	**NOP** -	-	None	
0011 01df ffff 34f	Rotate left f	**RLF** f, d	f(n) → d(n+1), C → d(0), f(7) → C	C	2,4
0011 00df ffff 30f	Rotate right f	**RRF** f, d	f(n) → d(n-1), C → d(7), f(0) → C	C	2,4
0000 10df ffff 08f	Subtract W from f	**SUBWF** f, d	f - W → d [f + W̄ + 1 → d]	C,DC,Z	1,2,4
0011 10df ffff 38f	Swap halves f	**SWAPF** f, d	f(0-3) ↔ f(4-7) → d	None	2,4
0001 10df ffff 18f	Exclusive OR W and f	**XORWF** f, d	W ⊕ f → d	Z	2,4

BIT- ORIENTED FILE REGISTER OPERATIONS

	(11-8)	(7-5)	(4 - 0)
	OPCODE	b(BIT #)	f(FILE #)

Instruction-Binary (Hex)	Name	Mnemonic, Operands	Operation	Status Affected	Notes
0100 bbbf ffff 4bf	Bit Clear f	**BCF** f, b	0 → f(b)	None	2,4
0101 bbbf ffff 5bf	Bit Set f	**BSF** f, b	1 → f(b)	None	2,4
0110 bbbf ffff 6bf	Bit Test f,Skip if Clear	**BTFSC** f, b	Test bit (b) in file (f): Skip if clear	None	
0111 bbbf ffff 7bf	Bit Test f, Skip if Set	**BTFSS** f, b	Test bit (b) in file (f): Skip if set	None	

LITERAL AND CONTROL OPERATIONS

	(11-8)	(7 - 0)
	OPCODE	k (LITERAL)

Instruction-Binary (Hex)	Name	Mnemonic, Operands	Operation	Status Affected	Notes
1110 kkkk kkkk Ekk	AND Literal and W	**ANDLW** k	k & W→ W	Z	
1001 kkkk kkkk 9kk	Call subroutine	**CALL** k	PC + 1 → Stack, k → PC	None	1
0000 0000 0100 004	Clear Watchdog timer	**CLRWDT** -	0 → WDT (and prescaler, if assigned)	TO, PD	
101k kkkk kkkk Akk	Go To address (k is 9 bit)	**GOTO** k	k → PC (9 bits)	None	
1101 kkkk kkkk Dkk	Incl. OR Literal and W	**IORLW** k	k v W → W	Z	
1100 kkkk kkkk Ckk	Move Literal to W	**MOVLW** k	k → W	None	
0000 0000 0010 002	Load OPTION register	**OPTION** -	W → OPTION register	None	
1000 kkkk kkkk 8kk	Return,place Literal in W	**RETLW** k	k → W, Stack → PC	None	
0000 0000 0011 003	Go into standby mode	**SLEEP** -	0 → WDT, stop oscillator	TO, PD	
0000 0000 0fff 00f	Tristate port f	**TRIS** f	W→ I/O control register f	None	3
1111 kkkk kkkk Fkk	Excl. OR Literal and W	**XORLW** k	k ⊕ W → W	Z	

Figure 18.5 PIC instructions. (Reprinted with permission of the copyright owner, Microchip Technology Inc. © 1995.) All rights reserved.

addressed directly or indirectly. Byte ordering is not an issue, since this is an 8-bit machine. Only 8-bit bytes are valid data types.

A full line of development and test tools for the PIC are available. A PC-based toolset under Windows includes a cross-assembler and linker, a discrete event instruction set simulator, and a real-time, ICE-based emulation. A fuzzy logic development system for the PIC series is available, as is a C compiler.

18.3.3 Floating Point

The PIC does not support floating point in hardware. A software package is available. This is not unusual for 8-bit processors. If you need floating point here, you're using the wrong chip for the application.

18.3.4 Cache

No internal cache is provided, and there is no specific support for external cache. Again, this product is intended for small, simple, well-defined applications. Data are kept in on-chip registers.

18.3.5 Memory Management

No specific memory management functions are provided in the PIC architecture.

18.3.6 Exceptions

On the 16C71, there are four interrupts: external, RTCC, A/D conversion complete, and on-change of certain I/O bits. Interrupt latency is one cycle. The 17C42 model supports eleven interrupt sources.

18.4 SUMMARY

RISC Features

Large register set—yes
Load/store—yes
Single-cycle execution—yes
Small instruction set—yes
Hardwired instructions—yes

Non-RISC Features

Multiple addressing modes—3 on 16C71

18.5 BIBLIOGRAPHY

"Development Systems Ordering Guide," 1994, Microchip Technology, Inc.

"Embedded Control Handbook," 1994/1995, Microchip Technology, Inc.

Frenger, Paul, "PIC 16C5x Series uP: The 8-bit RISC Microcontroller (Hardware Review)," Fall 1992, *SIG FORTH*, 4 (2): 27.

"Microchip Data Book," April 1994, Microchip Technology, Inc.

"Microchip Product Selection Guide," 1995, Microchip Technology, Inc.

"PIC 16C5X Microcontroller Application Notes, Sets 1–4," 1990, Microchip Technology, Inc. (note: also available on disk).

"PIC16C71 Data Sheet," 1992, Microchip Technology, Inc.

19

MISCELLANEOUS PROCESSOR ARCHITECTURES

This chapter contains information on various processor architectures that didn't, in my opinion, necessarily each deserve a full chapter, but should be discussed. Some of these chips are no longer available and some are just emerging. These include the Clipper, abandoned by Integraph in favor of work on the SPARC, and the Motorola 88k, now incorporated into the PowerPC architecture. We'll also look at the innovative but strange Intel iWarp. A section is included on RISC-influenced DSP chips such as the Texas Instruments TMS320C080, and the Analog Devices SHARC. We then look at four examples of proprietary RISC architectures including the nCUBE, KSR, MasPar, and IBM's. RIOS. We consider the AT&T microprocessor architecture, a victim of slow PDA sales. We cover the influence of RISC on CISC by looking at Motorola's 68060, and the Intel 80x86 family, particularly the Pentium competitors. Worthy of mention are National's Swordfish architecture, derived from its 32000 line (reference [1]), National's Piranha, the Zilog Hyperstone 32-bit RISC project from Hyperstone Electronics GmbH (reference [2]), Sinclair Research's 7600 (reference [3]), and Axis Technologies' AXT 6100 and 6200. As these and other projects develop, they will be included in future revisions of this book.

19.1 CLIPPER

19.1.1 Introduction

This section discusses the architecture of the Clipper family of 32-bit processors.

19.1.2 Background

The Clipper was originally developed at Fairchild Semiconductor in 1985 and began shipping in 1986. When Fairchild was acquired by National Semiconductor in 1987, the rights to the architecture were acquired by Intergraph Corporation, a manufacturer of high-end graphics workstations. Development of the Clipper processor was curtailed in 1994 due to Intergraph's work on a bi-endian mode for the SPARC architecture. Intergraph was also involved at the time in the Windows/NT port to the SPARC.

The Clipper architecture addressed high-performance workstation and embedded applications such as robotics. Unix was supported on Intergraph workstations, and graphics were one of the chip's strong points.

19.1.3 Architecture

The Clipper architecture was available in a family of implementations, ranging from CMOS to emitter coupled logic (ECL) implementations. First- and second-generation parts included the C100 and C300. The C300 had improved floating point and higher clock speeds, and was superpipelined. The C400, a third-generation part, was introduced in September 1990. In 1993, Intergraph dropped the planned 1994 introduction of the next-generation C5 project, an eight-pipeline affair, in favor of a relationship with SPARC and Windows/NT.

19.1.3.1 Hardware
The chip included an integral floating-point unit, and interfaces to the four-kilobyte instruction and data caches and memory management units in a Harvard architecture. Hardware scoreboarding was provided to avoid pipeline contention and stalls and for dynamic resource allocation. A user and a supervisor mode were provided in the hardware.

The Clipper parts were available as chips or in module form. Modules incorporated the CPU/FPU, MMUs, caches, and clock on one small (3x4.5-inch) module, with a 96-pin edge connector. Figure 19.1 shows the Clipper architecture.

The second-generation part, the C300, gained performance from higher clock

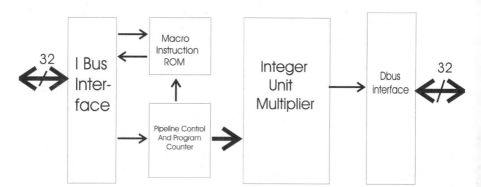

Figure 19.1 Clipper architecture. Courtesy of Intergraph Corporation.

speeds and a redesigned floating-point unit. The C300 maintained complete compatibility with the C100.

The last implementation of the Clipper architecture was the superscalar, superpipelined C400. It was able to issue two instructions per clock, and had a four-stage pipeline. Full 64-bit data paths were used between functional units. A 32×32 register file was incorporated on-chip. Almost all instructions except multiply and divide executed in one cycle. The associated FPU was pipelined, and had its own 16×64-bit register file. Three separate execution units handled add/subtract, multiply, and divide. A 32-bit add took four cycles, and a 64-bit divide took 30 cycles. Figure 19.2 shows a C400 system level block diagram.

On units through the C300, the instruction pipeline was three deep, and multiple issue of floating and integer instructions could occur. The integral floating-point unit was IEEE 754 compatible, but not pipelined. The integer pipeline had three stages: fetch, decode, and execute. Neither the C100 nor the C300 had a delayed branch because of the problems associated with the variable-length instructions. Branching, then, caused pipeline stalls in these units.

The multiple addressing modes tied up the sole ALU, further stalling the pipeline. The C400 incorporated a dedicated address adder and pipelined the floating-point unit. In fact, the C400 had nine distinct pipelines, including load/store and branch pipelines. The instruction pipeline was expanded to four stages by the addition of a write stage.

The C400 integer execution unit included hardware for multiplication and division, as well as a 32-bit barrel shifter. The C400 used no condition codes, but rather a general register was tested, and a branch occurred with two delay slots.

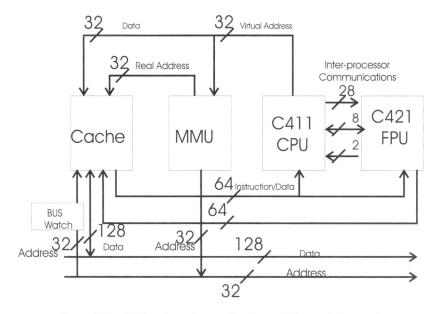

Figure 19.2 C400 system diagram. Courtesy of Intergraph Corporation.

The communications architecture between the CPU and the CAMMUs was Harvard, with 32-bit data paths, expanded to 64-bits on the C400. To the external world, a unified data path was used. Upon reset the processor went to unmapped supervisor mode, with traps and interrupts disabled and prefetch enabled. Instruction execution began at real address zero of the boot space.

The C100 operated at 25 or 33 MHz, going to 40 or 50 MHz for the C300 part. The C300 part was capable of being operated at 75 MHz. The C400 was introduced at 50 MHz. None of the Clippers provided JTAG support. The C400 CPU dissipated about seven watts at 40 MHz, using 5 volts. A one-volt swing on I/O lines was used to reduce power, a technique called *low voltage swing* (LVS).

The CPU portion of the C400 chip was available in a 299-pin PGA package, and incorporated about 160,000 transistors. The associated FPU also took a 299-pin package.

19.1.3.2 Software The Clipper architecture was of load/store format, with 101 instructions of single-cycle latency. Instructions were of variable length, being 16, 32, 48, or 64 bits. The operation code was always the first 16 bits of the instruction. Nine different operand-addressing modes were used.

Variable-length instructions provided an advantage in code density, at a cost of complexity in the pipeline. The basic four math operations were supported in integer and floating point. Logical operations included AND, OR, and XOR. Shifts and rotates could occur on words (32 bits) and longwords (64-bits). Delayed branches were not supported in the C100 or C300. The C400 supported delayed branches by means of a branch pipeline. A test-and-set instruction was also included. String manipulation instructions included compare, initialize, and move.

A macro instruction ROM implemented 67 functions in addition to the native 101. These included the conversion and string operations and most stack operations, among others.

Two sets of registers were included for user and supervisor usage. The C400 implemented a 32x32 register file with three read and two write ports. The floating point unit had its own 16x64 register file, also with three read and two write ports. The status registers included the program counter, the program status word (PSW), and the system status word (SSW), which defined interrupts, address translation, protections, and modes. Figure 19.3 shows the PSW and SSW layout in the Clipper.

Little-endian data ordering was used in the C100 part. Hardware support for big- or little-endian data access mode was provided with the C300 part, and was set upon reset. The Clipper supported 10 data types, including signed and unsigned bytes, half words, words, and longwords, as well as single- and double-precision floating point.

Clipper development and test tools were Unix hosted, and included Intergraph-developed optimizing compilers for C, Pascal, or FORTRAN. Output of the three compilers could be assembled and linked together. Other tools included the assembler, linker, librarian, and a downloader for embedded systems use, with a real-time debugger.

Numerous third-party languages and tools were available for the Clipper architec-

31 ... 24	23	22	21 20	19 ... 17	16	15	14	13	12	11	10	9	8	7	6	5	4	3	2	1	0
0	T	BIG	DSP	0	FR	FT	EFI	EFV	EFV	EFI	EFF UX	FI	FV	FD	FU	FX	C	V	Z	N

FIELD	MEANING
N	Negative
Z	Zero
V	Overflow
C	Carry out or borrow in
FX	Floating inexact
FU	Floating underflow
FD	Floating divide by zero
FV	Floating overflow
FI	Floating invalid operation
EFX	Enable floating inexact trap
EFU	Enable floating underflow trap
EFD	Enable floating divide by zero trap
EFV	Enable floating overflow trap
EFI	Enable floating invalid operation trap
FT	Floating-point trap
FR	Floating rounding mode
DSP	Delay slot pointer
BIG	Big endian
T	Trace trap

DSP	INSTRUCTION REQUIRING EXECUTION
0	Reserved
1	Reserved
2	Delay slot 1
3	Delay slot 0 & 1

FR	MEANING
0	Round to nearest
1	Round toward + infinity
2	Round toward - infinity
3	Round toward zero

FIELD	MEANING
IN	Interrupt number
IL	Interrupt level
EI	Enable interrupts
TYPE	CPU type
REV	CPU revision
FRD	Floating registers dirty
TP	Trace trap pending
ECM	Enable corrected memory error

FIELD	MEANING
DF	Disabled floating-point
M	Mapped mode
UU	User data mode
U	User mode
P	Previous mode

31	30	29	28	27	26	25	2423	22	21 ... 16	14 13 ... 9	8 7	... 4	3 ... 0
P	U	O	UU	O	M	DFM	ECM	TP	FRD	0	REV	TYPE	EI	IL	IN

Figure 19.3 Clipper PSW and SSW. Courtesy of Intergraph Corporation.

ture, ranging from the LISP, Prolog, and COBOL languages to a C-executive real-time kernel.

19.1.3.3 Floating Point
The Clipper floating point units were IEEE-754 compatible, and provided the four basic math operations and format conversion on single- or double-precision data. Eight floating-point registers were available. Follow-

ing the IEEE format, rounding modes were selectable, and the five floating-point exceptions (inexact, overflow, underflow, divide-by-zero, and invalid operation) were implemented.

19.1.3.4 Cache The Clipper cache was incorporated as part of the CAMMU. In the C100 and C300, there were 4-kilobyte instruction and data caches. Cache was two-way set associative, with a 16-byte line length. In the C400, a 128-kilobyte, direct-mapped, unified external cache was supported.

In the C400, cache coherency and snooping were supported, when the copy-back mode was being used. The cache approach was selectable, copy-back, or write-through. Any page could be designated as cacheable or not and with the appropriate strategy. On a per-page basis, read-only or read-write could be selected.

19.1.3.5 Memory Management The *cache and memory management* (CAM-MU) function was provided by a separate chip for the C100 and C300. It provided virtual-to-physical address translation, overlapped with cache accesses. It had five software-accessible registers. Both virtual and physical addresses were 32 bits. A 128-entry translation lookaside buffer supported virtual memory and multiprocessing, and hardware bus snooping was used to ensure cache consistency. Burst-mode transfers of 16 bytes were used between the processor and main memory. Figure 19.4 shows the address translation process and cache search in the Clipper.

The CAMMU incorporated three caches: a 4-kilobyte, two-way set-associative combined data/instruction cache; a quadword buffer; and a 128-entry TLB. Two-level page-based mapping was used, with a 4-kilobyte page size.

The TLB held the 128 most frequently used addresses. A system tag defined three physical spaces: boot, I/O, or program. The virtual address space was linear and had four regions: user and supervisor, code and data spaces.

For the coherency model, present, dirty, and accessed bits were kept on a per-page basis. Out-of-order execution was not supported. All I/O was memory mapped, with a separate I/O space.

19.1.3.6 Exceptions Exceptions used a vector table and included traps for anomalous internal events, interrupts from external sources, and supervisor calls invoked by the CALLS instruction. The C100 implemented 18 traps, 256 interrupts, and 128 supervisor calls. Traps included page fault, division by zero, memory protection violation, or privileged instruction violation from user mode. The C300 had the same configuration, but added two additional traps. The C400 had 56 hardware traps. A nonmaskable interrupt pin was available.

19.1.4 Summary

RISC Features

Large register set—32×32 + 16×64 fp
Load/store—architecture

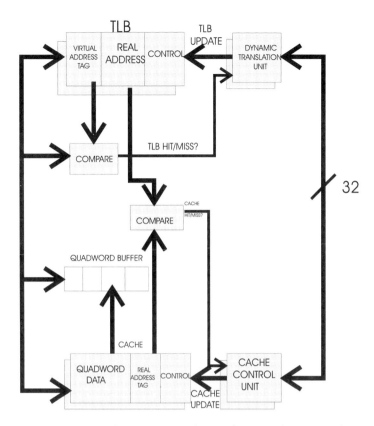

Figure 19.4 Address translation/cache search in Clipper. Courtesy of Intergraph Corporation.

Single-cycle execution
Small instruction set—101
Hardwired instructions

Non-RISC Features

Addressing modes—yes, 9
Macro instruction ROM, 67 additional instructions in addition to the native 101
Variable length instructions

19.2 MOTOROLA 88K

19.2.1 Introduction

This section presents a summary of Motorola's 88k family of RISC Microprocessors. We will look at the architecture of the chips, as well as their influence on the mainstream CISC 680x0 processors; their influence on digital signal processing such as the 96000; and their influence on the development of specialized devices for control—the 68332 and 88300. In addition, the design influences of the 88k on the Motorola/IBM/Apple PowerPC will be discussed.

19.2.2 Background

Motorola is more than a chip company. It has made its niche in embedded controllers, particularly for the automotive industry, as well as in communications and radio frequency (RF) devices. Motorola supplies processors, memories, and general logic chips to industry, as well as integrating its own line of Unix workstations. Active in communications, Motorola is venturing into the satellite communications business with its Iridium project. This ambitious project will see a series of spacecraft providing global communication services for voice and data users.

The 88k family was aimed at high-end workstations supporting Unix, and as an advanced generation of embedded control for automotive applications, requiring 32 bits. The 88k design effort has had an impact on Motorola's mainline CISC processors, the 680x0s, and Motorola's digital signal processors (DSPs) as well.

Motorola has also always been active in development of specialized processor devices for control. The 68332, derived from the 68000 family, and the 88300, derived from the 88k, are two such devices. They address the emerging market for 32-bit embedded controllers. The 88k also formed the basis of BBN's "Butterfly" massively parallel architecture, with 504 processors being used. Data General used the 88k in their AViiON line of minicomputers, and produced an ECL version of the 88k chipset as well.

Motorola's energies are now focused on the PowerPC line, and further development in the 88k family is unlikely. The 88k, although an exceptionally sophisticated design, met with limited acceptance. The planned 88300 model was never brought to market. For Motorola, the computer future lies with the PowerPC and the computer savvy of Apple and IBM.

19.2.3 Architecture

The 88k family consists of the first-generation 88100 CPU and the associated 88200 cache controller, which were later combined into one chip with the second-generation 88110 device. The 88k was a radical departure from Motorola's 68000 series. The 88k project influenced subsequent mainstream CISC designs, such as the superscalar 68060. Similarly, the RISC design experience gained by Motorola in developing the 88k was applied back to their advanced digital signal processor line, the 96000.

19.2.3.1 Hardware The 88100 processor is a 32-bit RISC design with five independent execution units and four pipelines, exploiting fine-grain parallelism to achieve performance. The 88k features a fully hardwired instruction, making no use of microcode for instruction decode. The architecture is Harvard, employing separate address and data buses for both instructions and data. Up to eight special function units (SFUs) are included on-chip. SFU 0 is the single-cycle integer/bit field

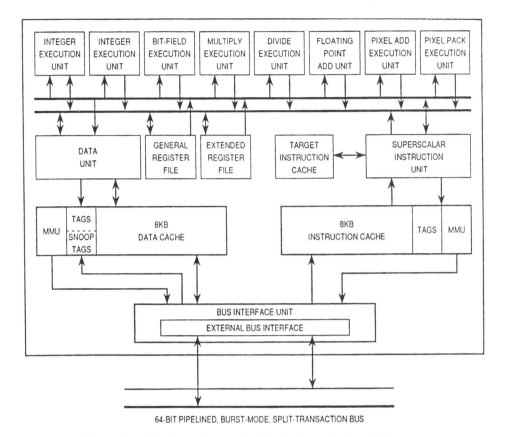

Figure 19.5 88100 architecture. Reprinted with permission of Motorola.

unit, SFU 1 is the floating-point multiplier/adder, and SFU 2–7 may be customized in the hardware for other tasks or emulations. SFU 1 contains two pipelined units for floating-point add and multiply. A new instruction can begin at each clock, but instructions can take more than one cycle to operate. The adder and multiplier operate concurrently. Figure 19.5 shows the 88100 architecture.

The associated 88200 device is called a *cache memory management unit* (CMMU). Since the 88100 has a Harvard-style memory bus, two 88200s can be used with one 88100. This results in separate data and code CMMUs. On the operand side, data memory accesses are pipelined. On the instruction side, one instruction per clock can be fed to the execution units. Internally, three 32-bit buses move two sources and the destination data between execution registers and registers. The combination of one 88100 and two 88200s, called a *processor node*, provides the basis for multiprocessor systems with shared memory and peripherals. Figure 19.6 shows an 88k processor node.

The second-generation 88110 combines the 88100 and 88200 into one device with over 1.3 million CMOS transistors. Called a *symmetric superscalar* architecture, it is capable of issuing two instructions every clock. There can be no data de-

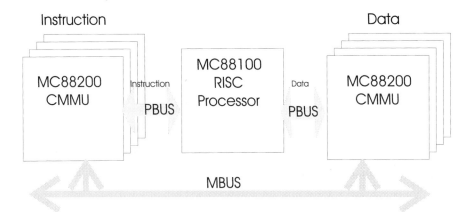

Figure 19.6 Processor node. Courtesy of Intergraph Corporation.

pendencies between the issued instructions, and the relevant execution unit must be available. This scheduling challenge in the instruction stream is the task of the optimizing compiler. There are 10 execution units: instruction fetch, data fetch, integer execution 1, integer execution 2, floating point add, bit field, multiply, divide, pixel add, and pixel pack. The 88110 has two register files. The instruction unit does I-fetches, and the data unit does the corresponding D-fetches. The floating-point and graphics units are implemented as Motorola special function units, with floating point being SFU 1 and graphics SFU 2. Up to seven SFUs can be supported by the hardware. The original intent was to have special function units to emulate other processors, such as the 68k family or possibly even the 80x86.

Internally, the 88110 uses 80-bit-wide buses between the various execution units and the register file. Feed-forwarding, or the passing of completed values to the next instruction step in the pipeline in parallel with their destination, is implemented. In this scheme, the results of one step do not need to be written into a register to be read on the next step. Rather, the results go to the destination register in parallel with going to the input bus for the following instruction's data read.

The 88k instruction pipeline consists of three stages: fetch, decode, and execute. The data pipeline is also three stages. The floating-point unit is pipelined, with separate adder and multiplier hardware. The 88100 has five independent execution units and the 88110 has ten.

19.2.3.2 Processor Busses The P-bus (processor bus) connects the 88100s to the 88200. This is translated in the CMMU to an M-bus (memory bus). This is not the same as the SPARC M-bus. In the 88110, the P-bus is internal to the device. The P-bus is synchronous and nonmultiplexed, and can transfer a 32-bit word each clock cycle. The P-bus uses 33-bit addresses and 32-bit-wide data. The M-bus is synchronous and multiplexed. It uses 32-bit address and data. The M-bus is sharable among multiple bus masters, by means of externally generated arbitration signals.

Upon reset initialization, the 88k processor begins execution at address zero. Up to a 25 MHz clock is supported. No JTAG support is provided in the 88100 or 200,

MC88100 INSTRUCTION SET CATEGORIES

Load/Store/Exchange Instructions
fldcr	Load From Floating Point Control Register
fstcr	Store to Floating Point Control Register
fxcr	Exchange Floating Point Control Register
ld	Load Register from Memory
lda	Load Address
ldcr	Load From Control Register
st	Store Register to Memory
stcr	Store to Control Register
xcr	Exchange Control Register
xmem	Exchange Register with Memory

Integer Arithmetic Instructions
add	Add
addu	Add Unsigned
cmp	Compare
div	Divide
divu	Divide Unsigned
mul	Multiply
sub	Subtract
subu	Subtract Unsigned

Floating Point Arithmetic Instructions
fadd	Floating Point Add
fcmp	Floating Point Compare
fdiv	Floating Point Divide
flt	Convert Integer to Floating Point
fmul	Floating Point Multiply
fsub	Floating Point Subtract
int	Round Floating Point to Integer
nint	Floating Point Round to Nearest Integer
trnc	Truncate Floating Point to Integer

Logical Instructions
and	And
mask	Logical Mask Immediate
or	Or
xor	Exclusive Or

Bit Field Instructions
clr	Clear Bit Field
ext	Extract Signed Bit Field
extu	Extract Unsigned Bit Field
ff0	Find First Bit Clear
ff1	Find First Bit Set
mak	Make Bit Field
rot	Rotate Register
set	Set Bit Field

Flow Control Instructions
bb0	Branch On Bit Clear
bb1	Branch On Bit Set
bcnd	Conditional Branch
br	Unconditional Branch
bsr	Branch to Subroutine
jmp	Unconditional Jump
jsr	Jump to Subroutine
rte	Return from Exception
tb0	Trap on Bit Clear
tb1	Trap on Bit Set
tbnd	Trap on Bounds Check
tcnd	Conditional Trap

Figure 19.7 88k instructions. Reprinted with the permission of Motorola.

but it is provided in the 88110. A user and a supervisor mode are implemented. Master and checker modes are possible, in which pairs of units are used, with a redundant unit comparing its derived outputs with those of the primary unit, and signalling discrepancies.

19.2.3.3 Electrical/Packaging Typical power dissipation for the 88000 is 1.5 watts. The processor is designed to operate at 5 volts. For packaging, the 88100 and 88200 use a 180-pin PGA. The 88110 is a 291-pin device.

19.2.3.4 Software The 88100 has a small set of 51 instructions (the 88110 has 66), providing the four basic math functions on integer and floating data, and the logical operations on register-held data. The instruction format is triadic register, with each instruction providing explicit source and destination register operand pointers. Only load or store operations address data memory. The 88110 includes new instructions for graphics, and additional floating-point support. The 88k instruction set is shown in Figure 19.7.

There is a 32×32-bit scoreboarded register file in the 88000. Thirty-one of the registers are general purpose, while register zero contains zero by definition. There is one "stale" bit per register. A scoreboard register contains one bit for each of 32 registers, with a zero indicating that the corresponding register is not in use. Although the registers are general purpose, certain conventions must be followed. For example, the hardware assumes R1 for subroutine return addresses, R30 is the frame pointer, and R31 is the stack pointer.

On the 88110, two eight-ported register files are supported. The general register file has thirty-two 32-bit registers. The extended register file has thirty-two 80-bit registers. R0 contains 0, and R1 contains the return address of a jump. Similarly, floating-point register X0 contains a zero. The eight ports include six output ports and two input ports. With this scheme, two parameters can be placed on two internal busses simultaneously, supporting dual-instruction execution. Thirty-five control registers are also a part of the architecture. Register scoreboarding is used to control data dependencies during out-of-order instruction execution, which is supported.

To expedite exception handling, shadow registers are kept for the program counters and scoreboard registers. This allows the pipeline context to be automatically saved at the end of each clock. When an exception occurs, the shadow freeze bit disables further shadowing.

Status and control registers include a processor identifier register containing the version and architectural revision of the part, a program counter, and a processor status register. There are 64 general control registers, and 64 possible floating-point control registers, of which nine are implemented. The 88200s have 21 control registers. The processor status register is illustrated in Figure 19.8.

The 88k is a load/store architecture, with several addressing modes for the load

31	30	29 28	27		10	9	4	3	2	1	0
MODE	BO	SER	C	Reserved			Reserved	SFD1	MXM	IND	SFRZ

MODE	= 0	Processor is in user mode.
	= 1	Processor is in supervisor mode.
BO	= 0	Big Endian byte order in memory.
	= 1	Little Endian byte order in memory.
SER	= 0	Concurrent instruction execution.
	= 1	Serial instruction execution.
C	= 0	No carry/borrow generated.
	= 1	Carry/borrow generated.
SFD1	= 0	SFU1 enabled.
	= 1	SFU1 disabled.
MXM	= 0	Misaligned memory accesses generate exceptions.
	= 1	Misaligned memory accesses truncate.
IND	= 0	Interrupt enabled.
	= 1	Interrupt disabled.
SFRZ	= 0	Shadow registers enabled.
	= 1	Shadow registers frozen.

Figure 19.8 Processor status register. Reprinted with the permission of Motorola.

and store instructions. These modes include register-indirect, with unsigned immediate, indexed, or scaled indexed. The instruction set of the 88k is built around a three-address architecture.

Either byte-ordering method (little- or big-endian) is selectable by a bit in the PSR register. It defaults to big-endian upon reset. Supported data types include signed and unsigned bytes, half words, and words (32-bits), as well as single- and double-precision floating point.

The 88k family is supported by a full line of software development and test tools, and a user/developer organization, 88-Open. Besides an assembler and linker, compilers for C and FORTRAN are available. Cross-assemblers and simulators are hosted on the PC. Unix is available for 88k systems.

19.2.3.5 *Floating Point* Floating point in the 88k is IEEE compatible, and implemented with two pipelines. Division is not pipelined, but the multiply unit has its own pipeline. There are eleven control registers in the floating-point unit. Single- and double-precision formats are supported, as are the four rounding modes of the IEEE standard. The four basic math operations plus format conversion and comparisons are provided. The square root operation is added on the 88110. Precise and imprecise interrupts are generated.

19.2.3.6 *Cache* The 88200 CMMU chip provides cache memory management to the main processor. These features are integrated into the 88110 design. The CMMU function implements demand-paged virtual memory management, as well as physical data caching. Also implemented are dual, fully associative address translation caches. The 88200 can map a page, defined as a 4-kilobyte entity on a 4-kilobyte boundary, a segment, 4 megabytes on a 4-megabyte boundary, or the entire 4-gigabyte user or supervisor space. A block, defined as 512 kilobytes on a 512-kilobyte boundary, can also be mapped. The code and data caches are 16 kilobytes, and a 56-entry page address translation cache as well as a 10-entry block address translation cache are included. For data reads from peripheral devices, cache avoidance is implemented.

In the MMU portion of the 88200, the I- and D-caches are 16-kilobyte, two-way set associative, and physically addressed. On the 110, these cache sizes are 8 kilobytes. In the D-cache, decoupled cache accesses allow cache accesses to continue during the time the cache is awaiting data from the bus in response to a previous miss. A subsequent miss halts cache accesses. This feature is more applicable to D-cache than I-cache because of the higher locality of reference in I-cache. Write-back and write-through modes are supported in the D-cache. Bus snooping is implemented for multiprocessing cache consistency, and a lockable bus tenure allows for access to synchronization semaphores. The 88110 uses a MESI cache coherency protocol.

Cache consistency for the instruction cache is maintained by a valid bit. For the data cache, items may be marked valid, modified, or shared/exclusive. Cache avoidance is provided for I/O. For the BTC, the 32 entries are fully associative. For the 88110, a 88410 secondary-level cache controller with multiprocessing support is also available.

19.2.3.7 Memory Management

19.2.3.7 Memory Management The 88200 MMU provides separate four-way set-associative translation and can implement different caching strategies for code and data. This is important, as the optimal scheme for caching op-code fetches is not necessarily the optimal for operands. The supported caching schemes are copy-back, write-through, don't cache, cache per page, cache per area, and cache per segment.

The MMU makes use of the technique of cache snooping to ensure cache consistency. This is, in effect, a hardware-implemented data-consistency protocol. Multiple copies of data items may exist for a read, but the first write to any item invalidates all the other copies and forces an update of cached copies and memory at the same time. Any subsequent writes are buffered in copy-back mode. Figure 19.9 shows the construction of the 88200 MMU.

A fault detection scheme is available with the 88k family, since all devices and interfaces are synchronous. Each component is configurable as master or checker. If the checker detects a mismatch on outputs, it asserts an error signal to the master, which is treated as an exception.

The 88200 provides supervisor and write protection at the page and block level, and can also implement cache avoidance at these levels. Two 88200 units, one for the instruction and one for the op-code spaces, implement a complete MMU functionality for the 88k processor. The CMMU interfaces the P-bus to the M-bus. Figure 19.10 shows the 88k address translation process.

Separate MMUs in the 88110 handle the instruction and data fetches. Separate supervisor and user code and data spaces are provided. Each MMU contains two address translation caches; one for page, and one for block translations. The page-address translation cache is 32 entry and fully associative. It handles translation of the

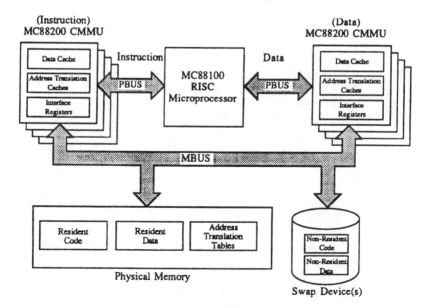

Figure 19.9 88200 MMU. Reprinted with the permission of Motorola.

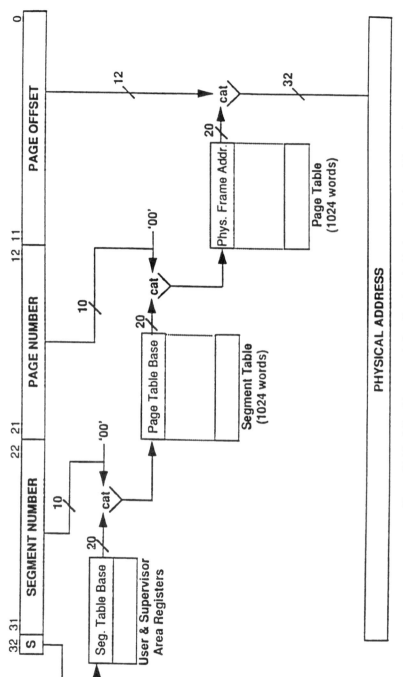

Figure 19.10 88k address translation. Reprinted with the permission of Motorola.

287

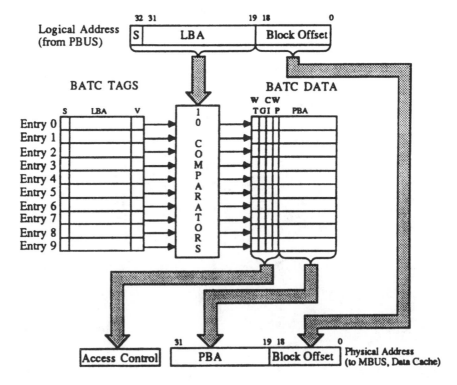

Figure 19.11 Block address translation cache. Reprinted with the permission of Motorola.

4-kilobyte page entities. The block-address translation cache is eight entry and fully-associative. It can be smaller, since block translations are done less frequently. Blocks range from 512 kilobytes to 64 megabytes in size. A pseudorandom replacement policy is used to replace lines in the caches. Figure 19.11 shows the block address translation cache of the 88k.

An interesting feature of the 88110 is the target instruction branch cache. Here, a 32-entry, fully associative cache holds the target instructions of the recently taken branches. The first two instructions of the branch target stream are held. The cache is virtually addressed and is invalidated when a context switch occurs.

19.2.3.8 Exceptions Exceptions in the 88k are defined as reset, external interrupts, privilege violation, bounds violation, divide-by-zero, overflow, and other errors or traps.

Exception processing is handled in the 88110, which utilizes a vector-base register, pointing to a memory page of all the exception vectors. An exception vector has two entries, the first being a branch to the routine, and the second being the first instruction of the exception handler. Thus, branch latencies are avoided. In the 88100, a history buffer is maintained. This is a FIFO of processor state, and is updated when an instruction completes execution. This information allows rapid resolution of out-of-order executions at exception time.

Exceptions are handled by a vector table of addresses starting at address zero. Exception handlers must wait for any pending memory accesses to complete. The scoreboard is cleared before the hardware branches to the exception handler address. Exceptions include external events such as reset or interrupt, and internal events such as errors in data or instruction access, misalignments, privilege violation, bounds violation, integer divide error, overflow error, and traps.

During reset the 88k enters supervisor mode, disables interrupts, freezes the shadow registers, flushes the pipelines, and clears the scoreboard registers. The vector table at address zero is accessed, and the first instruction is fetched from the reset vector location. After that, execution of instructions proceeds normally.

On interrupt the data pipeline is cleared, and the first instruction of the interrupt handler code is fetched from the vector address. The worst-case timing is three clocks, plus six processor bus (PBUS) cycles.

Possible floating-point exceptions include conversion overflow, unimplemented op code, privilege violation, divide-by-zero, underflow, overflow, and inexact. Also, an exception will be generated if the floating-point unit is accessed when it was marked as disabled in the PSR. A privilege violation is generated when a program at the user level attempts to access control registers. Overflow is defined as the case where a generated result is larger than the destination.

Exceptions may be precise (meaning the context is known), or imprecise (meaning the exception handler must reconstruct the processor context).

19.2.4 Summary

RISC Features

Large register set—yes, 32×32 and 32×80
Load/store—yes
Single-cycle execution—yes
Small instruction set—yes, 51 (100), 66 (110)
Hardwired instructions—yes

Non-RISC Features

SFUs

19.3 iWARP

The Intel iWarp is a VLSI instantiation of H. T. Kung's work on a parallel architecture, referred to as Warp. It was influenced by work at Carnegie-Mellon University on the earlier CMMP and CM* projects. Resembling the Transputer, the iWarp is a processor and memory unit that is hooked into networks of communication channels among processor elements. The original architecture for systolic computing arrays grew out of DARPA's interest in advanced computing and support via the Strategic Computing Program. The Warp architecture exhibits fine-grain parallelism in the sense that there are few calculations per I/O.

19.3.1 Introduction

The goal of the iWarp program was to develop a compute/communicate architecture that would scale in both dimensions. Message passing would exploit worm-hole routing for low overhead. Multiple logical connections on one physical channel would be possible, similar to Inmos' virtual link concept. Fine-grained, systolic communication would be supported. The iWarp is RISC-like in having one instruction per clock with a very-long-instruction-word (VLIW) architecture. The iWarp designers strove to achieve a balance between communication and computation that would address problems spanning the range from fine grained to coarse grained. In addition, they wanted state-of-the-art vector and scalar performance. Zero-overhead communication, like the Transputer's links, was desired.

19.3.2 Background

The iWarp architecture is systolic in the sense that data are pumped in "waves" throughout the processor system, much in the same way that the heart's systolic rhythm pumps blood throughout the body. iWarp chips are used to build scalable parallel processors.

19.3.3 Architecture

The iWarp achieves a communication-to-computation ratio of one to one. Each iWarp component consists of an integer and a floating-point computation section and a communication element. The communication element supports four full-duplex I/O channels of 160 megabytes/second input and output capability. The computation element supports 20 mips of integer operations, and 20 mflops of (single-precision) floating-point performance. The memory access of the computation element supports 160 megabytes/second. Figure 19.12 shows the architecture of the iWarp computation element.

19.3.3.1 Hardware The integer execution unit has an eight-kilobyte ROM for initialization and self-test. The floating-point unit includes an adder and multiplier that can operate in parallel; DMA support is provided. An event pin is used for interrupts, and a timer is included in the architecture. No memory management support is provided.

A communications element is integral to the processor, and is implemented with eight DMA channels. The communication element handles interprocessor data messages. In the message format, 20 bits contain a destination address; 4 bits are assigned for message control. A 32-bit word format is used.

The external memory interface is of a von Neumann style, with a 64-bit-wide data path and 24-bit address. Since iWarps are designed to be used in large parallel networks, the small address space affects only local memory, not total system memory.

A 40 MHz clock is required, which is divided by two internal to the chip. The iWarp chip draws 1 amp at 5 volts and 40 Mhz, for a total power of 5 watts. The device is packaged in a 271-pin PGA format.

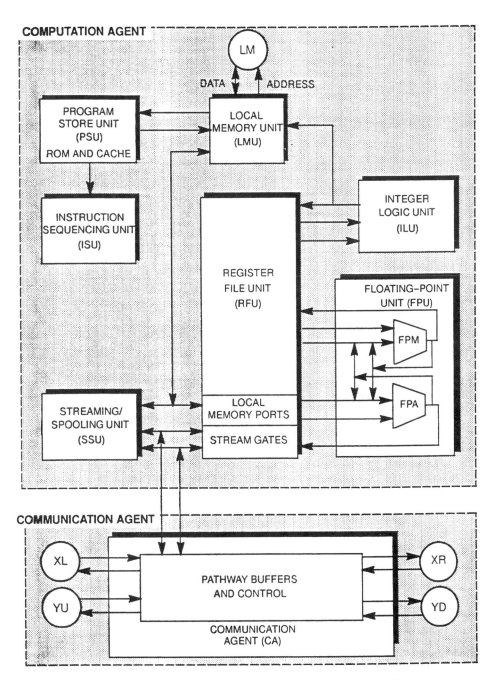

Figure 19.12 iWarp computation element. Reprinted by permission of Intel Corp., copyright 1991 Intel Corp.

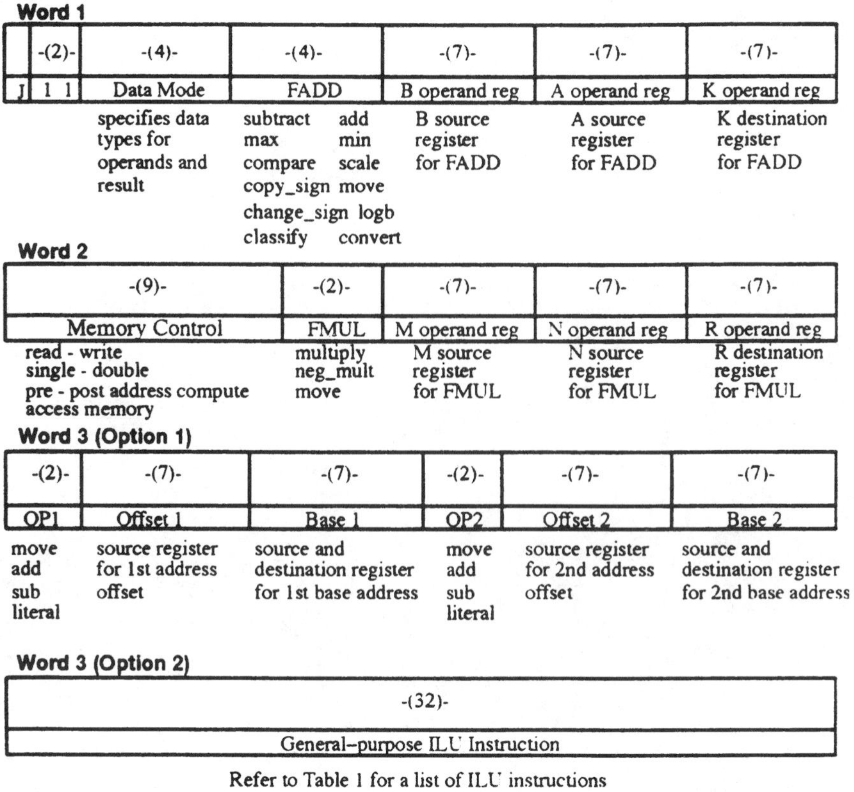

Word 1

-(2)-	-(4)-	-(4)-	-(7)-	-(7)-	-(7)-
J 1 1	Data Mode	FADD	B operand reg	A operand reg	K operand reg
	specifies data types for operands and result	subtract add max min compare scale copy_sign move change_sign logb classify convert	B source register for FADD	A source register for FADD	K destination register for FADD

Word 2

-(9)-	-(2)-	-(7)-	-(7)-	-(7)-
Memory Control	FMUL	M operand reg	N operand reg	R operand reg
read - write single - double pre - post address compute access memory	multiply neg_mult move	M source register for FMUL	N source register for FMUL	R destination register for FMUL

Word 3 (Option 1)

-(2)-	-(7)-	-(7)-	-(2)-	-(7)-	-(7)-
OP1	Offset 1	Base 1	OP2	Offset 2	Base 2
move add sub literal	source register for 1st address offset	source and destination register for 1st base address	move add sub literal	source register for 2nd address offset	source and destination register for 2nd base address

Word 3 (Option 2)

-(32)-
General–purpose ILU Instruction

Refer to Table 1 for a list of ILU instructions

Figure 19.13 iWarp instruction format. Reprinted by permission of Intel Corp., copyright 1991 Intel Corp.

19.3.3.2 Software General-purpose instructions on the iWarp are 32 bits in size. Following the VLIW philosophy, the iWarp also uses a 96-bit compute and access instruction format, with a 32-bit general-purpose format. A single VLIW instruction can perform a floating add, a floating multiply, two memory-address computations, and a memory access. Loop-decrement and branch evaluation take two cycles. Figure 19.13 shows the iWarp instruction format.

Integer math instructions perform add and subtract. Floating-point operations include add, subtract, multiply, divide, log, square root, comparison, and conversion. Shift/bit manipulation instructions include AND, OR, XOR, XNOR, find high bit, and set and reset bit. Flow control is implemented by calls, branches, and supervisor calls.

The register file contains 128 32-bit locations. It is 15-way ported, and can support nine reads and six writes in one clock. This allows both the computation agent and communication elements to access the registers simultaneously. The local memory unit has a 24-bit address bus and a 64-bit data bus. The program store unit implements a one-kilobyte instruction cache, and has startup and system routines in ROM. The integer and floating-point units operate in parallel. The floating adder is not pipelined, and operates in parallel with the multiplier. Single precision requires two cycles, and double precision requires four cycles from either unit. Supported data types on the iWarp include bytes, half words, words (32 bits), and double words.

iWarp tools are hosted on the Sun platform, and include a C and a FORTRAN-77 optimizing compiler, with language extensions for parallelism. Support tools also include a linker, debug monitor, and runtime environment. Math and Unix system call libraries are available.

19.3.3.3 Floating Point Full IEEE single- and double-precision floating point is provided. The adder can operate in parallel with the multiplier. The floating-point unit uses the general register file on the iWarp chip.

19.3.3.4 Cache The on-chip cache size of the iWarp is one kilobyte.

19.3.3.5 Memory Management No memory management features are supported. All I/O is memory mapped in the iWarp.

19.3.4 Summary

RISC Features

Large register set—yes, 128×32
Load/store
Single-cycle execution
Small instruction set
Hardwired instructions

19.4 RISC INFLUENCES ON DIGITAL SIGNAL PROCESSORS

This section discusses two key architectures in the RISC-influenced Digital Signal Processing line. These are Texas Instruments' TMS320C080 in section 19.4.1, and Analog Devices' SHARC in section 19.4.2. DSP influence on RISC is discussed in section 3.7.5. As DSP features are included in more and more architectures, the need for special purpose dedicated DSP chips can be questioned for all but the highest-end and lowest cost applications. Algorithms for compression of audio and video data, for handwriting and speech recognition, and for data communications can be implemented in DSP-derived extensions to RISC architectures. The emergence of the native signal processing (NSP) standard will drive the inclusion of DSP functionality in desktop systems.

19.4.1 TMS320

19.4.1.1 Introduction Texas Instruments' TMS320 family of digital signal processors was introduced in 1982. Since that time, new members of the family have been added with greatly enhanced capabilities. Starting with the 1982 model 32010, over 30 products in six generations have been produced. Some are fixed point only, but the later models support floating point. The TMS320C040 is rated at 275 mips. The C080 model announced in 1994, is capable of in excess of two giga-operations per second, and includes five processor units in one chip. Although these devices are marketed for classical digital signal processing applications, they are universal enough in feature to allow them to be considered for scientific calculation and embedded control applications. In addition, the TMS320 family is interesting in that it balances its processing power with interprocessor communication capability that nicely balances computation and I/O, like the Transputer or iWarp. As silicon manufacturing technology progresses, it should be possible to include more processor units, and more memory on the chip.

19.4.1.2 Background The C0x0 family uses many of the same techniques that RISC machines use to achieve performance: pipelining, superscalar architecture, and a large set of registers. However, they allow direct operand addressing. The instruction set is not really "reduced," but rather optimized for DSP tasks. Most instructions execute in one cycle, and parallelism is supported. The C080 model is marketed as a multimedia video programmer (MVP), and has four DSPs plus a RISC engine with a shared-memory MIMD architecture on one chip.

19.4.1.3 Architecture This section discusses the architecture of the TMS320 family of chips, with emphasis on the most recent and capable family member, the C080.

Hardware The C040 model achieves a large processor throughput by means of a superscalar design, allowing eleven operations per cycle. Although a large register set is provided on-chip, the architecture is not load/store. Operations are allowed on memory locations directly. A 128 word by 32-bit instruction cache is included. A four-stage pipeline architecture supporting delayed branches is used. Six DMA engines support six parallel data paths, and concurrent communications and computation. These 8-bit-wide ports support 20 megabytes per second of I/O each. The DMA controllers support variable indices, which provide for matrix and table addressing with different strides.

The C080 has four 32-bit advanced DSP engines, a 32-bit RISC control unit with floating-point capability, 50 kilobytes of shared SRAM, and 44 user registers. The SRAM array is segmented into 25 blocks of 4 kilobytes. Sixteen of these are accessible to any processor. The others are local memory and cache. The on-chip SRAM is crossbar-shared, and provides the MIMD architecture on the chip. The crossbar can switch every cycle. A single-cycle multiplier is provided, as is support for manipulation of bit fields and pixels. DRAM, SRAM, and VRAM can be directly controlled. Figure 19.14 shows the architecture of the TMS320C080.

Each of the four ADSP engines of the C080 consists of a program flow controller, a data unit (ALU), and two address units, all of which can operate in parallel. It has two kilobytes of I-cache, and eight kilobytes of D-cache. The 32-bit ALUs of the DSPs can be split into two 16-bit or four 8-bit ALUs. A three-stage pipeline is used.

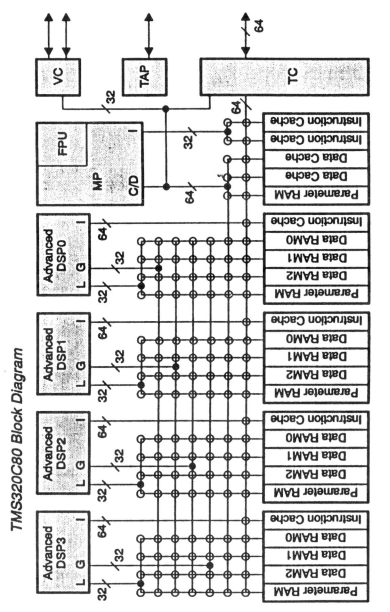

Figure 19.14 TMS320C080 architecture. Courtesy of Texas Instruments.

295

Each DSP engine has 44 user registers. The data unit includes a single-cycle, 16x16-bit multiplier. Each unit can perform three memory accesses per cycle, for the local instruction cache, the local data, or the global data. Three, zero-overhead loop counters are also available in the register file to support zero-overhead nested loops.

The RISC master processor (MP) unit has an integral floating-point processor and a scoreboarded 32 element register file. It uses a three-stage pipeline to support effective single-cycle execution. The RISC master processor has four-kilobyte I-cache, and four-kilobyte D-cache. The MP includes the floating point unit. It has a load/store architecture, and most operations take one cycle. The MP is optimized to efficiency C code.

The on-chip crossbar provides nonblocking interprocessor communications at a bandwidth of 4.2 gigabytes/second. It connects the processors to memory on a cycle-by-cycle basis. Up to five instruction fetches and ten data accesses per cycle can be initiated. A round-robin prioritization is used in case of resource conflict. The transfer controller handles all data and instruction movement, and DRAM refresh for the external memory. It interfaces directly to SRAM, DRAM, or VRAM. Dynamic bus sizing is supported.

Two on-chip video controllers provide timing and control of VRAM, and direct support for image capture and display using frame memories. There are two independent frames for capture (input) and display (output). Timing can be synchronized to external clock sources. The frame times generate horizontal and vertical sync signals, and frame blanking for PAL and NTSC format.

JTAG support is provided by the C080 and there is an emulation port that is a superset of JTAG. The device is available in a 305 pin CPGA, and operates at a supply voltage of 3.3 volts. Clock input to the device is 40 or 50 MHz.

Software TMS320C080 is not binary compatible with previous family members. The instruction set of the C0x0 family is regular, in that all 135 instructions are 32 bits long. Most execute in one cycle. The C080 actually has two instruction sets, one for the RISC engine, and one for the four ADSPs. The C080 uses a 64-bit-long-instruction-word format for the DSP engines. The RISC controller uses a 32-bit-wide instruction format. Both big- and little-endian data transfers are supported.

The master RISC processor has three instruction formats, short and long immediate, and triadic register. Support is provided for integer add and subtract, logical, and compare operations. Floating and vector-floating-point operations are provided. Program control is by conditional and unconditional branches and subroutine call. The architecture is load/store. Zero overhead loops are provided.

The DSP units use a 64-bit long instruction word, and support add, subtract, multiply, shifts, and logical operations on data words. The operations are specified in an algebraic format for ease of coding. All possible 256 Boolean combinations of three inputs are supported. The DSP units have eight data and six index registers, in addition to ten address registers. A 16x16 integer multiplier, and a 32-bit barrel rotator are also included. There are 12 addressing modes for data.

C080 tools are PC-Windows based, and include C/C++ compilers for the RISC master and the DSP processors, assembler/linker/loader, debugger, a simulator, and emulation facilities, aided by on-chip emulation circuitry accessed through the JTAG port. Software libraries are available for image and audio processing, 2D and 3D graphics, MPEG/JPEG, and so on. A resident microkernal is available for the RISC master processor that provides real-time multitasking, synchronization, and communications primitives. A real-time parallel-ICE unit is also available.

Floating Point On the C040, a floating multiply, and a floating add may be performed in parallel in one cycle. The reciprocal of a floating-point number can be calculated in one cycle, and extended from 8 to 32 bits of precision in seven more cycles. Using a floating multiply to complete the divide operation gives a total of nine cycles for floating divide. However, double-precision floating point is not supported in the hardware.

On the C080, the floating-point unit of the MP RISC engine is IEEE 754 compatible, and includes a set of vector floating-point instructions. It handles 32- and 64-bit formats. The floating-point section provides add, subtract, compare, and conversions within one unit, and uses a second functional unit for multiply, divide, and square root. The multiply unit is microcoded and seven-stage pipelined. The floating-point register file shares the scoreboarded integer registers. The double precision square root takes 28 cycles. A double precision add can be performed simultaneously with a single precision multiply and a 64-bit load or store.

Cache The C040 has a 128-word I-cache on chip. Each of the four DSP units of the C080 has its own two kilobytes of I-cache and eight kilobytes of D-cache. The RISC master processor has a 4-kilobyte I-cache, and a 4-kilobyte D-cache. These are four-way set-associative, and use an LRU algorithm. Data write back mode is supported.

Memory Management The C080 has a 32-bit address space. The 50 kilobytes of on-chip RAM is mapped into the lower 32 megabytes of the space, along with the memory-mapped registers. Bus snooping for multiprocessors is not supported.

Exceptions There are one level-triggered and three edge-triggered external interrupts to the master processor. The DSP units do not have interrupts, as the master processor handles those.

19.4.1.4 Summary

RISC Features

Single-cycle execution
Fixed instruction size
Small number of instructions
Large number of registers

19.4.2 SHARC

19.4.2.1 Introduction This section covers the Analog Devices ADSP-2106x SHARC (Super Harvard Architecture Computer) chip family. This is not a mainline RISC chip, but rather a high-end 32-bit DSP chip, designed with RISC techniques and influenced by expansion into multiprocessing. Many vendors are now shipping board-level products based on the SHARC chip, and other vendors have chosen it to replace traditional architectures in number-crunching applications. For example, Mercury Computers has shifted from the i860 chip to the SHARC and has married it with the PowerPC in a multicomputer architecture. Ixthos manufactures a full line of computation-enhancement products based on the chip. The SHARC unit has applications in image processing for sonar, radar, and medical applications, as well as display graphics, laser printers, instrumentation, and data acquisition.

19.4.2.2 Background This chip is designed by Analog Devices, an industry leader in analog products that branched out into high-end DSPs. The ADSP-21000 family consists of 32-bit floating-point DSPs of which the 21060 is the third member. Previous members were the 21010 and 21020, neither of which included on-chip memory. All are instruction-set compatible. Analog Devices worked closely with MIT's Lincoln Labs for signal processing applications for radar. Lincoln Labs influenced the MeshSP multiprocessor interconnect of the SHARC. Lincoln Labs' spin-off, Integrated Computing Engines, Inc., has constructed a 64-SHARC multiprocessor supercomputer for the desktop. The chip was initially fabricated by Sharp.

19.4.2.3 Architecture The 2106x architecture includes a CPU, memory, and connectivity in one chip. The 21060 features a 4-megabit (1/2 megabyte) on-chip static RAM and ten DMA channels. The 21062 is essentially the same, with a 2-megabit memory. The memory can be organized as 16, 32, or 48 bits wide and is dual ported. The chip is intended for multiprocessing. There is a three-stage instruction pipe (fetch, decode, execute). Figure 19.15 shows the SHARC architecture. There are two 40 megabit/second serial ports on the SHARC and 6 link ports that support 40-megabyte/second rates.

Hardware The superscalar SHARC features three computation elements, an ALU, multiplier, and barrel shifter, linked with a 10-port 32 x 40 register file. The ALU and multiplier operate on fixed- or floating-point data types.

Dual data address generators (DAGs) support strange but useful modes such as bit-reversed words and modulo-addressing for use with circular buffers. These modes derive from the DSP world. The DAGs support an indirect mode of data memory addressing using registers. Pre- or post-modify can also be specified.

Instruction execution is single cycle, and the loops are zero overhead, using a "do until"-type construct. The four independent buses allow two data accesses, one instruction fetch, and one DMA transfer in a single cycle.

The chip includes two bidirectional synchronous serial ports, six 4-bit-wide, 40-megabytes/second link ports, and a 48-bit-wide external "system bus" port. The links provide a 40 megabytes per second point-to-point transfer of data between

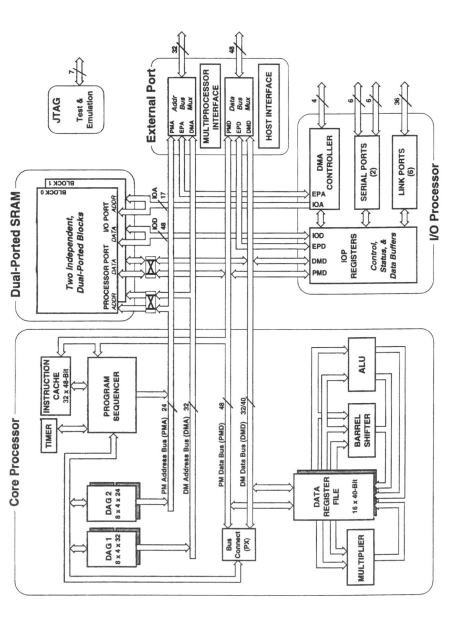

Figure 19.15 SHARC architecture. Cortesy of Analog Devices.

299

processors. This can be used to reduce contention for the common bus in data transfer between multiple processors. The serial ports operate at up to 40 megabits/second each, and feature companding. The six link ports allow a glueless connection to six nearest neighbors in a multiprocessor connection for SIMD or MIMD topologies. They transfer 8 bits per cycle. The system bus port uses a 32-bit address.

The DMA controller works between the chip's various I/O ports and the on-chip memory. The chip provides ten channels of nonblocking DMA. It operates at up to 160 megabytes/second. Autochaining of DMA transfers serves to minimize processor intervention. DMA resources are mapped into the global memory map and are freely accessible to any processor. DMA can involve external or internal memory resources. Any access by one processor to another processor's internal memory will be completely transparent to the second processor.

The processor can be booted from 8-bit-wide ROM, from a host processor, or from one of the link ports, similar to the Transputer. The integral programmable interval timer is 32 bits wide. It decrements every machine cycle and causes an interrupt upon reaching zero, when it is automatically reloaded from a register. The timer can be enabled and disabled under program control.

The part is fabricated in 0.6-micron two-layer metal, with an initial clock speed of 40 MHz. Power consumption is 3.6 watts for 5 volts, and the chip is now available at 3.3 volts. Due to the included 4 megabits of dual ported SRAM, the transistor count goes beyond 25 million. An IEEE 1149.1 JTAG interface is included, and a 240-pin PQFP is used.

Software Instructions for the SHARC are 48 bits in length, and there are 22 of them. There are four major groupings of instructions, and many instructions can be conditional. Data movement can be combined with arithmetic operation. The instruction groups are compute and move or modify, flow control, immediate data move, and miscellaneous. The compute group includes 43 different operations, specified in an "operate" field of 23 bits.

Fixed-point operations include add, subtract, AND, OR, XOR, NOT, min, max, and clip. The "clip" instruction allows the absolute value of a datum to be restricted to a hard limit. The operations on floating-point data include add, subtract, absolute value, compare, minimum, maximum, clip, saturate, reciprocal, and reciprocal square root. The saturate operation sets the result to the maximum value if the results are greater than the allowed maximum value for the specified data format. The reciprocal operation forms an 8-bit seed for 1./(operand), and the reciprocal square root forms a 4-bit seed for 1./(sqrt(operand)). Division is done by an iterative convergence process, and square root may be done by a Newton-Raphson algorithm. Arithmetic shifts and rotates are provided, as well as bit-set, bit-clear, bit-test and bit-toggle. Instructions are provided to extract leading zeros or ones, and for format conversion. The two data address generators implement up to 32 circular buffers in hardware, for streamlined DSP operations.

Jumps and calls can be direct, indirect, or PC-relative. Both delayed and nondelayed branches are supported. An on-chip PC stack holds up to 20 return addresses for subroutines and interrupts. An idle instruction puts the processor into a low-power mode, pending the next interrupt.

Data structures include IEEE 32-bit and extended 40-bit floating point, and 32-bit integers. Double precision floating point (64 bit) format is not supported. The 32-bit address space spans the internal 4-megabit (on the 21064) memory, and the internal memory of other processors in a multiprocessor configuration. The on-chip memory can be configured as 16-, 32- or 48-bit words, and is organized into two independent halves. Each half can be used for instructions or data. There is a register file of 32 registers, organized as 16 primary and 16 secondary. The register file is 10-ported.

The SHARC processors are well suited for use as data-flow architectures, or can be used in 2D or 3D mesh SIMD arrays. In the SIMD arrangement, a master processor provides instructions to the array and nearest neighbor connectivity is achieved though the data link ports. In an MIMD arrangement, each processor has its own control stream, as well as data stream. For cluster multiprocessing, the SHARC processors provide built-in support for up to six SHARCs on a common bus.

Software tools are hosted on a Sun or PC, and include the G21K optimizing ANSI C compiler, derived from GNU C, an assembler, linker, CBUG source-level debugger, runtime libraries, in-circuit emulator, evaluation board, and a simulator. Extensions to the C compiler include features for variably dimensioned arrays, vector math, complex data types, and circular pointers. An ADA compiler is also available from Meridian Software. An ICE emulator unit uses the JTAG mechanism, and runs under Microsoft Windows. It can handle full-speed operation and multiprocessor debugging, as well as single-stepping. A variety of third-party real time operating systems for the SHARC are also available.

Floating Point IEEE 32-bit and extended 40-bit floating-point calculations are supported in hardware. Sixty-four bit operations are not supported in hardware. The floating-point operations include add, subtract, absolute value, compare, minimum, maximum, clip, saturate, reciprocal, and reciprocal square root. The IEEE modes round-toward-zero and round-toward-nearest are supported. Divide takes six cycles, and reciprocal square root can be completed in nine cycles. There are three independent floating-point computation units for ALU operations, multiplication, and shifting.

Cache A two-way, set-associative, 32-word instruction cache is provided on-chip. This is sufficient for the type of tight loops that are typical in DSP-type applications. A least-recently-used replacement algorithm is used for the cache. The chip has a two- or four-megabit on-chip memory using internal SRAM. This is organized in two banks, and can support dual simultaneous operand fetch.

Memory Management Memory management features include support for multiprocessing provided in the form of bus-locking, message registers for software semaphores, and broadcast-write for reflective semaphores. Program memory can contain instructions and data, but data memory can contain only data. An internal path is provided to transfer data between the memory spaces. The two memory spaces can be divided into banks, with boundaries defined in registers. The program space can be divided into two banks and the data space into four banks. Different banks can have different numbers of wait states programmed, and different wait state methods. Memory page sizes are selectable in the range 256-32k words, to allow memory page boundary detection. Automatic wait-state insertion on page boundary crossing can be enabled. A 32-bit physical address is used. Support for multiprocessing is provided by a read-write-modify semaphore mechanism. Broadcast-write is also an option.

Exceptions Four external interrupt select pins are included in the architecture, with edge- or level-sensitivity selectable, as well as a reset. There are nine internal and eight user level exception sources. Interrupts are vectored, with a global- enable bit. The interrupt latency is generally three cycles, but operations that span more than one cycle can hold off interrupts. There is no NMI, except for reset, and an emulation instruction. A total of 32 vectors is provided.

19.4.2.4 Summary

RISC Features

Small number of instructions—22
Pipelined execution
Large register file
Single-word instructions

Non-RISC Features

Three addressing modes for jumps
Modulo addressing
Bit-reversed addressing

19.5 RISC-LIKE PROPRIETARY ARCHITECTURES

This section discusses the RISC-influenced proprietary chips. These chips are ones that are generally not available on the open market, but are designed for one company's internal use. The design decision to use a custom chip instead of a merchant chip is a complex one. A custom chip gives advantages, but does not ride the manufacturing volume curve of the merchant chips. Customers may be adverse to invest in a system with a processor that is a closed or proprietary design. On the other hand, a custom design can provide overwhelming benefits in certain areas. The design and testing can be done with emerging tools such that a custom design may be less than a generation behind the merchant chips. There are other subtle benefits—nCube, for example, does its chip design and simulations on its own massively parallel machines, giving it a simulation performance advantage. This section will discuss the custom RISC chip designs from the computer manufacturers nCube, KSR, MasPar, and IBM.

19.5.1 nCUBE

19.5.1.1 Background nCUBE is in the business of building massively parallel machines, based on its proprietary chip design and a hypercube interconnect. The nCUBE machines have been used in the "big science" class of problems, to host very large parallel databases, and for consumer applications such as video-on-demand.

19.5.1.2 Architecture The nCUBE machine is based on a proprietary chip design, currently 32 bits (the nCUBE2) and going to 64 bits (nCUBE3). This chip is currently fabricated by HP. A single chip plus DRAM chips makes a module; modules are combined on boards into systems. The advantage of nCUBE's approach is minimization of components; all necessary logic is built onto the single chip. This is similar to the Transputer T-800 and iWarp, but with more I/O channels. A "single-wide" module holds the chip plus 16 megabytes, with a "double-wide" module holding 32 megabytes. The I/O subsystem uses the same format modules, with different backend interfaces to support SCSI and other industry-standard interfaces. An nCUBE2 node supports up to 16 megabytes of memory on a board measuring 1" $\times$ 3.5". The nCUBE node has only the CPU and DRAM memory, with no glue logic required, because of the highly integrated CPU. This is the advantage of the proprietary design—reduced cost of the system level.

Interconnection among processor nodes in an nCUBE machine is via a hypercube topology. Each nCUBE2 chip has 13 I/O engines, one of which is used for I/O. Thus, an order-12 Hypercube is supported, or up to 4096 (2^{12}) nodes. The worst-case (longest-distance) communication is the order of the Hypercube, or 12 in this case. The nCUBE3 chip expands this to 16 DMA engines for interprocessor communication.

Hardware The nCUBE3 chip features a 64-bit ALU, and is superscalar. It initially operates at 50 MHz, but scales to 66 and 100 MHz. It targets 50 mips and 100 mflops at 50 MHz. It has a 16-kilobyte I-cache, and a 16-kilobyte D-cache, with virtual memory support and some new instructions. There are 18 communications channels on-chip, each 4 bits wide (2 in, 2 out). The channels operate at twice the clock frequency, or 50 megabytes/second peak each, 200 megabytes/second aggregate. The latency is less than two microseconds, with 200 nS internode forwarding. Adaptive routing is used for message transfer. Memory can be up to one gigabyte of synchronous DRAM, with an 800 megabytes/second bandwidth. The nCUBE includes 16 registers, and the nCUBE3 has 32.

The nCUBE3 chips use 0.5-micron, 3-level metal CMOS, operating at 3.3 volts, and using 3.26 million transistors. Thus, nCUBE design is not that far behind the merchant chip state-of-the-art. The company does its chip design and simulation on nCUBE machines. The chips feature low-latency channels and balanced I/O. The nCUBE2 chips operate at 25 MHz, with the nCUBE3 going to 50 MHz.

The nCUBE2(S) processor is packaged in a 108-pin package. The nCUBE3 is in a 348-pin package. The nCUBE2 processor operates at 5.0 volts, where the newer version has gone to 3.3 volts.

Software nCUBE has its own in-house compiler group, and tool developers. Each chip runs a 200-kilobyte microkernel (nCX), although the box and associated front end (SUN/SGI) runs Unix. Compilers for FORTRAN and C are available, as well as math and parallelization libraries, debuggers, and profilers.

Floating Point Full 64-bit IEEE-754 floating point is supported on the nCUBE chips. The optimized unit in the nCUBE3 chip is heavily pipelined, and can operate in a vector mode for eight single-precision operations per instruction. Divide and square root are supported.

Cache Eight kilobytes each of instruction and data cache are included on the nCUBE3 chip. The caches are physically addressed and two-way set associative.

Memory Management The nCUBE3 design includes support for virtual memory.

19.5.1.3 Summary

RISC Features

Single-cycle or superscalar operation

Non-RISC Features

Multiple operand addressing modes

19.5.2 KSR

19.5.2.1 Introduction Kendall Square Research (KSR) machines are based on their own chip design. The KSR1 chipset was fabricated by Sharp, with the KSR2 chipset being built by HP. The processor, implemented as a chipset, achieved two operations per cycle. Instruction-decode is hardwired, and pipelining is used. Up to 1088 processor units could be constructed in the KSR1. KSR had considered moving in the direction of standard chips in their next architecture, with use of the PowerPC.

19.5.2.2 Background KSR of Waltham, Massachusetts, was founded in 1986. The company manufactures the KSR1 and KSR2 general-purpose, highly parallel massively parallel processors (MPPs) using their patented AllCache memory system. Their focus shifted from scientific to commercial applications in early 1994. They stopped shipping hardware in September 1994, and are currently reorganizing the business.

19.5.2.3 Architecture There are six unique chips per processor in the KSR2. These include the CCU (cell control unit), the CIU (cell interconnect unit), the FPU (floating-point unit), the IPU (Integer-processing unit), the CEU (cell execution unit), and the DMA I/O unit. There are four each of the CCU and CIU chips. Two processors are provided per board, which then plugs into the backplane interconnect. The backplane actually can handle 20 slots or 40 processors total. Figure 19.16 shows the KSR architecture.

Hardware The KSR1 processor is implemented as a four-chip set in 1.2-micron CMOS. These chips are the cell execution unit (CEU), the floating-point unit, the integer and logical operations unit, and the external I/O unit (XIO).

The CEU handles instruction fetch (two per clock), and all operations involving memory, such as loads and stores. Forty-bit addresses are used, with the capability of expanding to 64-bit addresses later. The integer unit has thirty-two 64-bit-wide registers. The XIO has the capability of transfering 30 megabytes/second to I/O devices. This unit includes 64 control and data registers.

Software KSR instructions are any of six types: memory reference (load/store), execute, control flow, memory control, I/O, and inserted. Execute instructions include arithmetic, logical, and type conversion. They are usually triadic register in format. Control flow refers to branches and jumps. Branch instructions are two cycles. The programmer (or compiler) can implicitly control the "quashing" behavior of the subsequent two instructions that will be initiated during the branch. The choices are: always retain the results, retain results if branch test is true, or retain results if branch test is false. Memory control provides synchronization primitives. I/O instructions are included. Inserted instructions are forced into the instruction flow by a coprocessor. Inserted load and store are used for DMA transfers, and inserted memory instructions are used to maintain cache coherency. New coprocessors can be interfaced using the inserted instruction mechanism.

Floating Point IEEE standard floating-point arithmetic is supported. Sixty-four 64-bit-wide registers are included.

Cache In the KSR design, all of memory is treated as cache. A Harvard-style, separate bus for instruction and memory is used. Each node board contains 256 kilobytes of I-cache and D-cache, essentially primary cache.

19.5.2.4 Summary

RISC Features

Large register set
Load/store
Hardwired decode

19.5.3 MasPar

19.5.3.1 *Introduction* MasPar is unique in being a manufacturer of SIMD machines. In this approach, a collection of ALUs listens to a program broadcast from a central source. The ALUs can do their own data fetch, but are all under control of a

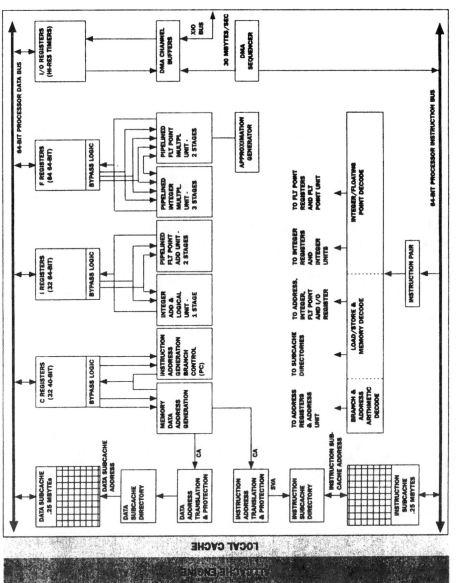

Figure 19.16 KSR architecture. Illustration is copyright by Kendall Square Research, 1990, 1991, 1992, 1993, and 1994.

306

central array control unit. There is a central clock. The emphasis is on communications efficiency and low latency. The MasPar architecture is designed to scale and to balance processing, memory, and communication. In a system, up to 512 processors can be used. MasPar uses a full custom CMOS chip, the MP2 PE, designed in-house and fabricated by various vendors such as HP or Texas Instruments.

19.5.3.2 Background The MasPar machines are specialized computer systems designed for data-parallel approaches, which match compute-intensive applications such as decision support and fine-grained parallel operations such as database searches. In a maximum configuration MP2 machine, the processing rate is 68 gips and 6.3 gigaflops.

19.5.3.3 Architecture The array control unit (ACU) handles instruction fetch. It is a load/store architecture. The MasPar architecture is Harvard in a broad sense. The ACU implements a microcoded instruction fetch, but achieves a RISC-like single instruction per clock. The arithmetic units, ALUs with data-fetch capability, are implemented 32 to a chip. Each ALU is connected in a nearest-neighbor fashion to eight others. The edge connections are brought off-chip. In this scheme, the perimeters can be toroid-wrapped. Up to 16,384 units can be connected within the confines of a cabinet. Figure 19.17 shows the MasPar MP2 architecture.

A global router, essentially a cross-bar switch, provides external I/O to the processor array.

Hardware The MP2 PE chip contains 32 processor elements, each a full 32-bit ALU with floating point, registers, and a barrel shifter. Only the instruction fetch feature is removed and placed in the ACU. The PE design is literally replicated 32 times on the chip. The chip is designed to interface to DRAM, to other processor array chips, and to communication router chips.

Each ALU, called a PE slice, contains sixty-four 32-bit registers that are used for both integer and floating point. The registers are, interestingly, bit and byte addressable. The floating-point unit handles single- and double-precision arithmetic on IEEE format numbers. Each PE slice contains two registers for holding the data memory address and the associated data item. Each PE also has two bit serial ports, one for inbound and one for outbound communication for the nearest neighbor. The direction of communication is globally controlled. The PEs also have inbound and outbound paths to a global router for I/O. A broadcast port allows a single instance of data to be "promoted" to parallel data. Alternately, global data can be OR-ed (demoted?) to a scalar result.

The serial links support one megabyte per second bit-serial communication that allows coordinated register to register communication between processors. Each processor has its own local memory, implemented in DRAM. No internal memory is included on the processors. Microcoded instruction decode is used.

The 32 PEs on a chip are clustered into two groups sharing a common memory interface, or M-machine, for access. A global scoreboard keeps track of memory and register usage. The path to memory is 16 bits wide. Both big- and little-endian formats are supported. Each processor has its own 64 kilobytes of memory space. Both

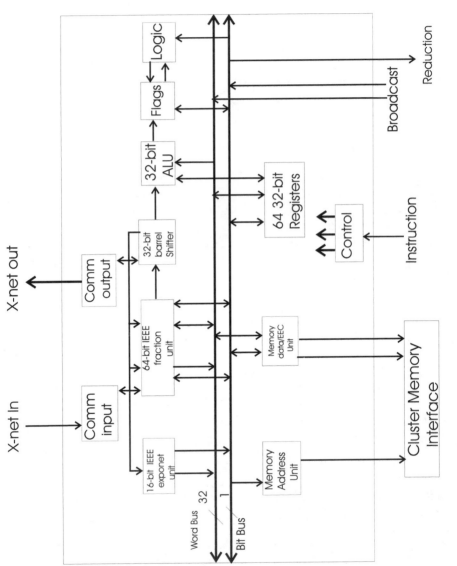

Figure 19.17 MasPar MP2 architecture. © Maspar Computer Corporation 1995.

direct and indirect data memory addressing are supported. Each PE has twenty-five 64-bit-wide registers.

The chip is implemented in 1.0-micron two-level metal CMOS, dissipates 0.8 watt, and is packaged in a 208-pin PQFP. A relatively low clock rate of 12.5 MHz is used.

Software The MasPar machines are front-ended by a host machine, usually a Vax. They are accessed by extensions to the languages FORTRAN and C.

Floating Point Full IEEE single- and double-precision floating point are supported in the MasPar architecture.

Cache There is no cache for the ALUs. Cache is not required, due to the memory interface operating at commensurate speed with the ALU data accesses.

Memory Management The ALUs do not implement memory management for data memory. The ACU uses demand-paged virtual memory for the instruction memory.

19.5.3.4 Summary

RISC Features

Load/store
Large number of registers

Non-RISC Features

Microcoded instruction decode
Multiple addressing mode for data

19.5.4 IBM RIOS 1 and 2

19.5.4.1 Introduction IBM's RISC microprocessors range from the early ROMPS-based RISC-PC, to the POWER family, to the newest Power-PC architecture. This section covers the RIOS chip family. There are two members: the RIOS 1 and 2. The RIOS 3 was phased out in 1994 by IBM in favor of substituting the Power-PC 630.

19.5.4.2 Background IBM Corporation certainly needs no introduction in the world of computers, producing machines ranging from laptops to mainframes. The RS6000 family of scientific computers is a 32-bit design for scientific workstations. The RS6000 family is based on the RIOS family of chips. IBM's POWER (Performance Optimization with Enhanced RISC) architecture defines a family of desktop and deskside machines with a wide spectrum of performance. The MCA bus is used, and the operating system is AIX, a Unix variant. The RIOS chip design was influenced by the IBM 801 Project, headed by John Cocke in building 801 of the Yorktown Heights Research Center in 1975.

IBM manufactures the RIOS chips for its own use, and does not make them available to customers except as integrated computer systems.

19.5.4.3 Architecture The first generation chipset, introduced in 1990, is referred to as RIOS 1, with a RIOS 2 being introduced in 1993. The chip sets are superscalar and pipelined. Figure 19.18 shows the internal organization of the RS/6000.

The RIOS 1 was introduced at 25 Mhz with 8 kilobytes of cache, and grew to 62.5 Mhz operation, with 32 kilobytes of cache. The RIOS 1 processor is capable of executing four instructions per clock. These have to be: one integer, one floating point, one branch, and one condition register operation. The RIOS 2 can execute six instructions per clock, and these have to be two integer, two floating point, one branch, and one conditional instruction.

Hardware The RIOS 1 architecture design uses a large register set and hardwired instruction decode. The interface to the on-chip I-cache is four words wide, to support the issuance of up to four instructions at a time. IBM's designers intended the architecture to be scalable to higher levels of instruction issue. Zero-cycle branches are enabled by a branch processor, with a wide interface to the I-cache. The fixed-point unit can do a multiply in three to five cycles, and a divide in 19 cycles. The integer unit handles 79 fixed point ALU operations, and 55 data reference operations.

The RIOS 2 derives from the RIOS 1, with expanded memory, widened data paths, and added functional units. The RIOS 2 has two complete integer and floating-point units.

The RIOS 2 consists of eight semicustom chips: instruction cache, four data caches, the fixed point ALU, the floating point ALU and a storage control unit. The prefetch buffer, filled from the I-cache, is 16 instructions deep. The instruction dispatcher decodes the first six instructions in the prefetch buffer. It also looks for branches in the seventh and eighth slots. Up to four floating and integer instructions can be dispatched per cycle, along with two branches, or one branch and one condition code modifying instruction. The dispatcher issues instructions in-order, and does not consider data dependencies.

A special branch unit in the instruction cache unit hides branches from the arithmetic units. This feature is called zero-cycle branching. Separate decoders allow working ahead on prefetched branch target streams. The instruction unit does not use branch prediction. There are two branch units. Two branches can be executed simultaneously, if the first is known not to be taken, using the condition code attached to the instruction.

The integer and floating-point units each can handle two instructions per cycle, although four can be dispatched to the unit and queued. The integer unit has two ALUs that are not the same. One has a three-input adder instead of a two-input adder, and has a multiply/divide unit for 36×26-bit data. The multiplier takes two cycles for integer multiplication. Division requires a table lookup, five multiplys,

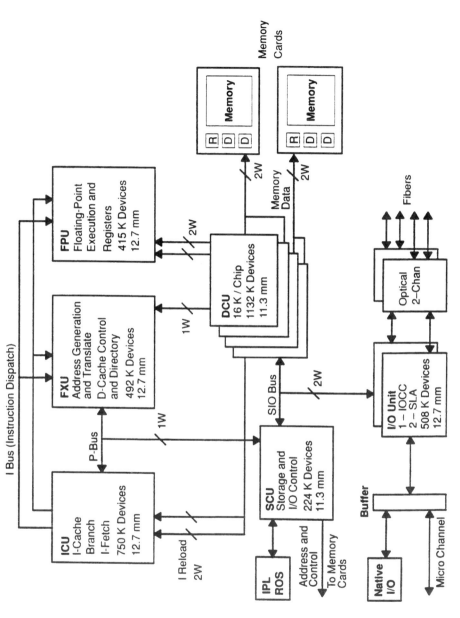

Figure 19.18 RS/6000 block diagram. Reprinted by permission from International Business Machines Corp. Copyright 1993 by International Business Machines Corp.

311

and two subtractions, and can be completed in 13 cycles. Data dependencies are checked in the arithmetic units. Both ALUs can operate together for complex string load and compare instructions.

Each of the CPU chips gets a built-in COP (common on-chip processor) for built-in self-test support. This occupies about 3 percent of the chip area. A serial interface links the COPs and a test facility. This system predates the JTAG standard.

Ball grid array (BGA) packaging is used for the low-cost version of the RIOS 1 and RIOS 2, in addition to the multichip module (MCM) configuration. The MCM is a very expensive packaging option to produce, but does combine the functional chips plus interconnect wiring. The module is configured as a 736-pin PGA for the RIOS 2. The RIOS 2 dissipates 65 watts, at 66.5 MHz.

Software   The instruction set includes 184 instructions. Supported data types include bytes, half-words, and words. The RIOS 2 adds quad-word (128-bit) load and store. Operations on unaligned strings are supported. Strings can be length defined, or null terminated. The RIOS architecture can support zero-cycle branches. Conditional branches use preset condition codes to assist the dispatcher.

Multiple-operand address modes are supported, including absolute, indirect, base-plus-displacement, and base-plus-index. The processor is big-endian, with special instruction support for handling little-endian data. In addition to the standard instruction set, there is a floating multiply-add instruction, and a branch-on-count, utilizing a dedicated count register.

Out-of-order execution is supported if there are no data dependencies. Register renaming is used for resource allocation. All registers are 64-bits-wide. There are 40 registers in the RIOS 1, and 54 in the RIOS 2. Only 32 are visible to the programmer at any one time. The register files are separate for the two execution units of the RIOS 2.

A full line of software development for the RIOS architecture is hosted under AIX. Tools include compilers for C/C++ and FORTRAN. Also available are an assembler, linker, debugger, simulator, and profiler. The simulator supports architectural and timing simulations. Emulators are available to run DOS and Macintosh applications under AIX.

Floating Point   The floating-point unit has a two-word-wide interface with the D-cache, and its own thirty-two 64-bit-wide registers. Register renaming is used to reduce data dependencies at runtime. Six rename registers and two registers for the divide operation are also included. Full IEEE floating point is supported. The floating-point unit implements 13 arithmetic instructions, including the usual add, subtract, multiply, and divide. A special instruction is the four operand multiply-add ($a*b+c$), with the same delay as either operation separately. This has four forms that allow multiply-add, multiply-subtract, negative multiply-add, and negative multiply-subtract. Multiply-add forms the basis for Newton-Raphson or series approximation to the transcendental functions. The RIOS 2 supports square root in hardware. The floating-point unit has two complete functional units and uses the integer ALU for operand address calculations. A six-stage pipeline is used. Data dependencies are resolved in the arithmetic units. FP execution can be out of order with respect to integer operations. The integer and the floating-point instruction streams are synchronized only at loads and stores. The Power 2 FPU uses a two-stage pipeline, and register renaming for multiple issue and execution support. The FPU can be accomplishing two loads, two stores, and two math operations simultaneously. Result bypassing is used to avoid pipeline stalls caused by read references to results not yet stored.

Cache The RIOS 1, a seven chip-set, includes 32 kilobytes of I-cache and 128 kilobytes of D-cache. The D-cache is four-way set associative, and store-back. Cache contents are always big-endian. The RIOS 2, a three chip-set, has 32 kilobytes of I-cache, and 256 kilobytes of D-cache. The cache is effectively dual ported to support two data loads or stores per cycle. The cache is virtually multiported because it is fast enough to sequentially support two accesses per cycle. The I-cache can supply eight consecutive instructions per cycle. The RIOS 2 has a two-way set-associative, 32 kilobyte I-cache, with its own I-TLB. There is an eight-entry target buffer for conditional branches. The data cache is four-way set associative and dual ported. It can be organized as 256 kilobytes accessed over an 8 word bus, or 128 kilobytes and a 4 word bus.

Memory Management The RIOS architecture has separate instruction and data translation lookaside buffers. These are both large and set associative. The D-TLB of RIOS 1 is 128 entry and two-way set associative. The RIOS 2 unit is 512 entry, and dual ported. They use an LRU refill algorithm. Hardware support is provided for reload and page table updates. The virtual address space for the RIOS 1 is 2^{52} bytes. A 32-bit read address is used. There are 16 segment registers, assigned to a memory or I/O space. Read and write protection is provided at the user and supervisor levels. The upper one megabyte of the real address space is reserved for ROM. I/O is memory mapped.

Exceptions There are nine different interrupt types in the RIOS architecture. Interrupt vectoring is used in the processing. Precise exceptions are guaranteed for integer instructions but not for floating-point instructions. Here, when an instruction causes an interrupt, the pipeline is stopped before the machine state can be altered by an interruptible instruction. In addition, the integer unit is kept from being more than two instructions ahead of the floating-point unit. The floating-point unit can get ahead of the fixed-point unit by up to six instructions. The floating point interrupts are imprecise.

19.5.4.4 Summary

RISC Features

Large register set—32+32×64
Load/store
Single-cycle execution

Small instruction set—184

Hardwired instructions

Non-RISC Features

Addressing modes (3)

String load and compare

Misaligned data support

19.6 ATT92010

19.6.1 Introduction

This section describes AT&T's entry into the 32-bit RISC design wars with the 92010 processor and associated chips. The 92010 addressed integrated computation/communication for the Personal Communicator market. When that market softened in early 1994, AT&T abandoned any further development of the chip.

19.6.2 Background

AT&T, a leader in the communications field, has been a major manufacturer of integrated circuits for a long time. Most of us haven't seen them because they were manufactured for internal use. AT&T is attempting to branch out into computation-communication products, where its marketing and extant communications reputation will help it gain market share. AT&T produced a 32-bit CISC processor, the WE3200, for its own use. In addition, it commercially provides a 32-bit DSP family, the DSP-32 series.

The 92010 chipset attempted to minimize the mips-per-watt factor, providing high performance for small, lightweight, battery-powered systems. The 92010 design requirements were driven by the Personal Communications market. AT&T saw this as a major market area for itself in the coming years. This is a classic consumer market; that is, it is cost-sensitive. The Personal Communications product provides integrated computation/communications in a small, lightweight package. Unique constraints for this class of product result in unique design requirements for the base RISC machine. Examples of Personal Communicators began to appear in the marketplace in 1992, with EO Corporation basing theirs on AT&T's processor. Competing products included the Apple Newton, and Tandy's Zoomer. When consumer demand for the first-generation products did not develop as expected, EO went out of business in early 1994.

The 92010 was the first in a planned series of processors from AT&T. It was accompanied by companion chips, including the 92011 System Management device. Also available in the family were the 92012 PCMCIA Controller, the 92013 Peripheral controller, and the 92014 video display controller for CRTs or flat panels. The 92020 processor doubled the size of the prefetch buffer to six kilobytes.

The 92012 PCMCIA Controller interfaces the AT&T processor to the personal computer memory card association (PCMCIA) bus, version 2.0. Block mode access is provided between the processor and the memory (or I/O) cards. This functions as a bus master in these transfers. Up to four card slots are supported. Thirty-two-bit data formats are mapped into dual 16-bit PCMCIA accesses.

The 92013 Peripheral Controller provides an interface from the 92010 to a subset of the industry standard architecture (ISA) bus, or AT-bus. Up to eight memory or I/O devices on the bus can be accommodated. Four channels of 8- or 16-bit DMA are provided, with the 92010 as bus master. The 92013 handles 92010's 32-bit accesses as two 16-bit or four 8-bit accesses. Memory and I/O accesses are supported by mapping the 92010 bus address into a 16-megabyte region on the ISA side. Up to 18 of these 16 megabyte regions are supported.

The 92014 Video Display Controller interfaces the 92010 bus to video memory for a CRT or LCD screen. An area of memory in the 92010 address space can be set aside for snooping by the 92014. Data transfers can be direct, or through a write-through buffer, implemented as a 256-word FIFO. Color LCD displays are supported with an external VRAM frame buffer, and the CRT data are output to external RAMDAC. Simultaneous operation of a CRT and an LCD device is possible.

The 92010 design is derived from the circa 1980 "CRISP" architecture developed by AT&T, which is optimized to run C code, and thus Unix. CRISP stands for *C-code reduced instruction set (processor)*. The primary influence of CRISP is seen in the lack of registers, and the use of a stack cache.

19.6.3 Architecture

The 92010 achieves a peak rate of slightly better than one cycle per instruction through a variety of techniques. It is not superscalar. Most instructions are inherently single cycle. A 3-kilobyte, three-way set-associate cache is provided for encoded instructions, and a 256-byte stack cache holds the top of the user stack on-chip. There is a 32-entry direct-mapped (1:1) decoded-instruction cache. Its high code density results in reduced memory requirements for applications. This has the twofold benefit of reducing power requirements for memory, and speeding applications. Figure 19.19 shows the architecture.

19.6.3.1 Hardware The prefetch decode unit incorporates a three-stage pipeline, as does the execution unit. Operand bypassing is used to supply results to subsequent operations in the pipeline without requiring a write followed by a read. This technique is called read-canceling. A single execution unit is included in the AT&T microprocessor. Integer multiply and divide is handled by on-chip hardware. The chip achieves a respectable 27k Dhrystone performance figure.

The 92011 System Management device augments the basic processor architecture by providing bus arbitration for up to five bus masters. It incorporates the system clock, interrupt controller functions, and DRAM control. It includes a real-time clock, and a synchronous serial and an asynchronous port. Two hundred and fifty-six bytes of battery-backed SRAM are also on-chip. The 92011 allows for graceful stopping and restarting of the main processor's clock. DRAM refresh can continue in stopped mode.

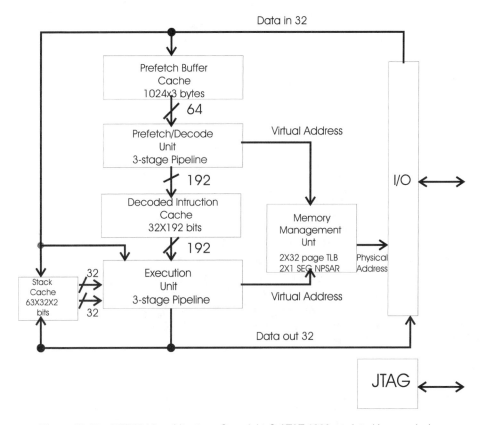

Figure 19.19 ATT92010 architecture. Copyright © AT&T 1992 reprinted by permission.

DRAM control supports fast-page-mode read and write, and has programmable timing for RAS and CAS. Self-refreshed DRAM may be used. Up to four banks of 1-, 4-, or 16-megabit DRAMs may be used. Figure 19.20 shows the architecture of the 92011 system manager.

Interrupts are provided from three external sources, or by internal events such as timer overflow. Certain instructions are not interruptible. Exceptions are used to signal program errors, such as division by zero or privilege violation.

Multiple bus masters are accommodated by a bus request/bus grant protocol, with the 92010 not necessarily the default master. An external arbiter is used.

The on-chip MMU includes dual 32-entry TLBs for paged or nonpaged segments. Address translation can be enabled or disabled. A 32-bit-wide von Neumann–type memory interface is used, with 32-bit physical addresses. Write buffering is not used. Either aggressive or demand prefetching of instructions is supported. For aggressive prefetch, the prefetch unit requests quad word chunks until a branch or jump is encountered. If the branch target is encoded, prefetching continues from the branch target. If not, prefetching ceases. In demand fetch, the execution unit takes a mispredicted branch. Demand prefetch, originating at the execution unit, is the default mode.

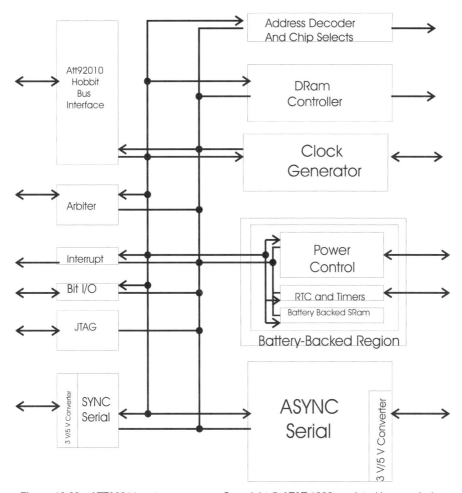

Figure 19.20   ATT92011 system manager. Copyright © AT&T 1992 reprinted by permission.

The 920x0 family chips are IEEE 1149.1 JTAG compatible, and include a 4-bit-wide port for boundary scan and test. The chip dissipates 250 mW at 3.3 volts, 20 MHz, and uses less than 50 microamps in standby. The associated System Management chip dissipates 90 mW, and less than 50 microamps in standby. The family is designed to work between 3- and 5-volt levels. The chip is packaged as a 132-pin plastic quad flat pack (PQFP). The system management chip is a 208-pin package. It is implemented in 0.9-micron CMOS.

19.6.3.2 Software   The 92010's instruction repertoire is small, consisting of only 44 different hardwired instructions. These are referred to as two and one-half operand instructions, which are instructions that specify two source operands and default to a known destination operand.

The instruction format allows for variable-length instructions. Pipelining is still feasible because there are only three formats, identified in the first byte. Instructions are identified as 1, 3, or 5 parcel, a parcel being 16 bits, or 2 bytes. Single-cycle execution is maintained. Code density distribution studies by AT&T have shown that over 70 percent of executed instructions are 2 bytes, with an average of less than 4 bytes per instruction. That compares favorably with 32-bit-wide fixed-instruction formats. The instruction formats are shown in Figure 19.21.

No floating-point instructions are included. Quite unlike other RISC architectures, the processor is a memory-memory architecture, with no specific load/store instructions.

The integer operations add, subtract, multiply, and divide are supported, as well as the AND, OR, and XOR logical operations. There is a left shift operation, and both an arithmetic and logical right shift. Logical comparisons are for equality, and for signed- and unsigned-greater-than.

Branch folding is used to reduce branches to zero cycles. This may at first appear to be magic, but it is just clever engineering. In essence, a branch instruction is folded back into the previous instruction such that the program counter is not incremented as would be the case for sequential instructions, but gets the branch value instead. The branch instruction disappears into the previous instruction. Of course, this works well for unconditional branches, but what about conditional ones? Each instruction has two next-PC (program counter) fields (one is the alternate next-PC), and branch prediction is done at the compiler level. A static branch prediction hint-bit is inserted by the compiler to assist the hardware in making the right guess. This reduces the nonsequential flow-of-control penalty. Neither delayed branch slots, nor load delays, are required in this scheme.

Program control is modified by call and return instructions, and op codes to allocate and free stack space and fill the stack cache. An unconditional jump instruction is included. A flush may be forced to the decoded instruction cache or the prefetch buffer.

The 92010 has no user-visible registers. To avoid penalties in addressing external memory, the 92010 caches the top 256 bytes of the stack on-chip into a circular buffer, with associated head and tail pointers. The interesting thing about a stack cache is that no tags are required. Since the cache is a FIFO data structure, only a bounds check is needed to determine if an item is present in on-chip cache. In a sense, the stack cache is like variable-length register windows. By AT&T's studies, the hit rate for data references is about 88 percent.

Control registers include the configuration register, the fault register, the JTAG register, interrupt and maximum stack pointer, program counter and program status word (PSW), shadow register, stack pointer, segment table and vector base, and two timer registers. The layout of the PSW is shown in Figure 19.22.

Unlike most RISC machines, the 92010 has multiple-operand addressing modes. There are seven operand addressing modes: immediate, direct and indirect absolute, direct and indirect stack offset, program counter relative, and register. In immediate and absolute modes, the 32-bit operand value is stored in the instruction itself. In

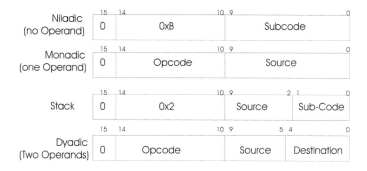

One Parcel Formats

A. Monadic (One Operand)

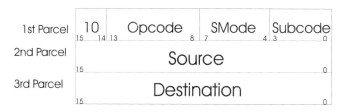

B. Dyadic (Two Operands)

Three Parcel Instruction Formats

Figure 19.21 Instruction formats. Copyright © AT&T 1992 reprinted by permission.

BIT(S)

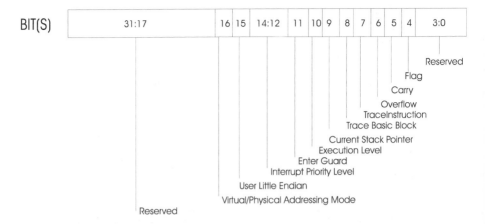

Figure 19.22 Program status word. Copyright © AT&T 1992 reprinted by permission.

stack offset mode, a signed 2's complement offset is stored in the instruction. The offset is added to the stack pointer. In stack-offset-indirect, the result of the addition is not the address of the operand, but the address of the address. Absolute indirect stores the address of the address of the operand in the instruction, and is used only for certain instructions, such as jump and call. Similarly, these instructions can use the PC relative mode, where the signed 2's complement value in the instruction is added to the address of the instruction to determine the operand address. In register addressing mode, access is provided to the internal registers. Jump/call instructions have four addressing modes: absolute, indirect, PC relative, and stack-offset-indirect.

High code density is maintained by the memory-memory architecture. In this scheme, memory access time is controlled by cached reads and writes. This optimizes the first (instructions/task) term of the performance equation (section 3.4.3), which is usually ignored by RISC designs. For example, the following is an illustration of the addition of two items in memory in both approaches:

Memory-Memory	Load-Store
Add A,B	Load A
	Load B
	Add
	Store A

Thus, if the memory-memory architecture can be made to work at the one-instruction-per-cycle rate, it has obvious advantages. Either big-endian or little-endian byte ordering can be handled by means of a settable bit in the PSW. Instructions can generally operate on signed or unsigned bytes, half-words, or words.

The 92010 development toolbox includes a cross-compiler (for C), a cross-assembler and linker, and a debugger. An in-circuit emulator is available, as well as a PC-board host for the 92010 chip.

19.6.3.3 Floating Point The first-generation 92010 does not support floating point.

19.6.3.4 Cache The 92010 uses a 3-kilobyte, three-way set-associative cache for encoded instructions, and a 256-byte stack cache holds the top of the user stack on-chip. In addition, there is a 32-entry direct-mapped (1:1) decoded instruction cache. The 92020 processor uses 6 kilobytes of cache.

There is no data cache per se, but the on-chip stack cache holds the top (most recently referenced) section of the user cache. This is a unique approach to caching a user data structure. The stack cache is implemented as a bank of sixty-four 4-byte registers in a circular structure, with a stack pointer and a maximum stack pointer. The stack pointer is the lowest addressed datum in the cache. The maximum stack pointer points above the highest addressed datum in the cache. If the address of a referenced data item lies between the two register values, the data are present in the stack. No facilities for secondary cache or multiprocessing/coherency modeling are provided.

19.6.3.5 Memory Management 92010's on-chip MMU, when enabled by setting the PSW virtual/physical bit to one, translates virtual to physical addresses in paged or nonpaged segments. The virtual address space is specified by a 32-bit address, and is divided into 1024 segments of 4 megabytes each. Paged segments are divided further into 4-kilobyte pages. Nonpaged segments can vary in size from 4 kilobytes to 4 megabytes. In the present page, a zero-cycle translation is possible. Translation makes use of map tables of physical addresses, which are 4 kilobytes. User and kernel access-rights bits are included. Data areas may be marked as read-only. Address translation in the chip is shown in Figure 19.23.

User and kernel segment identifiers are maintained, and segments can be marked with read/write permissions.

19.6.3.6 Exceptions Interrupts signal a need for servicing an external device or the timers. Exceptions signal errors in the executing program. Three interrupt input lines are provided, and the two timers can have timeout interrupts enabled. Seven levels of priority are allowed. A nonmaskable interrupt is supported. Interrupt latency is usually one cycle, since most instructions complete before the interrupt is serviced. Long instructions, such as divide, are interruptible. Exception conditions include division-by-zero, illegal instruction, privilege violation, and read/write faults.

Interrupts are handled and prioritized by the 92011 System Management chip. The 92011 has eight programmable input pins that it vectors to the five interrupt pins of the ATT microprocessor. Interrupt mask registers are provided.

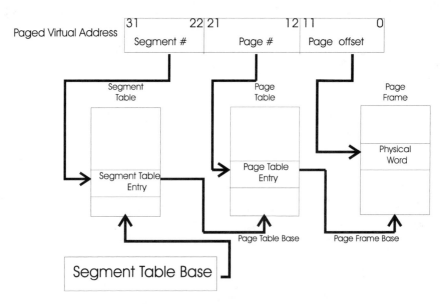

Paged Segment Address Mapping

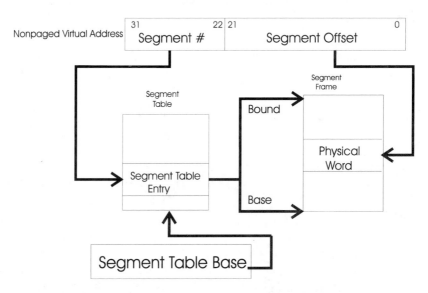

Figure 19.23 Address translation. Copyright © AT&T 1992 reprinted by permission.

19.6.4 Summary

RISC Features

Small instruction set
Single-cycle execution
Hardwired instruction decode

Non-RISC Features

Variable-length instructions
Memory-memory architecture
Multiple addressing modes
No registers

The AT&T microprocessor is a unique blend of CISC-like and RISC-like features. Like RISC machines, it has a small (44) hardwired instruction repertoire. It is pipelined in spite of having variable-length instructions. It achieves single-cycle execution or better, with branch folding. It is not a load/store architecture, but rather a memory-memory architecture. Also, unlike most RISC machines, the AT&T microprocessor has multiple-operand addressing modes. It achieves CISC-like high code density by using the memory-memory architecture to optimize the instructions/task term of the performance equation. Finally, it uses an on-chip data cache to minimize wait time for operands, but has no general-purpose, user-visible registers.

19.7 RISC INFLUENCES ON THE MAINSTREAM

This section discusses the influences of the RISC architecture on mainstream CISC families. This has become a major factor in new designs, as RISC is absorbed back into the mainstream. Techniques once thought too difficult to apply to CISC architectures are routinely appearing in them.

A common technique is to translate the variable length CISC instructions into fixed length, regular RISC instructions, and then execute these. Generally, one to five RISC instructions result. These look a lot like microcode, but result from hardwired translation logic, not a table lookup. Going back to the performance equation presented in Chapter 3, we see that if the benefit of streamlined RISC execution outweighs the increased number of instructions executed, the process makes sense.

The on-the-fly instruction translation costs hardware complexity, but is generally completed in the cache access time, thereby hiding the latency. The various complex addressing modes are left to an enhanced load unit to resolve. This approach is used on the Intel Pentium Pro Processor, the AMD K5, the Nx586, and the Motorola 68060.

A problem is presented by the self-modifying code, but this is handled by keeping the I-caches and the D-caches coherent. Another problem involves determining the actual boundaries of the instruction. This is a particular problem for 80x86 instructions.

Superpipelined architecture's such as those used in the Cyrix M1 are also being applied to legacy CISC instruction sets. The following table shows the various RISC techniques being applied to CISC processors.

processor	super-scalar	super-pipelined	out-of order execution	speculative execution	on-the-fly translate
80486	no	no	no	no	no
Pentium	yes	5-no	no	no	no
Pentium Pro Processor	yes	12-yes	yes	yes	yes
Nx586	no	no	no	no	yes
M1	yes	7-yes	yes	yes	no
K5	yes	5-no	yes	yes	yes
68060	yes	no	no	no	yes

19.7.1 80x86

The 80x86 family, from the 1978 vintage 8086 to the 1995 Pentium Pro Processor, are instruction-set compatibility-driven processors. Although each can execute the same base instruction set, generally the newer members of the family take fewer clocks to accomplish the same work. This is at the same time that clock speeds for the silicon have gone up more than tenfold. Internal parallelism has been used to achieve performance, while internal data paths have grown to 64 bits in width. Instruction-set backward compatibility with the circa 1978 8086 remains a key design driver for new family members. In the baseline 80x86 architecture, instructions can range from 1 to 15 bytes in length, with an average in excess of 2 bytes.

The Pentium Pro Processor processor, successor to the P5 Pentium, is four-way superscalar. It incorporates in excess of six million transistors and is fabricated in 0.6-micron technology. The Pentium Pro Processor was announced in Spring 1995. The follow-on is dubbed P7.

The Pentium processor, introduced in spring 1993, also maintains instruction-set compatibility with the previous 80x86 family members but has a significant array of features adapted from the RISC world. For example, it has 8 kilobytes of two-way set-associate unified cache on-chip, as well as a branch target cache. The design is dual-issue superscalar, with two integer units and one floating point.

In essence, the chip includes two i486 integer cores. Each has independent access to the cache, providing the ability to execute two instructions simultaneously. Instructions are not executed out of order. Another RISC-like feature is the 64-bit-wide external data bus. This helps to keep the on-chip caches and the pipeline filled. The two integer pipelines are not identical. Only one has a barrel shifter and the flag's unit. Figure 19.24 shows the Pentium architecture.

Good software tools always lag behind the hardware. To take advantage of the pipeline, the compiler has to properly rearrange the instructions. In real-world code demonstrations, the Pentium chip can execute between 1.5 and 1.8 80x86 instruc-

Pentium ™ Microprocessor

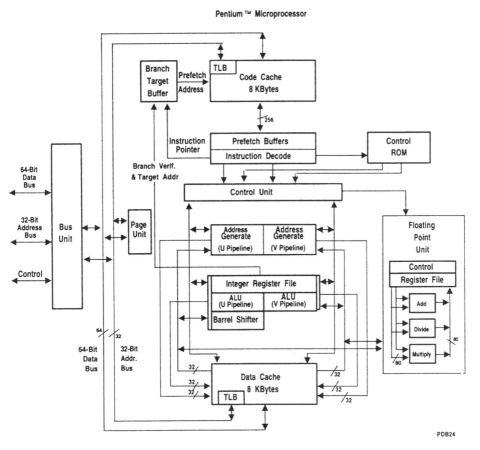

Figure 19.24   Pentium architecture. Reprinted by permission of Intel Corp. Copyright © 1993 Intel Corp.

tions per second. In actual practice, users see only about a 70 percent gain over the i486 without recompiled code. Self-modifying code is supported by having coherency maintained between the I-cache and the D-cache. This is a feature not found in mainstream RISC designs. Hardware support for the MESI cache-coherency protocol is included in the chip design.

The integral floating-point unit has been pipelined to support one-instruction-per-cycle rates. In addition, expanded multiply and divide hardware has been included, and other operations have been streamlined. The floating-point unit is essentially an eight-stage pipeline, with the first five stages provided by the integer units. The hardware adder and multiplier complete in three clocks, but can complete every cycle once the pipeline is filled. The divide hardware produces 2 bits per cycle for the quotient, giving a 32-bit quotient in 16 cycles. The Pentium chip features 8 kilobytes of on-chip cache. A second-generation unit will double the amount of level-1 cache.

PENTIUM SUMMARY

RISC Features

Single-cycle execution—mostly
Hardwired instructions—yes

Non-RISC Features

Large instruction set
Small register set
Many addressing modes, large instruction set
Not load/store; instructions can operate into memory
Compatible with previous CISC family members

19.7.1.1 The Pentium Competitors ®Intel's Pentium chip spurred several competitors at the high end of the CISC, 80x86-compatible world. These include the AMD K5, the Cyrix M1, and the NexGen Nx586. Each of these is a RISC-influenced design, and each, in turn, influenced CISC. This flurry of Pentium competitors is sometimes called the P5.5 generation, each striving to be somewhat better than the Pentium (P5). It remains to be seen whether the Pentium battleground is relevant, given the announcement of Intel's follow-on Pentium Pro Processor architecture. Competition from these vendors at the 686 (Pentium Pro Processor) architectural level is also expected, but Intel has an 18 month lead, as of early 1995.

AMD K5 The driving force behind the AMD K5 is Mike Johnson, director of advanced microprocessor development. The chip shows the influence of both the 80x86, and AMD's 29K. The K5 uses a 24-kbyte on-chip cache. The K5 development influenced AMD's work on the superscaler 29k. The K5 is a four-issue architecture, with one floating-point and five integer pipelines. Instructions for the 80x86 are translated into internal RISC-format instructions on the fly. Four instruction decoders are used, and a partial decode can be accomplished during the cache access time. Instructions for the 80x86 translate into one or more RISC instructions (ROPs). Four RISC instructions are dispatched per clock, although not all are necessarily derived from the same 80x86 source instruction. The instructions are dispatched into multiple execution units, consisting of two load/store units, two ALUs, a floating-point unit, and a branch unit. Figure 19.25 shows the K5 architecture. Complex 80x86 instructions, those that require more than 3 ROPS, go to a microcode ROM, and may result in hundreds of ROPs. This is a rare case. The average is 1.3 ROPs for 32-bit 80x86 code. Register bypassing, speculative execution, and register renaming are all used to expedite execution. Sixteen logical registers are used. Out-of-order execution is also supported with a reorder buffer to retire the results in order. Branch prediction first predicts all branches to be not-taken. If wrong, the prediction is reversed. The K5 was kept pin-compatible with the Pentium, and is expected to ship in 1995.

Cyrix M1 The M1 has dual 80x86 integer units each with a seven stage pipeline, and a 32-kilobyte, four-way set-associative cache on-chip. This cache is the primary D-cache, and the secondary I-cache. The primary I-cache is a 256 byte, fully associative unit. Very interestingly, the M1 provides 32 registers, of which only 8 are programmer visible at a given time. However, dynamic register renaming provides for more performance from the seven stage pipeline, with four level speculative execution and branch prediction. These chips are fabricated at IBM facilities, under an agreement with Cyrix. There is also an M1SC single pipeline version of the M1 which is housed in a 486DX4-compatible package. The 80x86 memory management scheme is supported, as well as a unique variable page size arrangement. 80x86 instructions may complete out of order, but results are written in program order, and exceptions are kept precise.

NexGen Nx586 The NexGen unit does not include an integral floating-point unit, but has beaten the other players to shipment, having been available in 1994. The Nx586 has been described as simply a very fast 486sx, but a unit supporting an external floating-point unit is planned. The device has 16 kbytes of I-cache and 16 kbytes of D-cache on-chip, as well as an integral secondary cache controller. It features three execution units in a superscalar architecture. Incoming 80x86 instructions are decoded into fixed length, 104-bit RISC86 instructions, which are then fed to the pipelines. Only one instruction is decoded and dispatched per clock but branch prediction is used. These chips are also fabricated in IBM facilities. NexGen's follow-on project, the Nx686, may provide some Pentium Pro Processor competition.

19.7.1.2 *Intel Pentium® Pro Processor*

The Pentium Pro Processor architecture from Intel, intended as the successor to the Pentium, was announced in February 1995. The chip features a unique double die, to encorporate a 256-kilobyte level-2 cache on the package. External cache is not required. The 8-kilobyte level-1 cache of the Pentium is maintained. A 64-bit-wide bus links the CPU and the secondary cache. The Pentium Pro Processor is a 12-stage superpipelined design, a technique that was once thought to be too difficult to apply to CISC. The Pentium Pro Processor decodes up to three 80x86 instructions per cycle, converting them into one to four fixed-length, RISC-like micro-operations called *u-ops*. These u-ops, then, lend themselves to out-of-order execution in the Pentium Pro Processor's superpipeline. A maximum of 5, and an average of 3 u-ops are dispatched per cycle. A technique called "dynamic execution" is used, in which up to 20 u-ops are in various states of execution at any given time. Speculative execution and branch prediction are also employed. Register renaming is used, with the register alias table (RAT). A branch target buffer is included to expedite the resolution of target addresses. The Pentium Pro Processor is designed to operate at 2.9 volts, to help control power dissipation. The chip dissipates an average 14 watts at 133 Mhz, and is packaged in a 387-pin MCM. The Pentium Pro Processor is expected to appear in 1995.

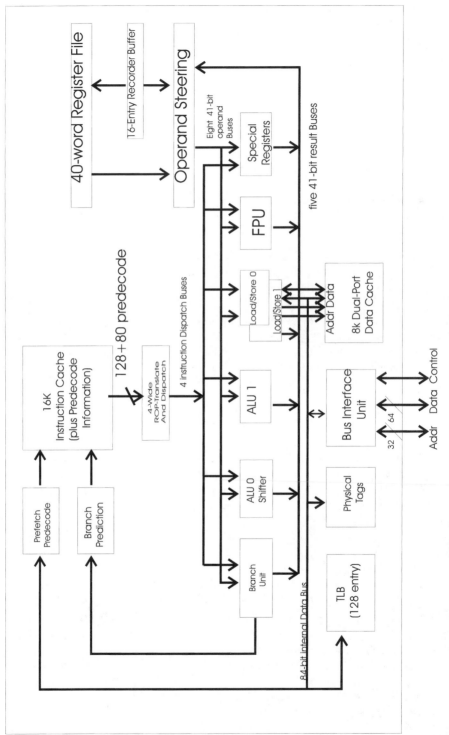

Figure 19.25 K5 architecture. Reprinted by permission from Advanced Micro Devices Inc., from K86 Family Microprocessor Editorial Background.

19.7.1.3 Summary

RISC-like Features

Superpipelined, out-of-order execution
Single-cycle execution (for the u-ops)
Register renaming
Speculative execution
Superscalar

Non RISC-like Features

Small register set (but large virtual register set)
Variable-length instructions (dynamically translated to fixed length)
Multiple addressing modes
Large instruction set

19.7.2 680x0

19.7.2.1 Introduction
Motorola's 68060 is the latest in the long-lived 68000 family. It is not a RISC processor. It is instruction-set compatible with previous 68k family members but has many features that were heavily influenced by RISC. For example, the processor is superscalar, pipelined, and has on-chip instruction and data caches as well as a branch cache. The processor uses 32-bit word size and addressing. The chip adapts the variable-length 68000 CISC instructions to fixed-length RISC pipelines by internal decoding. This is similar to the approach of Intel's Pentium Pro Processor and AMD's K5 in regard to 80x86 CISC instructions. A problem is presented by pipeline stalls, and this is partially addressed by a branch target cache.

19.7.2.2 Background
Motorola's 68000 processor was first introduced in 1978. It is a 32-bit architecture that was used by Apple Computer for its Macintosh processors. Motorola also makes a line of 8-, 16-, and 32-bit microcontrollers, and a line of DSP chips, as well as the PowerPC (Chapter 15). Motorola is also well known for its expertise in communications.

The "Coldfire" line of 32-bit processors is based on the 68k family for embedded applications. It has a streamlined 68k instruction set, based on the 68040 with some of the "difficult, but rarely used" instructions removed. These include instructions such as rotate, integer divide, and BCD-manipulation. Coldfire was announced at the fall 1994 Microprocessor Forum. It was heavily influenced by RISC techniques. It will also be available as an ASIC core. The Coldfire 5102 implements all of the 68040 instructions by software emulation.

19.7.2.3 Architecture
The internal bus architecture of the 68060 chip is Harvard, providing separate instruction and operand paths on-chip, which are combined

before interfacing off the chip. The 68k family uses variable-length CISC-type instructions that are hard to pipeline. Figure 19.26 shows the 68060 architecture.

Hardware The 68060 has an integral floating-point and memory-management unit. The MC68EC060 version has neither a floating point nor an MMU. The MC68LC060 has only the MMU. These chips address a spectrum of applications from the desktop through embedded systems.

The instruction fetch pipeline of the 68060 is four-staged. The variable-length nature of 680x0 instructions is decoded into fixed-length internal representations. These can be dispatched two at a time to dual execution units (primary and secondary), which are themselves four-stage pipelined. Out-of-order execution is not supported. A 96-byte FIFO decoded instruction buffer decouples the fetch and dual execute units. The secondary execution unit can be disabled in software for debugging purposes.

The branch cache allows zero-cycle branches in most cases. Branch folding allows the fetch stage to absorb the latency of the branch, and thus fetch and execute are decoupled for greater efficiency. Branch prediction is based on previous execution history.

A 64-entry address translation cache is four-way set associative. Most operations complete in one cycle. A separate register file is maintained for integer and floating-point operands. There are eight 32-bit-wide integer data registers, and eight 80-bit-wide floating-point registers. There are 15 control registers visible in supervisor

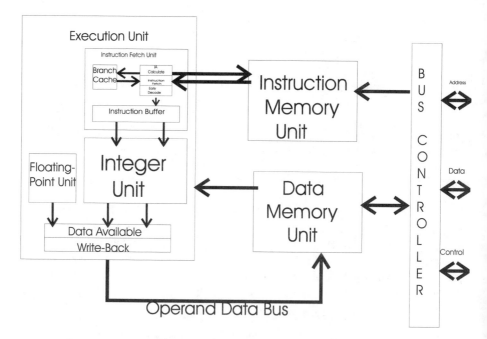

Figure 19.26 68060 architecture. Reprinted with the permission of Motorola.

mode. User mode also includes seven address registers and a stack pointer. These may be used as base address registers, and any of the registers can be used for indexes. The user-visible program counter contains the address of the executing instruction. An 8-bit condition code register is also provided. A four-entry store buffer decouples the output of the pipelines from the memory.

The 68060 includes an IEEE 1149.1-1993 JTAG test port feature. As an additional feature, the processor can be operated in a debug mode. This uses the same JTAG interface, but allows the processor to be operated in certain special modes. The processor can be halted and restarted, forced into an emulation mode, and access to the intermediate pipe stages can be obtained.

The 68060 is a fully static design, with built-in power management features. It operates at 3.3 volts. The chip is available in 206-pin PGA and 208-pin QFP packaging. Speed ratings of 40, 50, and 66 MHz are available. The unit dissipates between 4 and 5 watts.

Software and Programmer's View The 68060 is fully object-code compatible with previous members of the 680x0 family. This opens up a large universe of applications, languages, development tools, operating systems, and programmer experience. Any previous 680x0 software will run on the 68060 in user mode. Supervisor mode implements new features. Data structures include bits to 96-bit-wide extended precision words. Multiple complex addressing modes are possible.

Floating Point Full 64-bit IEEE 754-format floating point is supported in the 68060. The LC and EC variants have no floating-point unit, and take an exception when a floating-point instruction is encountered. This allows for emulation in software of the floating point features. The hardware floating-point unit is compatible with the previous 68881/882 units, and the internal unit on the 68040. A new instruction is included to explicitly select single- or double-precision rounding. Less-frequently-used instructions from the 881/882 set are emulated in software, through a trap mechanism. This includes the transcendental instructions, among others. The user has access to eight 80-bit floating-point registers.

Separate functional units are provided for add/subtract, multiply, divide, and misc. The floating-point unit operates in parallel with the integer units, but only one floating-point functional unit can be active at a time. The floating and integer units share the instruction decoding and operand fetch stages of the pipeline. One of four rounding modes commensurate with the IEEE model are selectable. The floating point unit can be disabled in software to reduce power consumption.

Cache An 8-kilobyte I-cache, four-way set associative and physically mapped, and an 8-kilobyte D-cache, also four-way set associative and physically mapped, are provided on-chip. The data cache is banked to allow simultaneous read/write access, and can be operated in write-through or deferred copy-back mode. The branch cache is a 256-entry, four-way set-associative, virtually mapped cache. The address translation cache in the instruction fetch unit is 64-entry four-way set associative. Memory mapped I/O regions are marked as cache inhibited. Bus snooping is used for multiprocessor consistency, although bus cycles can be flagged as "non-snoopable."

Memory Management Full 32-bit virtual to 32-bit physical memory management is provided in the 68060, except in the EC variant. This is compatible with the 68040's demand-paged virtual memory management unit, and it has dual 64-entry address translation caches. Snooping is provided for multiprocessor cache coherency. Four- or eight-kilobyte page sizes are supported. User and supervisor modes are provided on a page basis. Due to the internal Harvard architecture, dual MMUs serve the instruction and operand paths. There are 64 entry, four-way set-associative address translation caches in each MMU. They hold the most recently used virtual to physical address translations. If an address descriptor exists in the ATC, the translation process can be bypassed.

Exceptions Exception processing is vectored and is used for external interrupt events, access errors, traces, traps, or execution of specific instructions. If an address error occurs during the processing of an exception, the processor halts. The basic 68k exception model includes support for 256 vectored interrupts.

A restart model of exception processing is used. Exceptions recognized at the execution phase force later operations in the pipeline to be aborted. A new feature in the 68060 is that the first instruction of an exception handler is always executed, even if another exception is pending.

19.7.2.4 Summary

RISC Features

Pipelined execution (dual four-stage pipe in integer unit)
Superscalar design (2 I + F)
On-chip caches (256-entry branch, I- and D-cache)
Single-cycle execution (in most cases)

Non-RISC Features

Variable-length instructions
Multiple-operand addressing modes
Large instruction set (130)
Small number of registers (8)

19.8 FUJITSU FR20

19.8.1 Introduction

The FR family of 32-bit embedded processors is a reaction to offerings from Hitachi (Chapter 17), and NEC (Chapter 16). It is a blend of CISC and RISC thinking. As of this writing, the first chips are currently available only in Japan.

19.8.2 Background

Fujitsu has been producing its SPARClite processor (Chapter 10), aimed at the embedded market, for some time. The FR series is not compatible with this product, although it was influenced by RISC thinking.

19.8.3 Architecture

Targeted at embedded control, the FR includes embedded peripheral I/O functions such as eight channels of analog-to-digital and two channels of digital-to-analog conversion.

19.8.3.1 Hardware There are only sixteen 32-bit registers in the design, but they are mostly general purpose and orthogonal. R13 and R15 have special tasks related to memory addressing: R13 auto-increments, and R15 auto-decrements. A five-stage instruction pipeline is used. Most instructions are single cycle, and a 32x32 multiply can be completed in five cycles.

The processor is available as a megacell for an ASIC, providing the opportunity for customers to use the device as a building block in custom applications.

A DRAM controller is provided on-chip, as well as an eight-channel DMA controller, four UARTs for serial communications, up/down counters, and a set of capture-and-compare registers. A special peripheral accelerator interface (PAI) acts like a DMA controller, under the control of two special instructions to load and store data to an external coprocessor.

Available initially in a 5-volt version, the device will also operate at 3.3 volts. Power dissipation is 600 mW at 5 volts and 25 megahertz. A low-power sleep mode is included.

19.8.3.2 Software A limited set of 168 instructions is provided, and almost all fit within two bytes and execute in a single cycle. All instructions are two operand, with the destination being the same as the second source operand. The usual arithmetic, logical, load/store, and bit manipulation operations are provided. Unconditional and conditional branches using the status register are provided.

The logical operations can operate directly on memory, although without the auto-increment/decrement. Direct memory-memory moves are also supported. Fast machine state changing is provided by a multiple-register load and store operation. For multiprocessing, a byte-exchange instruction is indivisible. This provides a hardware interlock mechanism.

19.8.3.3 Cache The FR20 chip has a one-kilobyte instruction cache and a one-kilobyte data cache. These are two-way set associative, and can be locked on a line basis.

19.8.3.4 Memory Management The virtual address space of the processor is spanned by a 32-bit address, although the physical address space uses 24 bits.

19.8.3.5 Exceptions The FR20 features 12 external interrupt inputs.

19.8.3.6 Summary

RISC Features

Modest register set
Small, regular instruction set
Single-cycle execution

Non-RISC Features

Multiple addressing modes
Logical operations operate on memory
Memory-to-memory moves

19.9 REFERENCES FOR CHAPTER 19

[1] "National Unveils Superscalar RISC Processor," Feb. 20, 1991, *Microprocessor Report,* 5(3) p. 1.

[2] "Zilog Licenses Hyperstone as Core Processor," Sept. 19, 1990, *Microprocessor Report,* 4(16), p. 6.

[3] "Sinclair Launches Superchip," April 24, 1994, *Sunday Times of London*, Innovation section, p. 13.

19.10 BIBLIOGRAPHY

Clipper

Baxter, Arnold, "Code Restructuring for Enhanced Performance on a Pipelined Processor," 1991, IEEE, *COMPCON Spring '91 Proceedings.*

"Clipper C300 32-bit Compute Engine, Advance Information Data Sheet," Sept. 1988, Intergraph Corp.

"Clipper C400 Rev. 3 Programmer's Reference Manual," Feb. 1992, Intergraph Corp.

"Clipper Technical Description," April 23, 1991, Intergraph Corp. draft 3.0.

Hanson, Lee F., Brookwood, "The C400 Superscalar/Superpipelined RISC Design," 1991, IEEE, *COMPCON Spring '91 Proceedings.*

Hollingsworth, Walter, Sachs, Howard, Smith, Alan Jay, "The Clipper Processor: Instruction Set Architecture and Implementation," Feb. 1, 1989, *Communications of the ACM*, 32 (2): 200.

Hunter, "Introduction to the Clipper Architecture," Intergraph Advanced Processor Division, Sept. 1988, white paper.

"Introduction to the Clipper Architecture," Jan. 1990, Intergraph Corp.

"R.I.P. Clipper—Finally," Feb. 14, 1994, *Microprocessor Report*, 8 (2): 4.

Sachs, Howard G., McGhan, Harlan, Hanson, Lee F., "Design and Implementation Trade-offs in the Clipper C400 Architecture," June 1991, *IEEE Micro*, 11(3) p. 18.

Motorola 88k

"88open Sourcebook," 3rd ed., Nov. 1990, 88open Consortium Ltd. ISBN 0-9621938-3-6.

"DSP96002 IEEE Floating-Point Dual Port Processor User's Manual," 1989, Motorola, DSP96002um/ad.

"MC88000 Technical Pitch," undated, Motorola white paper, presentation slides.

MC88100 RISC Microprocessor User's Manual, Motorola, 2nd ed. Englewood Cliffs, NJ: Prentice-Hall, 1988. ISBN 0-13-567090-X.

"MC88100, Technical Summary," 1988, Motorola white paper.

"MC88110, Technical Summary," 1988, Motorola white paper, BR588/D.

MC88200 Cache/Memory Management Unit User's Manual, 2nd ed. Englewood Cliffs, NJ: Prentice-Hall, 1990. ISBN 0-13-567033-0.

"MC88200, Technical Summary," 1988, Motorola, BR589D/Rev. 1.

"MC88410, Technical Summary," March 1992, Motorola, MC88410/D.

Tucker, Michael, Coorpender, Bruce, "Programming the Motorola 88000," Blue Ridge Summit, PA: Windcrest/McGraw Hill, 1992. ISBN 0-8306-3533-5.

"Understanding RISC Processors," 1993, *Microprocessor Report*, Chapter 3, Emeryville, CA: Ziff-Davis. ISBN 1-56276-159-5.

iWarp

Annaratone, Marco, et al., "The WARP Computer: Architecture, Implementation, and Performance," Dec. 1987, *IEEE Transactions on Computers*, VC-36 (12): 1523–1538.

Borkar, S., Cohn, R., Cox, G., "Supporting Systolic and Memory Communication in iWarp," June 1, 1990, *Computer Architecture News*, 18 (2): 70.

Borak, Shekhan, et al., "iWARP; AN Integrated Solution to High Speed Parallel Computing," Nov. 14–18, 1988, *Proceedings of Supercomputing '88*, Kissimmee, FL.

Dally, William J., "A VLSI Architecture for Concurrent Data Structures," 1987, Norwood, MA: Kluwer Academic Publishers. ISBN 0898382351.

Figueiredo, Marco A., "An Architectural Comparison Between the Inmos Transputer T-800 and the Intel iWarp Microprocessors," Nov. 9, 1991, Loyola College, Dept. of Engineering Science, white paper.

Gross, T., Hinrichs, S., Lueh, G., "Compiling Task and Data Parallel Programs for iWarp," Jan. 1, 1993, *ACM SIGPLAN notices*, 28 (1): 32.

"Introduction to iWARP," Aug. 1991, Intel, publication 318150.

"iWarp Programmers Guide," Intel, 318151.

"iWarp Users Guide," Intel, 318158.

Swan, R., Fuller, S., Siewiorek, D., "Cm*—A Modular, Multi-microprocessor," 1977, AFIPS, *Proceedings, 1977 Fall Joint Computer Conference*, pp. 637–644.

RISC Influences on DSP

Bayoumi, Magdy A. (ed.), "Parallel Algorithms and Architectures for DSP Applications," 1991. Boston: Kluwer Academic Publishers. ISBN 0792392094.

Child, Jeff, "Higher Levels of Integration Come to DSPs," May 1994, *Computer Design*, 33, (6) p. 91.

"DSP: The Secret Is Out!" March 1994, *PC-Computing*, 7 (3): 188.

"DSPs Start Their Move to the Motherboard," May 1990, *Electronics*, p. 93.

Heath, Steve, "Microprocessor Architectures and Systems: RISC, CISC, and DSP," 1991, Newnes.

"MIT Building 64-processor Parallel DSP System," Feb. 14, 1994, *Electronic Engineering Times*, 784, p. 17.

"Parallel DSP System Integration," Oct 1993, *Microprocessors and Microsystems*, 17 (8): 460.

"Parallelism Pushes DSP Throughput," March 21, 1994, *Electronic Design*, 42(6), p. 151.

Smith, Michael R., "How RISCy Is DSP?," Dec. 1, 1992, *IEEE MICRO*, 12 (6): 10.

TMS320

"DSP and Parallel Development System for the TMS320C40," 1993, Transtech Parallel Technology.

Feigel, Curtis P., "TI Introduces Four-Processor DSP Chip; 320C80's Integral Crossbar, Parallel Operation Give Two Billion Ops," March 28, 1994, *Microprocessor Report*, 8 (4): 220.

"TMS320C4x User's Guide," May 1991, Texas Instruments.

"TMS320C80 Data Sheet," July 1994, Texas Instruments, SPRS023.

"TMS320C80 Multimedia Video Processor (MVP) Technical Brief," 1994, Texas Instruments, SPRU106A.

"TMS320C80 User Guide," 1994, Texas Instruments, version 1, TMDX3248559-07 (CD-ROM), order SPRC001.

SHARC

"ADSP-21060 SHARC Super Harvard Architecture Computer," Oct. 1993, Analog Devices.

"ADSP-2106x SHARC Preliminary User's Manual," 3/94 (Revised), Analog Devices.

"ADSP-21020, ADSP-21010 User's Manual," 1993, Analog Devices.

Bindra, Ashok, "$100k Supercomputer," May 22, 1995, *EETimes*, 849: 59.

"MIT Building 64-Processor Parallel DSP System," Feb. 14, 1994, *EETimes*, 784: 17.

"SHARC: A Bold New DSP Thrust by Analog; Analog Devices' Floating-Point Chip Sets New Integration Level," Dec. 6, 1993, *Microprocessor Report*, 7 (16): 10.

"32/40-Bit IEEE Floating Point DSP Microprocessor," Aug. 1993, ADSP-21020, Rev. B, Analog Devices.

Yee, Ronnin, "The SHARC Architecture for DSP Multiprocessing," 1994, *ICSPAT'94* Proceedings.

nCube

Dudzett, Bob et al., "nCUBE 3 Integrated MPP Node Processor," 1994, *Hot Chips IV Symposium Record*, Stanford University, Palo Alto, CA, Aug. 14–16, 1994.

"nCUBE 2 Systems Technical Overview," 1992, nCUBE Corporation, Foster City, CA.

"nCUBE 3 Technical Overview," 1994, nCUBE Corporation, Foster City, CA.

KSR

"Kendall Square Research Technical Summary," 1992, Kendall Square Research.

MasPar

Blank, Tom, "The MasPar MP-1 Architecture," January 1990, IEEE paper, CH12843.

"The Design of the MasPar MP-2: A Cost Effective Massively Parallel Computer," MasPar Corporation white paper.

Kim, W., Tuck, R., "MasPar MP-2 PE Chip: A Totally Cool Hot Chip," March 29, 1993, MasPar Corporation.

IBM RIOS I & II

Chakravarty, Dipto, PowerRISC System/6000. New York: McGraw-Hill, 1994. ISBN 0-07-011192-8.

Cocke, John, Markstein, Victoria, "The Evolution of RISC Technology at IBM," Jan. 1990, *IBM Journal of Research & Development*, 34 (1): 4–11.

"The 801 Minicomputer," April 1988, *SIGPLAN Notices*, 17(2): 39.

Garfinkel, Simson L., "The Grand Alliance," May, 1995, *RS/The Power PC Magazine*, 4 (5): 50–56.

Harris, Clive, *IBM RISC System/6000*. New York: McGraw-Hill, 1993. ISBN 0-07-707668-0.

Hopkins, Martin E., "A Perspective on the 801/RISC," Jan. 1987, *IBM Systems Journal*, 26 (2): 107–121.

"IBM Hardware Technical Reference General Information; RISC System/6000 POWERstation and POWERserver," IBM Corporation, 1990, SA23-2643.

IBM Journal of Research & Development, Jan. 1990, 34 (1).

"IBM Phasing out POWER Architecture," May 30, 1994, *Microprocessor Report*, 8 (7): 4.

"IBM Provides First Details of RIOS 2," Feb. 15, 1993, *Microprocessor Report*, 7 (2): 4.

"IBM Regains Performance Lead with Power2; Six-way Superscalar CPU in MCM Achieves 126 SPECint92," Oct. 4, 1993, *Microprocessor Report*, 7 (13): 1.

"IBM RISC System/6000 Technology," 1990, IBM Corporation, SA23-2619.

Leaver, Mike, Sanghera, Harden, IBM RISC System/6000 User Guide. New York: McGraw-Hill, 1993. ISBN 0-07-707687-7.

Levin, Frank and Thurber, Steve (eds.), "RISC System/6000 Power PC System Architecture," San Francisco, CA: Morgan Kaufmann, 1994. ISBN 1558603441.

Oehler, Richard R., Blasgen, Michael W., "IBM RISC System/6000: Architecture and Performance," June 1, 1991, *IEEE Micro*, 11 (3): 14.

"Understanding RISC Processors," 1993, *Microprocessor Report*, Chapter 9, Emeryville, CA: Ziff-Davis. ISBN 1-56276-159-5.

White, Steven W., Dhawan, Sudhir, "Power PC and Power 2: Technical Aspects of the New IBM RISC System 6000," 1995, IBM Corporation, SA23-2737.

AT&T Microprocessor

"ATT92010 Hobbit Microprocessor Data Sheet," Dec. 1992, AT&T.

"ATT92011 System Management Device Data Sheet," Dec. 1992, AT&T.

"ATT92012 PCMCIA Controller Data Sheet," Dec. 1992, AT&T.

"ATT92013 Peripheral Controller Data Sheet," Dec. 1992, AT&T.

"ATT92014 Video Display Controller Data Sheet," Dec. 1992, AT&T.

Berenbaum, Ditzel, McLellan, "Introduction to the CRISP ISA," 1987, *Compcon 87 Proceedings.*

"Hobbit: A High Performance, Low Power Microprocessor," 1993, *P. Compcon 93*, pp. 88–95.

O'Brien, Donald, "On the Origin of the Name 'Hobbit'," Winter 1989, *Mythlore*, 16 (2): 32.

"Understanding RISC Processors," 1993, *Microprocessor Report*, Chapter 12, Emeryville, CA: Ziff-Davis. ISBN 1-56276-159-5.

Pentium®

Alpert, Donald, "Architecture of the Pentium Microprocessor," June 1993, *IEEE Micro*, 13 (11), p. 11.

Anderson, Don, Shanley, Tom, *Pentium Processor System Architecture.* Reading, MA: Addison-Wesley Pub. Co. Mindshare Press, 1993. ISBN 1-881609-07-3.

Feibus, Michael, *"Pentium Power," Apr. 27, 1993*, PC, 12 (8): 108.

Halfhill, Tom, R., "Intel Launches Rocket in a Socket: Intel's New Pentium CPU Doubles the Speed of the Fastest 486," May 1, 1993, *Byte*, 18 (6): 92.

"Inside: Pentium or the 586," Apr. 27, 1993, *PC*, 12 (8): 4.

"Intel's Pentium Processor, Coming in March: One Very Hot CPU," Feb. 1, 1993, *PC World*, 11 (2): 67.

Leinecker, Richard C., "Processor-Detection Schemes," 1993, *Dr. Dobb's Journal*, 18 (6): 46.

"The Making of a Chip," Mar. 29, 1993, *Business Week*, 3311, p. 94.

Miller, Michael J., "Is There a Pentium in Your Future?" Apr. 27, 1993, *PC Magazine*, 12 (8): 81.

"New Era for Intel: The Supercharged Pentium PC," Mar. 22, 1993, *Electronics*, 66 (6): 4.

"An Overview of the Intel Pentium Processor," 1993, *P. Compcon 95*, pp. 60–62.

"PCI, Pentium Link Forged," Apr. 1, 1993, *Computer Design*, 32 (4): 40.

"Pentium Benchmarks," Feb. 1993, *PC Week,* 10.

"The Pentium Challenge," Mar. 22, 1993, *Informationweek*, 417, p. 14.

"Pentium Processor User's Manual," 3 vol(s), 1993, Intel, 241563-001.

"Preparing the Way for Pentium," Mar. 15, 1993, *Datamation*, 39 (6): 36.

Ruley, John, "Pentium Arrives," June 1993, *Windows*, p. 115.

Smith, Gina, "Field Guide to CPUs," Mar. 1, 1993, *PC/Computing*, 6 (3): 123.

Smith, Gina, "Will the Pentium Kill the 486?" May 1, 1993, *PC/Computing*, 6 (5): 116.

Subramaniam, Ramesh, Kundargi, Kiran, "Programming the Pentium Processor," June 1, 1993, *Dr. Dobb's Journal*, 18 (6): 34.

"A 3.3v 0.6 mm BiCmos Superscalar Processor," 1994, *P. ISSCC 94*, pp. 202–203.

Tredennick, Nick, "Computer Science and the Microprocessor," June 1, 1993, *Dr. Dobb's Journal*, 18 (6): 18.

Pentium® Competitors

"Coming Next Year: 586 vs. 586: CPU Proliferation Creates Need for Benchmarks to Sort Them Out," Oct. 24, 1994, *Microprocessor Report*, 8 (14).

Halfhill, Tom R., "AMD vs. Superman," Nov. 1994, *BYTE*, 19(11) p. 95.

Halfhill, Tom R., "80x86 Wars," June 1994, *BYTE*, 19(6), p. 75.

"NexGen Nx586 Straddles the RISC/CISC Divide," June 1994, *BYTE*, 19(6), p. 76.

"A 93MHz x 86 Microprocessor with On-chip L2 Cache Controller," 1995, *P. ISSCC 95*, pp. 172–173.

Ryan, Bob, "M1 Challenges Pentium," Jan. 1994, *Byte*, 19(1), p. 83.

Slater, Michael, "AMD's K5 Designed to Outrun Pentium," *Microprocessor Report*, 8 (14) Oct. 24, 1994.

Slater, M., "The P5.5 Generation," March 20, 1995, *EE Times*, (840), p. 18.

Slater, M., "X86 Competition Intensifies," Jan. 16, 1995, *EE Times*, (831), p. 39.

Intel Pentium Pro Processor

Colwell, Robert P., and Steck, Randy L., "A 0.6 mm BiCMOS Processor with Dynamic Execution," Feb. 1995, *IEEE ISSCC 95 Proc.*, San Francisco, pp. 176–177.

Rupley, Sebastian, and Clyman, John, "P6: The Next Step?," Sept. 12, 1995, *PC Magazine,* 14(15), pp. 102–118.

Schutz, J., "A 3.3V 0.6μ BiCMOS Superscalar Microprocessor," 1995, *IEEE ISSCC Proc.*, San Francisco, pp. 202–203.

Slater, Michael, "P6 Design Raises PC Performance a Notch," Feb. 20, 1995, *PC Week*, 12 (7): 6.

Stam, Nick, "Inside the P6," Sept. 12, 1995, *PC Magazine,* 14(15), pp. 118–130.

Stam, Nick, "The P6 from a Programmer's View," Sept. 12, 1995, *PC Magazine*, pp. 134–137.

680x0

Circello, Joe, "The Superscalar Hardware Architecture of the MC68060," 1994, *Hot Chips IV Symposium Record*, Stanford University, Palo Alto, CA, Aug. 14–16, 1994.

"M68060 Microprocessors User's Manual," M68060UM/AD Rev. 1, 1994, Motorola.

"Motorola Moves to Dominate Embedded World," April 4, 1994, *Electronic Engineering Times* (791).

"68060 Chip Rollout Answers Questions, Raises New Ones," May 1994, *Computer Design*, 33, p. 34.

Fujitsu FR20

"Fujitsu Starts New Embedded CPU Family," *Microprocessor Report*, 8 (13): 20.

20

CONTACT INFORMATION

20.1 KEY MANUFACTURERS:
ADDRESS, PHONE, FAX, BBS, E-MAIL

Advanced Micro Devices 901 Thompson Place Sunnyvale, CA 94088-3453	512-462-5425 800-222-9323, (hotline and literature) 800-538-8450
Advanced RISC Machines 20261 Beatty Ridge Road Los Gatos, CA 95030	408-399-5195 408-399-5196 (fax)
Analog Devices 1 Technology Way Norwood, MA 02062	617-461-3881 800-262-5643 617-821-4273 (fax)
AT&T Microelectronics 555 Union Blvd. Allentown, PA 18103	800-372-2447
Axis Technologies 4 Constitution Way Woburn, MA 01801-1030	617-938-1927 617-938-6161 (fax)

Bipolar Integrated Technology
1050 Compton Dr.
Beaverton, OR 97006

503-629-5490

Cyrix Corp.
2703 North Central Expressway
Richardson, TX 75080

214-234-8388

Cypress Semiconductor
390 N. First St.
San Jose, CA 95134

408-943-2600
408-943-2821 (applications)
408-943-2954 BBS 19.2k 8N1

Digital Equipment Corporation
146 Main St.
Maynard, MA 91754

800-344-4825
800-332-2717 (Alpha hotline)
508-568-6868

Fujitsu Microelectronics, Inc.
Advanced Products Division
77 Rio Robles
San Jose, CA 95134-1807

800-523-0034
408-943-9293 (fax)

GEC Plessey Semiconductors
Sequoia Research Park
1500 Green Hills Road
Scotts Valley, CA 95066

408-438-2900
408-438-7023 (fax)

Harris Semiconductor
P.O. Box 883
Melbourne, FL 32902

407-274-7000

Hewlett-Packard
Centennial Annex D2
Colorado Springs, CO 80901

719-590-1900
800-752-0900

Hitachi America Ltd.
2000 Sierra Point Parkway
Brisbane, CA 94005

415-589-8300
800-285-1601

Hyperstone Electronics, GmbH
Attn: Yoshi Kumagai
10050 North Wolfe Road, Suite 276
Cupertino, CA 95014

408-253-0283

Hyundai Elexs America
166 Baypointe Parkway
San Jose, CA 95134

408-473-9200

IBM Microelectronics
1000 River Rd.
Burlington, VT 05452

800-426-3333
800-PowerPC (800-769-3772)

ILC Data Device Corp.
105 Wilbur Place
Bohemia, NY 11716

516-567-5600
516-567-7358 (fax)

International Meta Systems, Inc.
23842 Hawthorne Blvd.
Suite 200
Torrance, CA 90505

310-524-9300

Integrated Device Technology
3001 Stender Way, Bldg. 3
Santa Clara, CA 95052-8015

408-492-8618
408-492-8674 (fax)
800-345-7015

Inmos
SGS-Thomson Microelectronics
1000 E. Bell Road
Phoenix, AZ 85022

602-867-6100

Intel Corp.
5000 W. Chandler Blvd.
Chandler, AZ 85226

800-955-5599 (literature)
408-987-8080
800-628-8686 (tech)

Intergraph Corp.
(no street address)
Huntsville, AL 35894

800-345-4856
info@intergraph.com

Kendall Square Research
170 Tracer Lane
Waltham, MA 02154

617-895-9400
617-890-0996 (fax)
ksr-info@ksr.com

LSI Logic Corp.
1551 McCarthy Blvd.
Milpitas, CA 95035

800-232-MIPS (6477)
408-433-8000
408-988-7447 (fax)

Matra MHS
2201 Laurel Wood Road
Santa Clara, CA 95056

408-748-9362

MasPar Computer Corp.   408-736-3300
749 N. Mary Ave.
Sunnyvale, CA 94086

Microchip Technology, Inc.   602-963-7373
2355 West Chandler Blvd.   602-899-9210 (fax)
Chandler, AZ 85224-6199

Mitsubishi Electronics America   408-730-5900
1050 E. Arques Ave.
Sunnyvale, CA 94086

Motorola Semiconductor   800-845-6686, 800-521-6274
6501 William Cannon Dr. W.   512-343-8940
Austin, TX 78735   Motorola@selectnet.bga.com

National Semiconductor   800-272-9959
2900 Semiconductor Drive   408-721-5000
Santa Clara, CA 95052

nCube   800-654-2823
919 E. Hillsdale Blvd.   415-508-5408 (fax)
Foster City, CA 94404

NEC Technologies, Inc.   800-366-9782
475 Ellis St.   800-729-9288 (fax)
Mountain View, CA 94039

NexGen   408-435-0202
1623 Buckeye Drive   408-435-0262 (fax)
Milpitas, CA 95035

NKK America, Inc.   408-982-8277
2350 Mission College Blvd.   408-982-9809 (fax)
Suite 380
Santa Clara, CA 95054

OKI Semiconductor, Inc.   800-654-6388
785 N. Mary Ave.   408-720-1900
Sunnyvale, CA 94086

Panasonic (Matsushita)   201-348-7000
1 Panasonic Way
Secaucus, NJ 07094

Performance Semiconductor   408-734-9000
610 East Weddell Dr.   408-734-0962 (fax)
Sunnyvale, CA 94089

Philips Semiconductors   800-234-7381
811 E. Arques Ave.   408-991-3445
Sunnyvale, CA 94088

Plessey—See GEC Plessey

Ross Technology   800-774-7677
5316 Highway 290 W.   512-892-7802
Suite 500   512-892-3036 (fax)
Austin, TX 78735

Samsung Semiconductor, Inc.   408-954-7000
3655 N. First St.
San Jose, CA 95134

SGS-Thomson—see Inmos

Sharp Microelectronics   206-834-8966
5700 N.W. Pacific Rim Blvd.   206-834-2500 (main)
Camas, WA 98607

Siemens Components, Inc.   408-777-4500
100950 North Tantau   408-777-4910 (fax)
Cupertino, CA 95014

SPARC Technology   415-336-0810
2550 Garcia Ave.
Mountain View, CA 94043

Texas Instruments   800-336-5236
P.O. Box 1443   800-232-3200
Houston, TX 77001   800-477-8924 (literature)

Toshiba America   714-455-2000
9775 Toledo Way   800-879-4963
Irvine, CA 92718   714-859-3963 (fax)

United Technologies   719-594-8081
Microelectronic Center   800-722-1575
1575 Garden of the Gods Road   800-645-8865
Colorado Springs, CO 80907

VLSI Technology   602-752-6873
8375 S. River Parkway
Tempe, AZ 85282

Western Design Center, Inc.   602-962-4545
2166 East Brown Road
Mesa, AZ 85213

Zilog   408-370-8000
210 E. Hacienda Ave.   408-370-8056 (fax)
Campbell, CA 95008

20.2 RISC CHIP MANUFACTURERS WORLD WIDE WEB ADDRESSES

The World Wide Web (WWW) has become a popular source of information. A subset of the Internet, the Web requires Browser software such as Mosaic or Netscape. Most high-technology companies have a presence on the Web. A Web address is referred to as a universal resource locator (URL). It starts with http, which stands for hypertext transfer protocol. The following list gives WWW addresses for some of the manufacturers of RISC chips. Information evolves quickly on the Web. Consider these addresses as starting points for exploration. At this time, we maintain a Web page at Loyola that contains all of these addresses. That page is located at http://sparkle.loyola.edu/localhtmls/risc.

Intel Corp.	http://www.intel.com/
Motorola	http://www.mot.com/SPS/PowerPC/
IBM	http://www.austin.ibm.com/
MIPS	http://www.mips.com/
Silicon Graphics	http://www.sgi.com/
Toshiba	http://www.global.net/toshiba.final.html
Ross	http://www.Ross.com
SPARC	http://www.sparc.com
TI	http://www.ti.com
CYRIX	http://www.cyrix.com

Inmos	http://www.pact.srf.ac.uk/inmos/
AMD	http://www.amd.com/
Advanced Risc Machines	http://www.systemv.com/armltd/
Harris	http://www.semi.harris.com/
Microchip	http://www.ultranet.com/biz/mchip/
National Semiconductor	http://www.commerce.net/directories/partici pants/ns/mvnshp.html
Samsung	http://www.samsung.com/
Zilog	http://www.zilog.com/zilog/
DEC	http://www.digital.com/
HP	http://www.hp.com/
NEC	http://www.nec.com/
Fujitsu	http://www.fujitsu.co.jp
QED	http://www.qedinc.com

20.3 RISC ORGANIZATIONS

Organization	Sponsor	For:
88Open	Motorola	88k
Fusion 29k	AMD	29k
Power Open Computing	Motorola/IBM	PowerPC
ProPA-RISC	HP	PA
Sparc International	Sun/Fujitsu/Ross	Sparc

20.3.1 Addresses

88Open Consortium Ltd.
100 Homeland Ct.
Suite 800
San Jose, CA 95112

Fusion 29K Program Manager   512-462-5159
AMD
5900 East Ben White Blvd., MS561
Austin, TX 78741

Power Open Association   408-366-0460
10050 N. Wolfe Road   408-366-0463 (fax)
Suite SW2-255   askus@poweropen.org
Cupertino, CA 95014

Precision RISC Organization   408-447-4249
19111 Pruneridge Ave.
Cupertino, CA 95014-9807

SPARC International   415-321-8692
535 Middlefield Road
Suite 210
Menlo Park, CA 94025

Independent Benchmarking Organizations

System Performance Evaluation Corporation   703-698-9600 (ex 325)
c/o National Computer Graphics Association   703-560-2752 (fax)
2722 Merrilee Drive   email: spec-ncga@cup.
Suite 200   portal.com
Fairfax, VA 22031

AIM Technology (Unix Systems Performance)   800-848-8649
4699 Old Ironsides Dr.
Suite 150
Santa Clara, CA 95054

Transaction Processing Council (TPC)   408-295-8894
c/o Shanley Public Relations   408-295-2613 (fax)
777 N. First St., Suite 600
San Jose, CA 95112

21

GLOSSARY OF TERMS AND DEFINITIONS

3GL	Third-generation (computer) language, COBOL, FORTRAN, C
4GL	fourth-generation (computer) language, nonprocedural
5GL	fifth-generation (computer) language—usually object oriented
68k	CISC architecture from Motorola
80x86	CISC family from Intel, 8086, 80286, 80386, 80486, etc.
88k	RISC architecture from Motorola
ABI	applications binary interface
acronym	a resident of Akron, Ohio
Ada	standard computer language, required for DOD projects
ADSP	advanced digital signal processor, 1 of 4 TMS320C080
AI	artificial intelligence
AIX	Advanced Interactive Executive, IBM's Unix
ALC	assembly language code
ALLCACHE	trademark memory architecture from KSR
Alpha	64-bit RISC architecture from Digital Equipment Corp.
ALU	arithmetic logic unit
AND	logical union function
ansi	American National Standards Institute
API	application programming interface
ARPA	Advanced Research Projects Agency

ASCII	American Standard Code for Information Interchange, a 7-bit code
async	asynchronous
ATM	asynchronous transfer mode—a WAN technology
AViiON	computer system from Data General
ASIC	application-specific integrated circuit
B1	a level of computer systems security defined by DOD
baud	rate of information transfer, in symbols/second
BEAR	bus error address register (Intel i860)
Bellcore	Bell Communications Research
BER	bit error rate
BiCMOS	technology blend of bipolar and CMOS
big-endian	having the least significant byte in a word on the right
B-ISDN	binary integrated services digital network
bit	the smallest unit of binary information
BLOB	Binary large object, usually applied to image data
Booth	Algorithm for fast binary multiplication
bpi	bits per inch
BSD	Berkeley Systems Distribution (Unix)
bus	a parallel data pathway
byte	a collection of 8 bits
C	computer language developed at Bell Labs in 1972; basis of Unix
C2	DOD security level for systems, providing controlled access
C++	object-oriented computer language; extention to C
cache	a small, fast memory between the processor and the main memory; temporary holding area
CAE	computer-aided engineering
CalTech	California Institute of Technology
CAM	content addressable memory
CAN	campus area network
CASE	computer aided software environment (tools)
CCITT	French acronym, *Comité Consultatif Internationale de Télégraphique et Téléphonique*
CD-ROM	Compact disk, read-only memory
channel	point-to-point connection between two processes
CHMOS	high-speed variation on CMOS
CISC	complex instruction set computer
CM*	early research multiprocessor at CMU

C.MMP	early research multiprocessor at CMU
CMOS	complementary metal-oxide semiconductor
CMU	Carnegie-Mellon University
COBOL	computer language, ANSI X3.23-1985
cold	computer output to laser-disk
comm	communications
companding	compressing-expanding
core	ancient term for main memory; refers to magnetic cores
CPGA	Ceramic pin grid array; packaging for integrated circuit
CPU	central processor unit
CQFP	Ceramic quad flat pack; packaging for integrated circuit
CSMA/CD	LAN access technique—carrier sense multiple access/collision detection
CWP	current word pointer; current window pointer
DARPA	Defense Advanced Research Projects Agency
DASD	direct-access storage device
datacomm	data communications
DB-2	database software from IBM
DBMS	database management system
D-cache	data cache
DCE	distributed computing environment—OSF approach to interconnectivity; also, data communication equipment
DEC	Digital Equipment Corporation
demux	demultiplex
DG	Data General Corporation
DMA	direct memory addressing—I/O to/from memory without processor involvement
DOD	(U.S.) Department of Defense
DOE	Department of Energy
DOS	Disk operating system
DRAM	dynamic random access memory
DSP	digital signal processing
D-tlb	data-TLB, see **TLB**
ECL	emitter coupled logic; a common mode logic that is fast and power hungry
ECC	error correcting code
EIA	Electronic Industries Association
EiSA	extended industry standard bus (32-bit) (see **ISA**)
E-mail	electronic mail

EMI	electromagnetic interference
EEPROM	electrically erasable programmable read-only memory
EPROM	erasable programmable read only memory
ESDI	enhanced small device interface
Ethernet	a bit serial LAN communication protocol; usually 10 megabits per second over coaxial cable
exa-	prefix, 10^{18}
FDDI	fibre distributed data interface
FIBRE channel	emerging standard for data transmission
FIPS	Federal Information Processing Standards
Floating point	a scientific/engineering representation scheme with a mantissa and an exponent
FUD	fear, uncertainty, doubt
Futurebus	a 32/64-bit backplane bus
GIGA	Prefix 10^9
GIPS	giga (10^9) operations per second
GFLOPS	giga (10^9) floating point operations per second
GOSIP	Government Open Systems Interconnection Profile
GUI	graphical user interface
Harvard	computer architecture characterized by separate instruction and data paths
HIPPI	high performance parallel interface, an ANSI standard
hot swap	to exchange modules without powering down
HP	Hewlett-Packard Company
HP-PA	HP's Precision Architecture chip
HP-UX	HP's Unix
hypercube	topology in which each node is the vertex of an Order-n cube
HyperSPARC	SPARC implementation from Ross Technologies
Hz	hertz, cycles per second
IBM	International Business Machines, Inc.
I-cache	instruction cache
IEEE	Institute of Electrical and Electronics Engineers
IEF	Information Engineering Facility
IGES	Initial Graphics Exchange Standard
i860	high-performance RISC chip from Intel; addresses floating-point performance
i960	RISC chip from Intel; addresses embedded and military markets
IC	integrated circuit
IDT	Integrated Device Technology

iMRC	Intel's mesh router component (chip)
Intel SSD	Intel Supercomputer Systems Division
I/O	input/output
IPD	interactive parallel debugger
IPI	intelligent peripheral interface
iPSC	computer line from Intel Corp.
ISA	industry standard architecture (16-bit bus); instruction set architecture
ISDN	integrated services digital network
ISO	International Standards Organization
I-tlb	instruction TLB, see **TLB**
iWarp	a processor architecture from Intel Corp.
JPEG	Joint Photographic Experts Group
JTAG	(IEEE) Joint Test Action Group
jukebox	automated handler for storage media
k	(prefix) 1024 (2^{10}), or 1000 (10^3)
Kerboros	communications security algorithm from MIT
kernel	a process providing basic services
KSR	Kendall Square Research, MPP vendor
LAN	local area network
Linpack	a benchmark for scientific applications
LIPS	logical inferences per second
LISP	AI language for list-processing, derived from McCarthy at MIT
little-endian	having the least significant byte of a word on the right
LOC	Library of Congress, roughly, 10 terabytes of text
longword	usually, a 64-bit word
LRU	least recently used (replacement algorithm)
LSB	least significant bit, or byte
Mach	multitasking Unix kernal from CMU
MAN	metropolitan area network
MAX	maximum
M-bus	memory bus architecture from Sun Microsystems
MCA	microchannel architecture (32-bit bus)
MCA-E	microchannel architecture—extended (64-bit)
mesh	topology in which nodes form a regular acyclic n-dimensional grid
MESI	modified, exclusive, shared, invalid cache protocol for multiprocessing
MFLOPS	Mega (10^6) floating point operations per second

Mhz	megahertz
micron	10^{-6} meter
MIMD	multiple-instruction, multiple-data computer architecture model
MN	minimum
MIPS	Mega (10^6) instructions per second; also, a company name
MISD	multiple-instruction, single-data computer architecture model
MIT	Massachusetts Institute of Technology
MMU	memory management unit
MOESI	cache coherency protocol: modified, owned, exclusive, shared, invalid
MOS	metal oxide semiconductor
Motif	GUI from OSF for X-Windows
MPEG	Motion Picture Experts Group; international standards for picture or image compression
MPP	massively parallel processor
MPU	main processor unit
MQUAD	metal quad flat pack
MSB	most significant bit, or byte
MTTF	mean time to failure
MTTR	mean time to repair
Mux	multiplex
NaN	not-a-number (bit pattern used for status in floating point)
NAND	logical negated AND function
NASA	National Aeronautics and Space Administration
NCR	computer manufacturer, formerly National Cash Register Co.
NCSC	National Computer Security Center
nCube	a computer company, and a computer
NEC	Nippon Electric Corporation, manufacturer of chips and computers
NFS	network file system
NIST	National Institute of Standards & Technology, (formerly National Bureau of Standards)
NMI	nonmaskable interrupt
NOR	logical negated OR function
NQS	network queuing system—batch software for networks
NXOR	logical negated exclusive OR function
OEM	Original Equipment Manufacturer
OLCP	on-line complex processing
OLE	object linking and embedding

OLTP	on-line transaction processing
OO	object oriented
OODBMS	object-oriented database management system
OOPS	object-oriented programming system
op code	operation code; instruction
opsys	operating system
OR	logical intersection function
OS	operating system
OSF	Open Software Foundation
OSF-1	Open Software Foundation OS, based on Mach
OSI	Open Systems Interconnection
OTP	One-time programmable
packet	a block of information
PAD	packet assembler/disassembler
PALcode	in DEC Alpha architecture, extends instruction set
palmtop	a small computer
PARC	Palo Alto Research Center, Xerox Corp.
PC	personal computer
PCI	peripheral component interconnect
PCMCIA	Personal Computer Memory Card Industry Association
P-code	pseudocode
PDA	personal digital assistant
PDN	public data network
Pentium	Intel processor, instruction-set compatible to 80x86 family; fifth generation
Peta	prefix, 10^{15}
PE	processor element, usually consisting of cpu, memory, I/O
PGA	pin grid array (package of integrated circuits)
Pipeline	an assembly line type processing of instruction execution
pixel	picture element
PLCC	Plastic leadless chip carrier; packaging for integrated circuit
PLL	phase-locked loop; used to synthesize clocks
PMMU	paged memory management unit
POSIX	Portable Operating System Interface for Unix—IEEE standard
PostScript	a page description language by Adobe Systems
PowerPC	RISC chip by Motorola, IBM, Apple Computer
PQFP	plastic quad flat pack (for integrated circuit)
PRDBMS	parallel relational database management system

PRISM	parallel reduced instruction set multiprocessor—Apollo Computer, Inc.
PSE	parallel software environment
PSR	processor status (state) register
PVM	(software) parallel virtual machine; a public domain package from Oak Ridge National Laboratory, Dept. of Energy
QFP	quad flat pack; packaging for integrated circuit
QPFP	quad plastic flat pack; packaging for integrated circuit
quadword	four words
queue	first in, first out data structure
R2000	early 32-bit MIPS RISC processor
R3000	32-bit MIPS RISC processor
R4000	64-bit MIPS RISC processor
R8000	64-bit MIPS processor, with speed of Cray Y-MP
R10000	64 bit MIPS RISC processor
RAID	redundant array of inexpensive disks
RAM	random access memory
RDBMS	relational database management system
ring	topology in which each node is connected to two others in a closed loop
RIOS	IBM RISC architecture; a chipset
RISC	reduced instruction set computer; also Research Institute for Symbolic Computation; also Ronneby Ingenjoersfoerening Soft Centre (Sweden); also Relegate Important Stuff to Compiler
ROM	read-only memory
RS-232-c	EIA specification for serial interconnect
RS/6000	IBM workstation
RTOS	Real-time operating system
S-bus	I/O bus from Sun Microsystems, Inc.
SCI	scalable component interconnect, IEEE 1596-1992 standard
SCO	Santa Cruz Operation, variant of Unix
SCSI	small computer system interface
SFU	special function unit (in Motorola architecture)
SGI	Silicon Graphics, Incorporated, computer manufacturer
SHARC	SuperHarvard Architecture, by Analog Devices
SISD	single-instruction, single-data computer architecture model
SIMD	single-instruction, multiple-data computer architecture model
SIMM	single inline memory module
Smalltalk	object oriented computer language

SMM	system management mode, used for power management
SMP	symmetric multiprocessor, or processing
SONET	synchronous optical network standard
SNA	systems network architecture
SP1, SP2	IBM RISC systems
SPARC	*sc*alable *p*rocessor *arch*itecture
SPEC	System Performance Evaluation Cooperative—vendor association
SQL	structured query language
SRAM	static random access memory
SRT	algorithm for digital divide
SSOP	Shrunk small outline package
stack	a first in, last out data structure
Sun	Sun Microsystems, Inc. computer manufacturer
SuperSPARC	SPARC chip from Texas Instruments, Inc.
SVR4	(Unix) system V, release 4
sync	synchronous; synchronized
T1	digital carrier at 1.544 Mbps
T3D	MPP machine from Cray Research, Inc.
TAB	tape automated bonding—low-cost packaging
TCP/IP	transmission control protocol/Internet protocol
TI	Texas Instruments, Inc. computer and chip manufacturer
Tera	prefix, 10^{12}
TIFF	tag image file format—image exchange standard
TIPS	Tera (10^{12}) operations per second
TFLOPS	Tera (10^{12})floating-point operations per second
TLB	translation lookaside buffer; used for virtual to physical memory mapping
TMC	Thinking Machines Corporation
torus	topology in which nodes form a regular cyclic *n*-dimensional grid
TPC	transaction processing council
tps	transactions per second
TQFP	thin quad flat pack
Transputer	a computer architecture from Inmos, Inc.
tree	acyclic graph; usually refers to a binary tree, where a node has two children
TTL	transistor-transistor logic
UART	Universal Asynchronous Receiver Transmitted

Ultrix	DEC Unix
Unicos	Unix variation from Cray Research, Inc.
unified cache	a cache memory that holds both instructions and data
USART	Universal synchronous/asynchronous receiver transmitter
Unix	operating system
USL	Unix Systems Lab
UV-PROM	ultraviolet (erasable) programmable read-only memory
VAX	Virtual Architecture Extended—32-bit minicomputer from DEC
VHDL	very high level hardware design language
VMS	operating system for VAX computers
VRAM	video RAM
word	a collection of bits; may be 4, 8, 16,18, 24, 32, 64, etc.
VESA	(bus) Video Electronics Standards Association
VLIW	very long instruction word
VLSI	very large scale integration; also, a company name
VME	Versa bus extended
VME-64	revision D of the VME bus specification; 64 bits
von Neumann	computer architecture, control flow, data and instructions share memory
VUP	Vax unit of performance; roughly, 1 mip
WABI	Windows application binary interface (under Unix)
WAN	wide area network
WIMP	window, icon, menu, pointer
Windows	operating system with GUI, from Microsoft Corporation
Windows-NT	Windows-New Technology Operating System
WORM	write once, read many (or mostly)
WWW	World Wide Web (of the Internet)
XDBbus	high-speed interconnect developed by Sun and XEROX-PARC
X-MP	supercomputer from Cray Research, Inc.
XOR	logical function, exclusive intersection function
X-windows	GUI, under Unix
X/Open	consortium for CAE
Y-MP	supercomputer from Cray Research, Inc. follow-on to X-MP

BIBLIOGRAPHY

Miller, Charles A. (ed.) *Information Technology Glossary*, Boston: Gartner Group, 1993.

Wilson, Gregory V., "A Glossary of Parallel Computing Terminology," Feb. 1993, *IEEE Parallel & Distributed Technology*, 1(1), pp. 52–67.

APPENDIX 1

FLOATING POINT

A1.1 INTRODUCTION

This appendix briefly describes the floating-point number representation, its usage and its rationale. There is nothing unique to the use of floating point in RISC architectures. It is an old computer technique for gaining dynamic range in scientific and engineering calculations, at the cost of accuracy. First, we look at fixed-point, or integer, calculations to see where the limitations are. Then, we examine how floating point helps expand the limits.

A1.2 DYNAMIC RANGE VERSUS ACCURACY

In a finite-word-length machine, there is a tradeoff between dynamic range and accuracy in representation. The value of the most significant bit (MSB) sets the dynamic range because the effective value of the most positive number is infinity. The value of the least significant bit (LSB) sets the accuracy, because a value less than the LSB is zero. The MSB and the LSB are related by the word length.

A1.3 NUMBER THEORY

In any fixed-point machine, the number system is of a finite size. For example, in an 18-bit word, we can represent the positive integers from 0 to $(2^{18})-1$, or 262,143. A word of all zeros equals zero, and a word of all ones equals 262,143. I'm using 18 bits as an example because it's not too common. There's nothing magic about 8-, 16-, or 32-bit word sizes.

If we want to use signed numbers, we must give up one bit to represent the sign. Of course, giving up one bit halves the number of values available in the representation. For a signed integer in an 18-bit word, we can represent integers from + to −131,072. Of course, zero is also a valid number. Either the positive range or the negative range must give up a digit so we can represent zero. For now, let's say that in 18 bits, we can represent the integers from −131,072 to +131,071, including 0.

There are several ways of representing the sign bit. We can have a sign-magnitude format, a 1's complement, or a 2's complement representation. In sign-magnitude, the magnitude representation for positive and negative numbers is the same. Most computers use the 2's complement representation. This is easy to implement in hardware. In this format, to form the negative of a number, complement all of the bits ($1 \rightarrow 0$, $0 \rightarrow 1$), and add 1 to the least significant bit position. This is equivalent to forming the 1's complement, and then adding one. One's complement format has the problem that there are two representations of zero, all bits 0 and all bits 1. The hardware has to know that these are equivalent. This added complexity has lead to 1's complement schemes falling out of use in favor of 2's complement. In 2's complement, there is one representation of zero (all bits zero), and one less positive number than the negatives. (Actually, since zero is considered positive, there are the same number of positive and negative numbers, but the negative numbers have more range.) This is easily illustrated for 3-bit numbers, and can be extrapolated to any other fixed-length representation. Remember that the difference between a signed and an unsigned number lies in our interpretation of the bit pattern. In Table A1.1, we see the same 3-bit pattern interpreted in four different ways.

Up to this point we have considered the bit patterns to represent integer values, but we can also insert an arbitrary binary point (analogous to the decimal point) in the word. For integer representations, we have assumed the binary point to lie at the

Table A1.1 Interpretation of Four-Bit Patterns

All Possible Three-Digit Binary Numbers	Equivalent Unsigned	Sign + Mag Integers	1's Complement	2's Complement
000	0	0	0	0
001	1	+1	1	1
010	2	+2	2	2
011	3	+3	3	3
100	4	−0	−3	−4
101	5	−1	−2	−3
110	6	−2	−1	−2
111	7	−3	−0	−1

far right side of the word, to the right of the LSB. This gives the LSB a weight of 2^0, or 1, and the MSB has a weight of 2^{16}. (The sign bit is in the 2^{17} position.) Similarly, we can use a fractional representation where the binary point is assumed to lie between the sign bit and the MSB; the MSB has a weight of 2^{-1}, and the LSB has a weight of 2^{-17}. For these two cases we have:

Representation	Binary Point	MSB	LSB
Integer	right of LSB	2^{16}	2^0
Fractional	right of sign	2^{-1}	2^{-17}

The MSB sets the range, the LSB sets the accuracy, and the LSB and MSB are related by the word length. For cases between these extremes, the binary point can lie anywhere in the word, or for that matter, outside the word. For example, if the binary point is assumed to be 2 bits to the right of the LSB, the LSB weight, and thus the precision, is 2^2. The MSB is then 2^{19}. We have gained dynamic range at the cost of precision. If we assume the binary point is to the left of the MSB, we must be careful to ignore the sign, which does not have an associated digit weight. For an assumed binary point 2 bit positions to the right of the MSB, we have an MSB weight of 2^{-3}, and an LSB weight of 2^{-20}. We have gained precision at the cost of dynamic range.

It is important to remember that the computer's arithmetic unit does not care where we assume the binary point to be. It simply treats the numbers as signed integers during calculations. We overlay the bit weights and the meanings.

A1.4 ADDITION AND SUBTRACTION OF SCALED VALUES

To add or subtract scaled values, they must have the same scaling factor; they must be commensurate. If the larger number is normalized, the smaller number must be shifted to align it for the operation. This may have the net result of adding or subtracting zero, as bits fall out the right side of the small word. This is like saying that $10^9 + .00001$ is approximately 10^9, to 13 decimal places of accuracy. Normalization refers to putting the numbers in a standard format, for example, with a known weight for the LSB.

A1.5 MULTIPLICATION

In multiplication, the scaling factor of the result is the sum of the scaling factors of the products. This is analogous to engineering notation, where we learn to add the powers of ten. In floating point, we add the exponents, multiply the mantissas (these operations can be done in parallel), and renormalize.

A1.6 DIVISION

In division, the scaling factor of the result is the difference between the scaling factor of the dividend and the scaling factor of the divisor. The scaling factor of the remainder is that of the dividend. In engineering notation, we subtract the powers of ten for a division. We subtract the exponents, divide the mantissas, and renormalize.

A1.7 RENORMALIZATION

In a normal form for a signed integer, the most significant bit is one. This says, in essence, that all leading zeros have been squeezed out of the number. The sign bit does not take part in this procedure. However, note that if we know that the most significant bit is always one, there is no reason to store it. This gives us a free bit in a sense; the MSB is a "1" by definition, and the next bit, (MSB-1)-th bit, is adjacent to the sign bit. This simple trick has doubled the effective accuracy of the word, because each bit position is a factor of two. Figure A1.1 illustrates the renormalization process.

A1.8 THE SUBTRACTION PROBLEM

The primary operation that will cause a loss of precision or accuracy is the subtraction of two numbers that have nearly but not quite identical values. This is commonly encountered in digital filters, for example, where successive readings are differenced. For an 18-bit word, if the readings differ in, say, the 19th-bit position, then

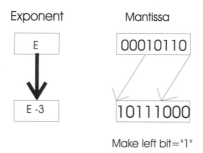

Exponent   Mantissa

E   00010110

E -3   10111000

Make left bit="1"

1. Shift Mantissa left 3
   net effect: Mantissa $* 2^3$

2. Subtract 3 from exponent
   net effect: number $* 2^{-3}$

Figure A1.1 Renormalization.

the difference will be seen to be zero. On the other hand, the scaling factor of the parameters must allow sufficient range to hold the largest number expected. Care must be taken in subtracting values known to be nearly identical. Precision can be retained by prenormalization of the arguments.

A1.9 OVERFLOW IN ADDITION OR MULTIPLICATION

During an arithmetic operation, if the result is a value larger than the greatest positive value for a particular format, or less than the most negative, then the operation has overflowed the format. Normally, the absolute value function cannot overflow, with the exception of the absolute value of the least negative number in 2's complement form, which has no corresponding positive representation, because we made room for the representation of zero.

In addition, the scaling factor can increase by one, if we consider the possibility of adding two of the largest possible numbers. We can also consider subtracting the largest (absolute value) negative number from the largest (in an absolute sense) negative number.

A1.10 SHIFTING AND ADJUSTING THE SCALING FACTOR

A 1-bit position left shift is equivalent to multiplying by two. Thus, after a one-position shift, the scaling factor must be adjusted to reflect the new position of the binary point. Similarly, a 1-bit position right shift is equivalent to division by two, and the scaling factor must be similarly adjusted after the operation.

A1.11 NUMERIC UNDERFLOW

Numeric underflow occurs when a nonzero result of an arithmetic operation is too small in absolute value to be represented. The result is usually reported as zero. The subtraction case discussed above is one example. Taking the reciprocal of the largest positive number is another.

A1.12 INEXACT RESULTS

As in the decimal representation, some numbers cannot be represented exactly in binary, regardless of the precision. Nonterminating fractions such as 1/3 are one case, and the irrational numbers such as e and pi are another. Operations involving these will yield inexact results, regardless of the format. However, this is not necessarily an error. The irrationals, by definition, cannot be exactly represented by a ratio of integers. Even in base ten notation, e and pi extend indefinitely.

A1.13 ROUNDING

When the results of a calculation do not fit within the format, we must throw something away. We normally delete bits from the right (or low precision side) of the word. There are several ways to do this. If we simply ignore the bits that won't fit within the format, we are truncating, or rounding toward zero. We choose the closest word within the format to represent the results. We can also round up by adding one to the LSB of the resultant word if the first bit we're going to throw away is a one. We can also choose to round-to-even, round-to-odd, round-to-nearest, round-toward-zero, round-toward-(+ infinity), or round-toward-(− infinity). Consistency is the desired feature.

A1.14 DYNAMIC RANGE REQUIREMENTS

If we look at typical physical constants, we can get some idea of the dynamic range that we'll require for "typical" applications. Recall, the mass of an electron is 9.1085×10^{-31} grams. Avogadro's number is 6.023×10^{23}. If we want to multiply these quantities, we need a dynamic range of $10^{23+31} = 10^{54}$, which would require a 180-bit word (10^{54} = approximately 2^{180}). Most of the bits in this 180-bit word would be zeros as place holders. Well, since zeros don't mean anything, can't we get rid of them? Of course.

We need dynamic range, and we need precision, but we usually don't need them simultaneously. The floating-point data structure will give us dynamic range at the cost of being unable to exactly represent the desired number.

A1.15 FLOATING POINT

Finally, we talk about floating point. In essence, we need a format for the computer to work with that is analogous to engineering notation, a mantissa and a power of ten. The two parts of the word, with their associated signs, will take part in the calculation exactly as the scaled integers previously discussed. The exponent is the scaling factor that we used. Whereas in scaled integers we had a fixed scaling factor, in floating point we allow the scaling factor to be carried along with the word and to change as the calculations proceed.

The representation of a number in floating point, like the representation in scientific notation, is not unique. For example:

$$6.54 \times 10^2 = .654 \times 10^3 = 654. \times 10^0$$

We have to choose a scheme and be consistent. What is normally done is that the exponent is defined to be a number such that the leftmost digit is nonzero. This is defined as the "normal" form.

In the floating-point representation, the number of bits assigned to the exponent determine dynamic range, and the number of bits assigned to the mantissa determine the precision, or resolution. For a fixed word size, we must allocate the available bits between the precision (mantissa), and the range (exponent). Each component has an associated sign.

Granularity is defined as the difference between representable numbers. This term is normally equal to the absolute precision, and relates to the least significant bit.

A1.16 DENORMALIZED NUMBERS

This topic is getting too far into number theory, and I will only touch on these special topics here. There is a use for numbers that are not in normal form, so-called denormals (denorms). A denorm has an exponent that is the smallest representable exponent, with a leading digit of the mantissa not equal to zero. An unnormalized number, on the other hand, has the same mantissa, but an exponent that is not the smallest representable. Let's get back to engineering . . . .

A1.17 OVERFLOW AND UNDERFLOW

If the result of an operation generates a number too large (in an absolute magnitude case) to be represented, we have generated an overflow. If the result is too small to be represented, we have an underflow. Results of an overflow can be reported as infinity (+ or – as required), or as an error bit pattern. The underflow case is where we have generated a denormalized number. The IEEE standard for floating point representation, discussed below, handles denorms as valid operands. Another approach is to specify resultant denorms as zero.

A1.18 STANDARDS

There are many standards for the floating-point representation, with the IEEE standard being the de facto industry choice. In this section, we'll discuss the IEEE standard in detail, and see how some other older industry standards differ and how conversions can be made.

A1.18.1 IEEE Floating Point

The IEEE standard specifies the representation of a number as +/–- mantissa $\times 2^{+/-\text{exponent}}$. Note that there are two sign bits, one for the mantissa, and one for the exponent. Note also that the exponent is an exponent of two, not ten. This is referred to as radix-2 representation. Other radices are possible but not in the IEEE scheme. The most significant bit of the mantissa is assumed to be a "1", and is not stored. Now, let's take a look at what this representation buys us. A 16-bit integer can cover a range of $+/- 10^4$. A 32-bit integer can span a range of $+/- 10^9$. The IEEE short real format, in 32 bits, can cover a range of $+/- 10^{+/-38}$. A 64-bit integer covers the range $+/- 10^{19}$. A long real IEEE floating-point number covers the range $+/- 10^{+/-308}$. The dynamic range of calculations has been vastly increased for the same data size. What we have lost is the ability to exactly represent numbers, but we are "close enough for engineering."

In the short, real format, the 32-bit word is broken up into fields. The mantissa, defined as a number less than one, occupies 23 bits. The most significant bit of the data item is the sign of the mantissa. The exponent occupies 8 bits. The represented word is as follows:

$$(-1^S)(2^{E+bias})(F1 \ldots F23)$$

Where F0 ... F23 < 1.
Note that F0 = "1" by definition, and is not stored.

$$S \ E0 \ldots E7 \ F1 \ldots F23$$

The term -1^S gives us plus when the S bit is zero and minus when the S bit is one. The bias term is defined as 127. This is used instead of a sign bit for the exponent, and achieves the same results. This format simplifies the hardware, because only positive numbers are then involved in exponent calculations. As a side benefit, this approach ensures that reciprocals of all representable numbers can be represented.

In the long real format, the structure is as follows:

$$(-1^S)(2^{E+bias})(F1...F52)$$

Where F0 ... F52 < 1.
Note that F0 = "1" by definition, and is not stored.

$$S \ E0 \ldots E10 \ F1 \ldots F53$$

Here, the bias term is defined as 1023.

For intermediate steps in a calculation, there is a temporary real data format in 80 bits. This expands the exponent to 15 bits, and the mantissa to 64 bits. This allows a range of $+/- 10^{4932}$, which is a large number in anyone's view.

In the IEEE format, provision is made for an entity known as not-a-number (NaN). For example, the result of trying to multiply zero times infinity is NaN. NaNs are status signals that particular violation cases took place. IEEE representation also supports four user-selectable rounding modes. Not all implementations of the IEEE standard implement all of the modes and options.

Although the IEEE standard is perhaps the most popular, numerous other representation schemes exist. We'll look briefly at two others in use—by Digital Equipment Corporation and IBM.

A1.18.2 Digital Equipment Corporation Floating Point—F,D,G

DEC F format is a single-precision mode, identical to IEEE. DEC D has the same dynamic range, but more precision is provided by more mantissa bits. DEC G has more dynamic range than D, by using more exponent bits. Digital's standard is in use by the VAX family of computers. DEC format does not allow for infinities or denorms, but does have reserved operands that work like NaNs.

A1.18.3 IBM—SP, DP

In the IBM representation, the double precision has more precision but the same dynamic range as the single precision. What is more important, this scheme uses radix-16 instead of radix-2 numbers. This provides a wider dynamic range than radix-2 schemes, with an increased granularity, resulting in reduced absolute precision.

A1.19 FLOATING-POINT HARDWARE

Floating-point hardware is a specialized, optimized computer architecture for the floating-point data structure. It usually features concurrent operation with the integer unit. Initially, floating-point units were separate chips, but now the state-of-the-art allows these functional units to be included on the same silicon real estate as the integer processor. The hardware of the floating-point unit is designed to handle the floating-point data format. For example, in a floating multiply, we simultaneously integer-multiply the mantissas and add the exponents. A barrel shifter is handy for normalization/renormalization by providing a shift of any number of bits in one clock period. Floating-point units usually implement the format conversions in hardware (integer to floating, called float; floating to integer, called fix), and can handle extended-precision (64-bit) integers. Both external and internal floating-point units usually rely on the main processor's instruction fetch unit. The coprocessor may have to do a memory access for load/store. In this case, it may use a DMA-like protocol to get use of the memory bus resource from the integer processor.

Floating-point hardware gives us the ability to add, subtract, multiply, and sometimes divide. Some units provide only the reciprocal function, which is a simple divide into a known fixed quantity (1), and thus easy to implement. A divide requires two operations, then, a reciprocal followed by a multiply. This may be quicker than the general case divide. Some units also include square root and some transcendental primitives. These functions are implemented in a microstep fashion, with Taylor or other series expansions of the functions of interest.

Signed Integer Range

10 bits	1×10^3 (a good approximation is: 2^{10} is approximately 10^3)
16-bits	3×10^4

Signed Integer Range

32-bits	2×10^9
64-bits	9.2×10^{18}
128-bits	1.7×10^{38}
256 bits	1.1×10^{77}

A1.20 FLOATING-POINT OPERATIONS

This section discusses operations on floating-point numbers. This forms the basis for the specification of a floating-point emulation software package, or for the development of custom hardware.

A1.20.1 Floating Point Add/Subtract

Before the addition can be performed, the floating-point numbers must be commensurate with addition; in essence, they must have the same exponent. The mantissa of the number with the smaller exponent will be right shifted, and the exponent adjusted accordingly. However, if the right shift is equal to or more than the number of bits in the mantissa representation, we will loose something. This is analogous to the case where we add 0.000001 to 1 million and get approximately 1 million. Subtraction, of course, is the addition of the 2's complement.

After the addition of mantissas, we may need to right shift the resultant by 1, and adjust the exponent accordingly, to account for mantissa overflow. This is analogous to the case of adding $4.1 \times 10^{16} + 6.3 \times 10^{16}$, with the result of 10.4×10^{16}, or $1.04 * 10^{17}$, in normal form.

If we add two numbers of almost equal magnitude but opposite sign, we get a case of "massive cancellation." Here, the leading digits of the mantissa may be zero, with a loss of precision. Renormalization is always called for after addition. For example:

$$1.23456 * 10^{16} \text{ plus} -1.23455 * 10^{16} = 0.00001 \times 10^{16} \text{ or } 1.0 * 10^{11},$$

in normal form.

A1.20.2 Floating Multiply

In multiply, we may simultaneously integer multiply the mantissas, and add the exponents. After the operation, we need to renormalize the results. Note that the multiply operation is simpler than the addition operation, because the numbers are ready to multiply, whereas in the addition or subtraction one, we may need to adjust the numbers before the operation.

A1.20.3 Floating Divide

The easiest division to do is a reciprocal, where the dividend is a known quantity. Some systems implement only the reciprocal operation, requiring a subsequent multiplication to complete the division operation. Even so, this may be faster than a division, because the reciprocal is much easier to implement in algorithmic form than the general-purpose division.

The Pentium Floating Divide Error In 1994, a subtle error was discovered in the floating-point divide algorithm of Intel's Pentium chip. This also affected the remainder function and transcendental functions dependent on divide. The problem was found to be independent of rounding mode. The divide errors pointed out the difficulties of designing test cases for full fault coverage of complex chips. The fact that it took several years for a large user community to notice the problem was also significant. Later analysis showed that the error occurred when the binary divisor's mantissa had these most significant bits:

1.0001

1.0100

1.0111

1.1010

1.0110

The reciprocal function was not similarily affected, providing a workaround for this problem. The chip design was changed and retested, and subsequent Pentiums (and P6s) do not have this particular problem.

A1.21 BIBLIOGRAPHY

"32-bit Microprogrammable Products, Am29C300/29300 Data Book," 1988, AMD.

"80387 Programmer's Reference Manual," 1987, Intel, 231917-001.

"Am29027 Handbook," 1989, AMD.

"ANSI/IEEE Standard 754-1985 for Binary Floating-Point Arithmetic," *IEEE*.

Barrenechea, Mark J., "Numeric Exception Handling," May 1, 1991, *Programmer's Journal*, 9 (3): 40.

Cavanagh, Joseph J. F., *Digital Computer Arithmetic Design and Implementation*. New York: McGraw-Hill, 1984. ISBN 0-07-010282-1.

"DSP96002 IEEE Floating-Point Dual Port Processor User's Manual," 1989, Motorola, DSP96002um/ad.

"Fractional and Integer Arithmetic Using the DSP56000 Family of General-Purpose Digital Signal Processors," 1993, Motorola, APR3/D.

Hwang, Kai, *Computer Arithmetic, Principles, Architecture, and Design*. New York: Wiley, 1979. ISBN 0471-03496-7.

"Likelihood of Pentium Chip Error," 1994, IBM Corporation white paper.

MC68881/882 Floating Point Coprocessor User's Manual, 2nd ed., Motorola. Englewood Cliffs: Prentice-Hall, 1989. ISBN 0-13-567009-8.

Nicely, Thomas R. "Bug in the Pentium FPU," October 30, 1994, Internet Posting.

Rowen, Chris, Johnson, Mike, Ries, Paul, "The MIPS R3010 Floating Point Coprocessor," June 1988, *IEEE Micro*, pp. 53–62.

Scott, Norman R., *Computer Number Systems and Arithmetic*. New York, NY: Prentice-Hall, 1985. ISBN 0-13-164211-1.

"Statistical Analysis of Floating Point Flaw in the Pentium (TM) Processor," Nov. 30, 1994, Intel Corporation white paper.

Appendix 2

EXAMPLES OF STUDENT PROJECTS IN RISC

This appendix shows some of the projects that were undertaken by the graduate students in EG-769, Introduction to RISC Architecture at Loyola College. The projects counted for 60 percent (later, 70 percent) of the student's grade. During the summer months, the student had 10 weeks to finish the project, but 14 weeks during the normal semester. Some projects expanded out to independent study.

As a guideline, projects could be oriented to hardware, software, or both. Students were given the widest latitude to choose and execute a project of interest to them and relevant to their work or personal interests. As most of the students in the Engineering Science Masters program were working professionals taking one or two courses a semester, the projects tended to reflect their interests at work. Where a project discusses a specific topic from this book, the chapter reference is given.

Selected Student Projects, 1989–1990

1. An Investigation into High-Speed Multiplication Techniques

   In this project, the student concentrated on optimizing the multiplication process by various hardware techniques. These techniques are applicable to specialized architectures for integer and floating-point multiply accelerators for RISC processors.

2. The Use of Optimizing Compilers in RISC Architectures

   For this paper, the student did an in-depth look at the use of optimizing compilers for RISC architectures, and the issues and tradeoffs. Optimization techniques were discussed in detail in Chapter 3.

3. MIPS Simulation

   For this project the student wrote an instruction level simulation of the R3000 processor (Chapter 6) in Pascal, for the PC. Full traces of instruction execution and register usage were provided. Not all of the R3000 op codes and features were included, due to time constraints.

4. Reduced Instruction Set Computer (RISC) Microprocessors as a Tool for Increased Performance from PCs

   In this project, the student looked at using several RISC chips to augment PC computational performance. These included the VL86C010 (Chapter 11), the Cypress SPARC CY7C601 (Chapter 10), and the 88100 (Chapter 5). The project considered the interface requirements and the software details.

5. DSP32—Transputer Interface

   In this project, the student designed and built an interface between the AT&T DSP-32 chip and the Transputer (Chapter 7). This took the form of a DSP-32 serial data stream to Transputer serial link adapter, plus associated software on both sides of the interface. The Transputer is frequently used as a communications agent for other RISC processors in large multiprocessor or parallel processor networks.

6. Double-Precision Floating-Point Processor Card Design

   In this project, the student designed a card to allow the use of the AMD 29C327 floating-point unit in the PC/AT architecture. Several of the AMD chips were donated to Loyola by AMD.

7. MIL-STD-1553 Remote Terminal Simulator

   For this project, the student designed and built a MIL-STD-1553 bus remote terminal simulator, using the DSP-32 chip from AT&T. MIL-STD-1553 is a common avionics serial bus. The remote terminal simulator is a debugging tool for network traffic.

8. Evaluation of the SPARC Processor Implementing a Digital Signaling Process (DSP) Algorithm

   In this project, the student implemented a finite impulse response (FIR) filter in the C language for the SPARC chip (Chapter 10). Simulated input data were provided for both white noise and a constant-amplitude, varying frequency sine wave. Fourier analysis of the filter output was applied. Different implementations of the filter were explored, to optimize runtime (frequency), and space. The goal of the project was a 100 KHz filter.

9. RISC Cache Graphical Software Simulator

   For this project, the student wrote a software-based cache simulator to allow exploration of various caching strategies. The project was implemented as 2,000 lines of Smalltalk code on the PC. Cache tuning could be explored by varying parameters for memory size, line size, replacement policy, and write policy in the cache. A debugger was included. Instructions were included similar to the MIPS R3000 set (Chapter 6).

Selected Student Projects, 1990–1991

1. A RISC-Based Encipherment Processor
    The student looked at the requirements of the OSI security model in terms of services, and evaluated how to implement this on an Intel i860 (Chapter 9).

2. Introduction to the EG-769 RISC Microprocessor
    In this project, the student designed a custom RISC machine from first principles. The derived machine had 32 instructions, 32 general-purpose registers, a branch address buffer of depth 32, a four-stage pipeline, output buffers, and a Harvard architecture. The student supplied example applications code for the proposed design.

3. Cache Considerations for RISC Architectures
    This in-depth survey examined cache theory and tradeoffs, as well as the specifics of caching in the SPARC, MIPS, 88k, 29k, Transputer, and i860/i960 architectures. (Chapters 10, 6, 5, 8, 7, 9, respectively).

4. Simulation of a Distributed Processing System Using an Occam Programmed Transputer
    In this project, the student defined and implemented simulation tools for distributed systems using the Occam language on the Transputer (Chapter 7). The specific example of automobile assembly was simulated.

5. Comparison of RISC and CISC Architectures with an Emphasis on Military Embedded Systems
    The student compared and contrasted the MIL-STD-1750A architecture with the SPARC, 29k, 88k, R3000, and i960 (Chapters 10, 8, 5, 6, 9, respectively). The MIL-STD-1750A is a standard avionics 16-bit architecture (Appendix 3).

6. Transputer-Based Artificial Neural Network
    The student implemented a multi-Transputer (Chapter 7) back propagation neural network with 35 inputs and 8 outputs. First, the network was designed, implemented, and tested on one Transputer, and later expanded to multiple Transputers. The effects on learning time were examined.

7. Database Performance on RISC Platforms
    In this project, the student considered the requirements from the database and large transaction processing world, and applied these to RISC processors. Software simulation was used, and various RISC architectures were compared to the 80x86 baseline. Examined were the 88k, R3000, Transputer, 80960, SPARC, and RISC/6000 (Chapters 5, 6, 7, 9, 10, 16, respectively).

Selected Student Projects, Summer 1992

1. The Selection and Application of a RISC Processor for a Ground Based Radar
    This project was related to the student's work. It involved the applicability

of a RISC processor for an embedded radar processor, to replace an existing 68020 CISC processor. The details and requirements of the application were presented, and a tradeoff was made with the MIPS R3000 (Chapter 6), AMD 29k (Chapter 8), and Motorola 88k (Chapter 5). The study predicted an expansion in the size of the applications software code, but an acceleration of the runtime. Cache memory issues were explored.

2. Memory Management in RISC

In this paper, the student explored the various techniques of memory management applicable to RISC systems. Details of caching were also explored and presented. The SPARC (Chapter 10) approach was examined in detail.

3. Replace Amharic Typewriter with a Personal Computer

In this interesting project, the student explored the design of a custom RISC-based laser printer controller to handle the Amharic alphabet, used in Ethiopia. There are 320 characters in the Amharic language, which is Semitic in origin. With more than (2^8) 256 codes, more than a single byte was required to express a character code. The project was based on the MIPS R3000 (Chapter 6). This was a classic embedded RISC application, involving Postscript font and codes conversion.

4. BESERK (Bare-Board/Embedded SPARC Elementary Real-time Kernel) Design

In this project, the student designed a real-time embedded operating system kernel for the SPARC architecture (Chapter 10). The requirements of a real-time kernel were explored, and bounced against the architectural features of the SPARC. The project was coded in prototype form to include functions for semaphore and task management and scheduling/rescheduling.

Selected Student Projects, Spring 1993

1. Definition of a one-bit RISC Processor

In this project, the student defined a 1-bit architecture, and wrote a simulator to test its operation. A 1-bit processor is combined with neighboring processors to provide operations on arbitrary size data structures. In a sense, it is the essence of the Transputer (Chapter 7). The simulation was written in the C language.

2. Native Alpha Instruction Simulator/Debugger

In this program, hosted on the campus VAX, the student provided a capability for instruction set simulation of Digital Equipment Corporation's Alpha architecture (Chapter 12). The simulator provided the full instruction set and addressing modes, except that the floating-point instructions were not included. The simulation has a Windows interface, and real-time trace is provided. Single-step mode is available. The simulation was written in VAX C.

3. FIR Filter Design Using an Eight-Bit RISC-Based Microcontroller

    In this project, the student implemented a five-tap FIR filter using the PIC 16C71 microcontroller (Chapter 17), which has an integral analog to digital port. A sampling frequency of 6.5 KHz was achieved. The filter implementation is a minimum parts count approach, but suffered from the lack of a multiplication operation in the PIC.

4. Elements of RISC, a Reduced Instruction Set Computer Software Simulator

    This was a very interesting project, in which the student picked up and extended the work of a previous student in the RISC class. In the 1990–1991 term, a student developed an architecture called the EG-769 Machine (named after the class number), which was a RISC machine designed from scratch. In the current project, the new student wrote a simulation of the operation of this machine, using the C++ language.

5. 88100

    In this survey project, the student did an in-depth investigation and report on the architecture of the Motorola 88100 (Chapter 5) processor. It was during the research phase of this project that the student learned that Motorola was deemphasizing the 88k in favor of the PowerPC architecture (Chapter 16).

6. RISC in Manufacturing

    In this report, the student derives the requirements for computing in manufacturing, and examines how RISC machines would meet these requirements. Various functions from the manufacturing floor were examined, including process planning and scheduling, related business functions, product design and simulation, quality control, shop floor control, and embedded machine control. The Next Generation Controller (NGC) Project of the U.S. Air Force Manufacturing Technology Group was explored. Issues of interfacing, language, and compatibility were discussed.

Selected Student Projects, Summer 1993

1. Implementing a Spine Position Monitor Using the PIC16C71 Microcontroller for Back Education and the Prevention of Back Injury

    In this preliminary design project, the student tackled the problem of generating clues for incorrect back position during heavy lifting. Incorrect back position leads to back injury during lifting. The PIC (Chapter 17) was the ideal candidate for measuring positions along the spine, and providing aural feedback to a user in a nonintrusive manner. Angle sensors were used to monitor the back position prior to a lift, to provide immediate feedback before a lift was attempted. Similar, commercially available units are expensive and cumbersome.

2. Is Networking Field Ready to Take a RISC?

    In this paper, the student explored the areas of commercial networking, particularly servers. He then examined whether RISC machines met the performance needs in this area.

3. Design and Simulation of a RISC Integer Unit

In this project, the student took an existing 4-bit computer design and converted it to a RISC design. The design was entered in ORCAD schematic capture package, and instruction execution was simulated. The design was a variation of a previous example from Tanenbaum [1]. This project could be extended and expanded in the future to include software tools for the architecture, and instantiation in a gate array, as part of Loyola's VLSI design class.

4. The IDTR3081 32-bit RISC Embedded Controller

In this paper, the student described the architecture of the MIPS IDT 3081 controller (Chapter 6) in depth, and compared and contrasted this unit with the Intel i960 (Chapter 9).

5. Pentium Power: Design Features of Intel's Newest Processor

In this survey paper, the student described an overview of the Intel Pentium Processor (section 19.7), with an emphasis on the influence of RISC design features on this mainstream CISC design. Comparisons were given of the Pentium, its earlier CISC relatives, and current RISC designs.

6. RISC Architectures for 3D Graphics

In this project, the student looked at the applicability of RISC machines for the highly specialized area of real-time 3D graphics generation. The paper started with an overview of the problem, describing the vector processing requirements for graphics. The graphics functions of the i860 (Chapter 9), the LR33020 GraphX Processor, and various DSP chips were examined.

7. Hewlett-Packard PA RISC Systems

In this survey paper, the student described the HP-PA RISC system's evolution and architecture (Chapter 14). Issues of compiler performance were explored.

8. Cache Memory in RISC Architecture

In this survey paper, the student explored the issues of caching in RISC systems, the various caching strategies for instructions and data, and cache policies.

9. Anatomy of an SGI Indigo

In this research paper, the student explored the architecture of the SGI Indigo Workstation, built around the MIPS R3000 processor (Chapter 6). The Indigo is a high-speed graphics engineering workstation.

Selected Student Projects, Summer 1994

1. The Intel 80960: A 32-bit RISC Implementation

In this survey paper, the student looked at the i960 family and the i960CA in depth. A comparison of generated code was made with the 80286, for a C-language routine.

2. Cache: A Bridge Between Data Storage and High Speed CPUs

    In this project, the student did an in-depth look at cache systems, particularly the caching schemes used on Intel's Pentium processor (19.6).

3. AM29205 RISC Microcontroller Used for Data Collection

    This project was concerned with reimplementing an existing, 68010-based analog data collection system to the AMD RISController.

4. The Porting of a Message Processing System from a CISC-Based Architecture to a RISC-Based Architecture

    In this paper, the student discussed the results of porting code from a VAX to an Alpha implementation. Both advantages and disadvantages of moving the I/O bound message passing code to the RISC implementation were covered.

A2.1 DESIGN AND CONSTRUCTION OF LOYOLA'S 64-NODE PARALLEL PROCESSOR

This section describes the design and construction of a 64-node parallel processor based on the Inmos Transputer, for the graduate engineering program at Loyola College. This project provided valuable hands-on experience to staff and students in the Dept. of Engineering Science. It also resulted in a valuable institutional resource for other programs, such as for the development of parallel software courses.

In June 1992, Loyola had most of the parts needed to integrate a 64-node parallel processor at the Columbia lab, thanks to generous donations from Inmos Corp. We had on hand sufficient T414 Transputer processors, over 500 pieces of SRAM memory, multiple copies of the development software system, and numerous technical reports and data books.

At the lab in Columbia, we set up a Transputer development workstation, hosted in a PC, that allowed us to develop code for the parallel machine in C, Pascal, FORTRAN, or Occam. This system, consisting of a single Transputer, is used for student projects. Later, we duplicated this development system.

Besides the experience gained by building and demonstrating this unit, other departments at Loyola were seen to benefit. Engineering Science was providing a resource that others could use. For example, ongoing projects at Loyola included using parallel processing for image processing research, using Transputers for embedded robot control, and setting up a parallel processing course. The 64 node architecture, utilizing 16 boards containing 4 nodes each is shown in Figure A2.1.

Our target was to do this project at a minimum cost, using existing and donated resources and student labor. Engineering Science would then provide the use of the machine as a resource to students in our program, and for other departments. The budget for parts was $4,000.

A four-node Transputer board was prototyped and designed by a Loyola alumnus.

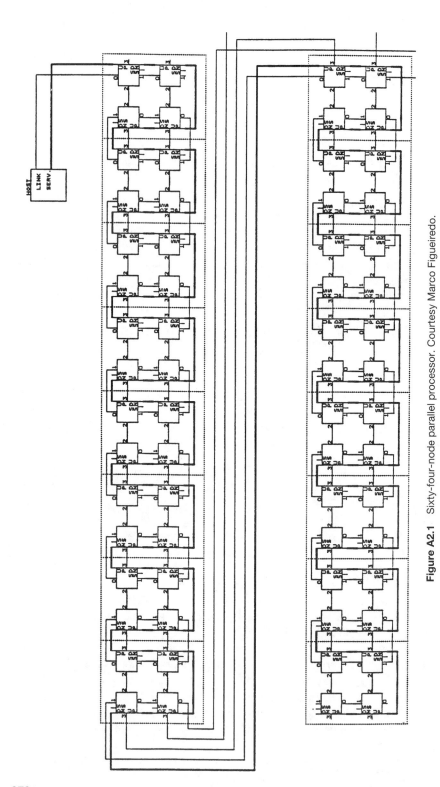

Figure A2.1 Sixty-four-node parallel processor. Courtesy Marco Figueiredo.

The four-node board was designed to be used as four one-node boards, or a single four-node configuration. We originally planned to procure several Augat-style wire-wrap boards. Each node of the parallel processor machine consists of a Transputer chip, a clock source, memory, and several "glue" chips. After a design for the node was completed, it was estimated to take three hours to wire-wrap, and two hours to check out and debug. Each Augat card could hold eight to ten nodes. However, experience with wire-wrapped Transputer systems showed significant electrical noise and interference problems with the memory interface. The circuit board approach was chosen. Sixteen of the boards plus two spares were produced, to house the donated Transputers.

Similarly, we originally planned to make use of the donated SRAM for the system memory. Each node was to have, at a minimum, 256 kilobytes of memory, for a total of 16 Megabytes of system memory. We did not have, however, enough pin-compatible memory to use for the 16 boards without doing several derivative designs. Thus, we switched to purchased SRAM chips for the design. The SRAM chips were the most expensive procured component of the system. In a Transputer system, the memory must be 32 bits wide, forcing use of four pieces of bytewide memory.

The quad board was able to use a single 5 MHz clock oscillator for all four nodes on the board. The Transputer's links were connected to their nearest neighbor, and the spare links were buffered off-board using TTL drivers. Inmos standard up-, down-, and system-control system resources were provided. A four-node processor board consumed less than 300 ma at 5 volts, with 256 kilobytes of external memory for each processor. The architecture of the four-node Transputer board is shown in Figure A2.2.

The boards were assembled, populated, and checked out over the summer of 1993 by students. All of the boards and chips worked as planned. After unit test, an integrated system was built up as interconnect cables were fabricated.

The system was completed in November 1993 with the design and construction of a power distribution board. Checkout was particularly easy, using the most rudimentary of software tools. The complexity of the system was much less than that of an integer processor of the same parts count, because in the case of the parallel processor, it was 64 identical, replicated circuits. Using only the public domain software utilities CHECK and MTEST we were able to debug the hardware in one evening. The software was able to identify the node that had an error, which then mapped to a particular board. For memory problems, we had the node and the byte, which mapped to a chip. In most cases a cursory visual inspection would reveal a missed solder joint, or an incorrect chip.

As of 1994, a card cage was being fabricated for the machine to protect the board interconnect cables. Plans were being made to connect the parallel processor's host machine, a 80386, to the network, and thence to the Internet. A graduate-level course on parallel programming was proposed, based on the machine. Faculty members were exploring the feasibility of using the machine for code previously run on a Cray. Studies of the SPRINT-2 architecture [2], a similar system using 64 Transputers, showed it to have an equivalent speed of execution to that of a Cray Y-MP.

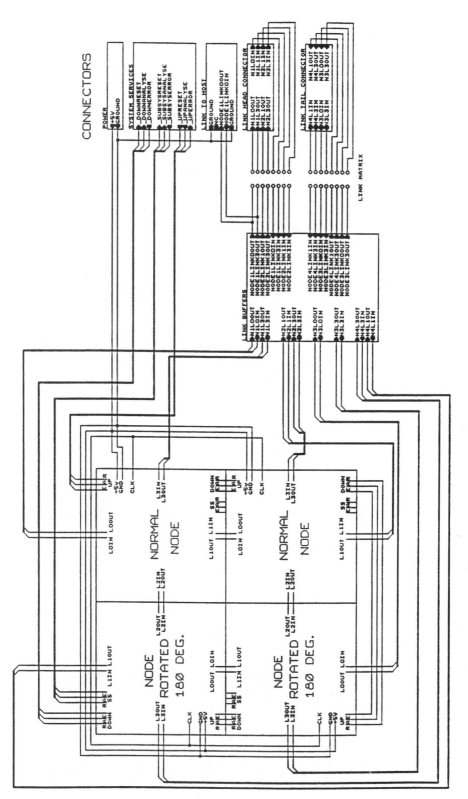

Figure A2.2 Four-node processor board. Courtesy of Marco Figueiredo.

REFERENCES

[1] Tanenbaum, Andrew S., "Structured Computer Organization," 1990, 3rd ed., Englewood Cliffs, NJ: Prentice Hall. ISBN 0138546622.

[2] DeGroot, A. J., Johansson, E. M., Fitch, J. P., Grant, C. W., Parker, S. R., "SPRINT—The Systolic Processor with a Reconfigurable Interconnection Network of Transputers," August 1987, *IEEE Transactions on Nuclear Science*, NS-34 (4): 873–877.

Appendix 3

RISC FOR AEROSPACE APPLICATIONS

A3.1 INTRODUCTION

Aerospace applications for RISC processors abound. Early space flight computers were generally custom designs, but cost and performance issues have driven the development of variants of commercial chips for these specialized applications. Aerospace applications are usually classic embedded applications, as discussed in Chapter 3. Military systems live in their own world, and a full discussion is not within the scope of this book. Civilian space applications are rather limited in number, and, until recently, almost exclusively meant NASA (National Aeronautics and Space Administration), ESA (European Space Association), NASDA (National Aero Space Development Agency—Japan), or some other government agency. MIL-STD-883 is the standard for testing and screening of parts. Specific issues of radiation tolerance are discussed in MIL-M-38510. Class-S parts are specifically for space flight use. Issues of radiation hardening and single-event upset hardening will be discussed in this section. Flight systems electronics usually require MIL-STD-883b, class-S, radiation-hard (total dose), single event upset (SEU)-tolerant parts.

RISC processors used in the field of aerospace, as with any semiconductor-based electronics, need to meet stringent selection, screening, packaging, and testing requirements and characterizations because of the unique environment. Most aerospace electronics, and the whole understanding of radiation effects, were driven by the Cold War defense buildup from the 1960s through the 1980s. This era was characterized by the function-at-any-cost, melt-before-fail design philosophy. In the 1990s, the byword is COTS—use of *commercial, off-the-shelf* products. Thus, instead of custom, proprietary processor architectures, we are now seeing the production of specialized products derived from commercial lines, such as IBM's RAD-6000, discussed below. In an era of decreasing markets, the cost of entry and of maintaining presence in this tiny market niche is prohibitively high for all but a few companies.

A3.2 RADIATION HARDNESS ISSUES FOR SPACE FLIGHT APPLICATIONS

A complete discussion of the physics of radiation damage to semiconductors is beyond the scope of this section. However, an overview of the subject is presented. The tolerance of semiconductor devices to radiation must be examined in the light of their damage susceptibility. The problems fall into two broad categories; those caused by cumulative dose, and those transient events caused by asynchronous very energetic particles. These will be experienced during a period of intense solar flare activity. The unit of absorbed dose of radiation is the *rad*, representing the absorption of 100 ergs of energy per gram of material. A kilorad (k-rad) is one thousand rads. At 10 k-rad, death in humans is almost instantaneous. One hundred k-rad is typical in the vicinity of Jupiter's radiation belts. Ten to twenty k-rad is typical for spacecraft in low Earth orbit, but the number depends on how much time the spacecraft spends outside the Van Allen belts, which act as a shield by trapping energetic particles.

Absorbed radiation can cause temporary or permanent changes in the semiconductor material. Usually neutrons, being uncharged, do minimal damage, but energetic protons and electrons cause lattice or ionization damage in the material, and resultant parametric changes. For example, the leakage current can increase, or bit states can change. Certain technologies and manufacturing processes are known to produce devices that are less susceptible to damage than others.

Radiation tolerance of 100 k-rad is usually more than adequate for low Earth orbit (LEO) missions, which spend most of their life below the shielding of the Van Allen belts. For Polar missions, a higher total dose is expected, from 100 k-rad to 1 megarad per year. For synchronous, equatorial orbits, which are used by many communication satellites and some weather satellites, the expected dose is only several k-rad per year. Finally, for planetary missions to Venus, Mars, Jupiter, Saturn, and beyond, even more stringent requirements must be met. For one thing, the missions usually are unique, and the cost of failure is high. For missions toward the Sun, the higher fluence of solar radiation must be taken into account. The larger outer planets, such as Jupiter and Saturn, have large radiation belts around them as well.

Leaders in the area of radiation-tolerant devices are companies that have addressed the military market. These include Texas Instruments, National Semiconductor, Harris Corporation, Performance Semiconductor, United Technologies, RCA/GE, Honeywell, IBM, SGS-Thompson, and GEC-Plessey.

Cumulative radiation dose causes a charge trapping in the oxide layers, which manifests as a parametric change in the devices. Total dose effects may be a function of the dose rate, and annealing of the device may occur, especially at elevated temperatures. Annealing refers to the self-healing of radiation-induced defects. This can take from minutes to months, and is not applicable for lattice damage. The total dose susceptibility of the Transputer has been measured at 35 to 50 k-rad with no internal memory (reference [1]). The internal memory or registers are the most susceptible area of the chip (3 k-rad; reference [2]) and are usually deactivated for operations in a radiation environment. An indicator of radiation damage is the increased power consumption of the device, and one researcher (reference [2]) reported a doubling of the power consumption at failure. Also, failed devices could begin to operate at a lower clock rate, leading to speculation that a key timing parameter was being affected.

Single-event upsets (SEUs) are the response of the device to direct high-energy isotropic flux (such as cosmic rays), or the secondary effects of high-energy particles colliding with other matter (such as shielding). Large transient currents may result from SEUs, causing changes in logic state (bit flips), unforeseen operation, device latchup, or burnout. The transient currents can be monitored as an indicator of the onset of SEU problems. After SEU, the results on the operation of the processor are somewhat unpredictable. Mitigation of problems caused by SEUs involves self-test, memory scrubbing, and forced resets.

The linear energy transfer (LET) is a measure of the incoming particles' delivery of ionizing energy to the device. Latchup refers to the inadvertent operation of a parasitic silicon control rectifier (SCR), triggered by ionizing radiation. In the area of latchup, the chip can be made inherently hard due to use of the epitaxial (epi) process for fabrication of the base layer (reference [3]). Even the use of an epi layer does not guarantee complete freedom from latchup, however. The next step generally involves a silicon-on-insulator (SOI) or silicon-on-sapphire (SOS) approach, where the substrate is totally insulated, and latchups are not possible.

In some cases, shielding is effective, because even a few millimeters of aluminum can stop electrons and protons. However, with highly energetic or massive particles (such as alpha particles, helium nuclei), shielding can be counterproductive. When the atoms in the shielding are hit by an energetic particle, a cascade of lower-energy, lower-mass particles results. These can cause as much or more damage than the original source particle. Shielding may cost from $10k to $30k per pound, delivered to orbit.

A3.3 RADIATION HARD PARTS

Processors and memory, as well as support and glue chips are available in rad-hard forms. If the technology or design cannot be made inherently rad-hard, then a special packaging approach can be used. This approach has been applied by Space Electronics, Inc. of San Diego, using a proprietary package to get 100 k-rad performance from repackaged commercial die from chips such as the 80386, as well as gate arrays, and digital signal processors. Rad-hard issues can also be addressed at the box or system level by redundancy techniques, dynamic reconfiguration, error detection/correction circuitry, and so on.

A3.3.1 Radiation Hardness of the Transputer

Although existing hand-selected units have flown and are flying in space, the application of Transputers for long-duration missions or flight-critical applications has yet to be proven. The University of Surrey, U. K., has extensive space flight experience with Transputers, and later sections of this appendix discuss current activities in the United States. Except for Hitchhiker-class short-duration shuttle-attached missions, rad-hard, class-S devices are needed. This section discusses the existing database of radiation testing on Transputer units.

One promising approach to using Transputer devices for space missions is to map the design to an inherently rad-hard technology. These technologies exist, and were developed based on military requirements.

The Strategic Defense Command (SDC), U.S. Army, has an ongoing rad-hardening program that has produced numerous digital devices, memory, and analog devices.

Reference [1] presents a projected Transputer orbital upset rate, based on the NRL "creme" program (*cosmic ray effects on microelectronics*, in Naval Research Laboratory (NRL) report 5901, Dec. 1986), which is reproduced in Table A3.1.

A comparison of the LET performance of several microprocessors shows the rather reasonable performance of the Transputer. For the upcoming Earth Observing System (EOS) missions, the parameters are: total dose 30 k-rads maximum for 7.5 years, with a maximum allowable SEU of 10^{-8} errors/bit-day. EOS missions are typical of a class of low Earth-orbiting satellites. The commercial Transputer meets the total dose requirements (with internal memory disabled), but does not meet the SEU criterion.

Chip	LET at latchup (MeV-cm²/mg)
IDT R3000	6.8
IDT R3000A	26.6
80386 CHMOS-IV	27.
Transputer	43.
LSI R3000	53.2
PS R3000A	59.7

Table A3.1 (Predicted) Transputer Orbital Upset Rate (/bit/day)

Orbit	Worst-Case Galactic Cosmic Ray	Worst-Case Solar Flare
500 km, 28 deg	4.1×10^{-6}	2.5×10^{-7}
900 km, 98 deg	8.6×10^{-2}	1.8×10^{-3}
Interplanetary	2.7×10^{-5}	6.7×10^{-3}

A3.3.2 Examples of Flight Systems Using Transputers

Examples of Transputer processor usage follow in the next few sections. We'll cover a robotic astronaut's assistant from Johnson Space Center, and several other satellite design examples.

A3.3.2.1 The EVA Retriever   The Extra Vehicular Activity (EVA) Retriever Project at NASA's Johnson Space Flight Center in Houston, Texas uses parallel processing techniques in a space robotic system. Transputers are used as computation engines and as communication links between other processors. This project is ongoing, and was begun in 1987.

The EVA retriever hardware is a vision, control, and manipulator subsystem using the existing Manned Maneuvering Unit (MMU). A prototype unit has been demonstrated on an air-bearing floor. The goal of the unit is to autonomously navigate through a series of obstacles to a desired target.

The initial phase of the project used four Transputers, linked with a rather narrow 375 kilobaud serial bus, and a laser tracker/video unit. The serial bus was abandoned in favor of using the Transputer's native link I/O, which provided an immediate 50-times-I/O speedup.

The phase-2 computation hardware included T800s for high-level and vision processing, an 80386 for path planning, and 68030s for arm and hand control. Another Transputer provided an interface between the 3D laser tracker and the rest of the control system. A diagram of the system is shown in Figure A3.1.

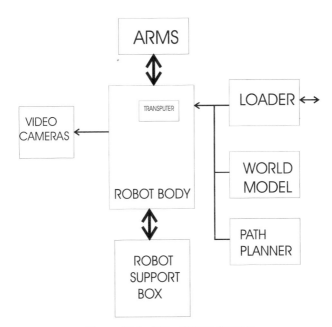

Figure A3.1   EVA retriever diagram.

The next phase of the EVA retriever involves a flight test, and this is predicated on the availability of flight-rated Transputer chips. The project has demonstrated its stated objectives.

A3.3.2.2 Space Computer Corporation Space Computer Corporation of California was under contract to DARPA to produce a "miniaturized, low-power parallel processor." Its approach was to use the Transputer as a communication element for vector coprocessors. A prototype system for guided missile applications was delivered in April 1990, and provided a peak processing throughput of 1.3 Gflops. Follow-on efforts focused on microminiaturization of the technology, using custom designed ASICs and wafer scale integration.

The applications for the resulting device include sensor image processing, and synthetic aperture radar (SAR) processing, including image compression tasks. The SCC-100 is a multinode device, with each node consisting of a Transputer, memory, and Zoran vector signal processor chips. The Zoran chips provide the computational throughput, and the Transputers provide communications and control. Flight units will require the availability of radiation-hard, military-specification integrated circuits.

A3.3.2.3 Coronal Diagnostic Spectrometer The embedded instrument controller for the Coronal Diagnostic Spectrometer (CDS) has been prototyped at NASA's Goddard Space Flight Center (GSFC) in Greenbelt, Maryland, using a T222 Transputer. This instrument is a part of SOHO/ISTP project (Solar Heliospheric Observatory/International Solar-Terrestrial Physics), jointly funded by the European Space Agency. This work is being done at GSFC, as part of the Laboratory for Astronomy and Solar Physics. Space flight qualification is of critical interest to this project, as they transform their laboratory unit to flight status. The flight unit, using a T800 processor, was delivered for a summer 1995 launch. The Transputer serves as an embedded controller, orchestrating the operation of the 1024×1024-element charge-coupled device (CCD) sensing element. The data system on the SOHO spacecraft also uses Transputers. Figure A3.2 shows the architecture of the CDS node.

A3.3.3 Radiation Tolerance of the MIPS R3000

Initial work on the flight version of the MIPS R3000 architecture took place at Sandia labs, with a working prototype being produced in 1989. The R3000 is favored for a number of flight projects, due to its 32-bit architecture, high throughput, and large number of support tools. It is, however, somewhat power hungry, which ripples through the system design, impacting, for example, the thermal design. The R3000 has the advantage of being an approved choice for avionics use (see section A3.4). The "Mongoose" (Figure A3.3) is a NASA/GSFC project based on the LSI Logic static R3000 core, plus DMA, counter-timer, and RS232. The Mongoose chips do not support floating point or the coprocessor interface. The Mongoose ar-

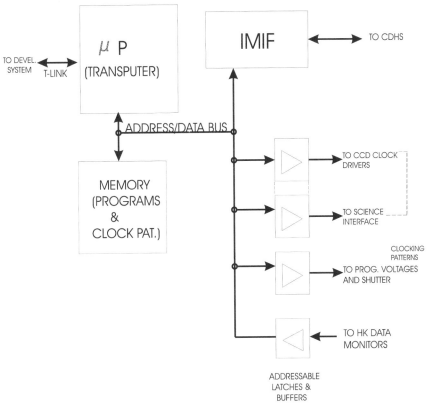

Figure A3.2   CDS node diagram.

chitecture is shown in Figure A3.3. Harris Electronics has produced the R3000 and
R3010 in rad-hard variants for various Navy space programs.

A3.3.4 RAD6000

The RAD6000 is a port of the RS6000 processor (Section 19.5.4 of Chapter 19) to
an inherently radiation-tolerant technology. The MC version, shown in early 1993,
is a six-chip version of the processor from the IBM RISC system 6000, model
320H. In the fall of 1993, IBM announced the SC, a one-chip version of the model
200 CPU. IBM was working on a rad-hard variant of the PowerPC architecture
(Chapter 15). This IBM group was subsequently sold to Loral Federal Systems, and
further development is in question.

The advantage of a radiation-hard version of a commercial chipset is the ability to
piggyback onto the existing set of software tools, applications, and development
environments. For the RS6000, this includes the languages Ada, C++, and
FORTRAN, and the AIX operating system, as well as several real-time and embed-

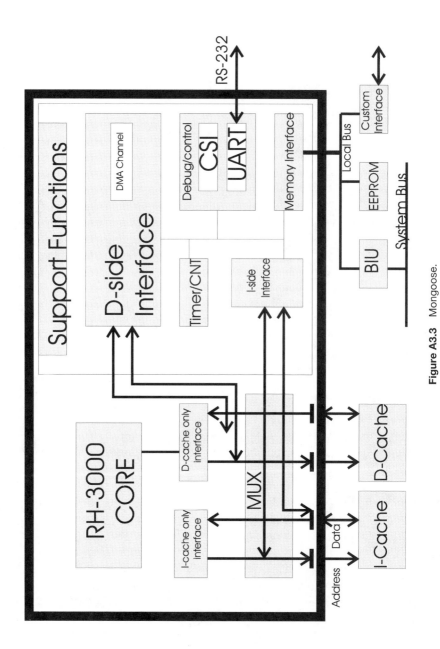

Figure A3.3 Mongoose.

ded kernels. The RAD6000 was used in a variety of military missions, including "Brilliant Pebbles," part of the "Star Wars" ballistic missile defense system. IBM integrated it into the Advanced Spaceborne Computer Module (ASCM).

A3.3.5 1750A Architecture

Avionics systems have favored the 1750A architecture, a 16-bit non-RISC design manufactured by a variety of companies. The 1750A is an instruction-set architecture, specified in MIL-STD-1750A. Different companies chose to implement different features, but the basic instruction specification is always used. A 1750A machine is not usually a RISC design, and the architecture specification does not address RISC issues. However, the United Technologies UT1750AR is a RISC microprocessor that implements the 1750A instruction set through an emulation ROM. United Technologies also makes the UT69R000 Microcontroller, a 16-bit RISC processor with a large number of registers and a Harvard bus structure

A3.4 JOINT INTEGRATED AVIONICS WORKING GROUP

The Joint Integrated Avionics Working Group (JIAWG), formed to provide commonalty in avionics for Navy and Air Force aircraft, was mandated to choose a 32-bit architecture as a follow-up to the 16-bit 1750A computers then in use. It chose not one, but two "approved" architectures for implementation of 32-bit processor systems in aircraft and weapons systems. These were the Intel i80960 (Chapter 5) and the MIPS R3000 (Chapter 6).

A3.5 SPACE STATION FREEDOM

The selected processor for the Space Station Freedom project is the non-RISC 80386 system, an Intel design flight qualified by Harris and IBM. The Space Station is planned to be placed in a 28-degree inclination orbit, at an altitude of 350 to 450 kilometers. Here it is expected to receive a dose of 100 to 1000 rad per year. The associated 80387 math coprocessor will also be used. Numerous other RISC and non-RISC chips will find application aboard the space station.

A3.6 REFERENCES

[1] Thomlinson, J. et al., "The SEU and Total Dose Response of the Inmos Transputer," Dec. 1987, *IEEE Transactions Nuclear Science*, NS-34 (6) p. 1803–1807.

[2] Thompson, J. A., Hancock, B. K., "Report on the Suitability of the Inmos T222 and C011 for Use in the Cluster Mission Radiation Environment," Feb. 7, 1990, University of Sheffield, UCL.

[3] Hunt, R. D., "Transputer Evaluation Phase 1, Completion Report," Nov. 6, 1989, Hampshire, UK: Spur Electron, Ltd.

A3.7 BIBLIOGRAPHY

"1553 Product Handbook," 1991, United Technology Microelectronic Center. 1553-PH-1-7-91.

Anderson, Richard E., "Radiation-Hardened Bulk CMOS Technology for Space and Weapon Systems," Nov. 1983, *IEEE NTC-83 Conference*, p. 68.

Burgess, Lisa, "Rad-Hard Technology: Shaking Down, Shaping Up," Nov. 1990, *Military & Aerospace Electronics.*

Ciecior, F., Arens-Fischer, W., Iglseder, H., Backhus, E., Rath, H. J., "A Transputer Based On-Board Data Handling System for Small Satellites," 1993, AIAA paper 93-4467CP, *Computers in Aerospace Conference Proceedings.*

Coe, Paul, D., "Rad-hard ICs," Oct. 1990, *Electronic Products.*

Cotarelo, María del Mar López, Johlander, B., "Total Dose Radiation Tests on Inmos T800, Final Report," Sept. 4, 1989, ESTEC.

Cotarelo, María del Mar López, "Proton Induced Single Event Upsets on Inmos T-800, Final Report," March 21, 1990, ESTEC.

Edmonds, "An Upper Bound Estimate of Heavy Ion-Induced Soft Error Rates in CMOS Devices Based on an Experimental Cross Section versus LET Curve," April 1990, Jet Propulsion Lab, NPO-17566/7071.

Elder, J. H., Osborn, J., Kolasinski, W. A., "A Method for Characterizing a Microprocessor's Vulnerability to SEU," Dec. 1, 1988, *IEEE Transactions on Nuclear Science*, 35 (6): 1, 1678.

Grimm, Keith A., "The Suitability of Transputers for Use in an Autonomous Free-Flying Robot," NASA/JSC, 1993.

Hass, K. J., Treece, R. K., Giddings, A. E., "A Radiation-Hardened 16/32-bit Microprocessor," Dec. 1, 1989, *IEEE Transactions on Nuclear Science*, 36 (6): 1, 2252.

Khan, M. Z., Tront, J. G., "Detection of Upset Induced Execution Errors in Microprocessors," 1989, IEEE Computer Society, *Eighth Annual International Phoenix Convergence on Computers and Communications Proceedings.* pp. 82–86.

Kinnison, J. D., Maurer, R. H., Carkhuff, B. G., "Radiation Characterization of the ADSP2100A Digital Signal Processor," Dec. 1, 1991, *IEEE Transactions on Nuclear Science,* 38 (6): 1, 1398.

Malhorta, M., "Fault Models of the UoSat Prototype Parallel On-Board Computer," 1993, AIAA paper 93-4472CP, *Computers in Aerospace Conference Proceedings.*

"The Military and Space Transputer Databook," 1990, SGS-Thompson Inmos.

"MIL-STD-1553 Designer's Guide," 3rd ed., 1990, ILC Data Device Corporation.

"NASA Gets a Glimpse of 200 MHz SPARC," Feb. 22, 1993, *EETimes*, p. 4.

Nicholls, J. P., "Report on Radiation Tolerance Testing of T425 Transputer," Feb. 9, 1990, Berkshire, U.K.: Satellites International, Ltd., SIL/TR00209.

Price, W., Goben, C., "Failure of CMOS Circuits Irradiated at Low Rates," Aug. 1990, NASA/JPL, *NASA Tech Brief,* 14 (8), JPL Invention Report NPO-17867-7361.

Sexton, F. W., Corbett, W. T., "SEU Simulation and Testing of Resistor-Hardened D-Latches in the SA3000 Microprocessor," Dec. 1, 1991, *IEEE Transactions on Nuclear Science*, 38 (6): 1521.

Sexton, F. W., Treece, R. K., Hass, K. J., "SEU Characterization and Design Dependence of the SA3300 Microprocessor," Dec. 1, 1990, *IEEE Transactions on Nuclear Science*, 37 (6): 1, 1861.

Shaeffer, D. L., Kimbrough, J. R., Denton, S. M., "High Energy Proton SEU Test Results for the Commercially Available MIPS R3000 Microprocessor and R3010 Floating Point Unit," Dec. 1, 1991, *IEEE Transactions on Nuclear Science*, 38 (6): 1, 1421.

"Single Event Test Method and Test Results of an Intel 80386," 1989, IBM Corporation.

Smith, Brian S., "Mongoose ASIC Microcontroller Programming Guide," Sept. 1993, NASA Reference Publication 1319.

"Transputer Evaluation Programme, Work Package 3, Package Study," Dec. 1989, Hampshire, UK: Spur Electron, Ltd.

"UT1750AR RISC Assembly Language Manual," Dec. 1991, United Technologies.

"UT1750AR RISC Microprocessor Data Sheet," June 1990, United Technologies.

Vail, D., "Estimating the On-Orbit Single Event Upset Behavior of a MIPS R3000 Microprocessor," Feb. 1991, Harris Corporation (GSFC study).

Zoutendyk, J., "Estimating Rates of Single-Event Upsets," Nov. 1988, *NASA Tech Brief*, 12 (10), item #152.

Yelverton, J. Ned, "Operation of Commercially-Based Microcomputer Technology in a Space Radiation Environment," 1993, AIAA 93-4493-CP, *Computers in Aerospace Conference Proceedings*.

INDEX